LW80

A - Saxon — 54

Kears: 4c/Nam - 137

THE LANGUAGE OF WALTER SCOTT

THE LANGUAGE LIBRARY

EDITED BY DAVID CRYSTAL

The Best English	G. H. Vallins
Caxton and his World	N. F. Blake
Caxton's Own Prose	N. F. Blake
Chamber of Horrors	'Vigilans'
Changing English (revised)	Simeon Potter
Chaucer's English	Ralph W. V. Elliott
Dictionaries British and American (revised)	J. R. Hulbert
A Dictionary of Literary Terms (revised)	J. A. Cuddon
Early English (revised)	John W. Clark
Early Modern English	Charles Barber
English Biblical Translation	A. C. Partridge
English Dialects	G. L. Brook
Finno-Ugrian Languages and Peoples	Peter Hajdu (trans. G. F. Cushing)
A First Dictionary of Linguistics and Phonetics	David Crystal
A Grammar of Style	A. E. Darbyshire
A History of the English Language	G. L. Brook
An Informal History of the German Language	W. B. Lockwood
Introduction to the Scandinavian Languages	M. O'C. Walshe
Jane Austen's English	K. C. Phillipps
John Donne: Language and Style	A. C. Partridge
Joysprick: An Introduction to the Language of James Joyce	Anthony Burgess
Language and Structure in Tennyson's Poetry	F. E. L. Priestley
The Language and Style of Anthony Trollope	John W. Clark
Language in the Modern World (revised)	Simeon Potter
The Language of the Book of Common Prayer	Stella Brook
The Language of Dickens	G. L. Brook
The Language of Gerard Manley Hopkins	James Milroy
The Language of Renaissance Poetry	A. C. Partridge
The Language of Shakespeare	G. L. Brook
The Language of Thackeray	K. C. Phillipps
The Language of Walter Scott	Graham Tulloch
Languages of the British Isles Past and Present	W. B. Lockwood
Modern Linguistics (revised)	Simeon Potter
The Pattern of English (revised)	G. H. Vallins
The Pitcairnese Language	A. S. C. Ross
Scientific and Technical Translation	Isadore Pinchuck
Sense and Sense Development (revised)	R. A. Waldron
The Study of Dialect	K. M. Petyt
Swift's Polite Conversation	Eric Partridge
Tudor to Augustan English	A. C. Partridge
The Words We Use	J. A. Sheard

Graham Tulloch

THE LANGUAGE OF WALTER SCOTT

A Study of his Scottish and Period Language

ANDRE DEUTSCH

First published 1980 by
André Deutsch Limited
105 Great Russell Street London WC1

Copyright © 1980 by Graham Tulloch
All rights reserved

British Library Cataloguing in Publication Data

Tulloch, Graham
   The language of Walter Scott – (Language library).
   I. Scott, *Sir* Walter, *bart* – Language
   I. Title II. Series
   828'.7'09   PR 5345

ISBN 0-233-97223-4

Printed in Great Britain by
Ebenezer Baylis and Son Ltd
The Trinity Press, Worcester, and London

Published and distributed in the United States and Canada by
Westview Press, 5500 Central Avenue, Boulder, Colorado 80301
Westview ISBN 0-86531-061-0
Library of Congress Catalog Card Number 80-51351

Published and distributed in India by
Clarion Books
(Indian Book Company)
GT Road, Shahdara, Delhi 110032

SUSANNAE UXORI AMICAEQUE

CONTENTS

Phonetic Symbols 8
Preface 9
Abbreviations 11
1 Introduction to Period Language 13
2 Scott's Reading of Medieval and Renaissance Authors 18
3 Period Vocabulary 25
4 Period Grammar 129
5 Introduction to Scottish Language 167
6 Scottish Sounds, Spelling and Vocabulary 182
7 Scottish Grammar 267
8 The Extent of Scots in the Novels 301
Appendix I 333
Appendix II 335
Select Bibliography 337
Index of Subjects 343
Index of Words 345

PHONETIC SYMBOLS

The following letters are used as phonetic symbols with their usual English values: p, b, t, d, k, g, f, v, s, z, h, w, l, r, m, n. Other symbols are used with the values indicated by the italicized letters in the key-words below.

CONSONANTS

ʃ	*sh*ip	θ	*th*in
ʒ	plea*s*ure	ð	*th*en
tʃ	*ch*in	j	*y*es
dʒ	*j*u*dg*e	ç	German i*ch*
ŋ	si*ng*	x	Scots lo*ch*
ɲ	French di*gn*e	ʍ	voiceless [w]

VOWELS

i	s*i*t	ɑ	German M*a*nn
i:	s*ee*	ɑ:	f*a*ther
y	German H*ü*tte	ɔ	h*o*t
ø	French p*eu*	ɔ:	s*aw*
e	*ge*t	u	p*u*t
e:	French *é*t*é*	u:	s*oo*n
a	f*a*t	ʌ	b*u*t
ə	fath*er*		

DIPHTHONGS

ei	d*ay*	ɔi	b*oy*
ou	g*o*	iə	h*ere*
ai	fl*y*	ɛə	th*ere*
au	n*ow*	uə	g*our*d

Square brackets are used to enclose phonetic symbols. A colon after a phonetic symbol indicates length.

PREFACE

SURPRISINGLY LITTLE has been written about Scott's language. In a note at the beginning of the Bibliography I have included a brief survey of previous studies. Many potential areas of interest are not touched on in this book. Merely as a writer of early nineteenth-century English, even in the non-archaic and non-Scottish passages, Scott's language is interesting to compare with present-day English. There is also the special kind of language he gives to the Presbyterians and Puritans in his novels and much more could be said about the sources of his language. However Scott's greatest contribution to the literary uses of language was certainly in his extensive use of Scots and of archaic or, as I have called it, 'period' language. Though others had used dialect and archaisms before, no one in English had used it so extensively and thoroughly. For this reason I have decided to limit my study totally to these two aspects of Scott's language. Furthermore, although there is some reference made to Scott's letters, journal and poems, the main emphasis in this book has been on his novels. Naturally the section on Scottish language concentrates on the novels with Scottish characters, but I have particularly concerned myself with those with extensive Scots dialogue rather than works with medieval and renaissance settings (like *The Fair Maid of Perth* and *The Monastery*) where the amount of Scots is restricted. Similarly the section on period language concentrates on the novels set in the Middle Ages and Renaissance where the period language is a consistent feature rather than those with later settings where it only occurs incidentally. The Scots in the novels has generally been appreciated, though not much studied except for a small number of articles and as an important source for the *Scottish National Dictionary*. By contrast much of what has been said, usually in passing, about Scott's period language has been unfavourable. I hope that this study will at least demonstrate its variety and inventiveness and the care Scott took in presenting it.

Part of this book was originally written as my PhD dissertation at Leicester University. My supervisor was Dr Ken Phillipps who was unfailingly generous to me with his time and advice, not just

Preface

in academic matters. I had other help at Leicester from my friends Lawrence Normand and Dhia Aljubouri. In the initial stages of my work I had much useful guidance from Associate Professor E. M. Liggins and Professor H. W. Piper at Macquarie University. I would also like to thank Professor Ralph Elliott for encouraging me to continue and expand my work on Scott. I had further encouragement from the late Professor Simeon Potter. My thanks to those who typed the manuscript: Sally Fraser, Toni Kennedy and Molly Scrymgour and to the staff of Flinders University Library. My greatest thanks go to my wife for the invaluable research assistance she has given me and even more for the patience and understanding with which she has suffered, over a number of years, my obsession with Sir Walter.

June 1979   GRAHAM TULLOCH
The Flinders University of South Australia

LIST OF ABBREVIATIONS

Full details of the editions referred to are given in the Bibliography. Arabic numbers following an abbreviation refer to a page number unless preceded by the sign § indicating a paragraph number. Roman numerals, following an abbreviation for one of Scott's novels, refer to part of the introductory material, whether by Scott or by Lang.

WORKS BY SCOTT

Ab	The Abbot	LLM	The Lay of the Last Minstrel
AG	Anne of Geierstein	LM	A Legend of Montrose
An	The Antiquary	Ma	Marmion
Be	The Betrothed	Minstrelsy	Minstrelsy of the Scottish Border
BD	The Black Dwarf		
BL	The Bride of Lammermoor	Mo	The Monastery
BT	The Bridal of Triermain	OM	Old Mortality
CC	Chronicles of the Canongate	Pi	The Pirate
CD	Castle Dangerous	PP	Peveril of the Peak
CRP	Count Robert of Paris	QD	Quentin Durward
DD	The Dream of Devorgoil	Re	Redgauntlet
FM	The Fair Maid of Perth	Ro	Rokeby
GM	Guy Mannering	RR	Rob Roy
HM	The Heart of Midlothian	SD	The Surgeon's Daughter
HD	Harold the Dauntless	SRW	St Ronan's Well
Iv	Ivanhoe	Ta	The Talisman
K	Kenilworth	TG	The Tales of a Grandfather
LI	The Lord of the Isles	Wa	Waverley
LL	The Lady of the Lake	Wk	Woodstock

OTHER ABBREVIATIONS

Abbreviations for Shakespeare's plays and for books of the Bible should be readily identifiable. Sometimes a Shakespeare abbreviation is followed by the word 'Folio' in which case the spelling used is that of the First Folio text (1623). Some other books are referred to by their author's name. They are listed in the final section of the Bibliography.

Abbreviations

Catalogue	Cochrane, *Catalogue of the Library of Abbotsford*
CE	Jespersen, *Chapters on English*
CT	Chaucer, *The Canterbury Tales*
DOST	Craigie, *A Dictionary of the Older Scottish Tongue*
DSCS	Murray, *The Dialect of the Southern Counties of Scotland*
EDD	Wright, *The English Dialect Dictionary*
EETS	The Early English Text Society
EMIH	Jonson, *Every Man In His Humour*
EMOH	Jonson, *Every Man Out of His Humour*
FQ	Spenser, *The Faerie Queene*
HF	Chaucer, *The House of Fame*
Life	Lockhart, *Memoirs of the Life of Sir Walter Scott, Bart*
MED	Kurath, *Middle English Dictionary*
MEG	Jespersen, *A Modern English Grammar on Historical Principles*
MMS	Grant and Dixon, *Manual of Modern Scots*
OED	Murray, *The Oxford English Dictionary*
PLD	'Phonetic Description of Scottish Language and Dialects' in *SND*
SC	Spenser, *The Shepherd's Calendar*
SND	Grant, *The Scottish National Dictionary*
STS	The Scottish Text Society
TC	Chaucer, *Troilus and Criseyde*

Chapter 1

INTRODUCTION TO PERIOD LANGUAGE

Ivanhoe was a turning point in Scott's career as a novelist. Up to its publication in 1819 all his novels were set in Scotland and all except one (*A Legend of Montrose* published earlier in the same year) were set after 1660. After *Ivanhoe* the majority of his novels were set before 1660 with medieval and renaissance settings and many were set outside Scotland. This change, which is often felt to have had far from beneficial effects on Scott's writing in general, certainly had major repercussions in the language of the novels, especially the dialogue. Scott reverted to something he had tried earlier in the less tractable medium of poetry. Distanced in time and often in place from his familiar eighteenth- and early nineteenth-century setting, he was forced to abandon the Scots dialect he had used so effectively in his previous novels; in its place he introduced a language reinforcing not locale but period, not Scottish but 'old'. This turning point has a particular interest for us because Scott, about to present his new novel to the public and wondering, no doubt, what effect his change of style would have on his popularity, paused to make some comments on what he was doing.

Of course it would have been open to him to do as his predecessors as historical novelists (if they can be called that) had done in their work. Of Clara Reeve's *The Old English Baron* Scott wrote:

> And 'were but the combat in lists left out,' or converted into a modern duel, the whole train of incidents might, for any peculiarity to be traced in the dialect or narration, have taken place in the time of Charles II, or in either of the two succeeding reigns (*Lives of the Novelists*, World's Classics edn, p. 203).

In fact *The Champion of Virtue*, the original title of *The Old English*

Baron when it was first published in 1777, is far more indicative of the author's real interests than that later adopted on its reprinting. We are told in the first sentence that the scene is set in the reign of Henry VI and this remains almost the only historical detail in the novel. Scott chose differently; not only did he provide an appropriate medieval background in political and social history for the twelfth-century setting of *Ivanhoe*, he also attempted to provide an appropriate linguistic setting. However, very little thought was needed to see that a popular novelist was in no position to rush to the opposite extreme to Clara Reeve and make his dialogue an exact copy of the language of the past. Through the mouthpiece of Laurence Templeton (the supposed author of *Ivanhoe*) Scott speaks jokingly in the Dedicatory Epistle of the 'motive which prevents my writing the dialogue of the piece in Anglo-Saxon or in Norman-French, and which prohibits my sending forth to the public this essay printed with the types of Caxton or Wynken de Worde' (*Iv* xlvii). We find in fact that the dialogue of *Ivanhoe* is not Anglo-Saxon or early Middle English but a mixed, artificially created language – a base of early nineteenth-century English with elements of earlier English added to give a flavour of 'oldness'. Nevertheless Scott did make at least two attempts to reproduce the language of the past in all its details. When he edited the Middle English poem *Sir Tristrem* he added a 'Continuation' in the same style and language as the original. Somewhat later he formed a characteristic scheme to publish, as genuine, a number of fake, supposedly seventeenth-century letters written by himself and his friends. Some sheets of the *Private Letters of the Seventeenth Century* were actually printed but Scott decided to abandon the idea and wrote *The Fortunes of Nigel* instead using some of the material. There are, of course, similarities in language between the 'Continuation' and Scott's poems and between the *Private Letters* and novels like *Nigel* and *Woodstock* but the author's fundamental aim is different. All the same, some of the comments Scott made about such imitation of older English are clearly intended to have relevance for the *Ivanhoe* kind of mixed, artificial language. 'Laurence Templeton' makes his comments after condemning as failures the poems of Chatterton, who in the eighteenth century tried to pass off as the genuine works of an unknown fifteenth-century poet called Thomas Rowley his own unskilful forgeries:

Introduction to Period Language

This was the error of the unfortunate Chatterton. In order to give his language the appearance of antiquity, he rejected every word that was modern, and produced a dialect entirely different from any that had ever been spoken in Great Britain. He who would imitate an ancient language with success, must attend rather to its grammatical character, turn of expression, and mode of arrangement, than labour to collect extraordinary and antiquated terms, which, as I have already averred, do not in ancient authors approach the number of words still in use, though perhaps somewhat altered in sense and spelling, in the proportion of one to ten (*Iv* xlix).

There are a number of points made here. Firstly that the number of obsolete words in earlier English should not be exaggerated. Certainly this is a trap Scott avoids in the novels and poems; a very large number of obsolete and unusual words are introduced but he takes care all the time that they are not spread too thickly on the page. In this, as in everything else, Scott shows his habitual solicitude for the ordinary reader, probably a stronger motive with him than any theory about the proportion of obsolete vocabulary in earlier English. His second main point is that attention should be paid to all aspects of the language and not just to vocabulary; it is further clear that his concern extended beyond the purely linguistic to the stylistic ('turn of expression and mode of arrangement') as well. These are important aspects of the present study although, for the moment, we are only concerned with vocabulary. The mention of 'words . . . perhaps somewhat altered in sense and spelling' alerts us to two further aspects of Scott's language. Like anyone who carefully compares an earlier phase of language with a later one, Scott realized that change of meaning in words which remain in use is at least as important in causing differences of vocabulary as the dying out of old words and the creation of new ones. Here again he had recognized a linguistic fact which was useful to him as a novelist. Unfamiliar words are often hard to assimilate in dialogue, although Scott became remarkably adept at explaining them without appearing to do so, but the meaning of a familiar word used in an unfamiliar sense is often easy enough to puzzle out in its context. Scott, as we shall see, made a lot of use of such unfamiliar senses of familiar words. On the other hand he relinquished any feeling of 'oldness' he might have gained from an antique spelling. The 'Continuation' of *Sir Tristrem* and the *Private Letters* have Middle English and seventeenth-century spelling respectively but the novels and poems have modern spelling. No doubt Scott felt archaic spelling would disturb and distract his readers but it is also worth remembering that at this stage the history of English phonology was little understood. By contrast when it came to dialect Scott made free use of phonological variation.

It will be noticed that I have used the term 'period vocabulary'. A more traditional term is 'archaic vocabulary' but this I have deliberately avoided from a feeling that the word 'archaic' suggests language which is actually genuinely old. In fact the language Scott used to suggest to his readers a sense of period, a linguistic setting to complement the historical setting, is frequently not genuinely old – it even includes some new coinages. Moreover just as all 'period' language may not be 'archaic', all 'archaic' language may not be 'period'. There is, for example, a long-lasting tradition for the use of jocular archaisms which Scott himself found congenial. Yet another of Scott's emanations, Mr Chrystal Croftangry, whose 'lucubrations' form, in their second series, *The Fair Maid of Perth*, tells us in his introductory chapter to the novel the tale of the visiting London apprentice who tries to remove the mark of David Rizzio's blood from the floor of Holyrood Palace. Mr Croftangry's own intervention saves the historic stain and the apprentice 'therefore took his leave, muttering that he had always heard the Scots were a nasty people, but had no idea they carried it so far as to choose to have the floors of their palaces blood-boltered' (*FM* 5). The term *blood-boltered* had lain dormant since Shakespeare had coined it for Macbeth's fearful cry: 'The blood-bolter'd Banquo smiles on me' (*Mac* IV i 123). In Shakespeare it means 'having the hair matted with blood' but Scott uses it as a mere synonym for *blood-stained*. Yet despite the word's antiquity its effect here is wholly humorous, the setting being in the Edinburgh of Scott's own day. This kind of jocular archaism is especially common in *Waverley* where the joke lies in the use of archaic diction to describe, for example, a very eighteenth-century innkeeper (*Wa* 296).

After a lapse of one hundred and fifty years it is difficult for us to identify obsolete, rare, newly coined and otherwise uncommon words when Scott uses them. While Scott himself occasionally offers us help, for the most part we have to rely on dictionaries for information. Dictionaries have their limitations. The readers for the *Oxford English Dictionary* did not read all eighteenth-century literature, nor did the editors record every appearance of

Introduction to Period Language

a word they had come across. Moreover if the editors generally gave a quotation for every century in which they found a word to occur they did not commit themselves to doing so in every case. According to the 'General Explanations' of the *OED* the quotations 'are arranged chronologically so as to give about one for each century, though various considerations often render a larger number necessary' (*OED* I xxii). The *OED* can occasionally be faulted, but as long as we recognize its shortcomings (and similar shortcomings in the new *Middle English Dictionary*, the *Scottish National Dictionary* and the *Dictionary of the Older Scottish Tongue*) they need not be disabling. The *OED* has just too many examples of words used by Scott which are not cited for the eighteenth century (that is, for the hundred years before Scott was writing), or cited in the eighteenth century and in Scott but not afterwards, or only cited for the eighteenth century in poets or historians or scholars before appearing in Scott or first cited in Scott, for all of them to be explained as an accident. He obviously did revive obsolete and obsolescent words and create new ones. Though it will always be possible to find uses of words by eighteenth-century authors where the *OED* does not record the word as used in that century, if we assume that where the *OED* gives no eighteenth-century example of a word, or a meaning of a word, that the word or meaning is, if not obsolete, at least very rare, we shall not often be misled.

Chapter 2

SCOTT'S READING OF MEDIEVAL AND RENAISSANCE AUTHORS

IN THE ACCOUNTS of Scott's early reading, Elizabethan literature looms particularly large. In a vivid passage in the autobiographical memoir Scott relates his first experience of Shakespeare in the theatre at Bath:

> The play was As You Like It; and the witchery of the whole scene is alive to my mind at this moment. I made, I believe, noise more than enough, and remember being so much scandalized at the quarrel between Orlando and his brother in the first scene, that I screamed out 'An't they brothers?' (*Life*, I 22).

Later he describes how he 'sate up' reading Shakespeare 'by the light of a fire' when he should have been in bed, and Spenser he 'could have read for ever' (*Life*, I 39). In the clearly semi-autobiographical account of Waverley's childhood reading the Elizabethan writers and Milton are singled out for special mention:

> He had read, and stored in a memory of uncommon tenacity, much curious, though ill arranged and miscellaneous, information. In English literature he was master of Shakespeare and Milton, of our earlier dramatic authors, of many picturesque and interesting passages from our old historical chronicles, and was particularly well acquainted with Spenser, Drayton, and other poets who have exercised themselves on romantic fiction (*Wa* 23).

The young Rokeby also shares Scott's love for Shakespeare:

> Hour after hour he loved to pore
> On Shakespeare's rich and varied lore,
> But turn'd from martial scenes and light,
> From Falstaff's feast and Percy's fight

> To ponder Jaques' moral strain,
> And muse with Hamlet wise in vain,
> And weep himself to soft repose
> O'er gentle Desdemona's woes (*Ro* I xxiv).

This early bias towards the Elizabethans continues in Scott's later life. But the literature of other periods is not excluded; Scott had read 'books of history, or poetry, or voyages and travels' and 'the usual, or rather ten times the usual, quantity of fairy tales, eastern stories, romances, &c' (*Life*, I 35). Most important of all he 'never read a book half so frequently, or with half the enthusiasm' as he first read Percy's *Reliques* (*Life*, I 39).

Yet it is at this point in the autobiography that Scott gives the first indication of moving outside this highly romantic fare:

> About this period also I became acquainted with the works of Richardson, and those of Mackenzie – (whom in later years I became entitled to call my friend) – with Fielding, Smollet and some others of our best novelists (*Life*, I 39).

Scott's reading was not at any time wholly restricted to one period, which is why the library at Abbotsford has books so diverse as Nils Idman's *Recherches sur l'ancien peuple Finois traduites du Suedois par M. Genet fils* (Strasbourg, 1778) and General Lachlan Macquarie's *Letter to Lord Sidmouth in Refutation of Mr Bennet's Statements* (concerning New South Wales; London, 1821). (See *Catalogue*, pp. 99, 31.)

Recent criticism has accepted that Scott is as much an Augustan as a Romantic and his thorough acquaintance with literature other than medieval and renaissance – the hunting ground of the Romantics – should not be forgotten. He was after all, the editor of Swift and Dryden. Saintsbury, who re-edited his Dryden, considered it 'one of the best edited books on a great scale in English' (Preface to his edition of Scott's Dryden, Edinburgh, 1882, I v). Scott provided the biographical introductions to Ballantyne's Novelists Library covering eighteenth-century novelists from Fielding to Mrs Radcliffe and edited Carleton's *Memoirs* (Edinburgh, 1808), which have been doubtfully attributed to both Swift and Defoe.

Scott also edited a considerable amount of material in the form of memoirs relating both to the Civil War and to the Restoration.

As he says, 'Memoirs are the materials, and often the touchstone, of history; and even where they descend to incidents beneath her notice, they aid the study of the antiquary and moral philosopher' (Advertisement to Scott's edition of Cary's *Memoirs* and Naunton's *Fragmenta Regalia*, Edinburgh, 1808, p. vi). In 1806 he published together the autobiography of Captain John Hodgson, who died in 1684, and the memoirs of Sir Henry Slingsby who lived from 1602 to 1658 (*Original Memoirs of Sir Henry Slingsby and of Captain Hodgson*, Edinburgh, 1806). In 1815 he resurrected a work which had been finished in 1679 but never printed. This is *The Memorie of the Somervilles*, a history of the family written by the tenth de jure Lord Somerville (1631–1693) and including a coverage of the author's own lifetime. Finally Scott brought out *Northern Memoirs Writ in the year 1658 by Richard Franck* (Edinburgh, 1821).

In the field of Renaissance literature Scott is more important for his advice and encouragement to others than as an editor himself. All the same he edited several works. There are more memoirs: those of Robert Carey, Earl of Monmouth (1560?–1639) and the *Fragmenta Regalia* of Sir Robert Naunton (1563–1635) – these two were published together (Edinburgh, 1808) – and the *Secret History of the Court of James the First* (Edinburgh, 1811) and there is one literary work, Rowlands' *Letting of Humours Blood in the Head Vaine* (Edinburgh, 1814; first published in 1600). More important than this is the fact that from 1822 Scott was involved in a scheme to produce an edition of Shakespeare. Scott was to prepare an introductory life and Lockhart to edit the text and write the notes. The scheme was later dropped and it is not known if Scott ever wrote his life of Shakespeare.* Some ten years earlier he was deeply involved in another project, the edition of Beaumont and Fletcher prepared by his protégé Weber. He helped Weber with his advice and by providing him with his marginal notes to his own edition of Beaumont and Fletcher's works. His interest in Elizabethan drama never waned; only his death prevented him from writing an article for the *Quarterly Review* on Peele and Webster (see *Letters*, XII 1).

Apart from Shakespeare Elizabethan dramatic literature was

---

* See W. M. Parker, 'Scott's Knowledge of Shakespeare', *Quarterly Review*, CCXC, (1952), 341–54. This article conveniently collects material about Scott's knowledge of Shakespeare and summarizes what little we know about his projected edition of Shakespeare's works.

comparatively neglected in the eighteenth century and even though a great deal was edited in Scott's lifetime he himself was exceptional in the extent of his knowledge of Shakespeare's contemporaries. In his library he had more or less full editions of Beaumont and Fletcher (Weber ed., *Catalogue*, p. 211), *Lyly* (p. 217), Marlowe (p. 346), Jonson (Gifford ed., p. 158), Peele (Dyce ed., p. 166), Massinger (Gifford ed., p. 209), and of course, Shakespeare (various editions: pp. 42, 62, 210). Besides these collected editions Scott was in constant search for first and early editions of individual plays and in this way he collected a number of plays by Webster, Marston, Thomas Heywood, Middleton, Rowley, Chapman and Shirley (*Catalogue*, pp. 213-15), all this in addition to what such extensive collections as Dodsley's *Old Plays* (*Catalogue*, p. 208) could give him. With such a library Scott's knowledge of Elizabethan drama was not superficial. His interest extended to prose and verse. He had, as we would expect from the description of Waverley's reading, the works of major poets like Drayton (*Catalogue*, pp. 42, 155, 192), Donne (p. 42), Sidney (p. 101) and Spenser (p. 187). After 1636 there was no edition of Lyly's *Euphues* until Arber's reprint appeared in 1868. Scott had early editions of both *Euphues: The Anatomy of Wit* and *Euphues and his England* (*Catalogue*, p. 102). His edition of Sidney's *Arcadia* was also an early one (*Catalogue*, p. 101). And again as well as the individual works he had modern collections like Sir Egerton Brydge's *Archaica: containing a reprint of Scarce Old English Prose Tracts* (London, 1815) in which amongst other things Scott would have found Nashe's *Christ's Tears over Jerusalem* and Gabriel Harvey's *Four Letters and Sonnets touching Robert Greene* (see *Catalogue*, p. 184). Scott's own *Collection of Scarce and Valuable Tracts* (generally called the 'Somers Tracts') which was published in thirteen volumes (London, 1809-15) contains a vast amount of mainly sixteenth- and seventeenth-century material. In another collection, John Nichols' *Progresses and Public Processions of Queen Elizabeth* (London, 1783), there appears Robert Laneham's *Letter* concerning the 'Entertainment unto the Queen's Majestie at Killingworth Castle' (*Catalogue*, pp. 265-6) of which Scott made considerable use in *Kenilworth*. Scott had more than one edition of this work; there was another in what he called 'a beautiful antiquarian publication termed *Kenilworth Illustrated*' (Chiswick, 1821) which also included the other account of the Kenilworth festivities, Gascoigne's *Princely Pleasures of Kenilworth* (K 484n, 487n; see also

Catalogue, p. 242). Thus of both major and minor Elizabethan literature Scott had a good collection.

Scott edited only one medieval text, *Sir Tristrem* (Edinburgh, 1804), which he believed to have been written by Thomas of Erceldoune. Few individual Middle English texts had been edited in this way by his time although there were collections and selections edited by Ellis, Weber and Ritson (*Catalogue*, pp. 105, 174). Moreover, so extensive is the quotation in Warton's *History of English Poetry* (London, 1775-1781; 2nd edn, 1824; *Catalogue*, pp. 105, 184) that it virtually constitutes an anthology of Middle English verse. Apart from this only a few works were available in print. Scott had access to some manuscript material – he quotes *Sir Orfeo* from the Auchinleck MS in the introduction to 'Tamlane' in the *Minstrelsy* (II 138ff) – and he had some transcripts of unprinted romances (*Catalogue*, pp. 103, 104). A good deal of the literature of the Middle English period was to have to wait for the coming of the EETS before it appeared in print. There was, for example, virtually nothing in print from the early Middle English period. (Warton had quoted a few of the Harley Lyrics and passages from other early works). Chaucer had gone through many editions – Scott had those of Speght (*Catalogue*, p. 154), Urry (p. 239) and Tyrwhitt (p. 155) – Gower was available (p. 42) and, though there was no modern edition of *Piers Plowman*, Scott had Crowley's 1550 edition (p. 173). Scott had also some of Lydgate's voluminous work (*Catalogue*, pp. 101, 156, 275). Nor was he ignorant of medieval drama; a certain amount had been published including two Roxburgh Club books – the Towneley *Judicium* (*Catalogue*, p. 276) and the Chester Mysteries (p. 275) – and some material on the Coventry plays (p. 249).

Finally tribute must be paid to Scott's Scottishness by mentioning the most important of the medieval Scots writers available at Abbotsford: the two great verse lives, *The Bruce* (*Catalogue*, pp. 4, 8, 173) and *The Wallace* (pp. 4, 8), and the works of Henryson (pp. 272, 281), Lindsay (pp. 21, 105, 173) and Gavin Douglas (p. 12). Lastly even if the index to the Abbotsford *Catalogue* has no reference to Dunbar, Scott had certainly read him (see e.g. *Letters*, X 366, 495). The reading of the Baron of Bradwardine as detailed in *Waverley*, though of narrow scope and of entirely different priorities from Scott's, includes some of Scott's favourite old Scottish authors: 'the Epithalamium of Georgius Buchanan, and Arthur Johnstone's Psalms, of a Sunday; and the Deliciae Poetarum Scotorum, and Sir David Lindsay's Works, and Barbour's Bruce, and Blind Harry's Wallace, and the Gentle Shepherd, and the Cherry and the Slae' (*Wa* 107).

This does not by any means exhaust the resources of Scott's collection of books but it does give some idea of its strengths and limitations in the field of English literature. Of eighteenth-century literature there is plenty, of sixteenth- and seventeenth-century literature a great deal both in minor, even ephemeral, work and in major work, especially the drama, and for the Middle Ages a much more circumscribed selection.

Scott's chapter tags are another source of information about the authors he remembered best. From *Waverley* onwards he put small scraps of verse at the heads of his chapters. In *Waverley* there are only five chapters so treated but later they became the rule rather than the exception. Scott's memory was prodigious. As he himself said, 'I always had a wonderful facility in retaining in my memory whatever verses pleased me', although naturally it was fallible: 'this memory of mine was a very fickle ally' (*Life*, I 36) and he felt none of the modern textual scholar's compulsion to check every word. His memory failing on occasions to come up with a suitable quotation – and considering the number of quotations he does use the extent of his memory is remarkable – Scott sometimes wrote his own lines, usually attributed to 'Old Play', 'Old Song', 'Old Ballad' or 'Anonymous'. Tom B. Haber ('The Chapter-Tags in the Waverley Novels', *PMLA*, XLV, (1930), 1140–49) has given a table of Scott's sources for the remainder. Shakespeare, who has already been frequently mentioned in this discussion of Scott's reading, proves his overwhelming importance for Scott by providing 202 chapter tags. He is much more important than anyone else; the next most important is Dryden with seventeen. (Swift, the subject of Scott's other major edition, furnishes only two tags – the fact that Scott's tags are invariably in verse probably accounts for this). After Dryden the greatest favourites are Crabbe (14), Pope (13), Byron (12), Coleridge (11), Jonson (11), Milton (10), Butler (10), Burns (9), Campbell (9), Wordsworth (8) and Spenser (8). Chaucer provides four epigraphs – as do Thomson, Southey and Gray. The importance of Augustan and contemporary poetry in Scott's mind is amply demonstrated even if this cannot be taken as an exact reflection of his tastes; they have little however to do with our present purpose. More to the point is the fact that the other

23

most frequent authors are sixteenth- and seventeenth-century and *not* medieval figures.

There are further quotations and allusions in the body of the novels and many others in Scott's letters and journal. Shakespeare again figures prominently but allusions to Chaucer collected by Caroline Spurgeon, (*Five Hundred Years of Chaucer Criticism and Allusion*, in 3 vols., New York, 1960. See vol. II, the years 1804–1832), Roland M. Smith ('Chaucer Allusions in the Letters of Sir Walter Scott', *MLN*, LXV, (1950), 448–55) and J. R. Schultz ('Sir Walter Scott and Chaucer', *MLN*, XXVIII, (1913), 246–7) are so numerous as to show that the four chapter tags from Chaucer scarcely reflect the degree of Scott's interest in him. Or did Scott's interest decline? Such at least is the opinion of Smith who considers that 'Ellis . . . seems in some measure to have been responsible for keeping alive Scott's interest in Chaucer' in the years from 1801 to 1805 'when their correspondence was at its height' ('Chaucer Allusions', p. 455). Whether this decline of interest took place or not (and the evidence is not wholly convincing) there is much more evidence of Scott's using the Elizabethans for his period language than of his using medieval writers.

Chapter 3

PERIOD VOCABULARY

OBSOLETE AND OBSOLESCENT WORDS

THE HISTORY of a few words will illustrate the wide spectrum from extreme doubt to virtual certainty over which the historian of the language ranges in any attempt to decide which of Scott's words were obsolete when Scott used them. The most doubtful cases are words which appear to have become obsolete in the eighteenth century. The *OED* records a number of words or senses of words used by Scott as falling out of use in the eighteenth century, although it fails to record their use by Scott. *Conscionable* 'conscientious' (*K* 68) seems oddly to have died out while *unconscionable* still lives on. The last *OED* example of *conscionable* is dated 1708 while the eighteenth-century instances of *conscionableness* in the *OED* (there are no later examples) are taken from dictionaries. The last citation of *curious* in the sense 'made with care or art' (*Iv* 453), a sense which has a respectable history from Middle English onwards, is dated 1760–72. *Miscarry* meaning 'come to harm' (*Ta* 510) is given as surviving no later than 1749. When Varney says of Amy that 'she takes state on her already' (*K* 64), meaning that she already assumes the dignity befitting a countess, he uses *state* in a sense of which the *OED* readers found no instance later than 1767 (*OED state* 19b). For *undertaker*, 'a promoter – an undertaker' says Scott in explanation (*FN* 168), the last *OED* quotation is dated 1779 and for *passage* 'a dice game' (*FN* 204), 1755 (*OED passage* 15). In all these cases the evidence of the *OED* may well be misleading in suggesting that the word was obsolete in Scott's time, especially when its last citation is dated as late as 1779. Equally the evidence could be accurate and Scott's use a revival. Passage, for example, was forbidden by law to be played after 1745 as the *OED*'s 1755 quotation records and, despite the notorious ineffectuality of anti-gaming laws, it is unlikely the game or its name was very familiar to Scott's readers.

Again, Scott takes the trouble of explaining *undertaker* implying that it was a rare if not an obsolete sense in which he was using the word.

These words are doubtful instances; even more so are cases where Scott himself is given as the last *OED* example but where eighteenth-century uses of the word are also cited. With most other authors we would take this to mean that the word was still current; in Scott's case we are entitled at least to call this in doubt. This applies to *cutter* 'bully' (*K* 45), *flat-cap* 'prentice' (*FN* 372), *gloze* 'expound' (*Mo* 52), *handicraft* 'artisan' (*K* 426), *injeer* 'intrude' (*Ab* 239), *lance-prisade* (*Wk* 640) – 'The lanspresado in the corporal's absence . . . doth all the corporal's duties' (Markham, *Soldier's Accidence*, 1625, p. 7), *lockeram* 'linen fabric' (*Ab* 24), *toledo* 'sword' (*Wk* 37) and *trangam* 'gewgaw' (*Ab* 267) – Scott also made use of a closely related word *trankum* (*FN* 361; *SRW* 280; *DD* III i 9). Finally Scott is also given in the *OED* as the last author to use both the verb *trinket* 'intrigue' (*Iv* 525, *K* 570) and its derivative nouns *trinketer* (*K* 156) and *trinketing* (*SD* 633). There is reason to suppose that at least some of these words, either in the senses given here or in all senses, were obsolete, if only recently so, when Scott put them in his novels, but they all remain highly doubtful cases.

A case almost parallel to these is that of *tuck* 'a rapier' (*Wk* 7). Although Scott does not provide the last example in the *OED* of this word, he is followed by only one other author, writing in *Harper's Magazine* in 1885, whose use is clearly historical and who needs to explain the word's meaning. *Tuck* is an interesting case because Scott himself provides us with evidence of the word's status by writing: 'a tuck, as it was then called, or rapier' (*Wk* 7).

Fortunately not all the possibly obsolete words in Scott are such questionable cases as those already mentioned. This is because, reflecting the pattern of Scott's reading, his favourite hunting ground for obsolete language was early Modern English. The majority of his possible revivals fell obsolete, according to the *OED*, between 1600 and 1700. Examples of words which seem to have become totally obsolete in this period are: *abye* 'atone, expiate' (*AG* 412; *K* 102), *bandog* 'mastiff' (*Ta* 662, *FM* 413, *K* 94), *barbican* 'outer fortification' (*Iv* 383, *FM* 603 *K* 428), *danske* 'Danish' (*Ab* 270), *drap-de-berry* 'woollen cloth from Berry' (*BL* 127, *RR* 436), *hest* 'command' (*Ta* 829, *HM* 222), *holytide* 'time of religious observance' (*LL* VI iii; used attributively *FM* 24), *leech* 'to cure' (*Iv* 234), *misproud* 'arrogant' (*Ta* 848, *AG* 73), *pennoncelle* 'a small flag' (*Ta* 487), which also appears, in the poetry, in the form *pensil* (*LLM* IV xxvii, *Ma* IV xxviii), *rudesby* 'a rude fellow' (*Mo* 195), *soldado* 'a soldier' (*FN* 218, *LM* 20), *sworder* 'cut-throat' (*FM* 103), *tregetour* 'juggler' (*Iv* 614). Furthermore there are some words, common enough otherwise, which Scott revived in obsolete specialized senses. Perhaps because the figure of a wolf found on some sword-blades was mistaken for a fox, a sword in the late sixteenth and seventeenth centuries is sometimes called a *fox*. Scott so uses it in *Kenilworth* (*K* 60, 466) and also revives the attributive use found at the same period: 'a good fox broadsword' (*Wk* 12).

A much smaller number of words in Scott's vocabulary fell out of use, according to the *OED*, during the sixteenth century; instances of this kind are: *bransle* 'kind of dance' (*AG* 601), *forayer* 'raider' (*LLM* IV xvii, *Ma* I xx), *malvoisie* 'malmsey' (*FM* 147), *palabras* 'idle words' (*K* 183) and *selcouth* 'strange' (*LI* IV xii). Again there are also familiar words used with unfamiliar senses. The original meaning of *secretary* was the one its etymology suggests: 'a confidant, one who knows a secret'. This was fully superseded about the end of the sixteenth century by the senses developed from it. We find it, appropriately, in the early seventeenth-century setting of *The Fortunes of Nigel* (*FN* 312) but also in the late eighteenth-century setting of *Guy Mannering* (*GM* 149).

These lists are selective; it is clear, however, that the bulk of Scott's obsolete language became so in the sixteenth and seventeenth centuries. Indeed, despite the fact that something like a third of Scott's novels are set in the Middle Ages – including some of his best-known novels – there are very few revived words and phrases in them which Scott could only have culled from Middle English. Chaucer seems to have given him *thunderdint* (*Iv* 448), *woodcraft* (*Ta* 846, *FM* 413, *Mo* 251), *yeomanly* (as an adverb; *Iv* 394), *viretot* (a word of uncertain meaning; *FN* 313) and possibly *heart-spone* 'the depression in the breast bone' (*K* 349). Dame Juliana Berners is the source for the hawking term *reclaim* 'recall' (*Mo* 320), and her namesake, Lord Berners, for *Tranchefer*, a name given to a sword, (*CRP* 238). With the exception of *heart-spone*, which had a limited dialectal survival, all these words were apparently not used after Middle English; they are all covered in more detail in the discussion of the contribution of these authors to Scott's vocabulary (see pp. 34–6). *Gramarye* 'magic' is another medieval word, this time taken from the ballad 'King Estmere' printed by Percy in his *Reliques*. Originally *gramarye*, a variant of *grammar*, meant 'learning'. Its meaning was later perverted to 'magic' reflecting the common association of learning with magic. It is a favourite word with Scott who uses it in his first major poem (*LLM* III xi), twice in *The Talisman* (*Ta* 649, 905) and again in his *Journal* (26 April 1826). *Coronal* in the sense 'a circlet for the head' survives until the mid-seventeenth century. For the nineteenth century the *OED* records its use by Lytton and Morris (*OED coronal* 1); Scott had in fact used the word in this sense before Lytton (*Ta* 644). However in the sense 'a circlet around a helmet' this word is wholly Middle English except that Scott so used it in *Anne of Geierstein* (*AG* 56; see *OED coronal* 1b). This may not be a conscious revival on Scott's part but merely an extension of the meaning of the word known to him from current usage. *Jape* 'a trick' (*K* 51) is, according to the *OED*, 'obsolete since *c.*1515 but used by Scott' (*OED jape* sb 1). The history of other senses of this word provides a reminder that in his revivals Scott is only part of a movement, though perhaps the most important part. The second *OED* meaning 'a device to amuse' is 'obsolete generally before 1600 (not used by Spenser, Shakespeare, or their contemporaries and recorded in seventeenth-century dictionaries as an old word) revived in literary use by Lamb and Barham' (*OED jape* sb 2), while the verb *jape* in its sense 'joke' is revived by Morris after being dormant some three hundred years (*OED jape* v 4).

Sometimes the question arises whether a word has been revived or recoined by Scott himself. *Paynimrie* is given in the *OED* as used by various medieval writers including Wyclif, but only in the sense 'paganism'. When King Richard in *The Talisman* talks of 'the Paynimrie' (*Ta* 628) he means not 'paganism' but 'the pagans, or Saracens, in general'. Other nineteenth-century writers follow Scott's, not Wyclif's, sense. Was Scott reviving the old word and extending its meaning or did he recoin *Paynimrie* on the model of *soldanrie* 'soldans, in general' (*Ta* 792), which, in its turn, he anglicized from the French *soudanrie* (see below)? With *palfrenier* 'man in charge of horses, groom' (*Mo* 491) the likelihood of the word being a revival from Middle English recedes even further. The only example before Scott in the *OED* is an obscure one from Caxton. Like Thackeray, in whose *Paris Sketch-Book* the word next appears after Scott, Scott must have been thinking of the Modern French *palefrenier* 'groom'. *Middle world* 'the earth' seems to be a very rare word as the *OED* cites only two obscure examples from medieval works and one from Scott – not, as it happens from one of the medieval novels but from the early eighteenth-century setting of *The Pirate* (*Pi* 389). On the other hand *middle earth*, with the same meaning, is a common term found until the end of the sixteenth century. An earlier form *middle e(a)rd* or *midlert* survived even longer in Scotland and was in literary use in Scott's own time (*SND middle* 1). Scott revived *middle earth* – or refashioned *middle eard* – in *The Bridal of Triermain* (*BT* I ix), being followed by Crabbe (*OED middle earth*). Since *middle earth* (and *middle eard*) are so much more familiar than *middle world* Scott may have merely used the latter as an equivalent without being conscious of its use in Middle English. Ruddiman in his early eighteenth-century edition of the late medieval Scots poet Gavin Douglas says that *middle eard* is 'a phrase yet in use in the North of Scotland among old people' (quoted in *SND middle* 1). Scott possessed a copy of this edition (*Catalogue*, p. 12). Did he have Ruddiman's comment in mind in making a native of the Shetlands use the term *middle world*?

Apart from the single word *cnihts* in *The Betrothed* Old English is used in only two of Scott's novels – *Count Robert of Paris* and *Ivanhoe*. Of the two only *Count Robert of Paris* is set in what we would now call the Old English period. Its hero is a Saxon exiled from England in the wake of the Norman Conquest and serving in the Byzantine Emperor's Varangian guard. The introduction, at times anachronistic, of Old English into *Ivanhoe*, set over a hundred years later, is principally due to the underlying theme of that novel – the conflict between Saxon and Norman which is to be resolved by the rise of the new Englishman. As it was, Scott – and, for that matter, his readers – being for the most part ignorant about Old English, is largely restricted to terms already made familiar by historians – terms like *thane* and *witenagemot*. These are dealt with further on. It is most unlikely that Scott revived any words direct from Old English, though the *OED* quotations suggest that he did so in the case of the word *folkfree* 'having the rights of a freeman' (*Iv* 438), with only *Ivanhoe* and the Anglo-Saxon Laws of Wihtræd cited. However the *OED* quotations for *esne* 'bondsman' (*Iv* 437) follow a similar pattern, but Scott almost certainly had this word from Spelman (see below).

Although Scott contributed to Modern English many words

current in the Scots of his own time – *awesome* (or *awsome*; RR 423), *cateran* (FM 41, Wa 167), *gruesome* (or *grewsome*; RR 423) *raid* (*Wa* 129n), *slogan* (FM 58, Ma VI xliii) – he seems to have drawn but little from the older Scottish tongue which he could not have also found in earlier English. From the title of Lindsay's *Ane Description of Peder Coffeis having no regaird till honestie in their vocatioun* (*c.* 1550) he took *pedder-coffe* 'pedlar' (*Mo* 436 – *pedder* is Scots for 'pedlar' and *coffe* is connected with the Scots verb *coff* 'purchase' (see *SND coff*). There are no other *OED* or *SND* quotations containing this combination besides Lindsay and Scott (*OED pedder-coffe*; *SND pedder*). Scott picked up the rare word *vasquine* 'a kind of gown or robe' (*Ab* 496) probably from a collection of records relating to the Scottish royal wardrobe published in 1815 (see below). The *OED* gives no examples of *pilgrimer* 'pilgrim' (*AB* 203) between the early seventeenth century and Scott. Subsequent use of the word, according to the *SND*, has been limited and the two instances of the word's use after Scott could well be literary rather than colloquial – one is from Carlyle. Apart from dialectal (including Scottish) use, *guesten*, meaning both 'to receive hospitality' and 'to entertain as a guest', is only found in Middle English. In later Scottish use it is seemingly confined to Scott and 'The Fray of Suport' in his *Minstrelsy* (I 291) and is marked archaic by the *SND*. It is not impossible that Scott himself introduced this word into the poem from his knowledge of older Scottish. His description of his sources makes it clear that a lot of editorial intervention was necessary to form his version: 'particular passages have become inexplicable, probably through corruptions introduced by reciters. The present copy is corrected from four copies, which differed widely from each other' (*Minstrelsy*, I 239). In *The Monastery* 'the godly Earl of Murray ... was to have guestened with the Baron of Avenel' (*Mo* 486). *Hership* is one of those relatively rare words on which Scott offers us a comment directly helpful in our connection; (these comments do, however, seem to be more common with Scottish words): 'Her'ship, a Scottish word which may be said to be now obsolete; because, fortunately, the practice of "plundering by armed force", which is its ultimate meaning, does not require to be commonly spoken of' (*HM* 624n). *Hership* is frequent in earlier Scots (see *DOST her(e)schip*) but the *SND* has no examples of its use after Scott except in the sense 'loss, ruin, destitution' which he does not use. The word occurs regularly in his Scottish novels set in the eighteenth century (*Wa* 137, *HM* 624, *RR* 359) with the implication that if the word was obsolete its dying out was only of fairly recent occurrence. Somewhat inaccurately for a Scottish word, it also appears in *Ivanhoe* where a footnote explains the meaning as 'pillage' (*Iv* 37). Scott also draws our notice to another recently obsolete word in writing of Bailie Macwheeble's 'apprentice (or servitor, as he was called Sixty Years since)' (*Wa* 593). Scott had special knowledge of Scottish law and lawyers and his assertion here that a lawyer's apprentice was called a *servitor* in the mid-eighteenth century highlights the inadequacies of even the best dictionaries – the *OED* gives no other examples later than *c.* 1660 (*OED servitor* 1d) and the *SND* cites only this use of the word (*SND servitor* 3). Scott also remarks that *maker* 'poet', an obsolete word many have taken up after him, belongs to older Scots. His note reads: 'Old Scottish for *Poet*; and indeed the literal translation of the original Greek ποιητής' (*FM* 36n). However *maker* is in fact also used in Middle English.

While *jack* 'a doublet quilted with iron' (to use Scott's own definition; *Mo* 95, also *Ab* 85) is used in Southern English, the more explicit but virtually synonymous *black-jack*, also used by Scott, (*Mo* 169, *FM* 135) seems to be unknown outside Scots. Indeed the *OED* cites only Douglas's *Aeneis* and Scott's *Monastery* for the word. Scott would also derive *jackman* 'soldier' (*FM* 54, 149; *Mo* 95, 428) from *jack* – he explains *jackman* as 'men wearing jacks, or armour' (*FM* 54) – but the *OED* disagrees with him seeing *jack* as the name *Jack* used generically for *man*. The *DOST* refuses to arbitrate between the two views. Whatever its etymology *jackman* was only used in Scotland and even fell out of use until revived by Scott. Of *unfriend* or 'false friend' (*Wa* 134, *FN* 267, *LM* 69) the *OED* says 'in early use chiefly Scottish and in the nineteenth century apparently revived by Scott' (*OED unfriend* 1).

The Baron of Bradwardine, with his usual tendency to lard his conversation with the pedantry of Scottish legal language, declares his fear of giving offence to the ruling powers if he and Waverley 'were to collect together the kith, kin, and allies of their houses, arrayed in their effeir of war' (*Wa* 633). Scott himself loved the ancient Scottish phrase 'bodin in effeir of war' – 'that is, not in dread of war but in the guise which *effeirs*, or belongs, to war; in arms, namely, offensive and defensive' (*FM* 54n). The circumlocutory expression is also found in *The Monastery* where

Christie of the Clint Mill boasts how 'the Baron of Avenel never rides with fewer than ten jackmen at his back, and oftener with fifty, bodin in all that effeirs to war as if they were to do battle for a kingdom' (*Mo* 468). 'Bodin in feir of war' (*feir* has the same meaning as *effeir*, 'array, guise') is, as Scott himself informs us, 'a frequent term in old Scottish history and muniments' (*FM* 54n; see *DOST bodin* 1b; *fere* n⁴ 2). The phrase was more or less obsolete, so it seems, by Scott's time – Bradwardine is no guide to current usage – and hardly used at all after him. One occasion where all were obliged, as part of their duties under Scottish law, to attend 'bodin in effeir of war' was the *weapon-schawing* (*FM* 59, *DD* I i) or *weapon-schaw* (*LLM* IV xxviii, *DD* I i) also spelt variously as *wappen-schaw* (*OM* 18) and *wappinshaw* (*OM* 582). Of course the initial events of *Old Mortality* take place at a *weapon-schaw* when, to quote Scott, 'the feudal array of the county was called out, and each crown-vassal was required to appear with such muster of men and armour as he was bound to make by his fief' (*OM* 18). According to the *OED wappenschawing* was unused in the eighteenth century while the only eighteenth-century citation for *wappenschaw* is from Herd's *Scottish Songs* of 1776 (II 121) a work in which we might expect to find some archaisms. In fact Scott's revivals from older Scottish have not had the good fortune which befell some of the current Scots words he used. *Awesome*, *gruesome* and *raid*, words used by Scotsmen in Scott's time, have all been assimilated into Modern English and are used wherever English is spoken. *Hership*, unlike its more fortunate synonym *raid*, has not been taken up after Scott either in that sense or when meaning 'plunder'. The short-lived revival of *black-jack*, *pedder-coffe* and *vasquine* has likewise been confined to Scott's work. *In feir of war*, *jackman*, *maker* and *pilgrimer* were not taken up by English writers and have been only sparsely used by Scottish ones, except *maker* which is common in literary criticism of Middle Scots poetry. *Unfriend* alone was used by English writers. These few words do however have one special interest. Most of Scott's unusual words are remarkable either for their Scottishness or their antiquity – reinforcing the setting either in place or in time. These few obsolete Scots words revived in the Scottish novels serve both purposes.

The use of the word *jape* by Lamb and Barham (see above) serves to remind us Scott was not alone in reviving words. The whole Romantic movement was involved to some extent with the revival of the language of some area of the past, whether it was the medieval or the renaissance past which particularly fascinated the individual poet. Before Scott had published even his earliest attempts at poetry, Southey had written his historical epic *Joan of Arc*. As Scott was to do, so did Southey; he revived a number of words including many used by Scott, though how far influenced the latter was by Southey it is hard to say. In *Joan of Arc* we find (sometimes with a slightly different spelling) the following words used by Scott: *arblast* 'crossbow' (VII 124; *cf. Ta* 681, *Iv* 383) *craven* 'a confessed coward' (X 458; *cf. FM* 309, *FN* 367); *jazeran* 'a coat of scale armour' (VII 184; *cf. QD* 19); *man-at-arms* (VI 300; *cf. CD* 18, *Ta* 583, *Iv* 89, *FM* 565, *Mo* 69): *mangonel* 'a catapult' (VIII 158; *cf. Ta* 580, *FM* 603) *poldroons* 'shoulder armour' (VIII 454; *cf. Mo* 491, *LM* 188). All of these had been obsolete from the seventeenth century or, in the case of *jazeran*, from the sixteenth century. *Pavesse* 'a large shield' (*Joan of Arc* VIII 345; *Ta* 798, *Iv* 361, *FM* 536) was, if not obsolete, then only known to antiquaries and historians. The phrase *cry craven* 'confess oneself beaten' used in Southey's *Madoc* (*Madoc in Wales* xv) – published in the same year (1805) as Scott's first long poem – is in the same position as *pavesse*, being apparently obsolete in the eighteenth century except for mention by the legal commentator Blackstone. *Cry craven* occurs in *Anne of Geierstein* (*AG* 100). Other revivals found in *Madoc* and used by Scott are *cowardlike* 'cowardly' (*Madoc in Wales* iv; AG 625) and *surcoat* 'a mantle worn over armour' (*Madoc in Wales* xv; *Ta* 487).

No other reviver of obsolete words before Scott had so many in common with him. *Ambushment* 'ambush' had been revived by Scott's friend William Stewart Rose in his *Amadis de Gaule* (1803), well before Scott used it in *Quentin Durward* published in 1823 (*QD* 543). Coleridge had used both *ivy-tod* 'ivy bush' (*K* 378) and *gramercy* (*Iv* 330, *K* 5) in *The Rime of the Ancient Mariner* which appeared in 1798. However in Coleridge *gramercy* is an exclamatory phrase meaning something like 'mercy on us', a rare sense which Coleridge perhaps had from Johnson (see the *OED*'s note, *gramercy* 2), while in Scott it has the more normal meaning 'thank you' or 'thanks'. Only Elizabethans, including Spenser and Drayton, had used *ivy-tod* before Coleridge; perhaps because of these associations the word also appealed to Tennyson.

Scott's debt to other writers in these cases is difficult to assess. Equally when others follow close on his heels in the use of revived words they need not be copying him. Scott had used the typically Elizabethan *viznomy* (a corruption of *physiognomy*) in *The Bride of Lammermoor* (BL 223) and *Kenilworth* (K 161) before Lamb used it in his *Essays of Elia* ('Distant Correspondents'), but Lamb's knowledge of Elizabethan literature was at least as extensive as Scott's.

Where did all these words come from? Most of Scott's words have, of course, innumerable possible sources. In the history of the language only a very few words are confined to one author. Most words must have become fixed in his mind by being encountered again and again in his reading. Others, though only encountered once, may still have stuck in his memory; occasionally we can guess what the source might have been. In just a few cases some additional information makes it possible to know with complete or near complete certitude Scott's actual source. If we examine the small proportion of words with discoverable sources we shall have a skeleton plan of the authors Scott drew on most.

In Middle English literature Chaucer is one of the few authors provably one of Scott's sources. The word *viretot* can only come from Chaucer. Its meaning is obscure but it probably means something like 'swift movement, rush'. According to the *OED* only Chaucer had used the word before Scott (*OED viretote*) and, in any case, the similarity between the two passages is such that Scott's example looks like an allusion to the Chaucer:

> Som gay gerl, God it woot,
> Hath broght yow thus upon the viritoot (*CT* I 3769–70).

> Here you come on the viretot, through the whole streets of London, to talk some nonsense to a lady (*FN* 313).

Scott at least sensed the meaning of this rare term, unlike Tyrwhitt who placed it in a list of 'Words and Phrases Not Understood' at the end of his glossary (*The Canterbury Tales*, 2nd edn, Oxford, 1798, II 651). In the same way its context leaves beyond doubt that *thunder-dint* (*Iv* 448, *Ma* I xxiii), a fairly rare Middle English word, is borrowed from Chaucer. The line in *Marmion*: 'Mid thunder dint and flashing levin' and the phrase in *Ivanhoe*: 'wild thunder-dint and levin-fire' are both almost word for word from the Wife of Bath's curse:

> With wilde thonder-dynt and firy levene
> Moote thy welked nekke be tobroke! (*CT* III 276–7)

Woodcraft 'skill in matters concerning forests especially the chase' (*Ta* 846, *QD* 162, *FM* 413, *Mo* 251), a word frequent in Scott, is rare in Middle English. Of the Middle English citations in the *OED* Scott could have known only that of Chaucer (*CT* I 110); the other text in which the word appears, *Sir Gawain and the Green Knight* (l. 1605), was not published until 1839. In the nineteenth century the word was used in the United States and in the British colonies to describe the skilled knowledge necessary to survive in forest conditions. This seems to be one of those words which went underground in the Elizabethan period only to reappear in the US, though it may have been recoined in the nineteenth century. In Chaucer it is the Yeoman who knows his woodcraft; Scott seems to have remembered his description in the General Prologue well since he also probably took from it the use of the word *yeomanly* as an adverb (*Iv* 394). Chaucer says of his Yeoman, appropriately enough: 'Wel koude he dresse his takel yemanly' (*CT* I 106). The *OED* records only Chaucer, Scott and, after him, G. P. R. James using the word in this way. Either from Chaucer or from dialect Scott took *heart-spone* 'the hollow in the breast bone' (*K* 349). The *OED* cites Chaucer (*CT* I 2606), an eighteenth-century dialect source and Scott (*OED heart-spoon*), but as the *EDD* has only English dialect examples (*EED heart* 1) and the *SND* does not have this compound it would seem to be no part of the Scottish dialect – Scott's most natural source of dialect material.

Another medieval author Scott certainly used is Dame Juliana Berners whose *Book of Saint Albans* published in 1486 deals with the subject of falconry. Scott had this work at Abbotsford (*Catalogue*, p. 208) and in a note on the word *singles* in *The Monastery* he makes reference to it: 'In the kindly language of hawking, as Dame Juliana Berners terms it, a hawk's talons are called his singles' (*Mo* 320n; see *Book of Saint Albans*, 1486, sig. A4). For another hawking term, *reclaim* in the phrase 'to come to reclaim', that is, 'to come when recalled', the *OED* cites only Dame Juliana and does not record Scott's use in *The Monastery* (*Mo* 320). The word occurs on the same page as that on which Scott makes reference to the *Book*. Scott might have also consulted Dame Juliana for some of the other hawking terms he uses but they are not uncommon words: *rifler* – a term used to describe birds which, in Scott's words, 'only caught their prey by the feather' – (*Mo* 321; *Saint Albans*, sig. A7v) and *casting* 'anything given to a bird to cleanse its throat' (*Mo* 321; *Saint Albans*, sig. A3v). Both, however, appear more widely than in Dame Juliana's work, as does *jesses* 'leather straps fixed around the hawk's legs' (*Mo* 318; *Saint Albans*, sig. B4v). Hawking language also occurs in a novel set in the late seventeenth century, *The Bride of Lammermoor*, where we find Lucy's brother talking of *singles* and *riflers* (*BL* 394).

From another sixteenth-century book on a similar subject – *The Noble Arte of Venerie or Hunting* – Scott took the words with which Charles of Burgundy calls on his hounds to chase the pseudo-herald: 'Hyke a Talbot! Hyke a Beaumont!' (*QD* 580). *Hyke* is a call to hounds (*OED hyke*) while *Talbot* and *Beaumont* are names given to them. The author advises his readers to 'halow vnto that hounde naming him, as to say *Hyke a Talbot*, or *Hyke a Bewmont, Hyke Hyke, to him, to him* &c' (1575, p. 112).

The novels and poems bear many testimonies in text and notes to Scott's love of the 'chivalrous pages of Froissart' (*Iv* 392n). Though Scott also possessed the modern translation by Johnes (Hafod, 1803–5; *Catalogue*, p. 28) – a magnificent volume printed on Johnes' private press – he first came to love Froissart in the early sixteenth-century rendering by Berners (*Catalogue*, p. 29) from which he usually quotes. Froissart's concentration on human incidents against the background of the warring of nations was congenial to Scott and his description of the minor details of medieval warfare must have had an effect on Scott's vocabulary. However the only certain borrowing from Berners I can point to is not from Berners' Froissart but from another work he translated from the French, *Arthur of Little Britain*. It is *Tranchefer* – a name given to a sword – (*CRP* 238) and according to the *OED* this word occurs only there (Utterson ed., 1814, p. 208) and in Scott. The book was at Abbotsford (*Catalogue*, p. 122).

Another medieval work is responsible for some of the very little Old English Scott uses – and even this proves to be inaccurate. In *Count Robert of Paris* Hereward the Saxon salutes the Byzantine Emperor:

> '*Waes hael, Kaisar mirrig und machtigh*' – that is, Be of good health, stout and mighty Emperor. The Emperor, with a smile of intelligence to show he could speak to his guards in their own foreign language, replied by the well known countersignal – '*Drink hael!*' (*CRP* 66).

There is no doubt why Scott considered the interchange particu-

Period Vocabulary

larly 'Saxon'. A tradition first mentioned and perhaps invented by Geoffrey of Monmouth has it that the formula was introduced into England by Rowena, queen to the first of the Saxon kings, Vortigern. Geoffrey's story and its subsequent appearance in English texts are dealt with in a note at the beginning of the *OED*'s entry for *wassail*. It is fairly clear that the *waes hael, drinc hael* formula was not as he suggests, current in the fifth century. Geoffrey is in fact our earliest authority for this interchange. Scott alludes to this tradition in *Ivanhoe* in Brian de Bois-Guilbert's toast to Rowena.* It is to be noted that he uses the later form, dating from the time when *waes hael* had come to be looked on as one word, *wassail*:

> And I ... drink wassail to the fair Rowena; for since her namesake introduced the word into England, has never been one more worthy of such a tribute (*Iv* 51).

Further on in *Ivanhoe* we find the drinking formula used in full:

> ... filling both cups, and saying in the Saxon fashion, '*Waes hael*, Sir Sluggish Knight!' he emptied his own at a draught.
> '*Drinc hael*, Holy Clerk of Copmanhurst!' answered the warrior, and did his host reason in a similar brimmer (*Iv* 222).

The *OED* notes that the formula 'in the twelfth century ... was regarded by the Normans as markedly characteristic of Englishmen' (*OED wassail* sb) and certainly Scott too intends us to take it that way. It may be an anachronism in *Count Robert of Paris* as Geoffrey of Monmouth, our first recorded authority for its use, wrote in the twelfth century, though the *OED* suggests that the interchange may have arisen amongst the Danish-speaking inhabitants of England somewhat earlier. The rest of the sentence in *Count Robert* is of doubtful accuracy too. *Kaisar*, a word Scott uses elsewhere in the traditional phrase *king and kaisar* (*Ta* 662, *FN* 198, *BL* 366), is more Middle English than Old English. *Mirrig und machtigh* looks, if anything, more like German than Old English – *mirig and meahtig* would have been a less idiosyncratic spelling.

The other piece of Old English in *Count Robert of Paris* is cer-

---

* The name *Rowena* which Scott was influenced to adopt for his heroine also it seems, originates with Geoffrey of Monmouth (see *Oxford Dictionary of English Christian Names*, s.v. *Rowena*). It is no more Old English, at least in this form, than Scott's *Cedric*, a mistake for *Cerdic* (ibid., s.v. *Cedric*).

tainly spurious; this too is found in *Ivanhoe* as well. The vituperative epithet *niddering* (*CRP* 369) or *nidering* (*Iv* 195, 608) is one of the several mistaken forms of the Old English *niðing* 'villain' originating in the 1596 printed text of William of Malmesbury where *niðing* was misread as *nid'ing* for *nidering* (*OED niddering*). The Saxonist Spelman perpetuated the mistake and a number of corrupted forms appear in the eighteenth-century dictionaries (Bailey: *niderling, niding*; Johnson: *niding*; Kersey: *niderling, niding*, but also *nithing*). The note Scott appends to the word on its first appearance in *Ivanhoe* indicates that he had it either from William of Malmesbury or from someone referring to him since the information he gives is recorded by that author:

> There was nothing accounted so ignominious among the Saxons as to merit this disgraceful epithet. Even William the Conqueror, hated as he was by them, continued to draw a considerable army of Anglo-Saxons to his standard, by threatening to stigmatize those who staid at home, as *nidering* (*Iv* 195n).

Wherever he got this spurious piece of Old English from Scott bequeathed it to his successors as a *sine qua non* of the Anglo-Saxon historical novel. Not much later we find Lytton, in his preface to the third edition of *Harold*, asking: 'would it indeed be possible ... to convey a notion of the customs of our Saxon forefathers without employing words so mixed up with their daily usages and modes of thinking as "weregeld" and "niddering"?' (*Harold*, Caxton edn., p. xvi). It even finds its way into Kingsley's Cambridge lectures *The Roman and the Teuton* (1864). Though the *OED* gives Lytton as the first to use *nidering* as an adjective – *niðing* is only used as a noun in Old English – Scott's use quoted above could possibly be adjectival too.

Shakespeare outdistances all others in the number of words for which he is Scott's demonstrable source. Shakespeare had coined *pouncet-box* 'a small box for perfumes' (*1 HIV* I iii 38) which Scott eagerly introduced as one of the accoutrements of a dandy into at least four of his novels (*Ta* 612, *Iv* 453, *FM* 292, *Mo* 350). Sometimes a word may be restricted solely to one author and his imitators so that it never is used without the first user of the word being in mind. *Pottle-deep* belongs only to Shakespeare and writers recalling him; the *OED* cites only Shakespeare's 'potations pottle-deep' (*Oth* II iii 57) and a late eighteenth-century example repeating the same phrase (*OED pottle* 4). I have only found Scott using *pottle-deep* in phrases modified from Shakespeare. In the narrative of *The Talisman* we find talk of 'pottle-deep potations' (*Ta* 802) and in the dialogue of *Anne of Geierstein* comes 'healths pottle-deep' (*AG* 540). The figurative meaning of *trench* – 'scar, or deep wrinkle' – is given only three times in the *OED*, in Shakespeare's *Titus Andronicus* (V ii 23), in Scott's *Quentin Durward* (*QD* 116) and in Godwin (*OED trench* 4). Another word used in a figurative sense is *pantaloon* 'old fool'. Only Shakespeare (*AYLI* II vii 158, *TofS* III i 37) and a later nineteenth-century author appear in the *OED* as using this word (*OED pantaloon* 2a) but Scott had in fact used it between them (*FN* 308).

In several cases the context reveals Shakespeare as Scott's inspiration. Lord Dalgarno's 'the fico for such outcasts of Parnassus' (*FN* 227) gives no clue as to where Scott discovered this fairly common Elizabethan expression of contempt; but when, in a novel slightly outside our period, the Restoration *Peveril of the Peak*, Buckingham says 'a fico for the phrase' (*PP* 638) Scott is remembering Shakespeare, as he uses the exact words of Pistol in *The Merry Wives of Windsor* (I iii 31). There is another reference to this phrase in the *Journal* (18 October 1826). It is Pistol too, but this time in another play, from whom Scott borrowed word for word Mike Lambourne's: 'thou diest on point of fox' (*K* 466; see *HV* IV iv 9). Scott here uses *fox* in the sense 'sword' which we came across earlier. No one is recorded in the *OED* as using this word after the later seventeenth century and before Scott (*OED fox* 6). *Pleached* is somewhat more common after the Elizabethan period. To *pleach* is to 'interlace branches and twigs to form a hedge'. There are no eighteenth-century instances of *pleach* or the participial adjective *pleached* in the *OED*, though Keats uses it in *Endymion* and many nineteenth-century writers follow his lead. Scott had come across the word in Shakespeare as he uses Shakespeare's slightly different sense of *pleached*, 'fenced, bordered or overarched with pleached boughs'. Shakespeare refers to a 'pleached alley' (*Much Ado* I ii 11), Scott to a 'pleached alley' (*QD* 325, *FN* 174) and a 'pleached walk' (*QD* 315). Shakespeare is also probably responsible for Scott's *six-hooped pot* (*K* 1); hoops were placed at equal intervals around a quart pot, and Jack Cade in part 2 of *Henry VI* promises that 'the three-hooped pot shall have ten hoops' (2 *HVI* V ii 75–6).

Certain archaic words in Scott are attested in the *OED* only in a few relatively minor authors other than Shakespeare. One tends to assume that Scott must have learnt such words from Shakespeare whom he knew so much better than any other authors, but this assumption may not always be well-founded – we shall see Scott taking words from very minor works, often ones that he had edited. *Bane* used in the sense 'to kill with poison' in *The Merchant of Venice* (IV i 46) and *The Abbot* (*Ab* 501) is otherwise only cited from Lyte's *Dodoens* (1578) and Warner's *Albion's England* (1589). Shakespeare uses *blue-bottle* as a nickname for a beadle (2 *HIV* V iv 22). It occurs again only in an obscure work called *The Miseries of Enforced Marriage* (1607) and then there is a long gap before it reappears in Scott (*OED blue-bottle* 2). Scott applies the term to servants (*Wk* 47). With other words there is more reason to suppose that Scott knew the alternative sources cited by the *OED*. For *bona-roba* 'showy wanton' (*K* 10, *FN* 281, *Pi* 573) the *OED* lists Shakespeare (2 *HIV* III ii 26), Scott and Dryden (*Kind Keeper* I i). Scott had edited Dryden and comments on the 'extreme indelicacy' of *The Kind Keeper* (*Works of Dryden*, 2nd edn, 1821, VI 9). The appearance of this word in Dryden makes it suitable for its use in *The Pirate*. For another word much liked by Scott, *cavaliero* – we have 'the cavaliero cuddy' (*FN* 9), 'this cavaliero citizen' (*FN* 217) and 'cavaliero Wildrake' (*Wk* 337, 428) – the *OED* cites Nashe's title *The Return of the Renowned Cavaliero Pasquill* (1589) and Shakespeare's 'Cavaleiro Slender' (*Merry Wives* II iii 76; see *OED cavalier* 2c). For *cullionly* 'base' the *OED* lists Shakespeare (*Lear* II ii 36), Scott (*FN* 213) and Milton's *Colasterion*. For *sheep-biting* 'wretched, miserable, debased' (*K* 466) the list is confined to early seventeenth-century sources – Shakespeare (*Measure* V i 354), Middleton's *Chaste Maid* and Fletcher's *Rule a Wife* – Scott's use not being covered in the *OED* citations. Finally for *unhouseled* 'not having received the Eucharist' (*Iv* 406, *FM* 579, *Mo* 203) the *OED* cites More, Shakespeare (*Ham* I v 77) and, for 1826, after Scott's use of the word, Southey.

For certain words the evidence of Shakespearean influence is more complicated. Two characters in Scott use the word *juvenal* 'youth'. The word appears in Shakespeare several times (*LLL* I ii 8, *MND* III i 100, 2*HIV* I ii 21). Its appearance in the speech of Don Armado in *Love's Labour's Lost* is the most important for our purposes, since Don Armado served as a model for Scott's Sir Piercie Shafton, the Euphuist, one of these two characters using *juvenal* (*Mo* 183). Probably Scott's other character to use *juvenal* (*K* 412), the pedant Erasmus Holiday, was also influenced by the pedantic Don Armado. The word however had currency outside Shakespeare – the *OED* records its use in Dekker and Webster's *Westward Ho* (1607) and Cotton's *Scarronides* (1664). However we can be certain Scott knew his Dame Crane's *palabras* 'mere words' (*K* 183) from Shakespeare, whose Dogberry uses it in *Much Ado* (III v 18) since two pages further on Dame Crane uses one of Dogberry's malapropisms – *comprehend* meaning 'apprehend, arrest' (*K* 185; *Much Ado* III iii 25). This variously corrupted word was however frequent about 1600. It may be significant that *palabras* is the subject of quite long notes in Johnson's variorum edition of Shakespeare (London, 1778, III 296); perhaps notes such as these in the edition he used helped to plant words in Scott's memory. He did possess Johnson's edition (*Catalogue*, p. 210) but on the other hand he was impatient of too many notes: 'A Shakespeare,' he wrote to Constable, '. . . has been often a favourite scheme with me – a sensible Shakespeare in which the useful & readable notes should be condensed and separated from the trash' (*Letters*, VII 79). Another of the words we have already mentioned, *bona-roba*, likewise received special attention in notes quoted by Johnson (Johnson's Shakespeare, V 529). But *taken in the manner* 'caught in the act' (*K* 201), the subject of long notes by Warburton, Steevens and Hawkins (*ibid.*, V 331), is a legal term which Scott may well have encountered in eighteenth-century writers on the law as well as in Shakespeare.

In this connection the word *lady-love* (*Iv* 369, *Ma* I xii) is a special case; Scott owes it not to Shakespeare, but to his editor Theobald. Theobald, in 1733, suggested *lady-love* as an emendation of the First Folio's 'ladies love' in a line from *Romeo and Juliet* now usually printed:

> . . . let there be weigh'd
> Your lady's love against some other maid (R & J I ii 101–2).

It is more than likely that Scott's attention was drawn to *lady-love* by the many notes stimulated in eighteenth-century editions of Shakespeare by Theobald's conjecture. In the *OED* Scott is the next to follow Theobald – in 1805 in *The Lay of the Last Minstrel* (*LLM* IV xix).

Shakespeare was for Scott the greatest of all authors, from the early days when he read him by firelight until the last years when he quoted him day after day in the Journal. The extent of Shakespeare's possible and probable contribution to Scott's period language is much greater than the few words listed so far. To take one example, all the following terms of abuse used by Scott appear in Shakespeare: *coistril* 'base fellow' (*FN* 302; *Tw N* I iii 44), *cullionly* 'base' (*FN* 213; *Lear* II ii 36), *hilding* 'worthless fellow' (*K* 397; *All's W* III vi 4), *misproud* 'arrogant' (*Ta* 848, *AG* 73, *K* 126; *3HVI* II vi 7), *panderly* 'bawdy' (*QD* 477, *Merry Wives* IV ii 125), *princox* 'pert fellow' (*K* 126, *FN* 625; *R&J* I v 90), *rampallian* 'ruffian' (*FN* 460, *2HIV* II i 67), *unthrift* 'prodigal' (*K* 37; *RII* II iii 122). Even when he used a common Elizabethan word Scott must often have had a passage from his favourite in mind. When he writes a note on the Elizabethan vogue word *humorous* he cites Shakespeare as an example: '*Humorous* – full of whims. Thus Shakespeare "Humorous as winter"' (*Mo* 270; see *2HIV* IV iv 34).

Besides Shakespeare, other Elizabethans, including Spenser and Jonson, are very prominent amongst those who make a demonstrable contribution to Scott's archaic vocabulary. Spenser's contribution is less than one might expect with this forerunner in archaic language. Scott was aware, no doubt, of the detrimental effect on the eighteenth-century archaising poets of too great a reliance on Spenser. Some words Scott may have owed either to Spenser or to his imitators or to both – *certes* (*Ta* 560), *faitour* (*QD* 307), *guerdon* (*Ta* 560, *AG* 108, *K* 115, *Mo* 407), *losel* (*AG* 147) and *singults* (*Mo* 396) belong to this category which is covered in the discussion of archaic poeticisms (see pp. 58–63). The word *miser* (*FM* 290, *Mo* 322), used in the sense 'wretch' and not with the modern restriction to 'an avaricious man', is peculiar in that Scott himself indicates its source. A footnote in *The Monastery* reads: 'Used in the sense in which it often occurs in Spenser, and which is indeed its literal import – "wretched old man"' (*Mo* 322n). In *The Fair Maid of Perth* Scott, always interested in semantic history, characteristically notes the lowering of the word's meaning: 'That is, miserable persons, as used in Spenser, and other writers of his time; though the sense is now restricted to those who are covetous' (*FM* 290n). As well as occurring in Spenser (*FQ* II i 8) the word occurs in Shakespeare (*1HVI* V iv 7) and others before Spenser.

Another word certainly taken from Spenser is *derring-do* (*Iv* 395). Scott's footnote explains this as 'desperate courage'. Actually this well-known mistake originates with Spenser. Chaucer, in *Troilus and Criseyde*, had written:

Period Vocabulary

> That Troilus was nevere unto no wight,
> As in his tyme, in no degree secounde
> In durryng don that longeth to a knyght (*TC* V 835-7).

Later Spenser, misconstruing this as a compound noun phrase, took it up and created the word Scott copied (*SC* Oct 65-6; *FQ* II iv 42). As with *nidering*, another error perpetuated by Scott, Lytton was his faithful follower (*OED derring-do*).

Three other Spenserian compounds resurface in Scott. Spenser's *errant-damozel* (*FQ* II i 19), used in *Kenilworth* (*K* 463) and *The Lady of the Lake* (*LL* VI ix), reversed to give *damosel-errant* (*K* 427) and *damsel-errant* (*AG* 330), and his *levin-brond* (*LLM* VI xxv). Finally *heben-wood* is, according to the *OED*, only used once between Spenser (*The Ruines of Time*, l. 618) and Scott where it first appears in *The Bridal of Triermain* (*BT* III xiii) and then in *The Fortunes of Nigel* (*FN* 125). *Heben* is a form of *ebon* or *ebony*.

Ben Jonson's traceable contribution to Scott's archaic language covers two isolated words and a number of terms used by Sir Piercie Shafton in *The Monastery*. Scott has taken the phrase 'peremptory gull' (*FN* 216) straight from Jonson (*EMIH*, Quarto I i 103) whose use of *peremptory* with this sense of 'utter, complete' is the only example recorded in the *OED* (*OED peremptory* 2c). An equally close copying identifies Jonson as the source of *provant* (*K* 409). (The provant was the soldier's allowance and, used attributively, as here, it suggests something of inferior quality). Stephano and Bobadil's exchange: 'This is a Toledo? pish . . . A poore prouant rapier, no better' (*EMIH*, Folio III i 163, 171) is compressed into the speech of one character: 'It is a poor provant rapier, and I warrant you he has a special Toledo' (*K* 409). The language borrowed from Jonson for Sir Piercie Shafton is especially appropriate to him. From two such fops as himself, Asotus and Amorphus in *Cynthia's Revels*, Scott borrows the pseudo-technical language of courtship: *accost, regard, address* and *close* (*Mo* 366). Amorphus introduces his protégé in these terms:

> Here is a gentleman, my scholer, whom . . . I am couetous to gratifie with title of Master, in the noble, and subtile, science of *Courtship*; For which grace he shall this night in court, and in the long gallery, hold his publique Act, by open challenge, to all *Masters* of the mysterie whatsoeuer, to play at the foure choice and principall weapons thereof, viz the *bare accost*, the *better regard*, the *solemne address* and the *perfect close* (*Revels*, IV v 91-9).

Piercie Shafton's account of his own boasted successes is couched in very similar terms:

> I cannot but allow, ... that in the alacrity of the accost, the tender delicacy of the regard, the facetiousness of the address, the adopting and pursuing of the fancy, the solemn close and the graceful fall-off, Piercie Shafton was accounted the only gallant of the time (*Mo* 366).

Apart from dropping all the adjectives, except *solemn* which he has transferred to *close*, Scott has followed Amorphus' terms exactly. Even the new noun *fall-off* which he introduces has a corresponding verb in an earlier scene in the play where Asotus and Amorphus practise for the coming contest:

> First you present your selfe thus; and spying her, you fall off, and walke some two turnes (*Revels*, III v 7–8).

As part of his aspiration to be the ideal courtier Sir Piercie prides himself on a fashionable knowledge of the terminology of duelling. Some of this duellist's language seems to come from Jonson. Halbert, his opponent, is incensed when Sir Piercie talks to him like this: 'Let us pause for the space of one venue, until I give you my opinion on this dependence' (*Mo* 289). Scott explains: '*Dependence* – A phrase among the brethren of the sword for an existing quarrel' (*Mo* 289n). Only Jonson is attested as using this word before Scott (*EMIH*, Folio I v 112; *Devil an Ass*, IV vii 13; see *OED dependence* 6b). *Venue* Scott does not explain – it means a bout of fencing. Though a word found much more frequently than *dependence*, especially in the alternative form *veny*, *venue* may have also have caught Scott's eye in Jonson since it occurs in the same scene of *Every Man in his Humour* as *dependence* (*EMIH*, Folio I v 149).

Sir Piercie's interest in the science of duelling reaches deeper than this:

> The English knight was master of all the mystery of the *stoccata*, *imbrocata*, *punto-reverso*, *incartata* and so forth, which the Italian masters of defence had lately introduced into general practice (*Mo* 288).

It seems likely that Scott had one 'Italian master of defence' in particular in mind when he wrote this passage. At Abbotsford there is a book which appeared in 1595 called *Vincentio Saviolo His Practise: In Two Bookes, The First Intreating of the use of the Rapier and Dagger*, *The second of Honor and Honorable Quarrels* (*Catalogue*, p. 119). Saviolo is the subject of a comment of Charles II on Sir Henry Lee in *Woodstock*; Sir Henry is a 'gouty old man who knows not, I dare say, a trick of the sword which was not familiar in the days of old Vincent Saviolo' (*Wk* 412). Scott and Saviolo are the only writers cited in the OED for *emboscata* (*Mo* 285) – Saviolo spells it *imboscata* (*Practise*, I i) – meaning 'ambush', another piece of Sir Piercie's affected diction (*OED imboscata*). It is reasonable to suppose that the 'Italian master' Scott had in mind in *The Monastery* was Saviolo though Scott could have had these words from elsewhere; the different spellings he uses may suggest that he often did so or they could simply mean that he was writing from memory. Saviolo has *imbrocata* (*Practise*, sig. H1), '*punta* either *dritta* or *riversa*' (*Practise*, sig. K2) and *stoccata* (*Practise*, sig. H4). Such knowledgeable listing of duelling terms is, however, frequent in Elizabethan drama. Jonson writes:

> I would teach these nineteene, the speciall rules, as your *Punto*, your *Reuerso*, your *Stoccata*, your *Imbroccata*, your *Passada*, your *Montaniv* (*EMIH*, Folio IV vii 76–9).

and Shakespeare:

> Ah, the immortal passado! the punto reverso! (*R & J* II iv 27–8).

Passado, or *passada*, another thrust in fencing, is also mentioned in both Scott (*Wk* 317) and Saviolo (*Practise*, sig. H4). It is Sir Henry Lee – a Shakespeare enthusiast as well as an enthusiastic duellist – who speaks of the *passado*. Both Sir Piercie and Sir Henry use the term *stramazon*, yet another thrust in fencing, but each has a different form of the word. Both *estramazone* (*Mo* 362) and *stramaçon* (*Wk* 342) have however been influenced by the French *estramaçon*. This word too occurs in both Saviolo (*Practise*, sig. F2) and in Jonson (*EMOH* IV vi 99).

Though Milton ranks high in the list of Waverley's reading, which we have said to be partly autobiographical, I have only found one provable borrowing from Milton in the period language of Scott's novels. *Scathed* meaning 'harmed or destroyed by fire' – 'a large broken scathed oak-tree' (*Mo* 57), 'the scathed vault' (the vault Wayland destroyed with gunpowder; *K* 211) – is either a deliberate or mistaken extension of the meaning of *scathe* 'harm', probably through association with *scorch*. It derives, so the OED conjectures, from an ambiguous passage in *Paradise Lost*:

> As when Heaven's Fire
> Hath scath'd the Forrest Oaks, or Mountain Pines,
> With singed top their stately growth though bare
> Stands on the blasted Heath (*Paradise Lost*, I 612–5).

The Scottish sources of Scott's period language have already been pointed out. *Pedder-coffe* 'pedlar' (*Mo* 436) came from the title of Lindsay's *Ane Description of Pedar Coffeis having na regaird till honestie in their vocatioun* (written about 1550) while *vasquine* 'a kind of gown or robe' (*Ab* 496) probably came from Thomson's *Collection of Inventories and other Records of the Royal Wardrobe and Jewelhouse* (Edinburgh, 1815, p. 132). Scott had the book at Abbotsford (*Catalogue*, p. 2). Also in this book Scott would have seen the noun *passement* 'lace' also used as a verb 'adorn with lace': both were rare though not as rare as *vasquine*. As far as I have discovered Scott only uses the participial adjective *passmented* (*Wk* 639, *HM* 356) or *passemented* (*FM* 64). (*Cf. Collection of Inventories*, pp. 31, 32.)

These are minor influences. In *The Fortunes of Nigel* reference is made to two books by a Scotsman which were of greater importance to Scott as an artist. At one point Prince Charles, hearing the king mention 'my book', is in dread that his father is 'going to recite the whole *Basilican Doron*' (*FN* 491) while earlier Lowestoffe assures Nigel that 'the King's counter-blast against the Indian weed will no more pass current in Alsatia, than will his writ of *capias*' (*FN* 295). James VI's *Basilicon Doron* and *A Counterblaste to Tobacco* are an important source of inspiration in *The Fortunes of Nigel*. James challenges Nigel as the central character in the book – he is certainly the most amusing – and the whole of his curious manner of speaking and a good deal of his character are based on his two books. Some of the best passages in the book – as when James defends David Ramsay's pedigree: 'They all wrought wi' steel, man; only the auld knights drilled holes wi' their swords in their enemies' corslets, and he saws nicks in his brass wheels' (*FN* 640) and so on – are telling parodies of the contorted logic of *A Counterblaste*'s arguments against tobacco. Again, Scott exploits to the full James' habit of larding his writings with scraps of Latin and homely proverbs. Scott also had warrant for James' swearing in *Nigel*; see the *Minstrelsy* (II 195) where Scott notes how the Scottish clergy reproved James for this habit. The printed versions of the *Basilicon Doron* have a more English kind of spelling than James' original manuscript but even so the language is markedly Scottish in many particulars.* It is true that James advises his son Henry not to use 'any rusticall corrupt leide' (*Basilicon Doron*, STS edn, I 179) but the very use of the word *leid*, from the fifteenth century only in Scotland used as a synonym for 'language', shows that by an 'uncorrupt' language he means the standard 'Inglis' of Edinburgh – indeed the *Basilicon Doron* was written four years before James ascended the English throne. Scott is thus provided with ample warrant for the racy Scots he has James speak in *Nigel*. James equally urges his son to avoid 'booke-language, and pen and inke-horne tearmes' (*Basilicon Doron*, I 179), but seems to be ignoring his own advice when, a few pages later, he speaks of 'writing, whiche is nothing else, but a forme of enregistrate speache' (*Basilicon*, I 183, 185). According to the *OED*, *enregistrate* is a nonce-word and it can justly be called an ink-horn term. Scott is therefore justified when he has the king describe himself as 'the very *malleus maleficarum*, the contunding and contriturating hammer of all witches' (*FN* 562–3). The monstrous word *contriturating* occurs in the *OED* with this single Scott quotation. Yet despite all this very accurate reflection of James' writings in *Nigel* I can find only one actual borrowing of an unusual word from either *A Counterblaste* or the *Basilicon Doron*. Funnily enough this does not occur in *The Fortunes of Nigel* but in *Anne of Geierstein*. It is *morgue* 'or haughty superiority of a knight and noble towards an inferior personage' as Scott describes it (*AG* 548; see *Basilicon Doron*, I 181) for which the *OED* cites only James, Scott and Matthew Arnold. However as the word is borrowed from French, Scott could easily have had it from that source; the fact that it is italicized in his text may mean that this is in fact the case. This seems to be the only contribution of James' works to Scott's period diction as such, and a very doubtful one at that. It is really a token of Scott's skill that he could imitate James' style so well without having to resort to borrowing individual words.

There were other works besides those of James himself that

* The *Basilicon Doron* exists in three versions – James' original manuscript version which has a purely Scottish spelling, the revised first edition of 1599 with English spelling and the even further revised edition of 1603. Scott had the 1616 edition of James' *Works* (*Catalogue*, p. 12) which follows, with some variations of spelling the 1603 text. My references here are to the 1603 text in the STS Parallel-text edition. Scott had in fact produced an edition of part of the *Basilicon Doron* - in his Somer's Tracts (Edinburgh, 1810, III 259–81) there is to be found a pamphlet called *The Dutie of a King in his Royal Office* which consists of the second book of the *Basilicon Doron* with a few paragraphs from James' *Speech at Whitehall* (1609).

could give Scott information about his language. Sir Anthony Weldon in a work which was one of the four Scott included in his collection *The Secret History of the Court of James the First* (Edinburgh, 1811) made this comment about James: 'Nor must I forget to let you know how perfect the king was in the art of dissimulation, or to give it his own phrase (*king-craft*)' (*The Court and Character of King James*, 1650, p. 102). Sure enough the king in *Nigel* protests that 'our secretary kens that point of king-craft, called refusing, better than we do' (*FN* 161). The sense is slightly different from Weldon's it is true, but Scott generally wrote from memory anyway. The word seems to be fairly common in the seventeenth century (there are three *OED* citations including Weldon for that period) but otherwise it only appears in nineteenth-century historians (1827, Hallam; 1874, Green). Was Scott responsible for bringing the word to their notice?

Scott, of course, made use of everything he read and, as we would expect, he is especially prone to quote from works that he had edited himself. Harold H. Scudder has pointed out ('A Queen at Chesse', *MLN*, XLII, (1927), 141–5) that the source of *martialist*, a word used several times in Scott (*Mo* 361, *FM* 218, *K* 222), is Sir Robert Naunton's *Fragmenta Regalia*, which, as we noted before, Scott edited in 1808. In *Kenilworth* he writes: 'Sussex was, according to the phrase of the times, a martialist; had done good service in Ireland' (*K* 222). This is almost word for word as Naunton had described him: 'he was indeed one of the Queen's martialists, and did very good service in Ireland' (Cary's *Memoirs* and Naunton's *Fragmenta Regalia*, Edinburgh, 1808, p. 208). In fact Scott owed Naunton much more than this. From Naunton he took one of the main themes of the novel's setting – the rivalry of Sussex and Leicester. In the novel this culminates in the scene where the two rivals both come before the Queen. Much of the build-up to this confrontation is borrowed from Naunton. Though not all the borrowings belong to our category of 'period language' they are worth considering in detail, so well do they illustrate Scott's methods of using his material. Scott describes how:

> Varney ... dressed out in the utmost bravery of the day, was stopped by the usher ... 'How is this, Master Bowyer?' said the Earl of Leicester. 'Know you who I am, and that this is my friend and follower?'
>
> 'Your lordship will pardon me,' replied Bowyer ...

Period Vocabulary

> 'Thou art a partial knave,' said Leicester . . . 'to do me this dishonour, when you but now admitted a follower of my Lord of Sussex.'
>
> 'My Lord,' said Bowyer, 'Master Raleigh is newly admitted a sworn servant of her Grace, and to him my orders did not apply.'
>
> 'Thou art a knave – an ungrateful knave,' said Leicester; 'but he that hath done, can undo – thou shalt not prank thee in thy authority long!' (*K* 260).

Though expanded to fit Scott's method of narration this is substantially the same as Naunton's account, though the unnamed follower has become Varney:

> Bowyer . . . one day stayed a very gay captain, and a follower of my Lord of Leicester's, from entrance; for that he was neither well known, nor a sworn servant to the Queen; at which repulse, the gentleman bearing high on my Lord's favour, told him, he might perchance procure him a discharge. Leicester coming into the contestation, said publicly, (which was none of his wont) that he was a knave, and should not continue long in his office (*Fragmenta Regalia*, p. 179).

Amongst other things Scott has taken over the term *sworn servant*, applying it however to Raleigh. Elsewhere in the novel he uses the nearly synonymous term *sworn man* 'henchman' when Leicester says 'Richard Varney is my sworn man' (*K* 104). Except in its general sense of 'a man bound by oath', *sworn man* was obsolete by Scott's time (*OED sworn* 2b), as presumably was also *sworn servant* which is not given in the *OED*. Scott goes on to relate how Bowyer complains to the Queen:

> The Spirit of Henry VIII was instantly aroused in the bosom of his daughter, and she turned on Leicester with a severity which appalled him, as well as all his followers.
>
> 'God's death! my Lord,' such was her emphatic phrase, 'what means this? We have thought well of you, and brought you near to our person; but it was not that you might hide the sun from our other faithful subjects. Who gave you license to contradict our orders, or control our officers? I will have in this court, ay, and in this realm, but one mistress, and no master. . . . Go, Bowyer, you have done the part of an honest man and a true subject. We will brook no mayor of the palace here' (*K* 261).

This is even closer to Naunton:

> Bowyer (who was a bold gentleman, and well beloved) stept before

him, and fell at her Majesty's feet, related the story, and humbly craves her Grace's pleasure; and whether my Lord of Leicester was King or her Majesty Queen: whereunto she replied, with her wonted oath, (God's death,) my Lord, I have wished you well, but my favour is not so locked up for you, that all others shall not partake thereof; for I have many servants, unto whom I have, and will, at my pleasure, bequeath my favour, and likewise resume the same; and if you think to rule here, I will take a course to see you forthcoming; I will have here but one mistress, and no master (*Fragmenta Regalia*, p. 180).

The phrase 'mayor of the palace' is just what Scott needs to round off his rather more novelistic account of the Queen's speech, but even this he has adapted from a hint offered by Naunton. The whole incident is offered by Naunton as proof that Elizabeth was 'absolute and sovereign mistress of her graces; and that all those to whom she distributed her favours, were never more than tenants at will' (*Fragmenta*, p. 181). Consequently, says Naunton:

... we find no Gaveston, Vere, or Spencer, to have swayed alone, during forty-four years, which was a well settled and advised maxim; for ... it starved all emulations, which are apt to rise and vent in obloquious acrimony, (even against the Prince), where there is only, *a major palatii* (*Fragmenta*, p. 178).

Major palatii was too good to miss and, translated, it is transferred to the Queen's own speech.

Though Scott did not edit Burt's *Letter from the North of Scotland* he contributed the 'History of Donald the Hammerer' to Jamieson's fifth edition of the work (Edinburgh, 1818). He was thus well acquainted with it, and his acquaintance bore fruit in the word *henchman* with which he has enriched present-day English. From the fourteenth to the seventeenth century *henchman* flourished in English in the sense Shakespeare used it – 'a page of honour' (*MND* II i 121). But after the early seventeenth century it is not heard of till the eighteenth century when Burt speaks of the use of the term *hanchman* in the Highlands: 'This Officer is a Sort of Secretary, and is to be ready upon all occasions, to venture his Life in Defence of his Master; and at Drinking-bouts he stands behind his seat' (*Letter*, London, 1754, II 157). Scott repeated the term in this special Highlands sense and with Burt's spelling in *Waverley* in the enumeration of Fergus MacIvor's retinue: 'his *hanchman* or right hand man' (*Wa* 144). In *A Legend of Montrose* Scott talks of the Laird's 'page, or henchman' (*LM* 48) but as the scene is the Highlands this seems to be a merging of the two senses. By using the spelling *henchman* Scott identifies the earlier *henchman* with the later *hanchman*, an identification which still remains doubtful (see *OED henchman* 2). It is however in the further extension of the word's meaning to cover the sense 'trusty follower' (*LL* II xxxv, *Mo* 429, *CD* 19) that it has become common in later English. Scott used the word with so general a sense that he could write: 'I have the Tweed for my henchman for about a mile' (*Letters*, II 531).

The small proportion of revived words for which one can discover Scott's source provides only a rough guide to the sources of his other revivals. A list of provable borrowings naturally gives such prominence to authors who favour new or unusual words since they provide the easiest cases to prove. However such a list does give us enough idea to be able to draw some conclusions. Firstly one sees the paramount importance of renaissance rather than medieval literature and above all the immense influence of Shakespeare. Secondly we can see how much Scott could extract from minor works – whether minor historical works like Naunton's and Weldon's or specialized treatises like Saviolo's. On a couple of days in October, 1826, Scott put down in his Journal some reflections on his imitators who he thought might eventually oust him:

> One advantage I think I still have over all of them. They may do their fooling with better grace but I like Sir Andrew Aguecheek do it more natural. They have to read old books and consult antiquarian collections to get their information – I write because I have long since read such works and possess thanks to a strong memory the information which they have to seek for. . . . Another thing in my favour is that my contemporaries steal too openly. Mr Smith has inserted in *Brambletye House* whole pages from De Foe's *Fire and Plague of London*.
>
> > Steal! foh! a fico for the phrase –
> > Convey, the wise it call –
>
> When I *convey* an incident or so I am [at] as much pains to avoid detection as if the offence could be indicted in literal fact at the Old Bailey (*Journal*, 18 October 1826).

Scott's efforts at concealment were not in vain; but the greatest bar to our discovering all his 'conveyings' is that to do so we would need a reading and a memory equal to his own – for most of us an impossible qualification.

WORDS FROM HISTORICAL WORKS

Much of the period language in Scott was not obsolete in his time but had come to be used only in specialized and limited contexts as, for example, the work of historians (including writers of literary history). Words known only in history books, however familiar, naturally have strong associations in the reader's mind with the past and, apart from helping to fill in the background of Scott's novels and poems, these words can add powerfully to our sense of a period flavour in the dialogue. The eighteenth century saw the real beginnings of the study of medieval history and literature which so blossomed in the nineteenth century. We have already seen how Percy's *Reliques*, an important book in this field, provided some of the most absorbing reading of Scott's childhood and he himself contributed to this study. How much Scott owed to historians and scholars rather than to original texts it is impossible to tell, and in any case the two must have worked together. Nevertheless it is fair to assume that when a word is specially dwelt on by eighteenth-century scholars this will have drawn Scott's own particular attention to it.

Some words used in historical works were more or less obsolete, so infrequent is their appearance; the names of some obsolete weapons belong to this category: *caliver* 'a kind of gun' (*K* 4) and *quarrell* 'a crossbow bolt' (*Iv* 383). Other words are taken up by all historians who tackle certain subjects. The structure of society being a primary concern of those who study history, there is no shortage of terms denoting the different ranks and institutions of society. These in fact make up a large part of what little Old English Scott uses. Hume in his *History of England* deals with the functions of the *thane* (London, 1823, I 208) and the *alderman* (I 207). The latter is the Old English *ealdorman* – not a functionary in a town (as the word has denoted since the thirteenth century) but a deputy of the king. As well as eighteenth-century historians Scott was acquainted with the works of the pioneering seventeenth-century Saxonist Spelman whose English works (in the 1723 edition) he had at Abbotsford (*Catalogue*, p. 235). Scott had evidently looked at Spelman carefully; when Cedric frees his bondsman Gurth he uses the formula: 'THEOW and ESNE art thou no more' (*Iv* 437). These two words occur together in Spelman's *Feuds and Tenures by Knight Service*, a treatise on the early development of the feudal system which would certainly have interested Scott. The *OED*'s readers and editors who recorded *esne* as obsolete from Old English and *theow* as obsolete from the fourteenth century until their re-appearance here in Scott missed Spelman's passing reference: 'their bondmen (whom they called *theowes* and *esnes*)' (*Reliquiae Spelmannianae*, Oxford, 1678, p. 11). In the same essay Spelman deals with the *thane* (*Reliquiae*, p. 16) and in another writes at some length about the *alderman* (*Reliquiae*, p. 53). Though the word *alderman* occurs at least four times in *Ivanhoe* it is never clear to the reader that it is meant to convey the special Old English sense. Wamba speaks of 'Alderman Ox' (*Iv* 11) in his famous speech on the significance of the different names for animals and meat, and later on he recites his pedigree: 'I am Wamba, the son of Witless, who was the son of Weatherbrain, who was the son of an Alderman' (*Iv* 102). But when he says to Cedric, offering to die on his behalf: 'I trust . . . that the son of Witless may hang in a chain with as much gravity as the chain hung upon his ancestor the alderman' (*Iv* 334) he conjures up, perhaps unintentionally, the traditional picture of the civic dignitary. Nor does the comment in Scott's note on *cnihts* that they always ranked 'above an ordinary domestic in the royal household or in those of the alderman and thanes' do anything to make the precise position of the *alderman* any clearer to the reader, merely implying that he held an exalted position. Furthermore Scott mistakenly considered *thane* to be synonymous with *franklin*. Cedric is described as being 'in rank a thane, or, as the Normans called him, a Franklin' (*Iv* 34). This comment arises, we may note in passing, from that same fascination with the dual language situation – triple if we include Latin – of earlier medieval England which led Scott to include Wamba's speech on animals and meats. Probably Scott is wrong in suggesting that a *franklin* and a *thane* are the same thing. Scott's description of Cedric as a *thane* is also possibly anachronistic but fits well with his portrayal of a character obsessed with the Anglo-Saxon past. The word *thane* is of course familiar to all readers of *Macbeth* but the Scottish meaning – 'the chief of a clan, ranking with an earl, and holding lands of the king' – was slightly different and by Scott's time obsolete though, due to Shakespeare, not forgotten; other senses like 'attendant', 'retainer' and 'warrior' had long since been forgotten. Later historians revived the spelling *thegn* to distinguish the Old English from the Scottish sense; *thegn* is the form preferred for example by Lytton.

Since the *witena-gemot* 'meeting of wise men' was the nearest the Anglo-Saxons came to a Parliament, the abiding interest in the origins of the English system of government ensured that this term was well aired from the Elizabethan period on. Hume spends several pages describing its functions, (*History of England*, I 200-4) while in 1821 Sharon Turner testifies to the continuing interest; in the preface to the third edition of his *History of the Anglo-Saxons* published that year he informed his readers that, in response to requests for 'more satisfactory information' he had expanded his comments on the witenagemot (7th edn, London, 1852, I ix). Scott's Saxons use it in *Ivanhoe* (*Iv* 357).

Sharon Turner also gave some attention to another term found in *Ivanhoe* – *cnihts* (*History*, III 110-1). Scott's interest in the semantic development of words as well as his limitations as a historian of language comes out in a footnote appended to the word *warders*:

> The original has *Cnichts*, by which the Saxons seem to have designated a class of military attendants, sometimes free, sometimes bondsmen, but always ranking above an ordinary domestic, whether in the royal household or in those of the aldermen and thanes. But the term cnicht, now spelt knight, having been received into the English language as equivalent to the Norman word chevalier, I have avoided using it in its more ancient sense, to prevent confusion (*Iv* 37n).

This sense of *cniht* is not peculiar to the 'Saxons' and appears throughout Middle English; Scott's information is otherwise accurate as regards to the English language though he makes a mistake in the French: *chevalier* is Central French; the Anglo-Norman equivalent was *chevaler*. It would be unfair, however, to stress these minor mistakes since Scott was probably the first author many of his readers had encountered who discussed things like change of meaning in a popular novel.

In Turner also, as he points out in a footnote (*Iv* 41n), Scott found *morat* 'a drink made with honey and flavoured with mulberries' and *pigment* 'spiced wine' (*Iv* 41). *Morat* appealed to other poets besides Scott: two years after Turner (the first to be cited in the *OED* for *morat* which he actually fashioned from the medieval Latin *moratum*) Campbell uses it in one of his poems and in 1829 Southey listed it with other old drinks; 'almost as obsolete as metheglin, hippocras, clary, or morat' (*OED clary* sb). *Pigment* is not found after the Middle Ages in this sense although *piment*, another form of the word with the same meaning, survived into the Elizabethan period.

For the background to *The Monastery* Scott used another early nineteenth-century work. A note to the word *misericord* (*Mo* 260) acknowledges material from the Rev T. D. Fosbroke's *British Monachism, or, The Manners and Customs of the Monks and Nuns of England*, first published in 1802, of which Scott had the second enlarged edition of 1817 (*Catalogue*, p. 184). As Scott would have found, Fosbroke's detailed study covered most of the background material on monastic life needed in the novel. The titles of the two officers whom the gourmet Abbot most values for their services – the *Kitchener* and the *Refectioner* (*Mo* 204) – both head chapters in Fosbroke. *Kitchener* is an old and rare word which Scott might have also seen in Dugdale's *Monasticon* but which he is unlikely to have come across elsewhere. *Refectioner* is not strictly a revived word but a translation of the Medieval Latin *refectorarius*. Elsewhere in the novel Scott uses Fosbroke's Latin terms: *biberes* 'the monk's allowances to drink' (*Mo* 473; *British Monachism*, 2nd edn, London, 1817, p. 58); *caritas* 'a cup of wine allowed to the monks' (*Mo* 473; *British Monachism*, p. 58n); and *frater ad succurendum* 'an inferior kind of lay brother' (*Mo* 206; *British Monachism*, p. 265).

The scholars of the eighteenth century, interested in the ballads as the first vestiges of medieval poetry that came before their notice, wished to establish their relation to medieval romances. In the process they incidentally revived the old spelling *romaunts* (see *e.g.* Percy's *Reliques*, Everyman edn, II 174). For Scott and Byron the spelling *romaunt* was a convenient differentiation from *romance*, which had become more or less synonymous with *novel*. Scott's medieval characters speak of *romaunts* (*FM* 550, *AG* 564) and the subtitle of *Childe Harold's Pilgrimage* is 'A Romaunt'. The word *lai*, which had been applied to a shorter kind of medieval poem, both lyrics and sung narratives, had, from the sixteenth to the eighteenth century, become a 'mere poetic synonym for song' (*OED lay* 1). It is, of course, in the restored medieval sense that the word is used in the title of *The Lay of the Last Minstrel*. Scott's major poems are the nearest modern literature has come to medieval romance though they are longer than what would have been called a *lai* in the medieval period. The term also finds its place in the novels (*Ta* 524, *AG* 180).

In the discussion of the relationship between ballads and romances it became necessary to define the role of the minstrel. This led to an acrimonious debate between Percy and Ritson on the minstrel's profession and social status. (Arthur Johnston's *Enchanted Ground* (London, 1964, pp. 95–9) traces the course of this somewhat embittered dispute). In the course of this various names for minstrels were bandied about. *Gleeman* was one of them; reading the *Reliques* Scott would have found a long note concerning the word *glee* (Old English *glig*) and its derivatives (*Reliques*, I 34–8). When he later came to edit *Sir Tristrem* he would have come across both *glee* and *gleeman* again. *Glee* occurs there with two meanings, each of them illustrated by Percy in his note and both reproduced in *Marmion* – 'musical entertainment' (*Sir Tristrem* I xxvii; *Ma* I xxv) and 'a musical instrument' (*Sir Tristrem* II x; *Ma* I iv). Both of these meanings were obsolete in normal English use though the first survived in the Scottish dialect. *Gleeman* (*Sir Tristrem* II lxvii) is used in *Ivanhoe* (*Iv* 227). When Scott introduced a female minstrel into *The Fair Maid of Perth* he called her a *glee-woman* (*FM* 175). While Percy offered no authority for this he did list *glee-maiden* (*Reliques*, I 35, 50) which Scott used in *The Lady of the Lake* (*LL* VI vi). On the other hand *glee-woman* is listed only once in the *MED* (*MED gle* 5). Perhaps Scott recoined this uncommon word by analogy with *glee-maiden* just as he probably coined *bower-lady* by analogy with *bower-woman* and *bower-maid*.

Another word for a minstrel raised into prominence in Percy's and Ritson's feud was *jongleur* (*Reliques*, I 30, 59), an altered or erroneous form of *jougler* (Old French *jogleor*) from which we get our word *juggler*. Scott understood the connection and in *The Talisman* the word means 'conjurer': 'No jongleur can show so deft a transmutation' (*Ta* 872).

The discussion of the origins of minstrelsy merges with the more general question of the history of music. This subject was well covered in the eighteenth century, most notably by Charles Burney's *General History of Music* (published in sections between 1776 and 1789) and Sir John Hawkin's *General History of the Science and Purpose of Music* (1776). Neither book is included in the Abbotsford *Catalogue* though it would be surprising if Scott was without knowledge of the work of Burney whose daughter,

Period Vocabulary

Fanny (the novelist), he met in London in 1826 (*Journal*, 18 November 1826). Scott does not seem to have held a very high opinion of early music:

> Saxon minstrels, and Welsh bards, were muttering prayers, and extracting mistuned dirges from their harps, crowds and rotes (*Iv* 598).

Demonstrating yet again his eager but uninformed interest in etymology, Scott's footnote to this passage repeats a false etymology which Burney too had upheld:

> The crowth, or crowd, was a species of violin. The rote a sort of guitar, or rather hurdy-gurdy, the strings of which were managed by a wheel, from which the instrument took its name (*Iv* 598n).

Burney had 'not the least doubt that the instrument called a rote, so frequently mentioned in our Chaucer, ... was the same as the modern *vielle* ... and had its name from the *rota*, the wheel with which its tones are produced' (*General History*, New York, 1957, p. 594n). If Scott had not read Burney he had read someone else who concurred with him. In fact the rote was a plucked or bowed instrument probably identical with the crowd. The two words have the same root as well – a word which a sixth-century Latin writer represented as *crotta* or *chrotta*. *Crowd* comes into English from the Welsh derivative *crwth*, and *rote* by a more roundabout route through an early Germanic borrowing taken into medieval Latin and French.

The influence of Percy and Ritson is felt in other fields besides minstrelsy. *Termagaunt*, the name given by medieval Christians to a supposed god they believed the Moslems to worship, is still a puzzle to modern scholarship. Like *glee*, *Termagaunt* was treated in a long note by Percy following 'King Estmere' (*Reliques*, I 112) and later in his *Metrical Romanceës* (1802) Ritson supplemented this by appending an even longer note on the subject to *Lybaeus* (*Ancient Engleish Metrical Romanceës*, London, 1802, III 257–62). Percy, quoting an example from *Sir Guy the Soudan*, noted that 'in the old romances [Termagaunt] is constantly linked with Mahound, or Mahomet'. Another instance Percy could have quoted but one which Scott would have known anyway is Spenser's:

> And oftentimes by Turmagant and Mahound swore (*FQ* VI vii 47).

Percy and Ritson reinforced Scott's memory so that in *The Talisman* we find Theodorick of Engaddi crying out:

> Down with Mahound, Termagaunt, and all their adherents (*Ta* 536).

When Ivanhoe first appears in that novel he is dressed as a pilgrim:

> A cloak or mantle, of coarse black serge, enveloped his whole body. It was in shape something like the cloak of a modern hussar, having similar flaps for covering the arms, and was called a *Sclaveyn*, or *Sclavonian* (*Iv* 44).

It seems very likely that Scott had obtained this word, not used since the Middle Ages, from an extensive note to *Horn Child* in the *Metrical Romanceës* (III 278) where all four examples quoted are spelt in this manner. The *OED* hesitates, in giving the root of this word, between *sclavus* 'slave' and *Sclavus* 'Slav' (*OED slavin*) the second being the derivation Scott adopted and expressed with his usual interest in etymology.

Historians often have recourse to invented terms of their own as well as those used in the past. We find *charger* (*Ta* 491), a modern term developed in the eighteenth century, used alongside *destrier* (*Iv* 566) or *dexter*, the Middle English word for a knight's horse or warhorse. Historians use both terms and so does Scott. *Destrier*, the form Scott uses, is Old French rather than Middle English but is favoured by eighteenth-century and later historians. *Morat* (*Iv* 41), which we earlier noted Scott had from Sharon Turner, is not an Old or Middle English word but an antiquarian coinage derived from the Medieval Latin *moratum*. Similarly, the term *mystery* used by two eighteenth-century writers on drama, Dodsley and Hawkins, to denote what we now generally call *mystery plays* or *miracle plays*, is not Middle English but an anglicization of the French *mystère* or Medieval Latin *mysterium*. Like Scott's own anglicizations and creations these new words form, paradoxically, part of the period language of the novels, since the ordinary reader associates them wholly with the past. The language of historians, even their neologisms, plays a large part in the make-up of Scott's period diction.

WORDS FROM POETRY

Apart from history books another haven for words otherwise

obsolete is poetry. Archaic diction has a place in most eighteenth-century poetry but in general it cannot be called an important one. However one branch of that poetry had a vital interest in archaic diction. Throughout the century a vogue continued for poems written in imitation of Spenser. The best-known of these is Thomson's *Castle of Indolence*. It is probably also the best, but there are many others like Croxall's *An Original Canto of Spenser*, Mickle's *Sir Martyn*, Moses Mendez' *Squire of Dames* and Gilbert West's *Education*. Even the scholar Fosbrooke – whose *British Monachism* Scott consulted in writing *The Monastery* – wrote a long Spenserian poem called (in most un-Spenserian fashion) *The Economy of Monastic Life*. Byron's *Childe Harold's Pilgrimage* comes at the end of this tradition and owes a little to it. At the beginning of the tradition was Prior in 1706 with his *Olde Humbly Inscrib'd to the Queen . . . Written in Imitation of Spenser's Stile*. His preface made quite clear how far his Spenserianism was to go:

> As to the style, . . . it was impossible not to have a mind to follow our great countryman Spenser; which I have done (as well at least as I could) in the manner of my expression, . . . having . . . avoided such of his words, as I found too obsolete. I have however, retain'd some few of them, to make the colouring look more like Spenser's. *Behest*, command; *band*, army; *prowess*, strength; *I weet*, I know; *I ween*, I think; *whilom*, heretofore; and two or three more of that kind, which I hope the ladies will pardon me, and not judge my Muse less handsome, though for once she appears in a farthingal (*Literary Works*, Oxford, 1959, I 230–31; modernized).

Prior does himself justice; he mentions no more than he intends to give. From the first stanza the poem proclaims itself solidly Augustan. Later writers were usually more liberal with their Spenserianisms but Prior's preface accurately foreshadowed the limitations of the Spenserian style. The constant imitation of one author imposes too great a uniformity of diction. All descended from the same source and, interbreeding amongst themselves, the Spenserians repeat each other in every stanza. *Sir Martyn* shows Spenserianism at its worse and illustrates how little rigid copying of one author could serve as a model for what Scott was doing:

> But certes you shall woo and strive in vain.
> Fast in his armes he caught her then ywis;
> Yfere they fell, but loud and angry then

The Language of Walter Scott

> Gan she of shame and haviour vild complain,
> While bashfully the weetlesse boy did look:
> With cunning smyles she viewd his awkward pain;
> The smyle he caught, and eke new courage took,
> And Kathrine then a kiss, perdie, did gentlie brook.
> (*Sir Martyn* I xix)

Certain words seem to be obligatory for the Spenserian poet: *certes* 'certainly', *depeinten*, 'painted', *eld* 'old age', *emprise* 'adventure', *eyen* 'eyes', *faitour* 'evil-doer', *guerdon* 'reward', *lever* or *liefer* '(I would) rather', *losel* 'sluggard', *lustihed* 'lustiness, vigour', *ne* 'nor', *perdie* 'truly', *prick* 'ride', *soothly* 'truly', *ween* 'think', *whilom* 'once upon a time', *wight* 'man', *yode* 'went'. On this Spenserian scrap-heap Scott was able to draw, but after a hundred years of association with minor poetry much of it was only at home in his verse. *Whilom* (*Ma* IV xi), *wight* (*Ma* III xxxix), and *yode* (*Ma* III xxxi) occur in the poems but I have not found them in the novels as period language, though the irreverent young Lord Dalgarno uses *whilome* jocularly in *The Fortunes of Nigel* (*FN* 200). (The jocular use of archaisms plays its part in the aims of some of the Spenserians). Generally when Spenserian diction does appear in the novels it seems to be confined to the medieval rather than the renaissance ones. In novels set in the Middle Ages we find *certes* (*Ta* 560; *Iv* 294), *emprize* (*Iv* 396), *faitour* (*QD* 309), *guerdon* (*Ta* 560, *AG* 108) and *losel* (*AG* 147). An exception is *lustihood* found in *Woodstock* (*Wk* 538). The word *singults* 'sighs' has so few quotations in the *OED* that it is very possible that it largely survived as a conscious recall of Spenser in whose works it first appeared (*FQ* III xi 12). Certainly this is likely when it is used in West's *Education*, a poem avowedly in imitation of Spenser (*OED singult*). In Scott I have only noticed it in the half-medieval, half-renaissance *The Monastery* (*Mo* 396).

It is not only the Spenserians who have archaic diction; in other poets the influence of Spenser may be felt as well. *Fray* 'to frighten', used frequently by Spenser (*e.g. FQ* I i 38), was taken up by Shenstone and reappears in Scott (*Wk* 95). *Fray* was almost certainly archaic in Shenstone – the eighteenth-century lexicographer Bailey marks it 'Spen.' (Spenserian) which usually indicates a word not in current use – but, as with possibly obsolete words, absolute certainty is impossible. *Maugre* 'in spite of' (*Iv* 449, *K* 24) is marked archaic by the *OED* editors and may well have been so in Scott's time despite a number of *OED* quotations for the later eighteenth century. Dr Johnson says: 'It is now out of use'. In the same category of probable archaisms are Gray's *haply* 'perhaps' (see *Iv* 393) and *press* 'thick of the battle' (see *Ta* 624).

Another writer one might perhaps expect to have some influence on Scott is Chatterton. However, his greatest influence on Scott seems to have been as an example of what to avoid, so that, as we saw before, in the Dedicatory Epistle to *Ivanhoe*, Chatterton stands as Scott's chief example of the wrong way to use archaic language. Apart from the fact that Chatterton was attempting something quite different from Scott – a full-scale imitation of earlier English – the great difference between the two authors is that Scott learnt the language of the past from texts while Chatterton, as Skeat long ago pointed out ('Essay on the Rowley Poems' in *The Poetical Works of Thomas Chatterton*, London, 1883, II xv–xix, xxx–xxxi), learnt it from dictionaries. Chatterton's language perpetuates the mistakes of the lexicographers but he also adds mistakes of his own of the kind we would expect from someone taking the meanings of words out of context. None of these mistakes, as far as I can see, Scott copied. Scott knew that a *bordel* was a 'brothel' (*AG* 366) and not, as Chatterton thought, a 'cottage' (*Aella*, l. 147), and although he popularized the term *slogan* 'war-cry' (*Ma* VI xviii, *LL* II xx, *FM* 58) under that spelling, Scott also recognized *slughorn* as another spelling of the same word (see *Minstrelsy*, II 34) unlike Chatterton and Browning who took it as some kind of horn (*Aella*, l. 691; 'Childe Roland to the Dark Tower Came', xxxiv).

The influence of the ballads on Scott's style and subject matter have often been commented on. However, when it comes to the kind of period vocabulary Scott liked to use in his novels they have less to offer than we might at first expect. Even in the poetry, where the stylistic influence of the ballads is more noticeable, the influence of written poetry on the vocabulary seems to be far greater than that of oral poetry. No doubt the very nature of traditional ballads has a lot to do with this. Although the ballads were transmitted from the past and retained some of the language of the past, they owed their survival to being repeated for generally poorly educated audiences. Consequently they tend to preserve only such old words as the listener can at least guess at the meaning of. Thus in Percy's version of 'Chevy Chase', printed from an old manuscript, we find the obsolete and obscure term *basnite* or *basnet* (*Reliques*, I 70) which Scott liked to use in his period language (*Be* 26, *Ma* VI xxi). But in the *Minstrelsy*, where the ballads are generally quoted from oral tradition, or from more recent written sources, the word only appears in 'Kinmont Willie' (*Minstrelsy*, II 60), a ballad in which, to say the least, a strong element of editorial rewriting has always been suspected (we have only Scott's version). 'Kinmont Willie' is by Scott's own account, 'preserved, by tradition, on the West Borders, but much mangled by reciters; so that some conjectural emendations have been absolutely necessary to render it intelligible' (*Minstrelsy*, II 55). When the equally recherché term *arblast* 'a kind of crossbow', another staple item in Scott's period language (*Ta* 681, *Iv* 383, *Be* 40), makes its solitary appearance in the *Minstrelsy* (in 'Kempion'; *Minstrelsy*, III 301) it proves to be in a stanza not to be found in Scott's main source for the text (see F. J. Child, *The English and Scottish Popular Ballads*, in 5 vols, New York, 1956, I 311). This use of *arblast* is the only one recorded in Child's very full glossary to his edition of the ballads. Scott records that 'the ballad of "Kempion" is given chiefly from Mrs Brown's MS with corrections from a recited fragment' (*Minstrelsy*, III 299). His editor Henderson felt 'this stanza was probably got from recitation' (III 301n) but it might well be Scott's own.

Nevertheless Scott almost certainly took at least two words from the ballads: *bower-woman* (*Ta* 784, *Mo* 22) and *bower-maiden* (*Be* 191). MED examples of *bower-woman* are limited to the fourteenth and fifteenth centuries (*MED bour* 5) and the *OED* has no further examples until the nineteenth century. However it appears in the *Minstrelsy* (II 270) in 'Rose the Red and White Lily'. Moreover an examination of Child's version of the ballad shows that Scott had the word from his original (Child's *Ballads*, II 419; Version A, st. 24). *Bower-woman* also occurs in Percy's *Reliques* (II 246) in 'Gil Morrice'. The synonymous *bower-maiden* likewise appears in the ballads (in 'Earl Richard'; *Minstrelsy*, II 234) Scott's source for these lines and this particular word being Herd's manuscripts ('Young Hunting', Version G, st. 1, in Child's *Ballads*, II 151). To these two Scott added his own further creation *bower-lady* (*Ta* 786).

Ballads and earlier literature are probably each equally responsible for Scott's use of the word *jack* meaning a 'protective jacket' (*Mo* 95, *Ab* 85). It occurs in 'Dick o' the Cow' (*Minstrelsy*, II 82) which in this respect faithfully reproduces Scott's source (Child's Version A, st. 33; see his *Ballads*, III 465, 468). *Leman*, retained in

'Brown Adam' (*Minstrelsy*, III 203) from the source Scott was using (Child's *Ballads*, II 374; Version A, st. 13), is far too common a word, though associated by Scott's time rather with the past than the present, for us to narrow its source to the ballads; nevertheless they probably played their part in making him use the word.

Though the ballads in his own *Minstrelsy* are only part of the ballad literature Scott knew, they do illustrate the kind of archaisms that can be expected to survive in orally transmitted literature. Much as Scott loved oral literature, its influence, in terms of actual word borrowing, does not seem to approach that of written literature.

VARIANT FORMS

Two things in favour with the Spenserians were spellings ending in *-e* such as *gentlie, weetlesse* and variant forms like *haviour vild*. Words only archaic in spelling did not fit into Scott's conception of period language in the novels. A few appear in the poems – *ladye* is used throughout Scott's first long poem (*LLM* I i &c) and *chapelle* is found in *Marmion* (*Ma* III xxix) – but even these prove on examination often to be introduced for the sake of the rhythm or the rhyme agreeable to the 'very remarkable license of varying the accents of words at pleasure, in order to humour the flow of the verse' which Percy attributed to the minstrels (*Reliques*, I 26). Scott never went to the lengths of Coleridge's original version of the 'Rime of the Ancyent Marinere' in the use of 'olde' spellings. The novels are virtually free from them, one exception being *papistrie* 'papistry' which for some reason Scott usually spells in this way in our novels (*Ab* 80, *K* 50, *FN* 85). On the other hand while he avoided speciously archaic spellings Scott saw a useful purpose for genuinely variant forms.

In many cases variant forms of the same word have had quite different fates. The aphetic *minish* (*K* 143, *FN* 261, *Wk* 43), although it was later revived by various nineteenth-century writers, seems to have fallen out of use about the beginning of the seventeenth century, yet the full form *diminish* has never been out of use since its introduction into English. *Botcher* (*K* 69) is a form of *butcher* only known in the sixteenth century and in Scott's revival. A similar difference in vowel is found between *nombles* and *numbles* 'the edible offal of a deer'. The *OED* does not record *nombles* (*Mo* 255) as an English spelling; Scott may have revived it from the Old French – as a French word it is used in *Ivanhoe* (*Iv* 58). *Deboshed* (*K* 50, *Wk* 44) is a form of *debauched* obsolete in English before the middle of the seventeenth century but lasting longer in Scotland. It was used in literary English after Scott 'with somewhat vaguer sense than *debauched*' (*OED deboshed*). *Rascaille*, the same word as *rascal*, is a fourteenth- and fifteenth-century spelling identical with the Old French *rascaille*. Scott seems to favour it for the early medieval novels (*Iv* 363, *Be* 28). Finally, according to the *OED*, the spelling *moyle* (*FN* 72) for *mule* is archaic in the nineteenth century.

The use of such minor variations from the standard must have seemed natural to a Scotsman. Every Scotsman soon becomes aware of a multitude of minor differences between English and Scots. Take a few lines from any Scots-speaking character in the novels and a host of vowel differences, if nothing else, are immediately evident. This applies even to the court-bred Sir Mungo Malagrowther in *The Fortunes of Nigel* with his *ane* 'one', *maist* 'most', *weel* 'well', *auld* 'old', *caup* 'cup' (*FN* 261). Add to this other variations – words shorter or longer by one or more syllables: *decored* 'decorated' (*Mo* 288, *BL* 128), *advisement* 'advice' (*RR* 52), *desiderate* 'desire' (*RR* 52) and such differences of ending as *custodier* (*Ab* 268) instead of *custodian* – and we have the chief kinds of variants Scott used in his period language. To a Scotsman's familiarity with the handling of variant forms Scott added his own collector's zeal. This combination achieves its most spectacular results in the words for *ambush*; there are no less than four variants: *ambushment* (*QD* 543), *bushment* (*QD* 542), *ambuscade* (*FM* 263, *QD* 542, *Wk* 41) and *emboscata* (*Mo* 285). *Ambuscade* was current in Scott's time, but *bushment* was obsolete and *ambushment* virtually so, while in *emboscata* Scott was reviving a word which had apparently been used only once before in English. *Harrowtry* (*K* 192) looks in context like a sub-standard form of *heraldry*. It is possibly not sub-standard; the *OED*, if it does not give this form of *heraldry*, nevertheless offers the spelling *harowed* for *herald* as current in the fifteenth and sixteenth centuries. The *OED* suggests a special reason for the revival of *damosel*, found in Scott in the Spenserian combination *errant-damozel* (*K* 463), namely 'to express a more stately notion than is now conveyed by *damsel*' (*OED damsel* 1). After Scott it was picked up by Rossetti for the title of his poem *The Blessed Damozel*, by which time it had been invested with quite different connotations from *damsel*. There was also a special reason for reviving the fourteenth- to seventeenth-century spelling *donjon* for the word *dungeon*. By using the spelling *donjon* for the primary sense 'the great tower or keep of a castle' (*Iv* 348, *AG* 47) Scott made possible an easy differentiation from the better-known second sense 'a secure prison cell' which he continued to spell *dungeon* (*Iv* 279). Before Scott the same spelling was used for both senses; later writers have maintained his useful distinction. *Bartizan* 'a parapet or battlement' (*Mo* 348, 392, *Wa* 111), one of Scott's best-known revivals, was believed by the *OED* editors to be Scott's corruption of the seventeenth-century spelling *bertisene* for *bertising*, a methathesized form of *bretising* or *bratticing* 'battlementing' (*OED bartizan*). *Bratticing* itself was obsolete by Scott's time. The larger number of Scottish uses of the word collected by the *DOST* showed that Scott's spelling is historically correct and that many similar forms also flourished in sixteenth- and seventeenth-century Scots (*DOST bartising, bartisan*).

Some of Scott's spellings and forms are his own. The two forms of the fencing term *stramazon* which he uses are both influenced, but in different ways, by the French *estramaçon*. *Estramazone* (*Mo* 362) takes from the French equivalent its initial *e* and *stramaçon* (*Wk* 342) its [s] pronunciation. Neither of these two spellings is attested elsewhere.

In describing the towers of Branksome Scott writes:

> On battlement and bartizan
> Gleam'd axe, and spear, and partisan;
> Falcon and culver, on each tower,
> Stood prompt their deadly hail to shower (*LLM* IV xx).

The word *culverin* is known in the fifteenth and sixteenth centuries with the meaning 'a small firearm' as in *Kenilworth* (*K* 243) and later from the sixteenth to eighteenth centuries meaning 'a large cannon' as in *Marmion* (*Ma* IV xxvii) but Scott is the first to use *culver* with one of these senses. Perhaps Scott was misled by the existence of *culver* 'a dove or wood-pigeon' identical in form but derived from Old English not, like *culverin*, from French and further led astray by the close proximity of *falcon* 'a kind of light cannon' (see also *OM* 268) which has a diminutive companion *falconet* (*OM* 268). Whether the aphetic *culver* is accidental or intentional, Scott has actually passed off a neologism as an archaism.

VOGUE WORDS

While many words are in vogue for a time and then pass out of use entirely, some go through a period of special popularity but afterwards still remain part of the living language though with diminished popularity. Sometimes a different, often a shorter form of the word has become more popular but without ousting it completely. *Laboratory* was by the nineteenth century probably the normal form, but *elaboratory* with the same meaning (*K* 175) still occurred down to Victorian times as a rather quaint variant. In the same way in our time the further shortening *lab* still has some competition from *laboratory*. Of *quacksalver* 'a quack doctor' (*K* 152) the *OED* says: 'very common in the seventeenth century; in later times largely superseded by the abbreviation *quack*' (*OED quacksalver* 1). Neither of the two older forms, then, appears to have been totally obsolete in Scott's time but, given the fact that they both occur in the romantically Elizabethan atmosphere of *Kenilworth*, both *quacksalver* and *elaboratory* would have had an Elizabethan ring to them for the better-read part of Scott's audience. Comments in the *OED* enable us to recognize other words in this category. *Nose-of-wax* (*FN* 165), a term of abuse, is described as 'very common *c*. 1580 to 1700' though it is attested later. *Unthrift* 'prodigal' (*K* 37) is 'frequent *c*. 1520 to 1690'. After that it seems to have been a somewhat rare word since Bailey marks it 'O'. (that is, old). *Statist* 'politician' (*QD* 521, *K* 355) may have been already archaic in Scott's time though it was used by Wordsworth. The *OED*'s description is 'very common in seventeenth century now archaic'. *Make-bate* 'trouble-maker' (*K* 458) is also marked 'archaic' with a note to the effect that it was common in the sixteenth and seventeenth centuries. Some of these words may, in fact, have been obsolete by Scott's time. Swift provides the last *OED* example before Scott (dated 1710) of *make-bate*; Scott himself is only followed by Macaulay.

Failing a comment by the *OED* it is hard to establish that a word had a vogue at a certain period. The term *actor* has now entirely superseded *player*; both were current in Scott's time but had *player*, used in *Kenilworth* (*K* 468), been more common in the sixteenth century than it was in the nineteenth?

Period Vocabulary

A hint of the meaning 'puritan' still hangs about the word *precise* on at least one occasion when used by Jane Austen (see Phillipps, *Jane Austen's English*, p. 54). Nevertheless it must have been much more commonly used in this sense in the sixteenth and seventeenth centuries when, as the *OED* points out, the related noun *precision* (*K* 21) was synonymous with *Puritan* (*OED precisian* a). In *Kenilworth* Leicester links *precise* with another word of related meaning, *professor*, using both in a slightly ironic fashion: ' "You are a grave professor of the precise sisterhood, pretty Mrs. Janet," said the Earl' (*K* 103). *Professor* 'one who makes open profession of religion' has a more complicated history than either *precise* or *precisian*. The last two *OED* examples are from Mrs Stowe's *Uncle Tom's Cabin* (1852) and *The Raiders* by Crockett (1894); the *OED* remarks: 'now chiefly Scottish and US' (*OED professor* 3b). Before that Scott had used the word in *Waverley* (*Wa* 284) giving it to a speaker of Scots dialect. If the word had become confined to Scotland by the time of the Waverley novels then this would be an interesting case of Scott returning a dialect word to its rightful historical place in English. *Professor* had been normal and frequent in Elizabethan English. *Malecontent* (*FN* 292) is another word especially common in Elizabethan English. For his play *The Malcontent* Marston was able to draw together the attributes of a well-known stock stage figure of the Elizabethan period, and if the word has never been quite obsolete it is particularly rich in Elizabethan connotations.

Groups of words can have a vogue in the same way as individual words. In the Elizabethan period there was a fashion related to the Elizabethan fondness for foreign words, for moulding words ending in *-ado*. *Poignado*, a reshaping of *poignard*, is a case in point. Mainly an Elizabethan word (*OED* quotations from 1567 to 1694), it resurfaced in *Kenilworth* (*K* 463). The foreign look is only superficial. The Spanish and Portuguese *-ado* is a masculine ending of the past participle as in *el Dorado* 'the gilded' (found strangely in *Kenilworth* as 'the Eldorado' (*K* 10) with a double article – the English and Spanish) and *tornado* 'that which is turned'. Legitimate borrowings like these account for only a small percentage of English words ending in *-ado*, represented in our novels by *reformado* 'an officer left without command but with rank' (*FN* 291) and *soldado* 'soldier' (*FN* 218, *LM* 20) – that is 'one who is paid' since *soldo* (Spanish *sueldo*) means 'military pay'. *Trinidado* 'a kind of tobacco' (*Wk* 129) is adopted from the

Spanish adjective for Trinidad. More frequently the *-ado* ending is what the *OED* calls an 'ignorant sonorous refashioning' of nouns in *-ade* borrowed from the French *-ade* (feminine) which corresponds to the Spanish *-ada* (see *OED* *-ado*). Of these bastard formations Scott has several: *bastinado* 'beating' (*Wk* 660) – Spanish *bastonada*; *camerado* 'comrade' (*K* 141) – French *camarade*; *pasquinado* 'lampoon' (*FN* 540) – French *pasquinade* (the French form is common in English); *passado* 'a forward thrust with the sword' (*Wk* 317) – Spanish *pasada*. To these words attested before this time, though in the case of *pasquinado* only once, Scott added one of his own manufacture, *gambado* which he usually puts in the plural as *gambadoes* 'horse's leaps and bounds' (*Mo* 260). It is adopted from the French *gambade* (Spanish *gambada*). *Gambade* itself had been borrowed into English much earlier on in the sixteenth century but had changed in form to yield our modern *gambol* (*gambade* – *gambawd* – *gambaulde* – *gambol*). As well as changing it to *gambado* Scott reborrowed *gambade* unchanged (*QD* 156). In the end *-ado* came to be used just as a foreign sounding optional extra: *poignado*, to return to our first example, has no nearer foreign model than *poignard*. Indeed, once established in the English consciousness, the ending *-ado* overruled any similar foreign ending: *mocado* 'a kind of cloth' (*K* 406) is a corruption of the Italian *mocajardo*. (From the same ultimate Arabic root as this word, *mohair* is also derived). Most of the words had only been used in the sixteenth and seventeenth centuries before receiving a new lease of life in the Waverley novels. *Bastinado*, if it was still used in the general sense 'beating' in Scott's time, was probably rare (*OED* *bastinado* 2); *mocado* is used by Richardson (1741) but probably in the mistaken sense 'mockery' (*OED* *mockado*). In *pasquinado* Scott revived a very rare word or, very likely, recoined it. The *OED* records only one instance of its use, dated 1600.

Similar pseudo-foreign forms are found ending in *-o*; these had a like vogue in Elizabethan times. *Coranto* 'a kind of dance' (*Mo* 208) was adapted from the French *courante* (also borrowed into English) or the Italian *coranta*. By the nineteenth century its use was confined to historical works. The Spanish word *huracan* appeared in English under a multitude of forms of which *hurricane* emerged as the form acceptable in Standard English from the seventeenth century on. Earlier, forms ending in *-ana* and *-ano* seemed like to predominate. In *Kenilworth* we find *hurricanoe* (*K* 56). The ending seems to have been influenced, as the *OED* notes, by a general misconception that all Spanish words ended in *-o* (*OED hurricane*). On the other hand *duello* (*Mo* 282; *Wk* 211) and *piccadilloe* in *piccadilloe-needle* (*K* 185) are true foreign words adopted respectively from the Italian *duello* and the Spanish *picadillo*.

Most of these words occur in the renaissance novels; whether genuine borrowings from abroad or foreign-sounding English creations – they all fit in with the general Elizabethan flavour by recalling the Elizabethan's love of foreign words.

NEW WORDS

In his examination of Scott's contribution to Modern English ('Sir Walter Scott's Contributions to the English Vocabulary', *PMLA*, LXVIII, (1953), 180–210) Paul Roberts differentiates Scott's attitude to the invention of new words from that of Joyce and Shakespeare:

> He had a clear though qualified interest in words as words. His interest was not Shakespeare's or Joyce's. A word to Scott was not a toy, something on which to try one's ingenuity or exercise one's inventiveness.... A word to Scott had a meaning, and that was the end of it. It was static (p. 203).

Compared to those two great creators of new words Scott is insignificant as a word coiner. But although, as Roberts further remarks, 'Scott did not essay any pure creations, like *kodak* or *gas*' (p. 202) he did nevertheless introduce a number of new words. Not all of these belong to our subject-matter but some do, since, in what is almost a contradiction of terms, Scott managed to create 'old' words, or what we might paradoxically call archaic neologisms. Other words convey no sense of period even though some of them occur in our medieval novels, for example *cragsman* 'mountaineer' (*AG* 38) which had appeared earlier in Scott in a Scottish form, *craigsman* in *The Antiquary* (*An* 91). But elsewhere Scott contrives to slip in new words as part of the apparently 'old' language.

Sometimes Scott bases his creation on an obsolete prototype, one particularly suggestive model being the string of Elizabethan words beginning in *mar-*, the best known of which is the pseudonym *Martin Marprelate*. On the same lines as this Scott gives us two new words: *mar-feast* (*K* 16) and *mar-company* (*AG* 364). A

The Language of Walter Scott

close parallel to this both in sense and method of formation are compounds beginning in *trouble-*. The OED lists a number of these mostly from late sixteenth- and seventeenth-century sources (*OED trouble* v III 6). The two nineteenth-century examples are from Lamb and Hardy, both writers who used archaic terms in their writing. Scott's *trouble-mirth* (*K* 585), which the OED also lists, without, however, supplying any quotations, could be a revival from this period but might equally be an innovation like *mar-feast* and *mar-company*. As well as *mar* and *trouble* one finds the further synonyms *spoil* used in this fashion. Scott is given in the OED, rather surprisingly, as the first to use *spoil-sport* (*K* 458). Whether or not Scott was the creator of this now common word he arranges for it a context in which it sounds very Elizabethan: 'Mike Lambourne was never a make-bate, or a spoil-sport, or the like' (*K* 458), where *make-bate*, yet another verb-noun compound, is a common sixteenth- and seventeenth-century word probably revived by Scott (see above).

This type of compound, verb plus noun to give noun, seems to be especially common in Elizabethan English – *crack-rope* 'gallows bird' (*QD* 590) and *tear-cat* (*K* 206) and *tearmouth* (*Letters*, V 339), terms applied to ranting actors, are all Elizabethan terms revived by Scott. Scott's creations *bleed-barrel* 'tapster' (*K* 335) and *swill-flagon* 'drunkard' (*AG* 448) follow this same syntactical pattern. *Swill-flagon* has the Elizabethan prototypes *swill-pot* and *swill-bowl* but the sole model behind *bleed-barrels* seems to be the general syntactical one. *Killbuck* is attested before Scott but in the sense 'fierce-looking fellow' (*OED killbuck* 1) and not in his sense 'the keeper of a deer-park' given as a nonce use by the OED (*OED killbuck* 2). A 'fierce-looking fellow' sounds more like a poacher than a keeper. Did Scott recoin the word or just remember it hazily?

There is close similarity between these compounds and others of Scott's creation like *Bend-the-bow* (*CRP* 23), *Cleave-the-wand* (*Iv* 320), *leap-the-ladder* (*QD* 589), *Fire-the-fagot* (*K* 44), *Lock-the-door* (*K* 470), and *hop-the-gutter* (*K* 447), the difference being merely the inclusion of the article. Some of these are used as nicknames and all owe something to the tradition of allegorical naming – compare Bunyan's Mrs Love-the-flesh and Mr Hold-the-world and Scott's own Mr Bide-the-bent (*BL* 410). Scott's use of these combinations – 'a peculiar coinage of noms-de-guerre' – was one of the similarities between his novels and poems by which J. L.

Period Vocabulary

Adolphus concluded that the novels, at the time anonymous, were written by Scott (*Letters to Richard Heber*, London, 1822, p. 281). Where these names or nicknames reflect the characters' occupation Scott perhaps had in mind as a prototype *Burn-the-wind*, a 'cant name' for a smith (*FM* 38). He had taken this word from Burns (see *FM* 38n). There is no special reason for considering them as period except in so far as any unfamiliar combinations are likely to be taken as archaic in Scott's setting. When Petit-André addresses the condemned Hayraddin both as 'my merry leap-the-ladder' (*QD* 589) and as 'my little crack-rope' (*QD* 590) the ordinary reader is hardly in a position to distinguish between the genuine archaism (*crack-rope*) and the sham one (*leap-the-ladder*). Another of Petit-André's horrible terms of endearment for his victims – *jerry-come-tumbles* (*QD* 242) – is likewise of Scott's creation and is probably assimilated by the reader in the same way.

Such seventeenth-century terms as *suburb-sinner* and *suburb-drab*, formed in reference to the fact that the prostitutes lived in the suburbs, are the model for Scott's neologism *suburb-wench* 'prostitute' (*K* 374). The basis of *sack-spigot* (*K* 338), another word invented by Scott, was the attested Jacobean term *sack-butt* 'a butt for sack (the wine)' (*K* 34). A spigot is a small peg to stop the vent-hole of a cask. *Bower-lady* (*Ta* 786) is, as we have already mentioned, coined on the model of the medieval *bower-maid* and *bower-woman*. *Six-hooped-pot* (*K* 1) is Scott's variation on Shakespeare's *three-hooped pot* (*2 HVI* IV ii 75). (Hoops were placed at equal intervals around a quart pot). Finally if *lyme-hound* (*K* 49) was an unknown term to some of Scott's readers, as seems likely, those readers probably thought of *lyme-dog* (*FM* 550, *AG* 147) – yet another of Scott's creations – as being archaic. *Lyme* or *leam* is another word for a leash and both of these compounds mean 'a hound kept on a leash'.

This process occurs in reverse as well; a current compound has one of its elements replaced by an obsolete term. Thus *lightning-bolt* gives way to the archaic-sounding but in fact new-coined *levin-bolt* (*FM* 163, *Mo* 180) by the substitution of the obsolete *levin* for the current *lightning*. From this it was only a short step to the formation of new compounds without any prototype in mind but with one archaic element. The best-known of these is *free-lance*, which occurs first in Scott, though now very similar. He uses it as the name of De Bracy's mercenaries; the usual term for them in *Ivanhoe* is *Free Companions* (*Iv* 479) but a couple of times Scott calls them *Free Lances* (*Iv* 476, 478). However it is in a figurative sense that it has been taken into Modern English. *Lance* in this compound means 'a horse soldier armed with a lance' although Scott also uses it in a less specific sense 'a lance, in other words, a belted knight' (*CD* 27; also *Ta* 517). Scott is given in the *OED* as the last to use the word to describe a horse soldier and it was presumably obsolescent in his time if not obsolete. *Rash-taffeta* (*K* 406) is a rather tautological combination as both *rash* and *taffeta* denote kinds of silk. Quite which kind of silk is intended here is not clear since *taffeta* has been used to describe different materials at different times. If, as seems to be the case from the *OED* quotations (*OED rash* sb^2), *rash* was obsolete in Scott's time the tautology was presumably intended to make the archaic word intelligible. The same applies to Scott's *donjon-keep* (*QD* 29); both *donjon* and *keep* in this new combination mean 'the great tower of a castle' and *donjon*, if not an obsolete word, has at least an obsolete spelling (see above).

It seems to be the fate of many of the words Scott restored to the language or created to be accepted in Modern English mainly in a figurative sense, for instance, *free-lance*, *henchman*, *slogan* and, one not mentioned before, *passage of arms*. *Passage* had been used to mean an exchange of blows between two combatants in the seventeenth century (*OED passage* III 13) but Scott formed the phrase *passage of arms* and applied it to the 'Gentle and Joyous Passage of Arms of Ashby' (*Iv* 172), in other words the tournament described in *Ivanhoe*. In writers of the later nineteenth century the phrase is generally used figuratively of verbal conflict.

One kind of combination which successfully *looks* period is words ending in *-craft*. Scott's *scholar-craft* (*Mo* 136) and *tailor-craft* (*Wk* 342) do not seem to have appeared before him. *Scholar-craft* is listed this once (*OED scholar* 5) and *tailor-craft* not at all in the *OED*. By Scott's time the addition of *-craft* had ceased to be a normal form of word-formation. We have already seen how Scott came to use the attested but, at the time he wrote, probably obsolete *king-craft* (*FN* 161).

One of the commonest forms of word-formation in English is the addition of *-er* to a verb to give a noun for the agent. These words are mostly without period connotation and if *marker* 'marksman' (*Mo* 241) and *mouther* 'flatterer' (*FN* 235) have any period flavour in the novels it has spilled over from their surroundings. However when the word added to is itself archaic the result will be an apparent archaism. Until Scott's time the noun *roister* 'bully' was identical with the verb. Whether out of ignorance or to avoid ambiguity Scott formed a new noun *roisterer* (*Mo* 281, *Ab* 195, *FN* 273). While the older noun *roister* had not apparently died out by Scott's time it had been especially common '*c.* 1550 to 1700' (*OED roister* sb). Scott's new word took on the Elizabethan ring of the more established form. Finally there is *halfling* (*Iv* 65) Scott's new way of describing a half silverling or old penny; presumably none but the expert numismatist took this to be anything but a genuine old word.

Since French was the second, and indeed often the first, language of early medieval England, it is not surprising that Scott occasionally englishes Old French as a substitute for reviving Middle English. *Soldanrie* 'soldans, in general' (*Ta* 792) is not a Middle English word but an anglicization of the Old French *soudanrie*. *Couching* – 'I am called Kenneth – Kenneth of the Couching Leopard' (*Ta* 516) – is the Old French heraldic term *couchant* made English by replacing the French with the English participial ending. A model for this kind of invention had been provided by words, like *mystery* from French *mystère* and *morat* from Latin *moratum*, used by historians and already the subject of our attention. Of course Scott had other functions for such words as well: *subtrist* 'somewhat sad' (*Ab* 452) is an anglicization of the Latin *subtristis*, but in the mouth of Doctor Lundin it is a piece of humorous pedantry rather than a period word. On the other hand Scott did not need to english the German *Lanzknecht* as *lance-knight* (*QD* 44) as this had already been done in the sixteenth century. The word has a curious history. It originates from the German *Landsknecht* (*Lands* 'of the country' plus *Knecht* 'servant') but even in German it was soon miswritten *Lanzknecht* due to a false etymological association with *Lanz* 'lance'. As well as being borrowed into English in the section by section translation *lance-knight*, *Lanzknecht* also came into English via the French borrowing *lansquenet*. In addition to *lance-knight* Scott tried the hybrid spelling *lance-knecht*. Such at least is the spelling in the 1829–32 'magnum opus' edition (XXXVIII 107); in the Border edition an attempt at greater logical consistency is made with the spelling *lanzknecht* (*Ta* 582).

Leaving aside anachronisms, and many of them are deliberate, Scott makes few mistakes. When he extends the application of a word, as he sometimes does, it is not always possible to know if it is done intentionally or in ignorance. The verb *cote* is used in hunting when one hound passes another. In Scott the hound *cotes* another animal:

> A most perfect creature of heaven . . . strength to pull down a bull – swiftness to cote an antelope (*Ta* 607)

> . . . no greyhound loves to cote a hare, as I to turn and course a fool (*K* 285).

Deliverly is found in earlier English as an adverb meaning either 'quickly' or 'deftly' but appears to have died out by Scott's time; in Scott it is found, uniquely, as an adjective meaning 'sprightly' – 'a deliverly fellow' (*Mo* 224). By the early nineteenth century the use of *gossipred* in its primary sense 'the relationship of godparents, spiritual affinity' seems to be only historical. Scott thought of the sense of *gossip* which we should now think of and used *gossipred* to mean 'the habitual action of a gossip or tatler' (*FM* 309, *Wk* 450). In *Quentin Durward* Scott speaks of a *sounder* '*i.e.*, in the language of the period, a boar of only two years old' (*QD* 160). This is incorrect; a *sounder* is the name given to a herd of swine – 'a sounder of wild swine' – as had been rightly explained in a work Scott knew, Strutt's *Sports and Pastimes of the People of England* first published in 1801 (London, 1876, p. 80). It is also correctly defined in *The Noble Arte of Venerie or Hunting* (1575, p. 100), that earlier authority on hunting which we have encountered before as one of Scott's sources. The fact that Scott explains the term, even if incorrectly, suggests it was not in normal use. (See also the *OED*'s 1824 quotation which would make good sense if applied to an obsolete word.) Finally, a well-known instance from the poems of Scott making a mistake – in *The Lay of the Last Minstrel* the word *warison* clearly means a 'note of assault':

> Either receive within thy towers
> Two hundred of my master's powers
> Or straight they sound their warrison,
> And storm and spoil thy garrison
>
> (*LLM* IV xxiv).

Previous to this *warison*, which became obsolete in the sixteenth century, has two main meanings 'wealth' and 'reward'. As the *OED* points out the source of Scott's mistake 'is probably the line "Mynstrells, playe vp for your waryson", in *The Ballad of Otterbourne*, which Scott had doubtless read in Percy's *Reliques*'

Period Vocabulary

(*OED warison* 5). The word in its new sense was associated with Scott by his contemporaries:

> As my friend Scott says 'I sound my warison'
> (Byron, *Don Juan*, XV lix).

WORDS FROM CANT DICTIONARIES

A small but interesting sub-section of Scott's period language is the cant terms. These are especially common in *The Fortunes of Nigel* and *Kenilworth*. Eric Partridge, who edited Francis Grose's *Classical Dictionary of the Vulgar Tongue* (third edition, 1796), felt Scott had drawn heavily on that work:

> The glorification of the underworld, or rather the vogue of its language in literature ... began in 1822 with Scott's *Fortunes of Nigel*, for which that greatest of historical novelists ransacked the *Classical Dictionary of the Vulgar Tongue* (E. Partridge, *Slang Today and Yesterday*, 3rd edn., London, 1950, p. 85).

Scott certainly consulted Grose – he had the edition of Grose which Partridge has since edited (see *Catalogue*, p. 156) – but equally certainly he used other books as well. There had been many books on cant before Grose, and Scott possessed a number of them: Thomas Harman's *Caveat for Common Cursetors* (first published in 1566; *Catalogue*, p. 140), Head and Kirkman's *English Rogue* (Head appeared in 1665; p. 131) and the *New Dictionary of the Canting Crew* by B. E., Gent. (1698; p. 131).*

Many of the terms used in Scott occur in all or nearly all of these works, including Grose. *Bien* 'good' (FN 295, PP 616), *harman beck* 'a constable' (FN 622) and *wap* 'copulate' (FN 409) can be found in all four (see Partridge, *Dictionary of the Underworld*, London, 1961, s.v. *bene, harman beck, wap*); *prig a prancer*

---

* Starnes and Noyes in *The English Dictionary from Cawdrey to Johnson: 1604–1755* (Chapel Hill, 1946) provide a list of cant glossaries and dictionaries (and general dictionaries which include cant) from Harman to Grose. Scott owned many of these apart from those already mentioned (the most important); of cant dictionaries and glossaries he had Head's *Canting Academy* (*Catalogue*, p. 134), Smith's *Compleat History* (p. 131), Carew's *Life and Adventures*, (p. 130), Parker's *Life's Painter* (pp. 115, 135) and *The Scoundrel's Dictionary* (p. 130), while the 1694 *Ladies' Dictionary* and Johnson's *Dictionary*, both of which he possessed (pp. 138, 266), contained some cant terms. With the works listed above this accounts for 11 out of the 24 items listed by Starnes and Noyes and shows how well equipped Scott's library was even in minor subjects like this. Scott had besides at least two plays important for their inclusion of cant terms, Brome's *Jovial Crew* (*Catalogue*, p. 212) and Shadwell's *Squire of Alsatia* (p. 217).

'steal a horse' (*K* 399) is suggested by the phrase *prigger of prancers* 'horse stealers' recurrent in all four and *gentry cove* 'gentleman' (*FN* 293) occurs in Harman, B. E., and Grose (*Underworld Dictionary*, *s.vv. prigger of prancers, gentry cofe*). The recurrence of certain words and phrases in all books of cant reflects not only the persistence of cant terms but also the habit of lexicographers of borrowing from their predecessors. One early book with a good deal of cant, Dekker's *Bellman of London*, has long passages plagiarized from Harman. On the other hand though some terms are repeated in some or all of these works, it is only in Grose that we may find almost every cant word used in *Nigel* and *Kenilworth*; moreover sometimes Scott's spelling indicates he had relied on Grose rather than on any other authority. Scott writes *bing avast* 'go away' (*FN* 296) like Grose (see Grose, Partridge ed., London, 1963, *s.v. bing*), and not *bynge a waste* like Harman (*Caveat*, Viles and Furnivall eds, London, 1880, p. 84) or even, considering he usually chooses modern spellings, *bing a wast*. Yet when Scott writes *cut boon whids* 'give good words' in *Kenilworth* (*K* 168) he is following neither Harman's *cutte bene whyddes* nor Grose's *cut bene whiddes* (*Caveat*, p. 84; Grose, *s.v. cut bene*) though he does use their explanation 'give good words'. It is perhaps significant that this phrase and *prig a prancer* (deducible from Harman's *prygger of prauncers*; *Caveat*, p. 42) are the only two cant terms I have noticed in *Kenilworth*. Harman's *Caveat* was written just at the time of the *Kenilworth* setting – the later sixteenth century – and is the only work Scott had (apart from the occasional play) which he could trust to give him information about Elizabethan cant. Though Grose has these terms his *Classical Dictionary* is not organized 'on historical principles' and he gives no indication of when words were first used and whether they were obsolete in his time. In general the language of *Kenilworth* has few anachronisms; it is presumably not by chance that the only cant terms in *Kenilworth* are accurately Elizabethan and can be found in an Elizabethan text Scott knew.

Much of the action of *The Fortunes of Nigel* takes place in the sanctuary of Whitefriars, called in cant 'Alsatia'. For this Scott drew on a Restoration play, Shadwell's *The Squire of Alsatia*, and this is one of the causes of anachronism in the novel. Both *decus* 'crown piece' (*FN* 396) and *smelt* 'half guinea' (*FN* 396) can be found in Grose but as they occur in the speech of an 'Alsatian' in Scott he certainly remembered that Shadwell had used them.

They are both listed in the original 'Explanation of the Cant' prefixed to *The Squire* (see Shadwell's *Works*, London, 1927, IV 201). Since the *OED* cites only Shadwell and Scott for *decus* and only Shirley (1635), Shadwell and Scott for *smelt*, *decus* at least could well be anachronistic for a novel which is early seventeenth century in its setting, but of course in these matters we have no *terminus a quo*.

Some of the cant in *The Fortunes of Nigel* also appears in *Peveril of the Peak*; one word which appears in both novels but not in Grose is *tour* 'look' (*FN* 295, *PP* 616). Harman has *towre* 'see' (*Caveat*, p. 84) but Scott apparently had this from Head whose 'Bing out, bien morts, and toure and toure' (*English Rogue* quoted in *Dictionary of the Underworld*, s.v. *bing*) Scott must surely have known when he wrote 'Why, the bien morts who bing out to tour at you . . .' (*PP* 616). The same passage perhaps also influenced: 'Tour out . . . tour the bien mort twiring the gentry cove' (*FN* 295).

The 'Alsatian bully'* Captain Colepepper claims that he 'plays as truly on the square as e'er a man that trowled a die – Men talk of high and low dice, Fulhams and bristles, topping, knapping, slurring, stabbing, and a hundred ways of rooking besides; but broil me like a rasher of bacon, if I could ever learn the trick on 'em' (*FN* 397). The terms *high and low dice*, *Fulhams* and *bristles* denote different kinds of loaded dice and are all given in Grose (*s.v. dice*); so too are *top* 'cheat', *slur* 'cheat at play' and *rook* 'cheat, particularly at play'. This leaves Scott with no authority for *knap* and *stab*. Possibly he had read Cotton's *Complete Gamester* (1674) though it is not at Abbotsford: 'Late at night when the company grows thin . . . and your eyes are dim with watching, false dice are frequently put upon the ignorant, or they are otherwise cheated by Topping, Slurring, Stabbing, &c' (quoted in *Dictionary of the Underworld*, s.v. *stabbing*).

Grose gives *trine* 'to hang' and *nubbing cheats* 'gallows' (*s.v. nubbing*) but Scott must have had some further authority for combining these two in *trine to the nubbing cheat* 'hang on the gallows' (Scott's explanation *Wk* 658) since the phrase *trine on the cheats* is found in the seventeenth century (see *Dictionary of the Underworld*, s.v *trine*). All the same *trine to the nubbing cheat* may be partly anachronistic since, while *chates* (a form of *cheats*) is found in the sixteenth century (*Underworld Dictionary*, s.v. *chates*), *nubbing cheats* is

---

* This is the name that was originally to have been given to Shadwell's *Squire of Alsatia* but it admirably suits Scott's character Colepepper.

attested only from the later seventeenth century. (The use of *cheat* instead of *cheats* is a mistake.)

A final comment on Scott's cant: two of Grose's terms have made their way into *Ivanhoe*: *give him leg bail* 'run away' (*Iv* 253; see Grose *s.v. leg*) and *hedge priest* (*Iv* 468) which Grose defines as an 'illiterate unbeneficed curate' and which is perhaps more slang than cant. The first phrase is only found in the eighteenth and nineteenth centuries – Scott may have also come across it in dialect use. As for *hedge priest*, Scott would have noticed this word in Shakespeare as well as Grose; Berowne in *Love's Labour's Lost* speaks of 'the pedant, the braggart, the hedge priest, the fool, and the boy' (V ii 543–4). Such combinations with *hedge* are innumerable from the sixteenth to eighteenth centuries; for example, *hedge-wine* 'poor wine' occurs in Shadwell's *Squire of Alsatia*, to choose a work already mentioned. Scott followed this practice and himself produced *hedge-parson* (*FN* 291), *hedge-inn* (*Letters*, IV 270–1) and *hedge-ruffian* (*GM* 284). To use such a compound in *Ivanhoe* is thoroughly anachronistic since they were unknown to Middle English.

FOREIGN WORDS

A Frenchman at Abbotsford said that Scott spoke 'le Francais du bon sire de Joinville' (*Life*, I 130), but if Scott was very much at home with medieval French he naturally felt the novels to be no place to air his knowledge. However it demands no great ingenuity and minimal knowledge of French to recognize *roi* and *reine* in their medieval forms *le roy* (*AG* 570) and *la royne* (*Iv* 91) or to translate the addressive in Prior Aymer's 'Benedicite, mes filz' as 'my sons' and thereby recognize the medieval spelling of the modern *fils*. Scott's use of the spellings *roy* and *filz* goes contrary to his practice with English words of generally preferring a modern spelling. In *belle amie* (*Ta* 766) – literally 'sweet friend' but here 'mistress' – he reverts to his normal practice; *belle amie* is a modernization of the Old French *belamy* which was adopted into Middle English and can be found in Chaucer (*CT* VI 318) and Spenser (*FQ* II vii 52). Another phrase which became an accepted part of English was *par amours* 'in sexual love' from which later evolved the term *paramour*. *Par amours* is very frequent in Scott (*CRP* 343, *Ta* 766, *Iv* 309, 500, *Be* 364, *FM* 244, *AG* 549) though the phrase had become obsolete in English by the end of the seventeenth century.

Period Vocabulary

When a term from Old French with no Modern French equivalent is introduced it is promptly explained by being coupled with synonyms:

> to acquire *los* and fame in this mortal life (*Ta* 595).
>
> such words as fame, honour, *los*, knightly glory (*AG* 481).
>
> immortal *los* and honour (*AG* 481).

In one case *los* is further glossed in a footnote: '*Los* – *laus*, praise or renown' (*Ta* 595). Another French word is disguised as the English sounding *gab*:

> Thou art one of the knights of France, who hold it for glee and pastime to *gab*, as they term it, of exploits that are beyond human power (*Ta* 499).

Scott's explanation is given at the foot of the page:

> *Gaber.* This French word signified a sort of sport much used among the French chivalry, which consisted in vying with each other in making the most romantic gasconades. The verb and the meaning are retained in Scottish.

(In spite of Scott's comment the word is not given with this meaning in the *SND*.)

Several of these words occur in the speech of Englishmen, reminding us of the special position of French in medieval England as the language of the upper classes. In *Ivanhoe* some characters are described as speaking Norman or French, some as speaking English (see especially *Iv* 45). In *The Talisman* Scott describes Richard as speaking firstly the Crusaders' *lingua franca*, then French, then English (*Ta* 810–2). He seems to make little distinction between French and Anglo-Norman and in saying that Conrade of Montserrat spoke 'in Norman-French, or the language of Ouie, as it was then called' (*Ta* 636) he appears not to realize that the latter term covers a wide group of dialects and not just Norman. Anglo-Norman – a language distinctly different from French of Paris in several respects – was the normal, almost the only, language of the ruling classes in England from the Conquest at least until the beginning of the thirteenth century. (The loss of Normandy in 1204 by Richard's successor John gave an impetus to the learning of English by the Normans who had formerly been able to consider themselves Frenchmen). It is doubtful therefore whether Richard could speak English at all, and if he could, whether he would have used it very often. Reversing the argument there seems to be little reason for making Henry Gow, shown throughout *The Fair Maid of Perth* as the champion of the lower classes, use the Old French term *gouge* 'wench' (*FM* 210), French being the language of the upper classes.

One use of French which extends beyond the medieval novels is hunting terms; these occur in *The Fortunes of Nigel* (*FN* 481) and *The Bride of Lammermoor* (*BL* 134–5) as well as in *Ivanhoe* (*Iv* 58). With his customary interest in the social significance of language Scott remarks of the terminology of hunting that 'As the Normans reserved the amusement of hunting strictly to themselves, the terms of this formal jargon were all taken from the French language' (*Iv* 58n). French is also the language of chivalry as Richard himself tells us in commenting on the supposed Nubian slave's use of the words *devoir* and *guerdon*:

> '*Guerdon* and *devoir*!' said the King, interrupting himself as he read . . . 'These Eastern people will profit by the Crusaders: they are acquiring the language of chivalry!' (*Ta* 812).

It is interesting that just as Scott made very little use of Old English in his novels so he makes little attempt to show French in its earliest form. In this he can be contrasted with Lytton who makes, for example, William the Conqueror swear '*Per la resplendar Dé*' (*Harold*, Caxton edn., p. 33).

The Latin, like the French, in the medieval novels has its greatest importance in reminding us of the variety of language spoken in the England of the Middle Ages – English for the lower classes, French for the upper classes, Latin for the learned. Most of the Latin in the medieval novels is spoken by monks and priests who made up the bulk of the literate population. Laymen venture only on the words of prayers like Richard's *confiteor* and *mea culpa* in *The Talisman* (*Ta* 768). The priests and monks generally divide their attention between the Vulgate and the rules of their own religious order – the Grand Master of the Templars quotes again and again from the ordinances of his order (*Iv* 492, 405–6, 520). In *The Monastery*, once again transitional between the medieval and renaissance eras, we are faced with an array of Latin terms covering all aspects of the monastic establishment. Scott has these from Fosbroke's *British Monachism* (see p. 55).

Period Vocabulary

By the renaissance period the emphasis has shifted to other languages. In particular, as we have seen, Spanish and pseudo-Spanish words ending in *-ado* and *-o* – *reformado* (FN 291), *pasquinado* (FN 540), *hurricanoe* (K 56) – occur frequently in the later-set novels. French has lost its predominant place but is still maintained as the language of chivalry. The newly made knights at Kenilworth 'were assailed by the heralds, pursuivants, minstrels, &c., with the usual cry of *Largesse, largesse, chevaliers tres hardis!* an ancient invocation, intended to awaken the bounty of the acolytes of chivalry towards those whose business it was to register their armorial bearings, and celebrate the deeds by which they were illustrated' (K 509). The French phrase appears in one of the poems incorporated into Laneham's *Letter* on the Kenilworth entertainment (*Letter*, Furnivall ed., 1890, p. 41) and presumably Scott had it in this novel from that source though the song was also printed in Percy's *Reliques* (Everyman edn., II 204–5). The same phrase occurs, translated, in *Ivanhoe*: 'Largesse, largesse, gallant knights' (Iv 107). We may also compare:

> Now, largesse, largesse, Lord Marmion,
> Knight of the crest of gold!
> A blazon'd shield, in battle won,
> Ne'er guarded heart so bold (*Ma* I xi).

There is Latin too in *Kenilworth* but of a quite new kind, not the religious-based Latin of the Middle Ages. The pedant Erasmus Holiday though he is a figure of fun is also, with his insistence on Latin conversation and classical allusions (K 146–59, 411–2), a type of the new renaissance scholar. However when we get to the novels set in the eighteenth century the pedantic use of Latin by characters like Bradwardine in *Waverley* does not convey any sense of the period as a whole but only adds to the individuality of the character.

OATHS AND EXCLAMATIONS

Religion is all-important to both the medieval and the renaissance worlds which Scott is anxious to create as backgrounds to his novels. Between the Renaissance and the Middle Ages are the fundamental differences brought about by the Reformation. Curiously, one of the most noticeable ways this important change is registered in our novels is through oaths and imprecations.

With the exception of Father Clement in *The Fair Maid of Perth*, all the Christians in the medieval novels are undoubting Catholics. The novels set in the earlier seventeenth century have only Protestant characters. Between lie the two Scottish renaissance novels and *Kenilworth*. In the two Scottish novels we see the struggle between Catholicism and Protestantism, the dominance slipping from the Church of Rome in *The Monastery* to the Reformers in *The Abbot*. In the Protestant setting of *Kenilworth*, set about the same time but in England where the Reformation came earlier, only the last vestiges of Catholicism remain.

In concentrating the evidence of the new religion in oaths, Scott was fitting in with history. The impact of the Reformation on the language, widespread everywhere, is perhaps at its most unmistakeable in oaths. The Reformation, even if it did not completely destroy, for Anglicans at least, the idea of the 'communion of saints', still dealt a death-blow to the popular conception of their power. In common speech the change was registered in the disappearance of the scores of oaths invoking the saints of which examples in plenty can be found in medieval romances. In the novels where the triumph of Protestantism is incomplete occasional invocations of the saints appear – in these cases an explanation can be found in the character or situation of the speaker. In *The Monastery* the Abbot Boniface, conceived by Scott as the incarnation of the dying Church of Rome, is rather pathetically fond of calling on the saints: '*Sancta Maria*' (*Mo* 71); 'Saint Jude be with us' (*Mo* 203); 'In the blessed name of Our Lady' (*Mo* 475). Mysie, the miller's daughter, is also a votary of the Virgin calling on 'Saint Mary! sweet lady' (*Mo* 169). In *Kenilworth* one minor Catholic character appears, Dame Crane 'the papist laundress', who swears 'by our Lady' (*K* 185). Lord Hunsdon, a Protestant, and a relative of that most Protestant of queens, Elizabeth, also swears 'By Our Lady' (*K* 544). There is a special reason in this case; Scott obviously remembers that Naunton in his *Fragmenta Regalia* had commented on Hunsdon's habits of swearing (Carey's *Memoirs* and Naunton's *Fragmenta Regalia*, in 1 vol., Edinburgh, 1808, p. 256). The gaoler at Kenilworth Castle, perhaps somewhat old-fashioned in his seclusion, swears by 'good Saint Peter of the Fetters' (*K* 469) – Arthur Philipson, a Catholic character in the medieval novel *Anne of Geierstein*, uses the same oath when he finds himself accidentally locked in a prison cell (*Ag* 296). It is interesting that both prisoner and gaoler see the imprisoned Saint

Period Vocabulary

Peter as their patron, although the gaoler may also be thinking of Peter's emblematic keys. The Kenilworth gaoler's companion, Mike Lambourne, is equally out of step with the spirit of the times with his oath 'by the pillow of the seven sleepers' (*K* 50) a reference to a medieval legend that seven young men imprisoned in a cave for their faith slept there for two hundred years. The slightly Romish but not very religious oath exactly fits Lambourne's character; generally indifferent to religion, he is yet unwilling to assume hypocritically the time-serving role of a Puritan, as he tells Varney when entering Leicester's service (*K* 120–1). He sees no need to throw off the habits formed under Mary's brief reinstatement of Catholicism when his friend Foster earned the epithet of *Fire-the-fagot* (*K* 21).

The saints are not called on in the novels set in the period following that of *Kenilworth* but in *The Pirate*, a novel set in the eighteenth century, invocation of the saints again appears. No doubt this reflects the isolated, archaic, almost feudal nature of society in the Orkneys and Shetlands where the events take place. (*The Bride of Lammermoor*, almost contemporary in period setting and located in mainland Scotland, has no such oaths). Nearly all the references are to a Saint Magnus; there are a number of saints called Magnus but it is clearly Saint Magnus of Orkney that is intended here. Magnus Troil, for obvious reasons, likes to invoke this saint: 'By the blood of Saint Magnus the Martyr' (*Pi* 221); 'so help me, Saint Magnus' (*Pi* 231); 'by the bones of Saint Magnus my ancestor and namesake' (*Pi* 454); 'Bones of Saint Magnus' (*Pi* 561) but other characters call on the saint as well: 'By Saint Magnus the Martyr' (Mordaunt Merton; *Pi* 245); 'by Saint Magnus' (Claud Halcro; *Pi* 375).

One of the advantages, in short, of this kind of oath which Scott was quick to exploit is that they can be made individually appropriate to the characters that use them. For the purpose of differentiating characters there is nothing to be said for choosing one Elizabethan-type oath like *Udslid* instead of another, say *Od's death*. With those oaths Scott can, by way of characterization, do no more than make one character swear, another not, a third infrequently. When it comes to saints each one has special connotations, though Scott does not always make use of them. Christie of the Clinthill, the mosstrooper (that is, more or less, a bandit), swears 'by Saint Giles' (*Mo* 114). There is no personal significance for the character here in the choice of oath though Scott has been careful to choose one of the saints popular in the Middle Ages; Chaucer's characters invoke him more than once (*CT* VIII 1185; *HF* 1183) and he is one of the two saints invoked in *Sir Gawain and the Green Knight* (l. 1644). This is not the only case in which Scott chooses a saint whose worship was particularly intense in the Middle Ages. In choosing to make Dunois swear by Mary Magdalene (*QD* 252), one of Robin Hood's men by Saint Nicholas (*Iv* 256), one of the English soldiers in Palestine by Saint Christopher (*Ta* 802) and old Martin by the Virgin (*Mo* 223), Scott was probably guided by the fact that these were popular saints in the Middle Ages.

Just once in the Protestant setting of *Woodstock* a character swears by a saint; the Anglican Wildrake's 'by St George' (*Wk* 179) is explained by his nationalism. National pride or prejudice explains many of the oaths in the Catholic novels as well. Ivanhoe, another Englishman like Wildrake, also calls on the Protector of England: 'Saint George strike for us' (*Iv* 394). Charles the Bold, the Duke of Burgundy, who is trying to raise a feif to the status of an independent kingdom, and his follower Crevecœur are both eager to emphasize this same saint's patronage of Burgundy: 'By Saint George of Burgundy' (*QD* 402, 441). Ivanhoe is one of the new men foreseen in the novel who will mingle the, at this stage, still antagonistic strands of Saxon and Norman – in Ivanhoe's own case Saxon birth with Norman manners. The distinction between Saxon and Norman is basic to the novel though probably more serviceable to Scott's art than historically accurate. For the characters who, unlike Ivanhoe, are more determined to insist on their Anglo-Saxon past Scott tries to devise oaths which sound Saxon. In part this is achieved by references to Germanic saints, since Scott was greatly interested in the cultural similarities between the different Germanic peoples, even to the extent of overestimating their importance. Scott certainly goes too far in relying on inter-Germanic influences when he gives the clown Wamba the name of a Visigoth king who figures in the legend of Saint Giles. Friar Tuck also illustrates this in swearing by the Visigoth king and saint Hermangild (or Hermenegild; *Iv* 447) and later in a string of names called forth by his drunkenness: 'Saint Dunstan, Saint Dubric, Saint Winibald, Saint Winifred, Saint Swibert, Saint Willick, not forgetting Saint Thomas a Kent and my own poor merits to speed' (*Iv* 231–2). The selection of saints in this wide-ranging invocation shows a certain bias towards Germanic figures. Saint Dunstan, the Anglo-Saxon archbishop and statesman, Saints Winibald (or Willibald) and Swibert (Swithbert?), Englishmen who were active as missionaries in North Germany and Holland, and Willick (Willigis), a German missionary, are more likely to appeal to the Anglo-Saxons than the Normans, who, despite their Germanic origins, had adopted the French culture. Saint Dunstan is a favourite of the Saxons throughout the novel. Friar Tuck invokes him again (*Iv* 326) and his lead is followed by two other Saxons, Anwold (*Iv* 671) and an unnamed 'boor' (*Iv* 621). On the other hand Thomas à Beckett, or, as he is called here, Thomas a (of) Kent, is a saint whom both Saxons and Normans are willing to have as their patron. The Saxon Gurth and the Norman Prince John both invoke his name: 'by the bones of Becket' (John; *Iv* 178), 'by St Thomas of Canterbury' (Gurth; *Iv* 327). Furthermore Dubric (more commonly known as Dubricius or Dyfrig) and Winifred (or Gwenfrewi) were Welsh saints made popular in England by the Normans. Dubricius first became important in England when the Normans claimed him as the founder of their see of Llandaff. In later medieval times he appears as the archbishop who crowns Arthur. Information about Saint Winifred is more or less legendary but her supposed relatives were Welsh and only after her reputed relics were taken to Shrewsbury in 1138 did her name become well known in England. Thus, despite a certain leaning towards a Germanic tradition, the friar's choice of patrons also reflects the Normans' adoption of Welsh traditions and the rise of *English* figures like Becket beside the *Saxon* ones like Dunstan. Another way of creating distinctively Saxon oaths is illustrated in Ivanhoe's reference to the English hero Hereward the Wake: 'by the soul of Hereward' (*Iv* 397). His father Cedric also uses the same oath (*Iv* 417) and, fittingly for the champion of the Saxons against the Normans, he looks back before the Norman Conquest to the earlier Anglo-Saxon conquest of England and refers to one of the first Saxons supposed to have come to England: 'By the soul of Hengist' (*Iv* 61). It is not easy to know how far the legends or names of Hengist and Horsa in fact survived in the thoughts of twelfth-century Englishmen unacquainted with Latin. It is also improbable, but not impossible, that the old Northern heathen mythology still survived in twelfth-century England; in any case Cedric's curse uses the Scandinavian names of the gods, not the English ones: 'may the foul fiend fly away with me and leave me in Ifrin with the souls of Odin and Thor' (*Iv* 338). Though Scott always calls Cedric a Saxon not a Dane, Coningsburgh, his home, is well within the Danelaw area. Likewise when the old woman Urfried or Ulrica appears 'yelling forth a war song such as was of yore raised on the field of battle by the scalds of the yet heathen Saxons' (*Iv* 430) her mythology too is more Norse than Anglo-Saxon. Scott himself admits that his inspiration has been Norse poetry not Anglo-Saxon (*Iv* Note VI). His use of the Norse term *scald* to describe the Anglo-Saxon poets is perhaps a further indication of his special interest in the *North* Germanic peoples. It seems that Ulrica's reversion to the pagan habits of her ancestors caught Lytton's imagination; the character of prophetess Hilda in *Harold* bears a strong general resemblance to that of Ulrica. She too, in searching for the identity of her race, reverts to paganism. A comparison can also be made with Scott's Norna of the Fitful Head in *The Pirate*.

Traditionally those who invoke the saints choose one who can be expected for some reason to be particularly sympathetic towards them. The reason for the supposed sympathy often lies in the stories or legends attached to the saint in question. We have already seen how Saint Peter, himself once a prisoner, is called on by prisoner and gaoler alike in Scott. Saint Dunstan has been mentioned as a saint dear to Scott's Saxons. For quite different reasons he is also dear to Henry Gow or Smith, the blacksmith in *The Fair Maid of Perth*. As Henry points out, Saint Dunstan was of the craft (*FM* 37) being a skilled metalworker; this was a well-known fact since the most famous legend about him relates how, when he was making a golden chalice, the devil appeared – the saint seized him by the nose with a pair of hot tongs. It is of Saint Dunstan then that Henry thinks when he swears (*FM* 218). Another even more superstitious oath is Gurth the swineherd's 'by the hog dear to St Anthony' (*Iv* 239). A pig is supposed to have been Saint Anthony's sole companion in the Egyptian desert. Finally Allan-a-Dale swears 'by Saint Hubert' (*Iv* 624). Saint Hubert, as the patron of hunters, can be expected to be the friend of Robin Hood's band living in the forest.

The custom of associating saints with the names of places at which they are worshipped survives in the modern Catholic church, for instance in 'Our Lady of Lourdes'. Such identifications provide Scott with some conveniently apposite oaths. Oliver

Period Vocabulary

Proudfute calls on 'St John of Perth' (*FM* 311) and his fellow townsman Simon Glover exclaims 'by St John' (*FM* 303) because, as Scott himself lets us know, Saint John was 'the patron saint of the burgh' (*FM* 428). The principal church in Perth was dedicated to Saint John the Baptist and from this the city was sometimes known as 'St John's Town'. In the novel Perth is referred to as 'this godly city of St Johnston' (*FM* 60). Its slogan was 'St Johnston's Hunt is up' (*FM* 345; also Note IX). Ivanhoe, home in England from the Crusades, swears 'by Saint John of Acre' (*Iv* 394). Acre was the second most important town of the Crusader Kingdom of Jerusalem and a centre of the activities of Ivanhoe's leader Richard Cœur-de-Lion. The conventual church of the Hospitallers in Acre was dedicated to Saint John, their patron. The city itself was sometimes called 'St John-de-Acre', to use the partially anglicized form of the name Scott has Ivanhoe refer to it by (*Iv* 60). Some saints are associated with particular families, thus Douglas in *The Fair Maid of Perth* swears 'by St Bride of Douglas' (*FM* 193) and again 'by St Bride' (*FM* 238), Saint Bride being the patron saint of his family. In *The Talisman*, Thomas de Multon, Richard's faithful follower, swears by 'Our Lady of Lanercost' (*Ta* 636). Scott refers to this Thomas under a bewildering varity of names including Lord de Vaux of Gilsland (*Ta* 592) and De Multon (*Ta* 606). He refers to a passage from Ellis mentioning a knight called Thomas de Multon as the companion of Richard I on his crusade (*Ta* Note I), but has confused this Thomas de Multon with a later member of the same family who had the same name but for whom this oath would have been more appropriate. *The Talisman* is set in the late twelfth century. In the mid-thirteenth century a Thomas de Multon married the heiress of the De Vauxs of Gilsland who had founded the priory of Lanercost in the 1160s. This was the first Thomas de Multon of Gilsland. Scott makes a second mistake; the priory church of Lanercost was not dedicated to the Virgin Mary but to St Mary Magdalene. Scott has nevertheless made a remarkable effort to fill out de Multon's speech with suitable details. He is more accurate in choosing Elspeth Glendinning's local saint: 'Blessed be Saint Waldhave' (*Mo* 85). Elspeth holds her lands from the Abbot of Kennaquhair, Scott's name in *The Monastery* and *The Abbot* for Melrose. One of the important early abbots of Melrose was Waltheof who was locally venerated as a saint. His name survives as a Christian name in the form *Waldive* until the seventeenth century in which the two novels are set; Scott's *Waldhave* is another spelling of the same name. A saint rather better known than Waltheof hides under Front-de-Bœuf's 'Saint Bennet' (*Iv* 358); it is Saint Benedict who is intended here under a form of his name frequent in the Middle Ages. When Louis XI in *Quentin Durward* uses a local designation of the same kind as Multon's 'Our Lady of Lanercost' it is with a special significance. His exclamation 'Saint Mary of Embrun' (*QD* 441) is just right for a superstitious prince who regards the saints as powerful local functionaries. Prince John's character is equally well revealed in his oath 'by Saint Grizzel' (*Iv* 101). He has listened more to the *lais* of the minstrels than to the lives of the saints. The story of Grizzel or Griselda, which Chaucer retold in *The Clerk's Tale*, was a favourite with medieval audiences, though perhaps not as early as this, but her name does not appear among the saints.

Another oath may be included here amongst oaths by the saints because it was evidently felt to be such, though etymologically it is not. *Halidom*, a word first found in Old English, means basically 'holiness' but this sense is unknown after the seventeenth century. Scott illustrates another sense 'holy place', probably by then obsolete, in *The Monastery* when he speaks of 'the Halidome, as it was called, of Saint Mary's' (*Mo* 14). However the most common meaning is 'holy thing, relic'; as such it was used in the oath 'by my halidom' but in this use the suffix is so frequently given the spelling of *dam* or *dame* that it has clearly been taken by popular etymology to mean 'Our Lady'. We even find the spelling *Holydame* (*HVIII*, First Folio text, V i 117). Scott's spelling follows the original form in King Louis' 'by my halidome' (*QD* 16), but in *The Fair Maid* he not only spells the word *holidame* but also replaces the traditional *my* with *our* – 'by our holidame' (*FM* 313) – making a reference to the Virgin unmistakeable.

The Reformation itself was followed by the rise of Puritanism, which, as Jespersen noted (*Growth and Structure of the English Language*, 9th edn, 1962, § 255), had a lasting influence on the swearing habits of Englishmen. Englishmen swear less often and less violently than men of other countries, largely because of Puritanism. Scott himself shows the effects of Puritan ideals in his genteel, non-swearing heroes and occasionally in a *G–d* for *God* (*FN* 483) and a *damn* disguised as *d—n* (*Wk* 33). When, with the Reformation, saint oaths fell into disfavour the other common form of medieval oaths – swearing by God or his attributes – rose into prominence. This is the form the characteristic Elizabethan oaths take. Medieval authors, always on the lookout for symbolic levels of understanding, compared the oaths to a second crucifixion. Chaucer picked up what was apparently a commonplace:

> Hir othes been so grete and so dampnable
> That it is grisly for to heere hem swere.
> Oure blissed Lordes body they totere, –
> Hem thoughte that Jewes rente hym noght ynough
> (*CT* VI 472–5).

But *God* oaths are rare in the medieval novels of Scott compared to *saint* oaths. One reason may be that Scott prefers to use the minced forms like *Cock* and *Ud* rather than *God* itself, as being less offensive, and, while these are known in Middle English, they only begin to proliferate in any number in early Modern English. Puritanism may well have been the immediate reason why disguised forms of *God* became so popular. Swearing becomes from this point on less and less openly religious. Only two of the many minced forms of *God* were, according to the *OED*, common before 1600: *Cock* and *Gog* (*OED God* 13). *Ud*, *Od*, and *'s* (the final *s* in *God's*) appear in the late sixteenth century but only become common in the seventeenth century. While the *OED* has no examples of *Gad* and *Z—* (as in *Zounds* and *Zooks*, both corruptions of *God's wounds*) before the beginning of the seventeenth century they were possibly also current earlier in the late sixteenth century and certainly shared the seventeenth-century popularity of *Ud*, *Od* and *'s*. *Ad* and *Adad* (probably a variant of *egad*) belong to the second half of the seventeenth century. There are many other minced forms of *God* – *Dod*, *Gar*, *Gom*, *Gum*, *Gud*, are a few of them – but they are not used by Scott. Some minced forms were still used in Scott's time as we can see in the contemporary setting of *St Ronan's Well*. Touchwood, who is however somewhat old-fashioned, exclaims '*Sbodikins* (*SRW* 222), a groom uses *Zounds* (*SRW* 128) – perhaps also in an old-fashioned way – Etherington has '*Slife* (*SRW* 479) and Mowbray comes out with *Egad* and *Gad* (*SRW* 173). These last two still had, of course, a long life ahead of them in the nineteenth century; to cite one example, Mr Bounderby with that affected hearty way of his uses *egad* in *Hard Times* (Penguin edn, p. 86).

With minor lapses Scott's novels broadly reflect the historical development of minced forms of *God* as outlined here. *Cock* and *Gog* are, as we have seen, the two medieval forms: Chaucer's Host swears 'for cokkes bones' (*CT* X 29) and the Green Knight 'Bigog' (*Sir Gawain and the Green Knight*, l. 390). Appropriately *Cock* is one of the few corruptions of *God* which finds its way into the medieval novels – Sir Patrick Charteris uses it in *Cocksbody* (*FM* 150). Apart from in the Shakespearean oath 'by cock and pie' (*K* 333, *FN* 437; *Merry Wives* I i 319) I have only noticed *Cock* elsewhere in Scott in *The Fortunes of Nigel*: *Cocksnails* (*FN* 92), *Cocksbones* (*FN* 615). *Cock* also appears, rather jokingly of course, in the *Journal* in *cocksnowns* (18 October 1826). In *Anne of Geierstein* we find *'sdeath* (*AG* 242) and in *The Talisman* the rather unlikely oath *'sdeath and hell* (*Ta* 607). However the initial *'s*, in contrast to *Cock*, is not historically accurate for novels set in the Middle Ages. In the medieval novels the uncorrupted word *God* is even less common than these rare corrupted forms. *God-a-mercy* occurs in *The Talisman* (*Ta* 748). This particular oath is attested in the later Middle Ages and through the Elizabethan period; Scott even thinks it suitable for the eighteenth-century setting of *The Pirate* (*Pi* 491). In this, as in other respects, the language of *The Talisman*, where it is Middle English at all, is the Middle English of the fourteenth and fifteenth centuries not that of the twelfth.

Minced forms of *God* are rare in *The Monastery* and *The Abbot*. Sir Piercie's *a' gad* (*Mo* 198) is seriously anachronistic. Even in the Caroline setting of *Woodstock* the derivatives of *agad*, *egad* (*Wk* 363) and *adad* (*Wk* 33) should, if strict historicity were to be observed, have no place. *Agad*, *adad* and *egad* all belong to the Restoration. (The apostrophe in Scott's spelling of *agad* is unwarranted – the first syllable of the word is the exclamatory particle *a*.)

Although the exact date of the setting of *Kenilworth* is not made clear – the outside possibilities are 1560 (the death of Amy Robsart) and 1612 (the last date possible for *The Winter's Tale*, a song from which is sung by one of the characters) – the historical events mentioned mostly cluster in the 1570s. If the evidence of the *OED* can be taken as exact to such a degree, the oaths used in *Kenilworth* began for the most part to be used in English in the last two decades of the sixteenth century. *Gog*, found in *Gogsnouns* (*K* 121) and not, to my observation, found elsewhere in Scott's novels, is primarily a sixteenth-century form, but *Ud* and *'s*, which provide the characteristic oaths of the novel, date only from the end of that century. In *Kenilworth* we find *Uds daggers* (*K* 44), *Uds precious* (*K* 56), *'snails* (*K* 403) and *'sblood* (*K* 330).

With the seventeenth-century novels the risk of anachronism is sharply reduced. At this period the language was almost overwhelmed with corrupted forms of *God*. Between them, *The Fortunes of Nigel* and *Woodstock* illustrate all the forms I have noticed in Scott except *Gog*. Three new ones are added – *Ad*, *Od*, and *Gad* – and *'s-* appears with the new spelling *Z-*. All these in fact developed about the beginning of the seventeenth century, so that Scott is now strictly in keeping with the line of historical development. There are six distinct forms and the array of oaths is impressive: *Adzooks* (*Wk* 115, 283); *Adzookers* (*Wk* 256); *Gad* (*Wk* 361, 362, 373, *FN* 184); *Gadzo* (*Wk* 230); *Gadzookers* (*Wk* 175); *Oddsfish* (*Wk* 87, 372, 374); *Ods death* (*FN* 93); *Odds pittikins* (*Wk* 61); *Ud's fish* (*FN* 93); *Cocksnails* (*FN* 92); *'swouns* (*FN* 184); *'sdeath* (*Wk* 266, *FN* 165, 398, 525); *Zooks* (*Wk* 88, 363, 642); *Zounds* (*FN* 289, 361); *Zouns* (*FN* 398, 525; this spelling is not recorded in the *OED*).

As this list illustrates with *Adzookers* and *Gadzo* (both meaning 'God's wounds') and *Odds pittikins* ('God's pity') the words associated with *God* also became corrupted. Some of these are used by themselves as oaths: *wounds*, particularly liable to corruption when associated with *God*, provides Scott's two corruptions *nouns* (*FN* 26, 289) and *oons* (*K* 403). Uncorrupted words are used in a similar way; 'blood and wounds' (*Wk* 86); 'by blood and nails' (*K* 57). Amid all the corrupted forms of *God* recorded in the *OED* one will search in vain for Michael Lambourne's *Cog* in *Cogswounds* (*K* 118). Probably not a deliberate invention, the word is added amongst the welter of possibilities probably without Scott being aware that his inventive faculty was at work.

As in the medieval novels the full name *God* is, here in the renaissance novels, rare. Queen Elizabeth in *Kenilworth*, however, is an exception with her 'God's pity' (*K* 242), 'God's death' (*K* 244, 261, 264), 'by God's day' (*K* 538) and 'God's life' (*K* 542). It is not just regal dignity which sanctions this exception, though it does have the effect of differentiating her swearing from that of others – actually evidence suggests that Elizabeth swore, if anything, more violently than her courtiers. The fact is that Elizabeth's swearing habits are well documented – a look at any one of her biographies will show how frequently oaths turn up in her letters and conversation. In the scene in *Kenilworth* where Elizabeth rebukes Leicester for his treatment of the usher Bowyer, already discussed in some detail in relation to Scott's source Naunton, we find that where Naunton says that the Queen 'replied with her wonted oath, (God's death)' (*Fragmenta Regalia*, 1808, p. 180) Scott has the same oath: ' "God's death! my lord," such was her emphatic phrase' (*K* 261).

Ninety per cent of the religious oaths in Scott's novels mention God (usually under a disguised form of his name) or the saints. Add to these two categories oaths on the cross (or 'rood') (*Ta* 517, *Ab* 125) and the mass (*Ta* 626, *Mo* 468) and virtually all religious oaths are covered. The effort to choose suitable oaths is maintained here. The formula 'by the cross of my sword' (*Ta* 493) is appropriate to the crusader Sir Kenneth; Cedric the Saxon's 'by the rood of Bromholme' (*Iv* 64) is chosen for the English not Norman-sounding *Bromholme*; 'by the blessed Rood' (*Wk* 27), though spoken after the Reformation, sounds natural for the high church Sir Henry Lee; while Tony Foster, the ex-burner of heretics, 'forgetting his Protestantism in his alarm', swears the thoroughly Romish oath: 'By the holy Cross of Abingdon' (*K* 51).

It is no accident that Robert Louis Stevenson when he wanted a name for a bad period language called it 'Tushery'. The first problem of the writer of period language is to make himself intelligible. Oaths and exclamations are small, almost meaningless, but unequivocally period elements; in this context they are invaluable. Not necessary to the sense, they do not interfere with it – the author can convey his meaning in pure modern English while the oath tacked on at beginning or end like a bookend adds the required period element. *Tush* is the ultimate example of the small, more or less meaningless oath. For all his ingenuity in integrating period words in a basically early nineteenth-century text Scott sometimes takes the easy way out. It is particularly hard to carry on a narrative in archaic language – archaized prose as a vehicle for translating historical accounts is now universally condemned. In the following speech, where Tressilian briefly recounts the events following the arrival of Varney at Amy Robsart's parental home, the only period element is the opening oath:

'No, by the rood!' replied Tressilian. 'Misunderstanding and misery followed his presence, yet so strangely, that I am at this moment at a loss to trace the gradations of their encroachment upon a family, which had, till then, been so happy. For a time Amy Robsart received the attentions of this man Varney with the indifference attached to common courtesies; then followed a period in which she seemed to regard him with dislike, and even with disgust; and then an extraordinary species of connexion appeared to grow up betwixt them' (*K* 137-8).

Scott's 'by the rood' is the most superficial kind of 'Tushery'.

Tush itself, *troth*, *forsooth*, and *marry* are the most easily transportable of tushery's props. Scott hardly needs them and at his best does not rely on them very much. *Tush* appears regularly (*Iv* 584, *Ta* 583, *K* 40, *Wk* 177) but not often enough to become annoying. *Troth* and *forsooth* are about as common as *Tush*. *Troth* (*Wk* 41) had become obsolete in Standard English by the eighteenth century, though it was still used in Scots (*An* 47, *HM* 428); *forsooth* (*Ta* 581, 683) was still used in early nineteenth-century literary English but only 'parenthetically with ironic or derisive statements' (*OED forsooth* b). This ironic tone had attached itself to *forsooth* in the eighteenth century; Scott sometimes (*Ta* 581) but not always (*Ta* 673) returns to the earlier straight sense 'in truth'. *Marry* is more of a favourite with Scott; he is fond of following it with an inverted verb: 'Marry are we' (*Iv* 455); 'Marry will I' (*AG* 231). *Marry* is of course a corrupted form of *Mary*; when the saint referred to is Mary the Egyptian, the resulting contraction is *Marry gipsy* further contracted to *Marry gip*. This is itself corrupted to *Marry gup* of which *Marry guep* would be a possible variant. The phrase is only attested in the literature of the sixteenth and seventeenth centuries. Scott made a double mistake by misreading *marry guep* as *marry quep* and using the phrase anachronistically in *The Betrothed* (*Be* 116). It also occurs, with greater historical accuracy, in *The Fortunes of Nigel* (*FN* 92).

Another apparently senseless exclamation borrowed from Elizabethan drama is 'what the good year' (*FN* 39). The puzzling term *goodyear* remains unexplained. Hamner, editing Shakespeare in 1744, suggested a spelling *goujeres* with the meaning 'the French disease'. This explanation is no longer accepted but it left its mark in dictionary spellings favouring a medial *j*. Consequently Scott has both 'what the good year' (*FN* 39) and 'who the good jere' (*K* 240). Possibly by analogy with 'what the devil', *goodyear* came to be used outside the usual phrase. *King Lear* has: 'The good yeares shall devoure them flesh and fell' (First Folio text, V iii 24) but the *OED* has no instance of Scott's phrase 'who the good year' (*OED goodyear*). If Scott accepted the conjecture made by Hamner about the meaning of *goodyear* this reference to venereal disease, for as such it would be intended, occurs in novels in which the subject is normally taboo. In this case it would be another instance of Scott's willingness to introduce subjects otherwise unmentionable when they can come under cover of unglossed, unfamiliar terms.

Not all Scott's characters swear. For reasons mainly literary rather than linguistic, such as the tradition of the genteel hero and Scott's own conception of the gentleman-hero and lady-heroine, Scott's heroes and heroines swear only rarely. This is also part of their general avoidance of period language. When they do swear they prefer oaths of which the religious significance has not been obscured and which can be considered as expressions of piety. Since Scott also avoids the full name *God* in oaths this largely limits them to medieval saint oaths, as minced forms of *God* do not have an obvious religious meaning. For this reason Scott's heroes and heroines swear more often in the medieval novels than in the later ones where the minced forms predominate. The same applies to other corruptions which are given, in the renaissance novels, only to less reputable characters. *Marry*, having lost its religious significance because it is no longer recognizable as the name of the Virgin, is given to the disreputable Ursula Suddlechops (*FN* 365) who is more or less a bawd. By contrast Isabelle de Croye, one of Scott's exemplary heroines, uses the unmistakeably religious 'Holy Mary' (*QD* 261) and 'Holy Virgin' (*QD* 256). This leaves few oaths for the renaissance novels; there the heroines do not swear and the heroes only very rarely, when they are provoked:

> 'Death and fury!' said Tressilian, transported beyond his usual patience (*K* 462).

Furthermore the oaths they do use are quite different from the full-blooded idiom of the minor characters; Edward Glendinning assures the Sub-Prior Eustace that he has seen the White Lady 'by heaven and earth' (*Mo* 454). These peculiar oaths also come in the medieval novels, as when another ostensible hero, Arthur Philipson, swears in poetic vein: 'by the White Swan' (*AG* 572). This can hardly be called profane language.

It cannot be to maintain their dignity that heroes and heroines do not swear since Scott's kings and queens, to whom dignity belongs *ex officio* (even James I can be dignified at times), are great swearers. Of course in the case of Elizabeth Scott was following historical evidence, as we have just noted. It is a commonplace that Scott's minor characters, including the royal figures, are often more real than the nominal heroes. Their habit of swearing is one of the contributing reasons towards this.

Since, in certain novels, Scott's heroes fill out the middle ranks of society, one is often left with a strange situation in which the characters who swear most are the two extremes of society – the highest and lowest – kings and peasants, nobles and menials, abbots and ruffians. No evidence suggests that the middle ranks of society were less prone to swearing than other ranks until the growth of Puritanism, a largely middle-class movement, with its embargo on oaths and curses. Puritan influence is important in only one of our novels – *Woodstock*. The hero, Markham Everard, is a Puritan. To the literary reasons for his not swearing is added a linguistic one. In the novel the line between the men who swear and those who do not marks the division between Cavalier and Roundhead, Anglican and Puritan. The principal Cavaliers, Sir Henry Lee and Roger Wildrake, swear profusely. Everard swears only once – in a fit of anger – and Scott carefully explains the significance of this happening:

> 'Damnation,' exclaimed the Colonel, in a tone which became a Puritan as little as did the exclamation itself (*Wk* 460).

(Even here *damnation* is more genteel than *damn*.) Several other Puritans in the novel swear at some point: the boorish and opportunist Desborough – *Adzooks* (*Wk* 283) – and Cromwell's blunt follower Pearson – *Zooks* (*Wk* 642). In both cases the speaker's character explains how he becomes an exception to the rule. As well as his normal part Roger Wildrake has to play the part of Everard's Puritan secretary. When he banteringly assumes the tone of the Puritans he exchanges his *egad* and *Zooks* for the mild exclamation *Lack-a-day* (*Wk* 89), still current in Scott's time (see *An* 11). *Woodstock* then is the only one of our novels in which a character's swearing or not swearing can be taken to have any relation to the period setting.

In the Middle English period French was the dominant outside influence on the English language. At the end of the Middle Ages other Romance languages begin to make their influence felt.

In the medieval novels of Scott oaths of foreign origin are usually French, in the renaissance novels Italian or Spanish. Richard Cœur-de-Lion, appearing both in *Ivanhoe* and *The Talisman*, uses two French oaths. There is nothing uniquely Anglo-Norman about these oaths but they do recall to the reader's mind the use of a kind of French by English Normans. In fact for Richard's oaths Scott's sources may well have been English rather than French literature: *mort de ma vie* (*Iv* 609) would have been early known to Scott through its use by the Duke of Bourbon in *Henry V* (III v 11). Richard's other French oath, *despardieux* (*Ta* 581), obtained a more lasting foothold in English, being known throughout the thirteenth and fourteenth centuries. Scott's medial *s* is intrusive and unhistorical – the Old French phrase is *de par dieu* – but the final *x*, though equally intrusive seems to have been common in English spellings; some of the Chaucer texts spell it this way (*CT* II 39, *TC* II 1058). *Certes* (*Ta* 712, *Iv* 294, *QD* 541) had an even longer history in English. Early adopted from Old French it survived into eighteenth-century literature, though Sterne's use of it is probably humorously anachronistic (*OED certes*). *My certes*, given to a Scottish speaker in *Quentin Durward* (*QD* 547), and the variation *by my certes*, given to another Scot in *The Abbot* (*Ab* 231), may in fact only be what the *OED* calls a 'literary' improvement on the common Scottish phrase *my certies* or *my certie* (*An* 337) – also corrupted to *my sartie* (*BL* 355) – in order to make it look archaic; or it may be genuine. The history of these phrases in relation to each other is obscure (*OED certie*).

In *Quentin Durward* there are Frenchmen to swear French oaths. The Germans swear in their own language too (*QD* 285-6). Scott passes on *Sapperment*, an oath which he had used for a German in *Guy Mannering* (*GM* 303), to a Liegois speaking the closely related Flemish language (*QD* 320). The French oaths warrant some attention on the score of a half-hearted attempt to give them an early French form. *Teste-dieu* (*QD* 467) and *Pasques-dieu* (*QD* 19, 20, 153) preserve a medial *s* which has disappeared in Modern French giving *tête* and *Pâques*. But *tête-bleu* (*QD* 20) in the same novel accepts the modern form. *Bleu* is a minced form of *Dieu* so that the oath has the same meaning as *teste-dieu* 'God's head'. *Cap de diou* (*QD* 244), which should have the same meaning as *teste-dieu* or *tête-bleu* reaches further back into the history of French. By the end of the Old French period *tête* had ousted *cap* or *chef* (from Latin *caput*) as the normal word for 'head'. Indeed it only survived in a few fossilized phrases, one of which has had an extension of life in English: *cap-à-pie*. The word which had been Latin *deus* and was to become French *dieu* 'god' in the intermediate period appeared as *diu* (*diou*).

Whereas with English exclamations *The Monastery* hovers between medieval (Catholic) and renaissance (Protestant), with foreign exclamations it belongs only to the renaissance. Sir Piercie Shafton favours the Italian, yet another element in his pretensions. The Italian interjection *via* is common in Elizabethan drama and is found with three different meanings; Sir Piercie uses it in two of these – 'onward!':

Thy death hour has struck – betake thee to thy sword – Via! (*Mo* 288)

and 'away! begone!':

... the Euphuist flung from him the mantle in which he was muffled. 'Via the cloud that shadowed Shafton!' said he (*Mo* 539).

A very similar instance occurs in *The Fortunes of Nigel*:

... Off, off, ye lendings!' he continued, in the same vein. 'Via, the curtain that shadowed Borgia!' (*FN* 293).

Michael Lambourne in *Kenilworth*, who like Sir Piercie aspires to be a courtier, provides us with examples of the word in its third sense, employed to dismiss a subject of conversation:

And what was Ralph Sadler but the clerk of Cromwell, and he has gazed eighteen fair lordships, – *via!* – I know my steerage as well as they.'
So saying, he left the apartment (*K* 110).

why, via, let that pass too (*K* 471).

Shakespeare uses *via* in all three senses (respectively 3*HVI* II i 182; *M of V* II ii II; *Merry Wives* II ii 161). From Shakespeare Scott has learnt Lambourne's exclamation *corragio* 'courage' (*K* 336; *All's Well* II v 98). Also significant for Lambourne's reputation is his Spanish oath *Voto a dios* (*K* 12). As another character says to him: 'I said you were speaking a little Spanish, as one who had been in the Canaries' (*K* 336). Lambourne is more than any other character in the novel the exemplar of the travelled Elizabethan man of fortune.

QUOTATION

One has only to read a few pages of the *Journal* to realize how often even Scott's private thoughts phrased themselves in another's words. He seems to have found often that a line or phrase of Shakespeare or some other author was in his mind to express his thoughts before any expression of his own was formulated; he thought naturally in quotations. In the latest edition of the *Journal* (W. E. K. Anderson ed., Oxford, 1972) under the index heading 'Shakespeare: his plays quoted' there are 148 entries. In the novels quotations short and long constantly mingle with Scott's own words. When Halbert Glendinning pronounces a spell and the White Lady appears to him Scott expresses Halbert's terror through lines from Coleridge's *Christabel*:

> These lines were hardly uttered when there stood the figure of a female clothed in white, within three steps of Halbert Glendinning:
> 'I guess 'twas frightful there to see
> A lady richly clad as she –
> Beautiful exceedingly'
> (*Mo* 139; see *Christabel*, I 66-8).

Scott makes these lines close the chapter. Even a rather trite sentiment from a poem contemporary with *Christabel* but now scarcely known, Campbell's *Gertrude of Wyoming*, sinks into his mind and emerges later to close a paragraph describing Cromwell:

> But the restraint upon his passion was but
> The torrent's smoothness ere it dash below (*Wk* 628).

A footnote quotes the original as:

> But mortal pleasure, what art thou in truth?
> The torrent's smoothness ere it dash below.

(See *Gertrude of Wyoming*, III v). The narrative of the novels frequently has catchy Shakespearean phrases embodied in it: 'coign of vantage' (*QD* 331; *Mac* I vi 7); 'daylight and champaign' (*QD* 337; *Tw N* II v 175); 'skyey influences' (*Mo* 237; *Meas* III i 9); 'in King Cambyses vein' (*K* 404; 1*HIV* II iv 430-1); 'high gravel-blind' (*HM* 464; *M of V* II ii 38). Scott quotes more often probably than any English novelist of equal stature. Clearly a not insignificant part of his thought-processes was quite naturally carried on in the words of others. This more than anything may explain why quotation forms a quite important part of the dialogue of his characters in certain of his novels. What was natural to himself he carried over to his created characters. At the same time this habit could be made to serve his special ends with regard to period language. In a perfectly natural way characters are able to quote sizeable passages from the works of their supposed contemporaries.

Of course, many quotations cannot have any part in the period language – as, for example, when Bletson quotes Chaucer in *Woodstock* (*Wk* 279). The language of Chaucer is too remote to appear part of the novel's period language. A distinction must therefore be drawn between characters who quote out of literary interest as Scott himself did – Die Vernon, with her frequent quotation of Spenser, is a good example – and those who quote plays or sing songs as part of the contemporary language of their time.

Sir Henry Lee in *Woodstock* is almost a caricature of Scott himself with his compulsive quotation of 'Will' Shakespeare. His quotations and allusions also make an important contribution to the linguistic setting. He quotes Shakespeare as a contemporary, a contemporary not of his old age, when the novel takes place (it is set in 1651, as its sub-title proclaims), but of his youth. The young around him look on Shakespeare as old fashioned. The fugitive king Charles talks of Sir Henry's 'atrocious complot with Will Shakespeare, a fellow as much out of date as himself, to read me to death with five acts of a historical play, or chronicle' (*Wk* 413). The contrast between young and old adds an extra dimension to the linguistic context, a point made by Thomas Crawford in his book *Scott* (Edinburgh, 1965, p. 81).

In quoting Shakespeare Sir Henry usually, but not always, acknowledges his source:

Thou word'st me, girl, . . . thou word'st me, as Will Shakespeare says (*Wk* 28, *cf. A & C* V ii 191).

I walk here in the hall, as Hamlet says (*Wk* 318; *cf. Ham* V ii 180).

a very palpable hit (*Wk* 318; *cf. Ham* V ii 294).

But my age is like a lusty winter, as old Will says – frosty but kindly (*Wk* 320; *cf. AYLI* II iii 52-3).

to over-red thy fear, as mad Will has it (*Wk* 572; *cf. Mac* V iii 14).

(See also *Wk* 29, 34, 72, 119, 403, 444, 457, 458.)

Sir Henry's daughter Alice follows in her father's footsteps:

> We must not go too fast – this craves wary walking (*Wk* 584; *cf. JC* II i 15).

and his son too, commenting at the same time on his father's habit:

> The pitcher goes oft to the well – The proverb, as my father would say, is somewhat musty (*Wk* 389; *cf. Ham* III ii 366).

King Charles, despite his disparaging remarks about Shakespeare, quotes him, but ironically, turning the line against Sir Henry (*Wk* 449; 1*HIV* IV i 110). Sir Henry returns with a line from the same scene which is modified both in order to fit the context and by passing through Scott's memory:

> I saw young Harry, with his beaver on (1*HIV* IV i 104)

becomes:

> You saw young Harry, with his beaver up (*Wk* 449).

In a more kindly mood Charles says to Markham who is to marry Alice Lee:

> If not, as your future father-in-law would say . . . this parting was well made (*Wk* 519; *cf. JC* V i 119).

While his own quotations and those he leads others to make draw on the literature of his youth, Sir Henry provokes his Puritan nephew Markham Everard into quoting a contemporary work – Milton's *Comus*, written for performance in 1645, and thus providing a much more up-to-date literary reference (*Wk* 455, 456). He does this by challenging Everard to produce a Puritan poet equal to his Shakespeare. When the Royalist Sir Henry discovers that the words (which he at first finds pleasing) are by Milton, best known to his age as a polemicist for the Parliamentary cause, he is very annoyed.

Roger Wildrake, whose conversation reveals another lover of plays, (*Wk* 118), is also responsible for quoting Shakespeare. He twists King Lear's words into a joke:

> Off – off, ye lendings, . . . borrowings I should more properly call you (*Wk* 500; *cf. Lear* III iv 111–2).

Reginald Lowestoffe, yet another play-lover, this time in *The Fortunes of Nigel*, uses the same quotation as, in thoroughly theatrical style, escorting Nigel into 'Alsatia' (the sanctuary of Whitefriars), he throws off his disguise at the entrance. The difference is that *The Fortunes of Nigel* is set in the reign of James I when the memory of *King Lear* was a recent one.

The effect of these quotations is to remind the reader continually that for the characters involved Shakespeare or Milton is a contemporary. Raleigh, quoting the first five lines of Spenser's Mutability Cantos to Edmund Tressilian, speaks of the author as his friend and makes clear his identity, at least for those who remember Spenser's full name: 'I had hoped thou wert in harbour, at least, my dear Edmund – But truly says another dear friend of thy name . . .' (*K* 226). As the earliest of the conflicting dates for events from political history mentioned in *Kenilworth* is 1579, this reference is probably too early if the Mutability Cantos were written after the first six books of *The Faerie Queene*. Some critics have however argued that the Mutability Cantos were part of the early work on *The Faerie Queene*, which was actually begun in this year, 1579. Spenser is also known to Leicester in the novel and is waiting to see him when Leicester comes from his audience with the Queen (*K* 282–3); in fact Spenser joined Leicester's household in 1578. After speaking to Spenser Leicester turns to Shakespeare and speaks to him: 'thou hast given my nephew, Philip Sidney, love-powder – he cannot sleep without thy Venus and Adonis under his pillow' (*K* 283). The reference to Sidney may be accurate enough here – though it is certainly not accurate for Sidney to be mentioned in *The Monastery* – but *Venus and Adonis* was published in 1593. A few pages further on Elizabeth, going down the Thames in a barge, listens complacently while Raleigh repeats some lines from 'a mad tale of fairies, love charms, and I wot not what besides' (*K* 295) as Leicester describes *A Midsummer Night's Dream*:

> That very time I saw, (but thou couldst not,)
> Flying between the cold moon and the earth,
> Cupid, all arm'd: a certain aim he took
> At a fair vestal, throned by the west;
> And loos'd his love-shaft smartly from his bow,
> As it should pierce a hundred thousand hearts:
> But I might see young Cupid's fiery shaft
> Quench'd in the chaste beams of the watery moon;
> And the imperial vot'ress passed on,
> In maiden meditation, fancy free (*K* 296; see *MND* II i 155ff).

Scott has adopted the suggestion first made by Rowe in 1709 that these lines refer to England's Maiden Queen, Elizabeth herself. *A Midsummer Night's Dream* was probably written in 1595 or 1596. Raleigh is not the only character in the novel who shows a knowledge of Shakespeare historically impossible in the 1560s and 70s – Wayland Smith sings songs from two plays written a decade into the seventeenth century, *The Tempest* and *The Winter's Tale*. Scott introduces part of Caliban's song as 'a stave from a comedy, which was then new, and which was supposed, among the more favourable judges, to augur some genius on the part of the author. We are happy,' continues Scott, 'to preserve the couplet, which ran exactly thus,–

> 'Ban, ban, ca Caliban –
> Get a new master – Be a new man' (*K* 211).

Scott has a tendency to misquote but his 'exactly' here may well be as humorous as is his choice of these lines in particular amongst all those that the author of 'some genius' wrote – certainly the lines deviate slightly from those in *The Tempest* (*Tp* II ii 97–8). Wayland also sings part of Autolycus' chapman song:

> Lawn as white as driven snow,
> Cyprus black as e'er was crow,
> Gloves as sweet as damask roses,
> Masks for faces and for noses.
>   (*K* 340; see *WT* IV ii 220–4)

The literary references are thus out of step by some fifteen to twenty years with the events of political history. This merely maintains a discrepancy between political and linguistic history found in other aspects of the novel's language – notably oaths.

Contemporary songs can be as useful as plays. Wildrake, that lover of plays or playhouses, is even more obviously a lover of songs and singing. He introduces a number of them into *Woodstock* mostly in fragmentary form (*Wk* 84, 85, 274, 354, 360, 659, 672). For most of these Scott does not name his source and some may be wholly or partly his own work. The last line of one – 'When the king shall enjoy his own again' (*Wk* 274) – is the refrain of an extremely popular song by Martin Parker who probably died in 1656, usually called by that name but originally entitled 'Upon Defacing of Whitehall'. It is an appropriately Cavalier song for this Cavalier gentleman. For another song

Period Vocabulary

(*Wk* 659) Scott gives the source in a note as Allan Ramsay's *Tea Table Miscellany*, an early eighteenth-century collection which preserved some songs written earlier. From Ramsay's 'If e'er I do well, 'tis a wonder' Scott has taken the first and sixth stanzas, but his comment that Ramsay's version is 'something very like' his own is actually an admission that he has changed the lines:

> I spent all my means
> On whores, bawds, and queans

to the less rakish:

> I spent all my means
> Amid sharpers and queans.

This is consistent with Scott's portrayal of Wildrake; the 'wild rake's' vices are not brought into very prominent view. King Charles also likes songs and hums to himself 'a well known ditty which he had picked up during his residence in Scotland' (*Wk* 488). What he has learnt are the last lines of Burns' version of the song 'Duncan Davidson'. Burns had in fact adapted these concluding lines from some extant earlier; Scott may have known this and, if not, he was certainly aware that a lot of Burns's material was traditional. The introduction of these lines into a setting some hundred years before Burns's time cannot be considered therefore as a very serious anachronism. Further on we find Charles exhorting Alice to join him in 'Patrick Carey's jovial farewell' (*Wk* 569) – adapted to fit the novel by the substitution of *Woodstock* for *Wykeham*. Scott had edited the *Trivial Poems and Triolets* of Carey (or Cary) in 1820 from a manuscript dated 20th August 1651 – the reference could hardly be more suitable in 'A Tale of the Year Sixteen Hundred and Fifty One' though whether Carey's poems were generally known at this time is another matter. (They were first printed in 1771). The host of the Black Bear is another lover of songs. One of his songs (*K* 134) is adapted from a sixteenth-century poem: 'This verse,' says Scott's footnote, 'or something similar, occurs in a long ballad, or poem, on Flodden Field, reprinted by the late Henry Weber'. On the following page we hear him sing another song to which a laughing footnote is attached: 'This verse of an old song *actually* occurs in an old play' (*K* 135; the italics are Scott's own). 'Old Play' is, as we have seen, the tag which Scott added to his made-up chapter mottoes. But this play, it seems, *actually* existed.

The Language of Walter Scott

When the Queen comes to Kenilworth Castle – the climax of the novel's historical pageantry – she is greeted by the Porter (*K* 483–4) with Scott's own version of lines by Gascoigne which had actually been used on the occasion (*K* 484n). Scott's imitation is obviously intended to render the rather disjointed style of the original more digestible. The original first line, for example, reads: 'What stirre, what coyle is here?' (Gascoigne, *Works*, Cambridge, 1907–10, II 92–3) but Scott has replaced *coil* with the more modern *turmoil* to give: 'What stir, what turmoil have we for the nones?' (*K* 483). (The phrase 'for the nones' is not present in the original Gascoigne poem; it both allows a rhyme and reinfuses an element of archaism into the more modern style of Scott's imitation.) However Scott may have originally intended to use Gascoigne's poem unchanged or to have changed it less. Earlier on in the novel when we first meet the Porter he is trying with very little success to learn his lines; we overhear him saying to himself: 'Here's a stir – here's a coil' (*K* 436).

In *The Abbot* too an attempt to find authentic material is maintained. The followers of the Abbot of Unreason sing an anti-Papist song (*Ab* 191–2) taken 'with trifling alterations' from a sixteenth-century collection 'A Compendious Book of Godly and Spiritual Songs . . . for avoiding of sin and harlotrie . . .' (*Ab* 192n).

Many scraps from plays and songs are introduced with the tag 'as the play says' or 'as the romance says'. In some cases the tag seems to carry no significance; the quotation does not seem on examination to reflect any special context; as, for example, in 'keep thee well from me, Sir Knight, as the romance has it' (*K* 49). Elsewhere the tag points the reader to a quotation from Shakespeare. Michael Lambourne turns to *King Lear* for his inspiration:

> I am younger and stronger than you, and have in me a double portion of the fighting devil, though not, it may be, quite so much of the undermining fiend, that finds an underground way to his purpose – who hides halters under folk's pillows, and puts ratsbane into their porridge, as the stage-play says (*K* 44).

Part of this is a free adaptation of the words of Lear:

> the foul fiend . . . that hath laid knives under pillow, and halters in his pew; set ratsbane by his porridge (*Lr* III iv 50–4).

In the same novel Amy Robsart's garrulous companion on the

way to Kenilworth Castle repeats a line which had become a cliché: 'But age has somewhat clawed me in his clutch, as the song says' (*K* 416–7). Thomas, Lord Vaux (1510–56) set this phrase out on a journey through many writers in a poem popular enough to be included in the early anthology, Tottel's *Miscellany* (1537, sig. X3), called 'The Aged Lover Renounceth Love':

> For age with stelyng steppes
> Hath clawed me with his cowche (ll. 9–10).

A half-century later the song was still popular and Hamlet's gravedigger sings it at his work (*Ham* V i 77–8). The reference to *King Lear* made by Lambourne is obviously once again too early for its setting but the lines from Vaux are strikingly appropriate given their great popularity.

Kenilworth is particularly rich in these tagged phrases. Varney, leaving a group centred around a woman giving birth to a child, makes a pun: 'and so, as the play says, "God be with your labour!"' (*K* 413). The source of this, if it exists, I have been unable to discover. In *The Fortunes of Nigel*, too, the label 'as the play says' is used to excuse a pun. The ill-clothed Scot Richie Moniplies is foolish enough to state his ludicrous pretensions to good birth:

> 'I am willing to do what I may to be useful, though I come of an honourable house, and may be said to be in a sort indifferently weel provided for.'
> 'Ay!' said the interrogator, 'and what house may claim the honour of your descent?'
> 'An ancient coat belongs to it, as the play says,' whispered Vincent to his companion (*FN* 25–6).

Vincent's pun may reflect the discussion of Slender and Shallow at the beginning of *The Merry Wives of Windsor*:

> *Slender:* All his successors gone before him hath done't; and all his ancestors that come after him may: they may give the dozen white luces in their coat.
> *Shallow:* It is an old coat.
> *Evans:* The dozen white louses do become an old coat well (*Merry Wives* I i 14–20).

One unusual example of quotation in *The Fortunes of Nigel* deserves special mention. Nigel is made to read a proclamation condemning the importunities of the King's debtors (*FN* 53) the wording of which is selected, as Scott tells us in a note (*FN* Note III), from real proclamations of the period. The Somers Tracts, which Scott edited, contained much material of this kind but not proclamations on this particular matter.

All the examples of quotations and songs mentioned so far are taken from the renaissance novels; a large part of them draw appropriately on Elizabethan drama. Scott makes less use of direct quotation and songs in the medieval novels. In *Quentin Durward* the hero displays an interest in literature uncommon in Scott's medieval heroes; he quotes six lines from a poem and reads a romance. Scott makes Quentin read a mythical Strassbourg edition of a poem which sets out:

> How the Squire of lowe degree
> Loved the King's daughter of Hongarie (*QD* 312).

This is not the spelling used in Ritson's edition of *The Squire of Low Degree* (in his *Ancient Engleish MetricalRanceës*, London, 1802), the only complete edition (and the only one containing these lines) that was available to Scott. The lines have been slightly modified to fit the context. Very likely Scott is quoting from memory. A few pages later Quentin remembers six lines from the same romance. Four Scott has made up or remembers from elsewhere as they are not to be found in *The Squire* in either of its two versions:

> 'Welcome,' she said, 'my swete Squyre,
> My heartis roote, my soule's desire:
> I will give three kisses three,
> And als five hundrid poundis in fee' (*QD* 335).

The other two:

> I have yknown many a page
> Come to be Prince by mariage (*QD* 335).

are definitely quoted from memory. Ritson's:

> For i have sene that many a page
> Have become men by mariage (ll. 373–4)

would have fitted the context just as well so the modification is clearly not forced on Scott by the context.

Period Vocabulary

Later the author makes Quentin, a Scot, quote the most famous lines of the medieval Scots poet Barbour:

> Ah, freedom is a noble thing –
> Freedom makes man to have liking –
> Freedom the zest to pleasure gives –
> He lives at ease who freely lives.
> Grief, sickness, poortith, want, are all
> Summ'd up within the name of thrall (*QD* 392).

This is the same mixture of the true text with Scott's additions as we have just seen in Quentin's romance. The first four lines vary only slightly from the original:

> A! fredome is a noble thing!
> Fredome mayss man to haiff liking;
> Fredome all solace to man giffis;
> He levys at ess that frely levys
>   (*The Bruce*, EETS edn, I 225–8).*

The last two are Scott's own though they roughly parallel the ideas of four more lines in Barbour:

> Na he, that ay hass levyt fre
> May nocht knaw weill the propyrte,
> The angyr, na the wretchyt dome,
> That is cowplyt to foule thryldome (I 233–6).

Scott had quoted Barbour at length before in the notes to *The Lord of The Isles* the main character of which, despite its title, is Barbour's hero Robert the Bruce.†

No doubt one reason why there is less quotation in the medieval novels is the greater difficulty of understanding Middle English,

---

* Scott had editions of *The Bruce* by both Pinkerton (London, 1790) and Jamieson (Edinburgh, 1820) in his collection (*Catalogue*, pp. 4, 173) as well as a small quarto of 1758 (*Catalogue*, p. 8). I have quoted here from Skeat's EETS text (London, 1870) which records no substantive variants from Pinkerton or Jamieson's texts in these lines.

† Scott quoted from Pinkerton's modernized text, the only one available to him at the time apart from the 1758 quarto, though he does mention Jamieson's text as forthcoming (*LI* Note LXXXI). In later editions Lockhart substituted Jamieson's text in the notes but only where the differences from Pinkerton's edition were more than a matter of spelling. The result in subsequent editions is a confusing mixture of texts with haphazard page, book or line references to whichever edition is being used.

a difficulty even greater with Middle Scots. Presumably it was to make them more intelligible that Scott rephrased Barbour's lines. There is also the fact that the amount of medieval literature available to Scott was limited. Yet probably the most important reason why Scott has his characters quote so much more often in the renaissance novels than in the medieval ones is this: no medieval author, not even Chaucer, ever succeeded in permeating Scott's total thought processes to the extent Shakespeare did. Most of the quotations in *Kenilworth*, *The Fortunes of Nigel* and *Woodstock* are of course from Shakespeare. Scott's characters quote Shakespeare because he himself could not avoid doing so.

HISTORICAL ACCURACY

Nowadays with the *OED* in our hands it is easy for us to criticize the historical accuracy of some of Scott's archaic language. Scott did not have the *OED* to help him and anyway he seems to have generally liked to rely on memory. One suspects that if he could have done so Scott would have found it cramping to write with the *OED* at his side, and would have had little sympathy for any imitator who did so. All the same, the *OED* provides us with a means of checking how accurate Scott was when the best aid at his command was a capacious memory.

Certainly Scott was not greatly worried by charges that he was guilty of anachronism. Sir Henry Lee in *Woodstock*, when told of D'Avenant's claim to be Shakespeare's natural son, protests:

> it reminds me of a verse in the puppet-show of Phaeton, where the hero complains to his mother –
> Besides by all the village boys I'm sham'd;
> You the Sun's son, you rascal, you be d--d!
> I never heard such unblushing assurance in my life! (*Wk* 451).

Scott in his footnote forestalls the criticism that this is anachronistic by himself making the charge and then dismissing it with a not-too-serious excuse:

> We observe this couplet in Fielding's farce of 'Tumble-down-Dick', founded on the same classical story. As it was current in the time of the Commonwealth, it must have reached the author of 'Tom Jones' by tradition – for no one will suspect the present author of making the anachronism.

What the reader sees here is however only the end of the process. The idea actually came to him as he was writing his *Journal*:

> Read a few pages of Will D'Avenant who was fond of having it supposed that Shakespeare intrigued with his mother. I think the pretension can only be treated as Phaeton's was according to Fielding's farce.
>
>   Besides by all the village boys I'm sham'd,
>   You the Sun's son, you rascal? – you be damnd.
>
> Egad I'll put that into *Woodstock*. It might come well from the old admirer of Shakespeare – then Fielding's lines were not written – what then it is an anachronism for some sly rogue to detect. Besides it is easy to swear that they were written and that fielding adopted them from tradition (*Journal*, 12 February 1826).

In the following pages rather than list all the anachronisms I have noticed (some have already been commented on in passing) I have confined my remarks to all the words to do with one subject – weapons, defensive and offensive – in order to give an idea of the degree of accuracy Scott achieved.

The methods and weapons of war are always quickly affected by advances in technology and are particularly open to change. Since the medieval and renaissance novels are set over a period of five centuries we would expect wide differences between them. In practice the process of the development of arms is to some extent obscured by Scott's mistakes. These mistakes are a mixture of linguistic and historical inaccuracies; he attributes weapons to ages in which they were not used and he gives weapons names only given to them at other times. Both a *partisan* (*Ta* 672) and a *head-piece* (*Ta* 487) are mentioned in the twelfth-century setting of *The Talisman*. However the *partisan* 'a long-handled spear with lateral cutting projections' was a sixteenth-century innovation, and though helmets were used throughout the Middle Ages, only in the sixteenth and seventeenth centuries were they called *head-pieces*.

The history of armour in its very simplest terms moves from the dominance of chain mail through to the later thirteenth century when there began to be attached to this chain mail small pieces of plate armour. These developed during the course of the fourteenth century into full plate armour which lasted until the sixteenth century, after which it became too heavy for the new methods of war. Lighter forms of protective dress developed as an alternative to plate. One of these was the *brigandine* – 'a flexibile tunic built up of small tin plates fixed together on a leather foundation' (J. Mann, *An Outline of Arms and Armour in England*, London, 1964, p. 41). It is not found before the fifteenth century. Scott reverses the line of development by mentioning a brigandine in *The Talisman* (*Ta* 798), that is before the time of the plate armour to which a brigandine was an alternative.

In keeping with the development of armour, particular parts like the helmet went through a series of transformations. At the time of the setting of *The Talisman*, the reign of Richard I, a barrel-shaped helmet was in use. This flat-topped *helm* became dome-like and was then, in the late fourteenth century, replaced by the conical *bascinet*, though the helm was retained for the ceremonial of tournaments. The *bascinet* (or *basnet*) was in its turn superseded about the middle of the fifteenth century by the *sallet*, which itself gave way, at the end of this long development, to the *morion* for footsoldiers, a *burgonet* being more normal for horsemen. Other names were also used; from the later sixteenth century a common and expressive name for a helmet was a *cask* or *casque*.

Once again *The Talisman* is strictly speaking at fault. Scott, by mentioning the morion there (*Ta* 846), has placed it at the beginning rather than at the end of this period of development. Moreover he has given it to a horseman for whom it would have been top-heavy. Yet the kind of helmet Sir Kenneth is described as wearing in the same novel is, in shape, exactly what a knight of the period might have worn: 'The flat top of his cumbrous cylindrical helmet was unadorned with any crest' (*Ta* 487). In *Marmion*, set in the early sixteenth century, we have helmets of various stages of development brought together – *basnet* (*Ma* VI xxi), *casque* (*Ma* I v), *helm* (*Ma* I v), *morion* (*Ma* I ix). *Casque* probably never had a particular sense. It was not quite obsolete in Scott's time although it had been invested with some special glamour by the appearance of the enchanted 'casque' in Walpole's *Castle of Otranto*. The *OED* quotations suggest that it was not in use until the late sixteenth century, but it would be hypercritical (and possibly, given the inadequacy of even the best dictionaries on such fine points, incorrect) to object to Scott's using it in an early sixteenth-century setting here in *Marmion* or in a mid sixteenth-century setting as in *The Monastery* (*Mo* 136). What is interesting is that *basnet* and *morion* too, although they had had – unlike *casque* – a particular meaning, in the context of the poem become for the reader no more than two colourful names for the same thing; Scott makes no attempt to differentiate the meanings. He was not the first to create poetic language by ignoring particulars for the sake of general meaning. The use of *helm* in this way had long since been sanctioned. Milton and Pope had already used it as a name for any kind of helmet and Morris was to do so later. The same happened to *falchion*, also used in *The Talisman* (*Ta* 487). It seems to have been a thirteenth-century development (Mann, *Arms and Armour*, p. 11) and the *MED* cites examples from the middle of that century on (*MED fauchoun*). Originally it meant 'a broad sword more or less curved with the cutting edge on the convex side' but by the eighteenth century was a poetic word for any sword: Gray, Dryden, and Keats use it so. Either Scott did not know what the particular meaning of *falchion* was or he too took it as a mere general synonym for *sword* since he describes a 'long broad, straight-shaped, double-edged falchion' (*Ta* 487).

One can hardly quarrel with *falchion* being used in *The Talisman* especially in view of the impossibility of knowing with complete accuracy the date at which any one weapon appeared. A perhaps timely reminder of the inadequacies of dictionaries for this purpose is provided by *aketoun*. The earliest *MED* example of *aketouner* 'a maker of aketouns' is for the same mid thirteenth-century period as *falchion* first appears in, but the earliest citation for the Arabic derived *aketoun* itself – an aketoun, appearing in Scott under the diverse spellings *hacqueton* (*Iv* 365) and *acton* (*FM* 675), was a 'quilted or padded jacket worn under the armour for comfort or protection' – is assigned the date 1338, nearly a century later. There can be no doubt that it is correctly used in *The Fair Maid of Perth* but it is perhaps anachronistic in *Ivanhoe*. There are other words which seem to be anachronisms from dictionary evidence but by a margin of years which leaves the question very much open to doubt. The earliest *OED* example of *mace* 'a heavy staff or club' is dated 1297. It occurs in *The Talisman* in the phrase *mace of arms* (*Ta* 488), for which the *OED* examples are insufficient to outline the full history (*OED mace* sb[1]). On the other hand though the earliest *MED* quotations for *mangonel* 'a military engine for casting stones' (*Ta* 580) are from the mid-thirteenth century, its use in *The Talisman* stands a good chance of not being anachronistic. Latin terms are very often modelled on the vernacular and a Latin form of the word, *mangunellus*, is found in at least one twelfth-century text from the British Isles

(Latham, *Revised Mediaeval Latin Word List*, London, 1965, *s.v. mangonellus*).

Even given the inadequacy of dictionaries, words for which the earliest *OED* citation is from the fourteenth or fifteenth century are almost certainly anachronistic when used in *The Talisman*. Towards the end of the thirteenth century mittens were added to protective armour by extending the sleeves of the mail hauberk (a coat of mail covering the torso; see Mann, *Arms and Armour*, p. 12). These, whether made of mail or, as later happened, of plate, were known as *gauntlets*. The *OED* dates its first example of the word *c.* 1420. Its use in *The Talisman* is thus inaccurate. This does not apply in other cases of its appearance: it is very probably accurate for the beginning of the fifteenth century (*FM* 601), certainly so for the mid-sixteenth century (*Mo* 491) and for the mid-seventeenth century (*LM* 188). *The Legend of Montrose* – source of the last example – is set at the end of the word's span of life in military use, since the *OED*, after frequent citations up to 1658 records only Hoole, the translator of Tasso, as using the word in the eighteenth century, with the one exception that in the fossilized phrase 'throw down the gauntlet' it has been in continual use since the sixteenth century (*OED gauntlet* 1a, c). The *pavesse* (*Ta* 798) or *pavisse* (*Iv* 361) 'a kind of large shield' may also have developed about the end of the thirteenth century though the *OED*'s examples date in this case from the late fourteenth century (*OED pavis*).

Quite certainly and seriously anachronistic in *The Talisman* and *Ivanhoe* are terms borrowed from the fifteenth, sixteenth, and seventeenth centuries. Though defences for the head of a horse are mentioned as early as the thirteenth century the particular kind known as the *chamfrein* or, in Scott's spelling, *chamfrom* (*Iv* 18) does not appear till the fifteenth century (earliest *OED* example 1465; *OED chamfram*). The *partisan* and *morion* have already been mentioned as belonging to the sixteenth and seventeenth centuries. So does *curtal-axe* (*Ta* 578), a much perverted form of *cutlass*. (Though *curtal-axe* had originally the same meaning as *cutlass*, namely 'a short broad cutting sword', it was often taken to signify some kind of battle-axe. The same weapon, carried by the murderer Bonthron, is referred to at one point in *The Fair Maid of Perth* as 'a bloody axe' (*FM* 325) and at another point as 'a curtal-axe' (*FM* 408). In *The Talisman* we read: 'Beside it ... lay a mighty curtal-axe, which would have wearied the arm of any other than Cœur de Lion' (*Ta* 578), a comment more appropriate to an axe than to a short sword.) At this later period too a hidden coat of mail was called a *secret*. Scott uses the term in *The Talisman* (*Ta* 924), *The Fair Maid* (*FM* 64) and *The Monastery* (*Mo* 317), but as the earliest *OED* example is dated 1578 it could only be historically valid in the last of these three novels. As already pointed out a helmet was only from the sixteenth century known as a *head-piece* though the term is found in *The Talisman* (*Ta* 487). Likewise though plate armour was used much earlier the term *proof*, found in Scott in the mouths of twelfth- and fourteenth-century men (*Ta* 721, *FM* 535), was not used to describe plate before the sixteenth century.

On the other hand it would be unfair to Scott to suggest that all mention of arms and armour in the two Cœur-de-Lion novels is anachronistic. History justifies Scott in mentioning the *arblast* 'a kind of crossbow' in both novels (*Ta* 681, *Iv* 383). The name is attested from the end of the Old English period (*OED arbalest*). In *Ivanhoe* Scott also makes reference to the missiles propelled by this crossbow, using both the general term *bolt* (*Iv* 362) and the specialized term *quarrell* (*Iv* 383). Citations for *bolt* date from the Old English period and for *quarrell* from 'ante 1225'.

The Fair Maid of Perth shows the conflict of dates usual in Scott's work – the death of Rothesay, which took place in 1401-2, is shown as preceding by only a few days the battle of the clans, which took place in 1396 – but it is a good two centuries nearer Scott's time in setting than *Ivanhoe* or *The Talisman*. The two centuries make a considerable difference to the degree of accuracy. *Mangonel* (*FM* 603) used correctly, in all probability, in *The Talisman* and *Ivanhoe* is equally historical for a late fourteenth-century novel but *acton* (*FM* 675), which might have been a mistake, and *pavesse* (*FM* 536) which almost certainly was a mistake for the earlier novels, are now no longer anachronistic.

On the other hand fifteenth-, sixteenth- and seventeenth-century terms which had been anachronistic in *Ivanhoe* and *The Talisman* remain so in *The Fair Maid*; this applies to *curtal-axe* (*FM* 408), *head-piece* (*FM* 135), *proof* (*FM* 535) and *secret* (*FM* 64). However *The Fair Maid* introduces some new terms not found in the Cœur-de-Lion novels. The protective jacket of leather sometimes quilted with iron called a *jack* was used in the fourteenth century and rightfully finds mention in the novel (*FM* 135). If, as Scott thought, the term *jackman* was originally meant to describe men who wore a jack – 'what were called jack-men, from the *jack*, or doublet quilted with iron, which they wore as defensive armour' (*Mo* 95) – then it was very likely in use at the same time as *jack* and thus correctly used in *The Fair Maid* (*FM* 149). On the other hand the *OED* disagrees with Scott's etymology, as we noted before. Moreover the earliest citations offered by both the *OED* and the *DOST* are from the sixteenth century. All this applies to the appearance of *jackman* in *Quentin Durward* (*QD* 117); but it cannot at any rate, be anachronistic in *The Monastery* (*Mo* 95, 428). *Mosstrooper*, 'a border freebooter', found likewise in both *The Fair Maid* and *The Monastery* (*FM* 141, *Mo* 99), is, according to dictionary evidence, anachronistic in both. If we are to believe the evidence of the *OED* quotations, *moss-trooper* had a short vogue in the mid-seventeenth century and then disappeared entirely till revived by Scott in the poetry (*LLM* I xix). According to Scott 'This was the usual appellation of the marauders upon the Borders' (*LLM* Note XIII). He goes on to quote Fuller's description of the moss-troopers in his *Worthies*, written in the mid-seventeenth century, where it is not made explicit how long the term had been in use (see *The History of the Worthies of England*, P. Austin Nuttal ed., in 3 vols., London, 1840, I 339–40). However in another section of his work Fuller also writes, in a passage quoted by the *OED*, 'a sprig of these borderers hath lately been revived (disguised under the new name of moss-troopers)' (*Worthies*, II 543) suggesting that the term was of recent invention. Scott concludes his note by saying: 'The last public mention of moss-troopers occurs during the civil wars of the 17th century, when many ordinances of Parliament were directed against them.' It is to this period that the *OED* references belong. Another term for an armed man, favoured by other writers as well as Scott, is *man-at-arms* (*CD* 18, *Ta* 583, *Iv* 419, *FM* 565, *Mo* 69). This useful word was unknown to eighteenth-century writers till Southey restored it to currency in 1795. The phrase was at first *man of arms* and the first *OED* quotation is from Gower; in the sixteenth century *man at arms* took over.

The other two medieval novels of our selection, *Anne of Geierstein* and *Quentin Durward*, both set in the later fifteenth century (at the time of the Wars of the Roses) have nothing like this wealth of material to offer. *Baldrick* 'sword belt' (*AG* 279, *Mo* 251) may – to judge from the possibly misleading selection of quotations in the *OED* – have become an archaic poeticism in the eighteenth century. After its use by Spenser the *OED* records only Pope (in his *Iliad*), Tennyson, Lytton and Dean Farrar as using the word. The first *OED* quotation is for about 1300. The sixteenth-century *proof* 'plate armour' appears anachronistically yet again (*AG* 443). *Quentin Durward* offers a few new words. A *jazeran* (*QD* 19) is 'a coat or jacket of scale armour'. It is first mentioned at the beginning of the fifteenth century and is therefore appropriate to *Quentin Durward*. Baldricks, jazerans and proof armour belong to our traditional conception of the medieval world; the *harquebus* represents the coming of the new world of gunpowder. Commines, whom Scott had studied in writing *Quentin Durward* (see his introduction and notes to that work), mentions this early type of portable gun as a recent innovation (see R. C. Clephan, *Defensive Armour and Weapons*, London, 1900, p. 222) and it is no doubt due to this comment that the word appears in *Quentin Durward* (*QD* 168). By the time Scott came to write, *harquebus* had come to be employed as a general name for any gun.

The *hagbut* (*Ma* V iii) and *hackbut* (*Mo* 426) mentioned in *Marmion* and *The Monastery* are the harquebus under a different form of the name. In the names of arms and armour, as in so many things, *The Monastery* and to a lesser extent *The Abbot* represent a transition between the Middle Ages and the Renaissance. Despite the coming of the *hackbut* we still find mention of the *cross-bow* (*Mo* 392); if armour is no longer an essential of war we still have the *casque* (*Mo* 136), *gauntlets* (*Mo* 491) and *poldroons* 'pieces of shoulder armour' (*Mo* 491) – *poldroons*, to judge by the *OED* entry, were in use until the mid-seventeenth century and are mentioned in *The Legend of Montrose* set at that period (*LM* 188). This heavy armour supplements the lighter protection afforded by the *jack* (*Mo* 95, *Ab* 85) already mentioned. Perhaps black was the normal colour of this garment since it is also called a *black-jack* (*Mo* 169). *Marmion*, close to these two sixteenth-century novels in a lot of its diction, has the same word in another compound *steel-jack* (*Ma* V ii). *The Monastery* is the first of our novels to mention the *dudgeon-dagger* (*Mo* 248), a must in all the renaissance novels (*K* 42, *FN* 14, *Wk* 115–16) even if Scott misunderstood what it was, as we will see further on.

To digress for a moment, these two novels have two more mistakes with daggers, but of a different kind from these anachronisms. The meaning 'hilt of a dagger', rightly belonging to the

French *poignée*, is given to *poignet* (*Mo* 214), a name given to a hand or wrist ornament (*OED poignet* 1), and a dagger is called a *stilet* (*Ab* 61). This latter was normally 'a surgical probe' but Browning and Meredith adopted Scott's extension of the word's meaning.

If the names for daggers proliferate, the names for a sword also become more numerous. Possibly this reflects the way the sword is becoming more and more a symbol of rank and a decoration rather than a weapon of defence. Snobbishness as well as an eye for quality adds value to the sword from Bilbao or Toledo – *bilboa* (*Wk* 501), *bilbo* (*Wk* 41), *bilboa blades* (*K* 255), *toledo* (*Wk* 37). A sword can also be called a *tuck* (*Wk* 7) or a *fox* (*K* 60, *Ab* 195), the latter also being used attributively – 'a good fox broadsword' (*Wk* 12).

The increasing reliance on fire-arms finds expression in mention of the *caliver* 'a kind of musket' (*K* 4). The first notice of this weapon recorded in the *OED* is dated 1658, so for *Kenilworth*, set somewhere in the last decades of the sixteenth century the reference is highly topical. To the embarrassment of his son, King James, in *The Fortunes of Nigel*, shows his fear of yet another new kind of gun which came into use about this time. This is the *snaphaunce* (*FN* 487). Another spelling of the word, *snap-haunche*, suggested to Scott the meaning 'a spring trap' only found in his *Quentin Durward*: 'Take heed you step not off the straight and beaten path in approaching the portal. There are such traps and snap-haunches as may cost you a limb, which you will sorely miss' (*QD* 77; see *OED snaphance*). Scott's meaning – the result of his persistent interest in etymology – is more expressive than the real one.

Scott's use of *poignet* and *stilet* involves mistakes of another variety but none of the words from the renaissance novels dealt with here appear to involve inaccuracy of historical dating. The nearer we come to the renaissance period the less the amount of anachronism in Scott's novels. Scott's reading is so much better for the Elizabethan period than for the medieval, especially the early medieval period, that he is continually obliged to fall back on Elizabethan material to fill out the linguistic background of the medieval novels. For all this he does attempt to make some differentiation of the early and late medieval worlds, and if his differentiation is not as subtle as that between Elizabethan and Jacobean England the great familiarity of renaissance English literature both to himself and his readers made his task there so much easier. Moreover we all do something like Scott when we look back into the past. A kind of historical foreshortening is at work – the further we look back into history the larger the period of time we lump together as roughly the same. We feel equally free to generalize about the Renaissance (some two centuries) and the Middle Ages (some four centuries) and feel that the eleventh and fourteenth centuries were no more different from each other than the fifteenth and sixteenth centuries.

But just to admit that everyone shares a partly simplified view of the past is not to do Scott justice. The whole viewpoint of historical accuracy is, in absolute terms of the value of Scott's art, too narrow – even if the narrowness must be accepted as part of the nature of this study. The inaccuracies of dating which a modern scholar with the unfair advantage of possessing the OED can point out do not destroy Scott's achievement. He used minor detail carefully, if not always accurately, to build up a picture of worlds quite different from that he and his readers lived in. If Scott was not the first to recognize that the past was very different from the present he was the first to make a popular novel reflect this difference in its most minute details. And it is his ability to handle a multitude of minor details within the framework of his novels that makes him so great a writer.

THE PROBLEM OF INTELLIGIBILITY

The greatest difficulty for a writer using archaic language is how to make it intelligible. In writing the Scottish novels Scott had had ample experience in making unfamiliar Scots words understandable to his English reading public so that he was not at a loss when he faced the problem of making archaic language intelligible in *Ivanhoe*. The first and most necessary condition, as with the Scots dialogue, was not to use too much of it. The bulk of the meaning is conveyed in current modern English. But even a slight flavouring of archaism brings in a number of archaic words.

The most straightforward and obvious way of explaining a word is to gloss it. A footnote at the bottom of the page has the advantage of not disturbing the stylistic pattern of the sentence but cannot be too often resorted to without making a popular novel look like a scholarly text. Thus *destrier* is simply glossed 'warhorse' (*Iv* 566n), *dortour* 'dormitory' (*Iv* 465n). Sometimes these notes are more extended either covering several words: 'The arblast was a cross-bow, the windlace the machine used in bending that weapon, and the quarrell, so called from its square or diamond-shaped head, was the bolt adapted to it' (*Iv* 383n), or pointing out the source of Scott's information: 'These were drinks used by the Saxons, as we are informed by Mr Turner: Morat was made of honey flavoured with the juice of mulberries; Pigment was rich and sweet liquor, composed of wine highly spiced, and sweetened also with honey' (*Iv* 41n) or even covering something so extended as a summary of the semantic development of *knight* (*Iv* 37n).

In the narrative there is no reason why Scott should not incorporate the explanation as he goes along. When *arblast* reappears after *Ivanhoe* in *The Betrothed* it is explained by the addition of 'or crossbows' (*Be* 40) and in *Quentin Durward* Scott speaks of 'a jazeran, or flexible shirt of linked mail' (*QD* 19). Sometimes these explanations also inform the reader that the term is now out of use: 'He wore large hose made of calves-leather, and a tuck, as it was then called, or rapier of tremendous length' (*Wk* 7). Another element introduced is etymology: 'what were called jackmen, from the *jack*, or doublet quilted with iron, which they wore as defensive armour' (*Mo* 95). This etymology has been questioned (see above) but it is interesting that Scott chooses to explain a word by an etymological breakdown. His interest in etymology was in fact of long standing. In Scott's notebooks of the year 1792 Lockhart found 'several pages of etymologies from Ducange' (*Life*, I 201). In his first long piece of prose fiction – the conclusion to Strutt's *Queenhoo Hall* – this interest manifests itself in the explanation of *bandog*: 'the keeper entered, leading his bandog, a large blood-hound, tied in a leam or band, from which he takes his name' (*Queenhoo Hall*, Conclusion by Scott, chap. iv; see *Wa* lvii). One sometimes doubts whether Scott's etymological notes were as interesting to the general reader as they are to the scholar. He cannot let the town name *Plessis* go by without comment: 'These woodlands comprised a noble chase, or royal park, fenced by an enclosure, termed in the Latin of the Middle Ages *Plexitium*, which gives the name of Plessis to so many villages in France' (*QD* 12). 'What care we ... whether Saragossa be derived from Caesarea Augusta' says Scott, with reference to Southey's 'tendency to augment a work already too long by saying all that can be said of the history of ancient times appertaining to every place mentioned' (*Journal*, 19 October 1826). What he objected to was excessive use of small details, what he had the day before called 'a dragging in historical details by head and shoulders, so that the interest of the main piece is lost in minute descriptions of events which do not affect its progress'. However he confesses in a well-known passage that 'I have sin'd in this way myself – indeed I am but too conscious of having considered the plot only as what Bayes calls the means of bringing in fine things'. In a lighter vein much fun is made in *The Antiquary* of Oldbuck and Sir Arthur's hypotheses based on the etymology of *Benval* (*An* 73–4). Scott's interest in etymology, not being adequately catered for by the best dictionaries of his period, sometimes led him astray. The word *viliago* 'villain, scoundrel' was borrowed from the Italian *viliaco* and used by Shakespeare (2*HVI* IV viii 49) and others of the period. Scott associated it with *village*, wrote *villagio* and used it to mean 'rustic' (*Mo* 180). The mistaken etymology did not originate with Scott; Theobald emended Shakespeare's *villiago* to *villageois*, a reading followed by Johnson (Johnson's Shakespeare, London, 1778, VI 405). Etymology is really part of the wider subject of semantic development. Scott's footnotes on the two appearances of *attaint* cover different parts of the word's history. In *The Monastery* he discusses the origin of the term: '*Attaint* was a term of tilting used to express the champion's having attained his mark, or, in other words, struck his lance straight and fair against the helmet or breast of his adversary. Whereas to break the lance across, intimated a total failure in directing the point of the weapon on the object of his aim' (*Mo* 210n), while in *Ivanhoe* he traces its later use: 'This term of chivalry, transferred to the law, gives the phrase of being attainted of treason' (*Iv* 111n). While Scott is right in suggesting that it is the same noun (and verb) *attaint* which is used of a hit in tilting and the process of attainder (see *OED attaint* ppl a, v) his attempt to explain how this came about is misleading. In fact *attaint* (which originally meant 'to condemn someone') came to refer primarily to the 'corruption of blood' by association with *taint* with which its aphetic form coincided, though the etymology and meaning were distinct. Another familiar phrase – *to the outrance* (*FM* 385, *K* 90) – Scott also traced back to tournaments: 'the combat was understood to be at *outrance*, that is, the knights were to fight with sharp weapons, as in actual battle' (*Iv* 106).

Dialogue offers the writer little chance to explain his terms in passing. Only very rarely is Scott so clumsy as to allow his speakers to explain their own unfamiliar terms:

> ' "His garrison," ' proceeded the minstrel, reading, ' "consists of a lance with its furniture," What then a lance, in other words a belted knight, commands this party' (*CD* 27).

More often Scott relied on some manipulation of the context to explain his terms. This is usually skilfully done and his ineptitude in the handling of *mangonel* in Wilkin Flammock's speech in *The Betrothed* is exceptional:

> They are taught also, these Flemings, by the practice of their own country, the attack and defence of walled cities and fortresses, and are especially skilfull in working of mangonels and military engines (*Be* 33–4).

Military engines seems to be included merely to explain *mangonels* 'catapults' and has too much the air of a textbook to sound natural in the mouth of a twelfth-century merchant. The thing is done better with *tregetour* 'juggler':

> I had not gained admittance into my own castle, had I not been supposed to be the attendant of a juggler ... I say the sewer thought I was dressed to bear a part in the tregetour's mummery ... (*Iv* 614).

Mangonel and *tregetour* were both obsolete terms that most of Scott's readers would have been hard put to define. Sometimes only a little manipulation is needed:

> 'But what liquor is there?'
> 'Only a bottle of Alicant, and one of sack, with the stone jug of strong waters.' (*Wk* 63).

Alicant and *sack* are kinds of wine.

One consequence of leaving words to explain themselves is that this may impose limits on the precision of our understanding; any particular sense is easily lost. We guess *Alicant* is a wine but we do not know if it is sweet or dry. It is in fact a strong sweet Spanish wine, the last *OED* citation being from the late seventeenth century. *Clary* and *bastard* equally proclaim themselves drinks – 'a cup of clary' (*K* 11), 'a cup of bastard' (*K* 33) – but of what kind? Both terms were no longer in normal use by Scott's time. *Clary* was spiced wine, *bastard* a sweet Spanish wine. *Kitchener* and *Refectioner* occur together in *The Monastery* (*Mo* 204).

Period Vocabulary

Though they are two distinct officers in a monastery, particularization is not necessary to Scott's purposes; the indication of the general nature of their functions given by their titles is sufficient.

A method Scott has of rendering unusual words intelligible by stringing them together when they are of related meaning makes it impossible to convey a precise sense, but gives the reader all the information he actually needs:

> In the house, many of the gentlemen betook themselves to cards or dice, and parties were formed at Ombre, at Basset, at Gleek, at Primero, and at other games then in fashion; while the dice were used at various games . . . as Hazard, In and In, Passage and so forth (*FN* 220).

> . . . he is the well known and general referee in all matters affecting the mysteries of Passage, Hazard, In and In, Penneeck and Verquire, and what not – Why, Beaujeu is King of the Card-pack and Duke of the Dice-box (*FN* 204).

Some of these names would have been familiar to Scott's readers. *Ombre* was a common game in the seventeenth and eighteenth centuries. Sterne had mentioned *primero*; *gleek* is given in the *OED* in historical contexts for the eighteenth century. *Passage* is last attested in the *OED* here in *Nigel* and the last example given for *basset*, excluding its use by Macaulay in his *History of England* (1849), is in the Prologue to Rowe's *Royal Convert* written in the early eighteenth century. *In and In* is very likely a revival not being attested after the end of the eighteenth century in the *OED*. The reference to *penneeck* is anachronistic as the *OED* examples all date from the Restoration period whereas *The Fortunes of Nigel* is set in the reign of James I. Its vogue seems to have been shortlived. Not mentioned in the eighteenth century it is referred to historically in Scott's later years. *Verquire* is also a mistake; the game was not played outside the early eighteenth century. At least six unfamiliar words have been introduced. Whether he is historically accurate or not Scott has unobtrusively conveyed the general meaning of all of them and this, in the second passage, without disturbing the natural flow of his dialogue. All the same the information conveyed is in fact minimal. In passages like this it becomes obvious that Scott's terms are often not there as details of social history but as colourful items in themselves, introduced for their own sake.

The romantic foreign names for the various thrusts in fencing are certainly brought into the novels for colour alone. They denote movements far too complicated to explain. This applies both when Scott speaks in some detail of Sir Piercie Shafton's proficiencies:

> The English knight was master of all the mystery of the *stoccata, imbrocata, punto-reverso, incartata*, and so forth which the Italian masters of defence had lately introduced into general practice (*Mo* 288)

and when Sir Henry Lee mentions in passing the *passado* (*Wk* 317) and the *stramaçon* (*Wk* 342). Hunting too had a jargon of its own to match that of duelling: Cedric the Saxon shows some knowledge of it even as he disclaims any intention of using it:

> I can wind my horn, though I call not the blast either a *recheate* or a *morte* – I can cheer my dogs on the prey, and I can flay and quarter the animal when it is brought down, without using the new-fangled jargon of *curée, arbor, nombles*, and all the babble of the fabulous Sir Tristrem (*Iv* 58)

and, in a novel set much later – *The Bride of Lammermoor* – the same desire to introduce colourful terminology for its own sake is evident. Bucklaw's delight in the bloodiest part of hunting has alienated Lucy; however showing little concern about this he throws himself into the business of cutting up the animal 'wrangling and disputing with all around him concerning nombles, briskets, flankards and raven-bones, then the usual terms of the art of hunting, or of butchery, whichever the reader chooses to call it, which are now probably antiquated' (*BL* 135).

Obsolete or archaic nouns can be made intelligible by the use of suitable adjectives. The danger in this is that the writer will fall into tautology. However tautological phrases are allowable in the language of abuse so often tautological in real life: 'thou lazy losel' (*AG* 147); 'unbelieving miscreants' (*Ta* 583) – *losel* means 'a lazy man', *miscreant* 'an unbeliever'. Both terms were probably little known outside poetry in Scott's time. When Colepepper speaks of 'base, skeldering, coistril propositions' (*FN* 302), the first adjective explains the other two, both seventeenth-century terms and equally abusive. Tautology is just another of Sir Piercie Shafton's affectations – nevertheless it also serves to explain the obsolete term *outrecuidance*. Scott can make Sir Piercie speak of Halbert's 'outrecuidance and orgillous presumption' (*Mo* 283) but in De Bracy's more forthright speech he finds it more suitable to explain the word by a footnote gloss: 'presumption, insolence' (*Iv* 131n). Another form of tautology practised by Scott, evidently again in order to make unknown words intelligible, is compounds like *donjon-keep* (*QD* 29) and *rash-taffeta* (*K* 406). In both compounds both elements have the same meaning but one or each pair is unfamiliar either from being an obsolete word (*rash*) or from having an obsolete spelling (*donjon*).

Of course intelligibility is not invariably a problem. Sometimes Scott's archaisms consist of only a slight change of meaning or usage: the adjective *main* cannot now be used comparatively but in Elizabethan times it could, with the sense 'highly important, momentous' (*OED main* 5). So in *Kenilworth* Mike Lambourne speaks of 'a more main concern' (*K* 466). Other revived words are self-explaining compounds like *bear-ward* 'bear-keeper' (*K* 293, *Wk* 155), *lance-knights* 'knights with lances' (*QD* 44) and *sack-butt* 'a butt for sack (a white wine)' (*K* 34) – not to be confused with *sackbut* 'a kind of trumpet' (*Ma* IV xxxi). The meaning of *parish-top* (*K* 327) is straightforward though we may be surprised to hear that there was such an institution as 'a whipping top kept for the exercise of the parishioners'. If weight is given to both elements, the compound *backfriend* is ambiguous and it has been used in two contrary senses: 'true friend' and 'false friend'. The latter sense had not passed out of use by Scott's time (*OED backfriend* 1) and is found in two of the novels under consideration (*FN* 267, *Mo* 429). For the much rarer sense 'true friend' we have to look to *Quentin Durward* (*QD* 82). The *OED* offers only one other example of the word used in this sense, from Nashe's *Lenten Stuffe* (*OED backfriend* 2). The literal meaning of *tear-cats* is obvious but it does not provide much clue to the figurative sense 'swaggerer, bully'. The context helps a little: 'I do not ... pretend to be ... one of those ruffling tear-cats who maintain their master's quarrel with sword and buckler' (*K* 206). Only those familiar with Elizabethan drama will recognise this stock phrase applied, with the verbal phrase *tear a cat*, to ranting actors. If Onions in his *Shakespeare Glossary* is correct and this phrase was 'specifically associated with ranting on the stage' then the application of it here to noblemen's retainers is an extension of Elizabethan usage.

In some cases where only half of the compound is familiar the sense is only partially conveyed. *Dudgeon-dagger* (*Ab* 61, *K* 42, *FN* 14, *Wk* 115–16), a word unknown in early nineteenth-century

English before Scott took it up, means 'a dagger with a hilt of dudgeon wood' but in most contexts it is sufficient for Scott's purposes that his readers will certainly realize that it is some kind of dagger even if they do not know *what* kind. Moreover the word calls up romantic associations with the hallucinatory dagger of Macbeth:

> I see thee still;
> And on thy blade and dudgeon gouts of blood
> (*Mac* II i 45–6).

On the one occasion when Scott decides to be more explicit he is wrong: 'a large knife hilted with buck horn, or, as it was then called a dudgeon-dagger' (*Mo* 247–8). *Turn-broche* (*FN* 255, last example in the *OED*; also *Mo* 206) may be understood by comparing *turn-spit* – it has the same meaning – but *rere-suppers* needs Scott's note to yield its full meaning: 'The supper took place at an early hour, six or seven o'clock at latest – the *rere-supper* was a postliminary banquet, a *hors d'œuvre*, which made its appearance at ten or eleven, and served as an apology for prolonging the entertainment till midnight' (*Wk* 272n). The word is also explained, in a shorter footnote, on its appearance in *Ivanhoe* (*Iv* 236). Outside the fourteenth to seventeenth centuries the *OED* cites only Scott's use of this word. *Wastel* is 'bread from the finest flour'. Readers of *The Monastery* need to know this to understand how complete an epicure the Abbot is in speaking of *wassel-bread* (*Mo* 220). There can be no doubt that Scott is here thinking of another religious person who was rather too much of an epicure – Chaucer's Prioress feeds her dogs 'With rosted flessh, or milk and wastel-breed' (*CT* I 147). The spelling *wassell*, incidentally, is due to confusion with *wassail* which is sometimes spelt *wassel* (e.g. *Ma* V vii). The more correct *wastel-bread* is also found in the same novel (*Mo* 153) along with *wastel-cake* (*Mo* 347), a compound apparently first found in Scott. The term *wastel* was, it seems, obsolete by the end of the seventeenth century though it was revived, especially in historical contexts, in the nineteenth.

The reader who shares Scott's interest in etymology will easily understand words used with a meaning nearer the etymological sense than the modern one. Looking at Rebecca, Urfried asks: 'Outlandish, too, ... What country art thou of? – a Saracen? or an Egyptian?' (*Iv* 303–4). *Outlandish* is here used in its primary sense 'foreign' – the sense we would expect it to have from its derivation. By Scott's time this had been replaced, by a process of association, with the normal modern sense 'strange'. *Chaplain* in *Ivanhoe* (*Iv* 326) means 'the priest of a chapel'. Again in Scott's time this primary sense had been more or less superseded by the meaning 'a priest attached to a household or other body of people'. *Rudesby* 'a rude fellow' (*Mo* 195) can be explained by any reader through its derivation from *rude*; the OED quotations suggest a Scott revival, the last example before *The Monastery* being dated 1601. Other obsolete words are likewise understood by reference to closely related current words: *secret* explains another noun itself familiar in a different sense – *secretary* 'confidante' (*FN* 312). Scott had already used *secretary* in this sense in *Guy Mannering* (*GM* 149) this being the OED's last recorded use of the word in this meaning following the penultimate use after a gap of two centuries. *Conscionable* 'considerate' (*K* 68) is explained by its negative *unconscionable* which for some reason survived the death of the positive in the eighteenth century and is still with us now. Perhaps its similarity to the current *rascallion* (*Wk* 92) or *rapscallion* as well as its context makes Richie Moniplies' *rampallian* 'scoundrel, ruffian' easier to understand: 'I was almost strangled with my own band by twa rampallians, wha wanted yestreen, nae farther gane, to harle me into a change-house' (*FN* 460). *Rampallian* is an Elizabethan word. The verb *bane* 'to poison' (*Ab* 501) was obsolete in Scott's time but was nevertheless easily comprehended by his contemporaries because the noun was still used, if only figuratively, with the same meaning 'poison'. Even obsolete figurative language is useful to Scott: surely even those forgetting Shakespeare, the only author before Scott to use *trench* figuratively to mean 'a scar or deep wrinkle' – 'Witness these trenches made by grief and care' (*TA* V ii 23) – would work out its meaning in Guthrie's retort to Le Balafré ('The Scarred'): 'Thou name ladies' love with such a trench in thy visage!' (*QD* 116).

With all these devices there yet remain some words which Scott simply did not explain. Isaac's characteristic comment on the wounded Ivanhoe: 'he is a good youth, and my heart bleeds to see the gore trickle down his rich embroidered hacqueton, and his corslet of goodly price' (*Iv* 365) does little to enlighten the reader as to the meaning of *hacqueton* 'a stuffed jacket or jerkin worn under the mail'. Being embroidered it cannot be either mail or plate but that is the limit of the help Scott offers. The majority of Scott's readers, it is safe to assume, would not have encountered the term before as it had been virtually obsolete since the seventeenth century. *Corslet*, on the other hand, which means 'armour for the trunk of the body' – worn, in fact, over the *hacqueton* – is a common word in eighteenth-century heroic poetry. It occurs also in Scott's poetry (*Ma* V ii). The point is, of course, that the reader can share the joke about Isaac's miserliness without knowing precisely what a hacqueton, or for that matter a corslet is.

Scott must have always had several audiences in mind, the basic division being between those who were ignorant of the language of the past and those who were well read in it. Henry Crawford's remark that Shakespeare is 'part of an Englishman's constitution' (*Mansfield Park*, p. 338) puts before us an ideal to which only a few of Scott's readers would have conformed. No more than a small minority of his readers would have understood each Shakespearean, or indeed Elizabethan, word Scott used. While making sure the general drift of his meaning was never in doubt and thus catering for the ordinary reader, Scott offered his better-read reader the pleasure of identifying and understanding the archaic language. We must however ask ourselves if there was not one case where Scott saw a special advantage in this dual audience.

It would be wrong to accuse Scott of not dealing with sexuality outside marriage – it is for instance an important part of the plot of *The Heart of Midlothian*, one of his most admired novels, even if he yielded to pressure to expunge the incident by which it was to have played an equally important part in *St Ronan's Well* – but it is true that his characters are reticent in talking about illicit sexuality. However in *The Fortunes of Nigel* and *Kenilworth* – the only two novels using a lot of archaic language which deal in any detail with the underworld of crime and misdemeanour – the ban on speaking about sex is partly lifted. One of the reasons seems to be that the meaning can be hidden behind unfamiliar words, being clear only to those well acquainted with earlier literature – readers already inured to the literary treatment of the subject. The dual audience operates in a different way in a case in the *Minstrelsy* where the readers are divided into those who can read Latin (and who have presumably read classical references to sexual matters) and those who cannot. After reading in 'Jamie Telfer of the Fair Dodhead' the rather implausible account of how the Captain of Bewcastle lost the love of ladies for ever because he:

> was run thro' the thick of the thigh,
> And broken was his right leg bane (*Minstrelsy*, II 11)

only some of Scott's readers will be enlightened as to the true cause by his note: 'The editor has used some freedom with the original in the subsequent verse. The account of the Captain's disaster (*teste laeva vulnerata*) is rather too *naïve* for literal publication' (*Minstrelsy*, II 17). Giles Gosling's insinuation that Laurence Goldthred is wasting his money on loose women may pass unsuspected: 'Let cards and cockatrices do their worst, thy father's bales may bide a banging for a year or two' (*K* 11) he says. One could easily mistake *cockatrices* as referring to some kind of gambling when, in fact, it is a word for 'prostitutes'. *Waistcoateer* (*FN* 295), with the same meaning, is in context less ambiguous though its meaning is still not immediately obvious:

> 'I know the face of yonder waistcoateer,' continued the guide, 'and I could wager a rose-noble from the posture she stands in, that she has clean head-gear and a soiled night-rail.'

The word *night-rail* 'night-dress' further serves to slightly obscure the meaning for the modern reader but it was still in normal use in Scott's time. The same word *waistcoateer* conceals the insinuation about Jin Vin's habits or associates in Dame Suddlechop's flattery: 'Thou knowest well, that, from Mrs Deputy's self down to the waistcoateers in the alley, all of them are twiring and peeping betwixt their fingers when you pass' (*FN* 362). An elementary knowledge of Latin will enable us to guess that the *bona-robas* some of Scott's low characters talk about (*K* 10, *FN* 281) must be showy women but something more is needed to tell us that they will be wanton too. *Bona-roba* and *waistcoateer* had both been obsolete since the seventeenth century: *cockatrice* was used in the eighteenth century and may or may not have been current in Scott's time. Another word for such a woman is *light o' love* which as well as signifying 'a woman capricious in love' can mean 'a harlot'. The reader can make a good guess at the meaning when Henry Gow says to Louise:

> I have been a *galliard*, a reveller, in my day; but it's best to be plain ... and so, my quean, you and I must part sooner than perhaps a light-o'-love such as you expected to part with – a likely young fellow (*FM* 207).

But with a word obsolete from the sixteenth century he cannot be certain how deep the insult is intended to be. It is interesting in this respect that Henry Gow is a rare thing in Scott, a hero with a past, and here, where it comes out, it is disguised by archaic language. The term occurs again in *The Fortunes of Nigel* when John Christie wrongly accuses Nigel of seducing his wife (*FN* 504); in this particular case it would be hard not to understand the meaning. When Elizabeth applies the term to Amy Robsart it is used in its less damning sense 'a woman unconstant in love' referring to her desertion of Tressilian (*K* 357). The literary reference which made *Lindabrides* a 'sort of court name for a female of no reputation' (as Scott's footnote puts it; *Wk* 517n) was lost for most nineteenth-century readers and the word had become obsolete. Perhaps because it is the heroine, Amy Robsart, that Mike Lambourne refers to as a *Lindabrides* in *Kenilworth* (*K* 26) there is no explanatory footnote there. In *Woodstock* Wildrake apologizes for having called Alice a *Lindabrides* (*Wk* 517).

In *Anne of Geierstein* the one descent to the underworld is similarly veiled in archaic language. *Bordel*, meaning 'brothel' and not, as Chatterton thought, 'cottage', replaces the more offensive current word and neutralizes or at least softens any offence in the innkeeper's remark: 'who the foul fiend presses on the Golden Fleece at such an hour, as if he thundered at the door of a bordel?' (*AG* 366). After the mid-eighteenth century, *brothel* was the normal form and *bordel* was so far unfamiliar that Chatterton could make the ludicrous mistake of having two lovers declare: 'We wylle ynn a bordelle lyve' (*Aella* l. 147). Any possible offence is also avoided by not explaining *dowsets* 'the testicles of a deer', obsolete since the seventeenth century:

> monarchs were sometimes said to have . . . amused themselves with broiling the *umbles*, or *dowsets*, of the deer upon the glowing embers with their own royal hands (*Wk* 53).

Obsolete language has allowed Scott to extend his subject matter in a direction where it might otherwise have been inhibited.

One question remains. One does not know if Scott knew the meaning of *ingle* 'a boy favourite (in a bad sense)' as the *OED* delicately puts it, when he made Michael Lambourne use the strange greeting 'my dear friend and ingle, Tony Foster' (*K* 43). If Scott did understand *ingle* – and he knew his Jonson where the word occurs – then this passage has a special interest. Scott does not usually make any reference to the subject of homosexuality

[handwritten note at top: JFC's grammar is seldom 'american' — except when meant to be parodic?]

Chapter 4

PERIOD GRAMMAR

INTRODUCTION

'Rowena,' said De Bracy, 'art thou, too, deceived by the common error of thy sex, who think there can be no rivalry but that respecting their own charms? Knowst thou not there is a jealousy of ambition and of wealth, as well as of love; and that this our host, Front-de-Beouf, will push from his road him who opposes his claim to the fair barony of Ivanhoe, as readily, eagerly, and unscrupulously as if he were preferred to him by some blue-eyed damsel?' (*Iv* 296).

'SPENSER, in affecting the Ancients, writ no language,' said Jonson. Certainly the extract above is 'no language' in the sense that it is neither the language of the past nor the language of the present. The choice of diction reflects its early nineteenth-century provenance but for a writer of that period to use *thou*, the simple present unaided by the auxiliary *do* in a question ('knowest thou not'), and the combination of demonstrative and possessive pronoun in 'this our host' is unusual. What Scott desired and achieved was, of course, a mixed language – a nineteenth-century sentence structure with a few elements of grammar belonging to the past. The catalogue of Scott's archaisms of grammar which makes up most of this chapter may leave an impression that Scott used archaic grammar all the time. In fact just as the archaisms of diction never become so frequent in Scott as to produce a dialogue totally Anglo-Saxon, Anglo-Norman, or Middle English in vocabulary, so archaisms of grammar are equally the exception rather than the rule. Some of Scott's archaisms are extremely rare in his work – I have noted only two examples of the construction 'the man's daughter of the house' replaced in present-day English by the group genitive: 'the man of the house's daughter' (see § 1). One archaism of grammar alone provides serious opposition to its modern equivalent: this is *thou* for modern *you* (see § 2). *Thou* apart, the grammar of Scott's period dialogue is always predominantly that of his own day.

The elements of archaic grammar are much the same as those of archaic vocabulary. In each case by far the most significant element results from the resuscitation of obsolete or obsolescent language. Usages of grammar, like words, once they start to die, are often a long time doing so. In examining the extent to which usages were dead or dying when taken up by Scott we shall face again patterns already familiar to us in the examination of obsolete and obsolescent vocabulary. A certain number of the constructions Scott adopted for his period language were well and truly dead by the time he came to them. The use of *beest* as a form of the second person singular of the verb *to be* after *if* and *though* is not attested in the *OED* after the late seventeenth century. It appears however in *Ivanhoe*: 'an thou beest a man' (*Iv* 10; *an* means 'if' – see § 31). Equally unknown to the literary English of Scott's period is the omission of *thou* as the subject of a verb in an interrogative sentence: 'art dead? art stupified?' (*Iv* 469; see § 14). Even more frequent than these totally obsolete usages are usages not obsolete but in various ways obsolescent. Obsolescence usually implies restricted usage, often usage that is restricted to poetry. *Him* for modern *himself* and *be* for modern *are* (see §§ 8, 33) are allowed in poetic usage in Scott's time though no longer normal in prose. The influence of the Bible in the preservation of older usages can be felt too. The appearance of *ye* and the *-th* ending in Scott – usually, but not always, with religious characters – owes a lot to the translators of the Authorized Version. (Of course, Biblical usage has an important influence in the novels on the grammar of strongly religious characters – Catholic priests, Puritans, Presbyterians and also, interestingly, Moslems – but this is outside our scope since the main aim is to impart a religious rather than an archaic tone.) Some formerly frequent usages became restricted to use only with certain words. There is evidence that Scott reopened the scope of some such restricted usages as well. In Jane Austen the present without the auxiliary *do* in interrogative sentences is restricted to the verbs *come* and *say* except in a few very dramatic passages; in Scott this older construction has a wider scope (see § 36). To what extent Scott expanded the scope of contemporary usage by drawing on both poetic and fossilized constructions it is not easy at this stage to say. The attempt made further on to decide how archaic some of Scott's usages were can be sometimes little more than a guess. However, the frequency with which constructions turn up which seem, on what evidence we have, to have been unusual for his period leaves little doubt that his grammar in his period dialogue where it was not archaic must often have sounded at the least old-fashioned.

In examining Scott's period diction we have labelled one element of it 'vogue words'. A corresponding 'vogue grammar' can also be discerned. Some words, while by no means ceasing to be used, are yet so much more frequent at or so much more characteristic of one period that Scott could use them as an element of period language. These are our 'vogue words'. Such predominant association with one period is less common with points of grammar than with words. Some such associations have however attached to three constructions – the idiomatic *your*: 'Your Turk never coughs in his cup' (*Ta* 802); the apparently pleonastic use of *it* in phrases like 'you coy it' (*FM* 193); and another pronominal construction, the ethic dative 'I hears me the lattice open' (*K* 24; see §§ 6, 7, 10). The first two are still found occasionally even in English of the present day but much less frequently than in Elizabethan English, where they are relatively common.

It will be noted that one example of the idiomatic *your* occurs in a novel, *The Talisman*, set about four centuries before the Elizabethan period; *The Fair Maid of Perth* too, in which the apparently pleonastic *it* occurs, is set about two centuries before the same period. If the reason for the appearance of these two constructions lies in their predominantly *Elizabethan* connotations then they nevertheless appear in novels set well before that time. This raises the whole question of historical appropriateness to period, already an important issue in regard to vocabulary. In the mixture of current and archaic grammar that makes up Scott's dialogue in the medieval and renaissance novels, the archaic element does not necessarily belong to the period appropriate to the novel in question; he was too keen on success as a writer to mystify his readers by too appropriate a grammar for the period in novels like *Ivanhoe* and *The Talisman*, let alone the eleventh-century *Count Robert of Paris*. The *-self* forms of the pronoun (now always used for the reflexive and occasionally, in apposition to the simple pronoun, to add emphasis) only began to develop in late Middle English. In conformity with his practice of using an eclectic grammar of old and new, Scott both follows the older usage with the simple pronoun – 'I will but arm me' (*Ta* 677) – and introduces the *-self* forms used in his own time – 'I will myself undertake thy revenge'

(*Ta* 510). As a matter of fact this mixture of forms would have been possible in renaissance English but is unknown to the early Middle English period to which *The Talisman* belongs. Also inappropriate to period is the use of the -*self* form in *The Talisman* in a way normal only in early Modern English as in: 'Themselves sought out the bait' (*Ta* 835) where it is emphatic but not in apposition to the simple pronoun as in present-day usage (see § 5). Equally the unemphatic use of *do* in positive statements found in *The Talisman* and in *Ivanhoe* (see § 38) is neither appropriate to the twelfth century nor the current usage of Scott's time. *Do* is not (except in a causative sense) found as an auxiliary in early Middle English. In later Middle and early Modern English it is in use in both emphatic and non-emphatic contexts. By Scott's time it was always emphatic in positive sentences. Where a usage common in Middle English becomes more restricted in use in early Modern English, Scott generally observes the restrictions of the later period. In earlier Middle English, *mine* and *thine* appeared in attributive use before consonants and vowels. By the beginning of the Modern English period they only appear before a vowel and *h* and this is how they are used in Scott (see § 9). The placing of a particle between adjective and noun, found in Middle English with an article placed between, by early Modern English lingers only in complimentary phrases with an intermediate possessive pronoun (see § 18). Once again Scott limits himself to the circumscribed usage of the Elizabethans rather than enjoying the greater freedom of Middle English. Many constructions are common to early Modern English and Middle English, amongst them the use of *thou* (see § 2), of the -*th* inflection (see § 32), and of the simple rather than the expanded tenses (see § 34), as well as numerous usages also common to the English of Scott's own day; but where Scott makes use of constructions not found over the whole Middle English and early Modern English period he almost always chooses those confined to later rather than earlier usage.

In addition to obsolete and vogue words, both paralleled in obsolete and vogue grammar, another important element in Scott's period diction is pseudo-archaic words or archaic neologisms. These seem to have virtually no parallels in grammar. Scott's period grammar usually seems to be based on previous usage even if it is not always historically accurate. One possible fake must be mentioned. The reflexive use of the verb *warrant* as in 'I warrant me' (*Ta* 748) meaning 'I'll be bound', is completely unknown

Period Grammar

before Scott. The OED neatly describes it as 'quasi-archaic' (*OED warrant* v 5b; see § 46).

A word must be said about the influence of Scott's contemporaries. The importance of poetry as a storehouse of archaic usage has already been emphasized. Both in his poems and in his later period-novels Scott belongs to the whole school of Romantic (and pre-Romantic) poets who saw the English of the Elizabethan period, in particular the English of Shakespeare and Spenser, as the natural quarry for a new poetic language different from that of the Augustans. When Scott shares with Keats the retention of *mine* and *thine* in attributive use (see § 9) and the obsolete past participle *foughten* (see § 33), with Shelley the use of *be* for modern *are* (see § 31) and with both Byron and Shelley the reflexive use of the simple pronoun (see § 8) – all of them archaic usages – he belongs to this tradition. What distinguished Scott was the more wide-ranging enthusiasm with which he pillaged Elizabethan sources and his use of them specially to provide period dialogue.

Considerable problems of intelligibility are raised by the use of archaic vocabulary and they have been dealt with in a previous chapter. With all the expedients Scott thought up to render unfamiliar words intelligible, there is a limit on the amount of period diction he could introduce without making his novels unintelligible to the great bulk of his readers. On the other hand, apart from the occasional risk of ambiguity (see § 15), period grammar rarely endangers intelligibility in this way – *him* used reflexively is not any more difficult to understand than *himself* and, despite the absence of the prop-word *one*, no reader should have any difficulty in realizing that in: 'my mistress is a good lady, and a virtuous' (*Ab* 77) both *good* and *virtuous* refer to *lady* (see § 18); though the arrangement of the adjectives is romantically remote to the modern ear, it is not confusing.

The main limitation on the use of archaic grammar is provided by considerations of euphony. Scott was aware that writers like Chatterton were not only difficult to understand but awkward and ugly as well. The reader is not therefore tired by the repetition to *thou* when it threatens to become cumbersome. Only occasionally do we find clumsy forms like 'thou blasphemest' (*Ta* 506) and 'thou accountest' (*K* 544). Similarly while Scott often uses a negative without auxiliary – 'I know you not' (*Iv* 293; see § 35) – he rarely sacrifices euphony for the sake of an archaism in as clumsy a way as he does in the first chapter of *Ivanhoe*: 'If the two legged wolf snap not up some of them ere nightfall, I am no true man' (*Iv* 9). Sometimes too an inconsistency of grammar maintains the consistency of the rhythmic pattern of the sentence (a device not unknown to the Elizabethans); in Saladin's proverb a second *-th* inflection would perhaps have disturbed the rhythm:

> When the rich carpet is soiled the fool pointeth to the stain – the wise man covers it with his mantle (*Ta* 753).

At times an obsolete and rather clumsy inflection indicates a slightly ironic tone, as when Wilkin Flammock assures Father Aldrovand that the business in hand has nothing to do with him: 'Reverend father . . . it altogether respecteth secular matters' (*Be* 59).

What follows is a descriptive list of the principal archaisms of grammar employed by Scott. In each case an attempt is made to determine how archaic the usage would have been to Scott's original readers. In some cases, given the nature of our evidence, the conclusions can only be doubtful. A few usages not archaic in Scott's time but archaic to us are also covered in passing.

NOUNS

1. I have noticed only one example in the narrative of the medieval and renaissance novels of the construction which, in Modern English, has been superseded by the group genitive: in *The Fortunes of Nigel* Duke Hildebrod refers to Martha Trapbois as 'the man's daughter of the house' (*FN* 410). The construction is however also found in *The Pirate* with 'the king's daughter of Norway' (*Pi* 421). The modern construction: 'the man of the house's (King of Norway's) daughter' is first recorded in Chaucer though in his work the older usage prevails in the greater number of cases (Mustanoja, p. 79). By the early seventeenth century (the period of the setting of *Nigel*) this usage would have been rare but not totally impossible (see Jespersen, *CE* § 129); a century later (the time of the setting of *The Pirate*) it was quite obsolete. Scott's historical sense was nevertheless not completely at fault. Magnus Troil is talking about 'the Frawa-stack off Papa, where the King's daughter of Norway was shut up to keep her from her lovers' (*Pi* 421). The allusion is to a tale clearly fit for a ballad and it is from a ballad, *Sir Patrick Spens*, that Scott has picked up this

very phrase. The relevant stanza as printed in his own *Minstrelsy of the Scottish Border* reads:

> To Noroway, to Noroway,
>   To Noroway o'er the faem;
> The King's daughter of Noroway,
>   'Tis thou maun bring her hame. (*Minstrelsy*, I 225).

The phrase has clearly been chosen to reinforce the romantic nature of Magnus' tale.

PERSONAL PRONOUNS

2. By Scott's time the use of *thou* for the second person singular pronoun had become archaic in all normal literary and colloquial contexts. *Thou* and other pronouns and adjectives associated with it – *thee, thy, thine, thyself* – are extremely frequent in the dialogue of our novels. This is the most frequent archaism in Scott's work and in fact its occurrence outnumbers that of the modern equivalent use with *you*. Even at the end of the sixteenth century the replacement of *thou* by *you* (and *ye*) had been more or less accomplished. In Shakespeare both *thou* and *you* (singular) appear. Franz (§ 289ff) and Abbott (§ 231ff) attempt to reduce Shakespeare's use of these pronouns to rule, but a residue of examples remain, for which none of these rules provides adequate explanation. One is at a loss to provide any reasoned explanation for sentences like: 'If thou beest not immortal look about you' (*JC* II iii 7). Scott's works show alternations of pronoun equally inexplicable; inexplicable, that is, if one tries to make Scott's usage follow rules: 'whosoever thou art, it is discourteous in you to disturb my thoughts' (*Iv* 28). Even stranger is the hesitation between *thou* and *ye* (singular) in the following: 'thou shalt this day see the naked breast of a Saxon as boldly presented to the battle as ever ye beheld the steel corslet of a Norman' (*Iv* 417). Any attempt to explain the wavering between *thou* and *you* forms in Scott according to rules will break down after, at the most, a page. Halfway through *Ivanhoe*, after Cedric's party has been captured by De Bracy and taken to Torquilstone, three crucial interviews take place: Front-de-Bœuf and Isaac, De Bracy and Rowena, Bois-Guilbert and Rebecca. Let us take one of these: the confrontation of Rowena and her would-be suitor. Both speakers begin with *you* forms (see *Iv* 293ff). In his second speech De Bracy passes to *thou* forms incidentally reviving

an obsolete usage of the reflexive pronoun on its own: 'To *thyself*, fair maid, . . . be ascribed whatever I have done' (*Iv* 293). The simple object pronoun would be used here in present-day English (see § 5). Is De Bracy, then, in using *thou* venturing on familiarity? Rowena also uses *thine* (contemptuously?) when speaking in ironic tones, but returns to *you*, as De Bracy has done meanwhile, in making another bitter and equally contemptuous comment. Following that De Bracy inside one speech uses *thou*, *your* and *thy*:

> proud damsel, *thou* shalt be as proudly encountered. Know then, that I have supported my pretensions to *your* hand in the way that best suited *thy* character (*Iv* 294).

Is this an unsure attempt at a warmer tone? The conversation continues with the same alternations for another page until it finally settles into consistent *thou*. At the end De Bracy is slightly scornful but still wooing Rowena after a fashion – neither the *thou* of contempt nor the *thou* of affection would seem appropriate. Again, even if Rowena is pleading, she is hardly likely to have dropped into the familiar *thou*. The best explanation of all this is not in terms of historical usage but in terms of style. The *thou* form is difficult to the modern ear, lengthening, as it does, the verb into forms nowhere as easy to pronounce as the almost uninflected modern verb. While Scott's use of *thou* forms very often becomes tedious, at other times it is saved from annoying us by the intermixing of *you* forms. For example he avoids the ugly past forms ending in -*st* (except the simple *didst* and *hadst*). Such effects are hard to illustrate as they extend over chapters rather than pages. Certainly, too, many examples of inconsistency are mere carelessness – meticulousness in such a matter would have been unlike Scott. He would only be careful in what he considered worth the trouble and inconsistency serves his purposes here as well as careful regularity. It is surprising how little we notice the inconsistency until we look for it.

The only rule that Scott appears to follow with any approach to regularity is the polite *you* to superiors. On the other hand superiors do not consistently use *thou* to inferiors. In *Kenilworth*, at the fateful meeting between Amy and the Queen, Elizabeth generally addresses Amy as *thou* but falls several times into *you* (*K* 536–9) and later addresses Varney with both *you* and *thou* (*K* 546–7). The Queen's words to Amy are those of a jealous woman and *thou* falls happily into this more passionate and high-flown dialogue; this as much as anything probably governs the choice of *thou*. Meanwhile Amy and Varney always speak to the Queen with *you* and *Your Grace*. Sometimes indeed, Scott makes the complete social distinction – in the archery contest in *Ivanhoe* Prince John throughout uses *thou* to Locksley and Hubert, his inferiors, and they *you* to him (*Iv* 180–7).

3. Far less frequent than *thou* is *ye*:

How named ye the Templar? (Cedric; *Iv* 41).

Oh, my brave lances, if ye knew how hard your captain were this day bested, how soon should I see my banner at the head of your clump of spears (De Bracy; *Iv* 403).

Ye are friends and allies of our reverend father in God, Aymer, Prior of Jorvaulx, ... ye owe him aid (Ambrose, a monk; *Iv* 359–60).

Ye be knaves! ye lie! ... it was you and your gormandizing companions that drank up the sack (Friar Tuck; *Iv* 449).

What order is this among ye? Be ye Turks or Christians, that handle a churchman? – Know ye what it is, *manus imponere in servos Domini*? (Prior; *Iv* 453).

And you, ye beef-devouring, wine-swilling English mastiffs, get ye to your guard again, and be sure you keep it more warily (Richard; *Ta* 808).

If ye find holy men labouring with their hands, and serving God in the desert, hurt them not, neither destroy their dwellings. But when you find them with shaven crowns, they are of the synagogue of Satan! – Smite with the sabre, slay, cease not till they become believers or tributaries (Saladin, quoting the 'successor of the Prophet'; *Ta* 512).

'Hark ye ... ye have supped this evening – have ye not?'
'It is a point of wisdom, ye owl.' (Rudolph, Sigismund; *AG* 147).

Originally *ye* was nominative, *you* accusative. In the fourteenth century *you* began to be used for *ye* and in the fifteenth *ye* for *you*. From then on they were virtually interchangeable although certain writers still differentiated carefully, including the translators of the Authorized Version. Thus we have within a few years of each other the Authorized Version's regular *ye* nominative, *you* accusative – 'Ye have not chosen me, but I have chosen you'

(*John* xv 16) – and Shakespeare's complete reversal of this pattern – 'Stand, sir, and throw us that you have about ye' (*Two Gents* IV i 3). In general too, *ye* appears in Scott with plural sense although in the example from *Anne of Geierstein* quoted here the meaning of *ye* is singular. The introduction of *ye* here is probably due to the presence of the tag *hark ye* (often found, well after *ye* was normally obsolete in conversation, in the contraction *harkee*; see § 42). There are, however, more weighty reasons for the use of *ye* at other points. Scott is slightly more regular in his use of *ye* than in his use of *thou* and *thee*. *Ye* is particularly favoured by the devout, no doubt due to its frequency in the Authorized Version. Scott also seems to have felt the use of this pronoun a good way of suggesting the religiosity of Moslem language. The language of Saladin in the quotation above sounds somewhat like the strongly Biblical cast of speech adopted by Scott's Presbyterians. Apart from its use by religious characters *ye* is frequently an expression of anger or contempt – several of the speeches quoted are made in such tones. In the poetic usage of Scott's time, moreover, *ye* was common in apostrophes; this has had its effect on Scott too. It is in an apostrophe that *ye* makes a solitary appearance in Jane Austen being given fittingly to Marianne Dashwood (*Sense and Sensibility*, p. 27; see Phillipps, p. 167). Unlike *thou*, *ye* is never maintained in Scott for more than a few lines. As the speeches of Saladin and Friar Tuck quoted above show, Scott quickly reverts to *you* even when there has been no change in the tone of the dialogue.

4. The use of *it* for *he* or *she* can still be heard in our own day in baby-talk – 'it's a good boy, isn't it' – but had a much wider currency in Shakespeare's time (see Franz, § 297). Phillipps notes its appearance in Jane Austen but only where 'our attention is being drawn to something other than the person' (p. 166) as in an example from *Emma*:

> Miss Nash thinks her own sister very well married and it is only a linen draper (*Emma*, p. 56).

The *it* directs our attention at the marriage rather than at the linen draper. Shakespeare does not share this limitation with Jane Austen:

> It is the prettiest villain; she fetches her breath as short as a new-ta'en sparrow *(T & C* III ii 32-4)

nor does her contemporary Scott:

> It is an art this French King of ours has found out, to fight with other men's swords, ... Ah! it is the wisest prince that ever put purple on his back *(QD* 73).
>
> Nevertheless it is a good youth – See, Rebecca! see, he is again about to go up to battle against the Philistine *(Iv* 127).
>
> I saw him look back ... 'tis a very devil for mischief *(K* 181).

Following the Shakespearean rather than the Austenian pattern Scott's usage seems to have been archaic.

5. The pronoun in *-self* can be used now only reflexively or in emphatic apposition to another pronoun. This was not always so, as Scott was aware:

> where ourselves were in presence *(Iv* 474).
>
> Ask himself, if thou wilt not believe me *(Ta* 536).
>
> ourself will be the chamberlain of the royal Richard *(Ta* 902).
>
> Yourself told me *(Wk* 308).

Constructions of this kind seem always to have been rare and generally to have become archaic or poetic by the eighteenth century, if we are to judge by the examples given in the *OED*. In Scots we still find something similar where *himself* is applied to the 'chief person in any body or institution' *(SND himself* 2). The *-self* pronouns are once again in our own day moving into wider usage in Standard English, a movement traced by Brian Foster in *The Changing English Language* (Penguin edn, pp. 232-4). Two cases occur amongst these examples of the royal plural – the speakers are Prince John and Saladin. The earlier form *ourself*, when superseded by the modern *ourselves* (see Mustanoja, p. 147), was retained as an editorial and royal plural. It can also be found in the emphatic use of the kind familiar to us today: 'we have ourself been deemed a proficient' says King René, on the subject of minstrelsy *(AG* 564).

6. The ethic dative, so frequent in Shakespeare – 'I will roar you

as gently as any sucking dove; I will roar you as 'twere any nightingale' (*MND* I ii 85–7) – is only rarely found in Scott; I have found only the following examples in the medieval and renaissance novels:

> he will change you his purpose as often as the trimmings of his doublet (*Ta* 583).
>
> I hears me the lattice open (*K* 24).

Visser's summary of the life of this construction is very much to the point in our study: 'The first indubitable examples – apart from *Patience* heading the list – seem to date from the beginning of the sixteenth century. From the end of the sixteenth century there is a remarkable increase in frequency reaching its height in the dramas of the Elizabethan and Jacobean periods, especially in the colloquial prose passages. In the nineteenth century there is a considerable decline, with the result that in Present Day English the construction is hardly ever used in natural diction' (Visser, I § 695; see also Franz, § 294). It is noteworthy that it was the Elizabethan period in which this construction was in vogue – as always Scott's search for archaisms begins with the Elizabethans, even here where the first example occurs in *The Talisman* set just before the end of the twelfth century. In the second example, which actually occurs in an Elizabethan novel, *Kenilworth*, the grammar is further complicated by the use of the sub-standard *hears* as an inflection of the first person. This is found sometimes in Modern Scots when, as here, the present is used as a dramatic past (see chapter 7 § 28).

7. A vague object *it* of indefinite meaning sometimes follows the verb in English. Its purpose is not always clear though sometimes it serves to aid a grammatical conversion as when Shakespeare uses nouns as verbs: *prince it* (*Cym* III iii 85), *devil-porter it* (*Mac* II iii 20). Shakespeare is fond of this idiom (see Franz, § 295 for numerous examples) and it is largely on the strength of this that the construction comes to be mentioned here. Though found in Scott's time in Jane Austen's work (Phillipps, p. 166) and not extinct in present-day English (*OED it* pron 9), the construction seems to have a special vogue in Elizabethan English, although it is possible that the apparent vogue at this time of this idiom –

and others like impersonal *your* (see § 10) – is due to the greater reflection of colloquial language in the largely dramatic literature of the Elizabethans. These are decidedly colloquial idioms. With *coy it* 'act coyly' and *ruffle it* 'swagger' Scott merely copies other authors but both phrases were obsolete in the early nineteenth century:

> Her lips, thou foolish boy! and Catherine, coy it not (*Ab* 622).
>
> you coy it (*FM* 193).
>
> He must ruffle it in another sort (*K* 50).

Scott certainly remembered *coy it* from Rowe's *Jane Shore* (*Works*, London, 1756, II 126) a favourite play of his childhood – his memory was prodigious even for small details like this. *Ruffle* as a verb was totally obsolete by the eighteenth century and Scott was responsible for reviving it in two other uses – as an intransitive verb meaning 'to contend with' (*Ab* 411) and in the further phrase *ruffle it out* (*Wk* 484). Besides these Elizabethan usages Scott furnishes his own *masquerade it*: 'masquerading it in your guest's lodgings' (*K* 131) and *brusque it*: 'I'll e'en brusque it a little' (*Wk* 135). The addition of *it* to *brusque* brings about a grammatical conversion from adjective to verb. Scott is, according to the *OED*, the first to use *brusque* as a verb though those who follow him use the verb without *it*. As for *masquerade it*, the *OED* fails to record what is apparently a creation of Scott's; Franz however cites the same phrase from Disraeli (Franz, § 295).

8. Well before Scott's time the *-self* forms had become the normal expression of the reflexive and the usages which follow are therefore archaic:

> I cannot ... revenge me for my disappointment on him (*Ta* 907).
>
> I ventured me thither in disguise (*Ta* 836).
>
> there ne'er was gentleman but who belted him with his brand (*Ab* 27).
>
> your Grace should have held you prepared (*Ab* 340).

However the use of the simple pronoun as a reflexive is very frequent in Scott, occurring in narrative as well as dialogue:

The Bernese then wrapped him in his cloak, and, lying down on the straw ... was in a few minutes fast asleep (*AG* 217).

Perhaps this frequency is due to the vigorous life the idiom still had in verse:

> Like one who loved beyond his nature's law,
> And in despair had cast him down to die
> (Shelley, *The Zucca*, ll. 43–4).

9. By the beginning of the Modern English period both *mine* and *thine* in attributive use were confined to positions before a vowel or *h*. *Mine* is still so used in the eighteenth century. After 1756 the *OED* quotes for the use of *mine* qualifying a following noun only a clearly poetic example dated 1871. The *OED*'s selection is inadequate at this point as Keats, for one, used *mine* in this way between those two dates: 'mine eyes' ('I stood tip-toe upon a little hill', l. 206); 'mine host's Canary wine' (*Lines on the Mermaid Tavern*, l. 6). All the same it looks as if by the early nineteenth century the use of *mine* attributively was confined to poetry. The same applies to *thine*, which after Ben Jonson, in the *OED*'s instances, likewise only occurs in the context of poetry. Scott uses these two only in the approved positions: before a vowel: 'thine influence' (*Iv* 297), and before *h* 'this mine high office' (*Mo* 477; for this use of a possessive in conjunction with a demonstrative pronoun see § 13). Blackmore and Kingsley, followers of Scott's pioneer lead in archaizing, are given by Franz (§ 326b) as employing this same usage in their historical novels.

10.

Your Turk never coughs in his cup or stints in his liquoring (*Ta* 802).

I do not, like your modern grandees, turn off my followers the instant they are useless (*K* 4).

Your Spaniard is too wise a man to send you the very soul of the grape (*K* 5).

Your pottle of sack is a fine shoeing horn to pull on a loyal humour, and a merry one (*K* 472).

This indefinite *your* has probably always been a colloquialism.

Period Grammar

Even today its life in speech is assured (see Phillipps, p. 168n). Jane Austen uses it – 'I know nothing of your furlongs, but I am sure it is a very long wood' (*Mansfield Park*, p. 95; see Phillipps, p. 168) – and Scott gives it to a character in a near contemporary novel, *The Antiquary*:

> your old remembered guest of a beggar becomes as well acquainted with you as he is with his dish (*An* 48).

However, the character in question – Jonathon Oldbuck, the antiquary – amongst his many idiosyncracies can count other seemingly anachronistic archaisms. Scott's original readers on reading this passage may well have thought more of the common speech around them than of literary parallels. However, if literary parallels are to be thought of, (and *Kenilworth* in particular is a novel which continually demands such references), then they are easiest to find in the Elizabethan period, as is the case with all colloquialisms. Anyone who has read *Hamlet* must think of Hamlet's lines:

> Your worm is your only emperor for diet: we fat all creatures else to fat us, and we fat ourselves for maggots: your fat king and your lean beggar is but variable service (*Ham* IV iii 22–6).

11. The following constructions – pronouns used with qualifying prepositional phrases – though they appear in both narrative and dialogue are certainly not normal early nineteenth-century English:

He of the Lion Heart (*Ta* 571).

her of the dark tresses and nobly speaking eye (*Ta* 838).

him of Gilsland (*Ta* 594).

He of the Fetterlock (*Iv* 471).

The *OED* (*he* 4b) calls this construction archaic and cites only three examples of its use – from Shakespeare, Milton, and Keats. Both Keats and Scott seem to be copying Shakespeare and Milton. Very probably the construction has always been 'poetic' rather than 'archaic', to follow a distinction made by the *OED* in other instances. The last of the four phrases quoted appears in the narrative.

12. I find I have noted only one example of the periphrastic possessive phrase as in: 'I had laughed in the very face of thee' (*K* 109). Examples of this construction can be found in Middle English (Mustanoja, p. 158) and it has been noted in Shakespeare (Franz § 323) but it seems to have died out in Standard English after the early Modern English period. However, its use in Scott may be explained by the fact that it still survives in Scottish usage (see chapter 7 § 5).

13. The use of a personal possessive pronoun alongside a demonstrative pronoun – 'this our host' (*Iv* 296), 'that thy law' (*Ta* 507), 'this mine high office' (*Mo* 477; *cf* § 9) – has yielded in later Modern English to a periphrastic and, according to Fowler (*Modern English Usage*, 2nd edn, *of* 7), illogical usage with *of*: 'this host of ours'. The periphrasis first appears in the fourteenth century and after early Modern English becomes the normal way of expressing such relationships. The presence of the earlier idiom in the King James Bible: 'this my son was dead, and is alive again; he was lost, and is found' (*Luke* xv 24) will have kept it alive for some of Scott's readers.

14. For five centuries English speakers have been more and more reluctant to invert the increasingly normal subject-verb-object word order. In the case of the second person singular the special -*st* ending reduced the need for the pronoun *thou* and it was frequently omitted in interrogatives:

Why dost not answer? (*Iv* 304).

art dead? art stupified? (*Iv* 469).

wouldst mount? wouldst fly? (*Mo* 320).

How wouldst like such beverage thyself? (*Ta* 800).

Art weary of thy life? (*Ta* 752).

With the disappearance of *thou* from speech and writing the usage naturally dies. Consequently Visser cites many examples (I § 5) of this omission up till the eighteenth century, when *thou* was moribund, but for the nineteenth century he has only dialectal uses (from George Eliot and Hardy).

RELATIVE PRONOUNS

15. The omission of the relative pronoun is one of the most distinctive usages of English. Where the relative would have been the object the usage continues unhampered even now: '*Waverley* was the first novel Scott wrote' but for a long time English has not allowed constructions like Shakespeare's:

> I have a kind of self resides with you (*T & C* III ii 155).
>
> My father had a daughter lov'd a man (*TwN* II iv 109).

where the subject is omitted. The only modern instances of an omitted subject relative are after introductory phrases like *there is, here is, we have*. Even then it is doubtful if a colloquial speaker would nowadays choose to say: 'We've got no end of people can come' rather than 'We've got no end of people that can come'. In Jane Austen the usage is already excluded from the best English (Phillipps, p. 172). Scott had, on the other hand, no objection to this construction:

> it is thy love must buy his protection (*Iv* 297).
>
> Here is a fellow, now, comes down the walk (*FN* 186).
>
> We had a clever French fellow at Newark would have done the job in the firing of a pistol (*Wk* 620).

Furthermore he allowed himself the unrestricted (Shakespearean) range of omission:

> the English are the choicest soldiers ever wore armour (*QD* 186).
>
> I could tell that of him would lose him favour (*K* 84).
>
> Misfortune to him would deprive him of an iota of it! (*Mo* 479).
>
> I know that shall make Varney uphold me sober (*K* 471).

The decline of this construction in Modern English can no doubt be attributed to its tendency towards ambiguity illustrated in the last two examples; for example, Scott's: 'I know that shall make Varney uphold me sober' means not (as it could only do nowadays) 'I know that thing shall make . . .' but 'I know that which shall make . . .'

INTERROGATIVE PRONOUNS

16. In the same way as it is now used in indirect questions,

whether was used up to the eighteenth century in direct questions with the meaning 'which of two' (*OED whether* 1a). Perhaps the use is substandard in the mouth of the apprentice Jin Vin:

> whether do you manage the wherry or we, master? (*FN* 464).

ARTICLES

17. Early nineteenth-century writers enjoyed a freedom to omit the article which is not now so widely allowed. Omission of the article before a preposition is common enough in present-day English but only in standard phrases: 'in bed', 'in town', 'to heart', 'to church'. Jane Austen's omissions have a wider scope: 'She was at window' (*Persuasion*, p. 78); 'Dinner was on table' (*Emma*, p. 298; see Phillipps, p. 174). Scott also omits the article before window: 'look out at window' (*Ab* 148); 'She put her head out at window' (*Ab* 152). Apparently the omission before *window* was idiomatic at that period. Perhaps more idiosyncratic is Scott's further omission of the article before less common words in prepositional phrases: 'thou wilt be read of in chronicle' (*QD* 253); 'record in song or in book of tourney' (*Iv* 293).

The article also fails to appear, to our way of seeing it, in certain cases following the verb *to be*. Phillipps cites an example from Jane Austen: 'She is niece to Sir Thomas Bertram' (*Mansfield Park*, p. 293; see Phillipps, p. 175) but Scott's examples are perhaps more widespread:

> I will be true prisoner (*Iv* 430).
>
> I will be true companion to thee (*Ta* 493–4).
>
> I am friend of the cross (*Ta* 536).
>
> as I am true Scottish man (*Ta* 595).
>
> He is good lord and true (*Ta* 721).

The recurrence of the adjective *true* (in four out of five of these examples) suggests the existence of some underlying formula. If it exists it is also reflected in Shakespeare who has: 'A mellifluous voice, as I am true knight' (*TwN* II iii 57) amongst other examples of the article after *to be* (see Franz, § 277). This omission of the article before a predicative noun is, according to Mustanoja (p. 269), frequent in Middle English.

Also frequent in Middle English is the omission of the article

Period Grammar

after a negative, *never* or *ever* (Mustanoja, p. 270). This is again especially common in Scott:

he shall draw bowstring no more *(Iv* 47).

no man wearing chain and spurs *(Iv* 293).

She is a sweet and a lovely a creature as ever tied snood over brown hair *(Mo* 155).

There ne'er was gentleman but who belted him with the brand *(Ab* 27).

if ever I trust bumpkin with bonny Bayard again *(K* 406).

all the tears that ever woman's eye wept *(Ta* 740).

Lastly Scott has examples of the omission of the article before a noun, complement to indefinite *it*:

it is comfort to think that we leave behind us on earth those who shall be as wretched as ourselves *(Iv* 304–5).

it is pity of their lives that these Templars are not so trusty as they are disciplined and valiant *(Iv* 639).

Phrases like these are very common in Old English and in Middle English but from the sixteenth century on become less and less common. Examples are extremely rare in the nineteenth century. For 'it is pity' Visser offers no examples later than the mid-eighteenth century (I § 255). The idiom is best known in the title of Ford's play *'Tis Pity She's a Whore*.

ADJECTIVES

18. The normal word order in English allows for the adjective to precede the noun it qualifies, but a number of phrases where the adjective is traditionally post-placed remind us of the influence French has had on our language. The phrase *knight-errant* suggests how much the tradition of romance in particular owes to France. *Knight-errant* has been the prototype or 'matrix formation' to use Barbara Strang's term (see Strang, § 54), of a large number of compounds, some of which preserve the exceptional word order. First follows *knight adventurous*, found in Chaucer (*CT* VII 909). Then Spenser added *errant damozell* (*FQ* II i 19) and *errant damzell* (*FQ* III i 24). Scott took up this creation both in the form Spenser had offered: *errant-damozel* (*K* 463) and, recalling *knight-errant*,

with the adjective post-placed: *damosel-errant* (*K* 427), *damsel errant* (*AG* 330). Then following Spenser's lead, but this time thinking of *knight adventurous*, he gives us *damsel adventurous* (*QD* 561). Scott's innovations do not stop here. *Knight* has been even more often combined with nouns than with adjectives: *knight banneret, knight companion, knight commander*. Scott extends the list with *Knight Ranger* (*Wk* 55) used to describe Sir Henry Lee who is ranger of the king's park at Woodstock.

Two more phrases with a post-placed adjective occur. *Art magic* (*FN* 196) is a traditional phrase, found for instance in the King James Bible (*Wisd* xvii 7). The phrase 'voice potential' – 'the Lord Abbot hath in this matter a voice potential' (*Mo* 368) – is borrowed from Shakespeare (*Oth* I ii 13). In present-day English it would have a quite different meaning with *potential* as a noun – here *potential* is the adjective with its etymological meaning 'powerful'.

In medieval and Elizabethan literature the pronoun is sometimes placed between adjective and noun; only in addressives – 'good my lord', 'sweet my lady' – does this usage survive the Elizabethan period, but not long enough to make the following normal for Scott's time:

Good my murderer (*Ab* 534).

Reverend my lord (*Mo* 521).

The construction is frequent in Richardson but dies out by the end of the eighteenth century.

When there are two adjectives qualifying a noun, one adjective is sometimes placed after the noun and they are arranged like this:

a fair man he was, and a goodly (*Mo* 120).

My mistress is a good lady, and a virtuous, and a well-doing lady, and a well-spoken of (*Ab* 77).

Thou art a good child, . . . my Catherine, and a faithful (*Ab* 361).

A most rare medicine . . . and a commodious (*Ta* 750).

In present-day English this arrangement of adjectives has been modified by the addition of what Sweet called the 'prop-word' *one* and (frequently) the adverb *too*: 'a good child, and a faithful one, too' we would say nowadays. Kellner, after citing examples from Old English to Ben Jonson, gives only Carlyle and Thackeray for continuing the construction into Modern English (Kellner, § 472). Neither of these authors is a good guide to normal nineteenth-century English – Carlyle has a liking for archaism and the Thackeray example is from a novel, *The Virginians*, set in the eighteenth century. On this evidence the purpose of Scott's examples is to contribute to the sense of archaism.

ADVERBS

19. One adverb with many characteristically Elizabethan and seventeenth-century uses is *even*. Chiefly in the colloquial form *e'en*, it is prefixed to verbs with a vague force which we should now express by *just*. The *OED* quotes from Udall's *Ralph Roister Doister*: 'If she despise you e'en despise ye hir againe' (*OED even* adv 8b). In Scott, we have several instances of the revival of this archaism:

> but since he is so unsocial to Christians, e'en let him take the next stall to Isaac the Jew's (*Iv* 67).
>
> remembering Rainsborough's fate, I e'en jumped the window (*Wk* 201).
>
> but, as you say, it is needless talking of it. Let us e'en go and see (*Wk* 275).

Besides occurring before verbs in this way, *even* is also found prefixed to a subject, object or a predicate (*OED even* adv 8b) to emphasize its identity:

> such self-confidence is even the worst symptom of the disorder (*Ab* 64).
>
> it is even this which our adversaries charge against us (*Ab* 443).

Not far removed from this, as Bradley points out in his essay 'Shakespeare's English' (*Shakespeare's England*, Oxford, 1916, II 559), is the use made familiar to us from the Authorized Version, in which *even* precedes a repetition or an explanation, with a sense something like 'namely' or 'that is to say' as in: 'the son of this bondwoman shall not be heir with my son, even with Isaac' (*Gen* xxi 10). With his usual sensitivity to the rightness of an archaism, Scott puts this Biblical idiom into the mouth of one of his Puritans in *Woodstock*, not the only use of Biblical language in the creation of their distinctive mode of speaking:

Take from him his arms, and let us bring him before the chosen Instrument, even our General (*Wk* 647).

20. *Something* and *nothing* were once freely used as abverbs as in:

I got something too deep into his secrets (*K* 203).

something my name may avail (*Ta* 517).

my old dame Joan is something dunny (*Wk* 43).

my thoughts came slower ... and something duller, than those of other folk (*AG* 279).

Scott may have been old-fashioned to use *something* as an adverb. The *OED* says of the usage that 'Except as an archaism this use chiefly survives in combinations which admit of the word being felt as a noun' (*OED something* B). In various uses Scott is once the last and twice the second to last writer cited. The fact that *something* as an adverb also appears in the narrative:

'I said Grahame, sir, not Grime,' said Nigel, something shortly (*FN* 296)

need not rule out its being old-fashioned. Scott's more unusual language often appears, as we have seen, outside period dialogue.

Nothing, too, seems to have been obsolescent or archaic as an adverb in the nineteenth century. Both *something* and *nothing* survive in combination with *like*: 'It was nothing like I imagined it'; but, to follow the distinction made by the *OED*, they can be felt in this combination as nouns. In both examples of *nothing* as an adverb that I have noted in Scott the word qualifies the verb *doubt*:

I nothing doubt it (*Wk* 45).

nothing doubting that the good cause shall triumph (*Iv* 536).

The phrase 'nothing doubting' occurs in the Bible (*Acts* xi 12) and may have influenced Scott here.

21. *Sufficient* is not now used as an adverb; we could not now say:

the fellow foins well – very sufficient well (*Wk* 320).

After appearing quite commonly in the sixteenth and seventeenth centuries as an adverb *sufficient* seems to have fallen into comparative disfavour according, at least, to the not unassailable evidence of the *OED*. The last citation is from W. A. Miles (1826). Perhaps both Miles and Scott were being old-fashioned. The piling up of adverbs – 'very sufficient well' – recalls the adverb clusters of Elizabethan English.

22. *Well* is one of our most common adverbs yet we could not now write:

I well trust he exaggerated (*K* 90).

I well thought that your blinded race had their descent from the foul fiend (*Ta* 525).

It is nevertheless hard to pin down what makes these quotations sound strange to our ears and almost impossible to know how they sounded to Scott's first readers. The nearest example provided by the *OED* amongst its examples of *well* used 'as an intensive to strengthen the idea implied in the verb' is taken from the Stonor Papers: 'In trowthe I hadde wil hopide that your horsis shulde a ben here as this night' (*OED well* adv 13). This use has now been restricted, particularly to verbs of pleasing (*OED well* adv 13b) or reinforcing an auxiliary as in 'I can well believe', 'I may well decide'.

23. A similar restriction of usage has occurred with *never* when used, as a simple negative without temporal sense, with an imperative:

Never shame his Highness for that (*QD* 252).

Never look at me with so sad a brow (*K* 71).

Never think shame for the matter, my girl (*Pi* 335).

Sometime between Shakespeare, from whom Franz cites plentiful examples of this use of *never* with an imperative (Franz, § 407), and our own time its currency became limited to use with *fear* and *mind*.

PREPOSITIONS

24. *A* as a preposition is a worn-down descendant of Old and

Middle English *on*. It is not now in evidence except in temporal distributive phrases like *three times a day* and (if, indeed, they now survive) in verbal constructions like *go a begging*. However, the preposition really survives in many combinations which are now looked on as single words, for instance, *afloat, alive, around, asleep*. *A* was also very common as used in Scott in the mild asseveration 'A God's name' (*Wk* 352). *OED* citations for this phrase end with Pope.

25.

I have found the use on't (*K* 4).

Elizabethan English often has *on* where we would expect *of* and especially in phrases like *on me* 'of me', *on's* 'of his' and *on't* 'of it'. According to Onions this was 'originally often an actual difference of idiom, but from Elizabethan times often resulting from confusion of *of* and *on*, both of which were reduced to *o*'' (*Shakespeare Glossary, on* prep).

26.

a man is well helped of these lazy churchmen when he hath most to do (*Iv* 360).

The *OED*'s summary of the history of this use of *of* 'introducing the agent after a passive verb' is this: 'The regular word for this is now *by*; . . . but *of* prevailed till *c*. 1600, and is still in literary use, as a biblical, poetic, or stylistic archaism' (*OED of* V 15). After the early eighteenth century its incidence does not seem to have been high.

27.

It were a sin, with wind and weather to friend, to lose so lovely a morning (*AG* 603).

Saint Thomas a Kent, and my own poor merits to speed (*Iv* 232).

God to aid (*Journal*, 31 May 1826).

Only in certain phrases (*call to witness, take to wife*) does this Old and Middle English usage where *to* means *as* now survive. Scott's use of it was already archaic; there are no *OED* citations between

Spenser and Swinburne. When an indubitably archaic usage like this occurs in the *Journal* we are once again reminded how deeply the language of the past had entered Scott's consciousness and that, even if he makes archaism serve a special purpose in his historical romances, it came uncalled to his mind even in his private meditations.

28. *Upon* has fallen out of favour with us. Jane Austen uses it with much more freedom than a modern novelist would find natural (see Phillipps, p. 194). So, too, with Scott:

> the stern necessity which is upon us (*K* 102).

> I could no longer . . . tarry upon your successive delays (*Mo* 513).

Biblical precedents like: 'The Philistines be upon thee, Samson' (*Judg* xvi 14) probably gave a quotation like the first a suggestion of archaism even in Scott's day.

CONJUNCTIONS

29. *An* or *and* has the same meaning as *if*, *and* being the original form, shortened to or respelt *an*. These conjunctions are also covered in the discussion of the subjunctive (see § 43). The following quotations illustrate the full range of possibilities; *an*, *and* and *and if*:

> an ye suffer a second impostor to be palmed upon you, I will have your eyes torn out, and hot coals put into the sockets (*Iv* 358).

> For hunting only, and please you (*Ta* 625).

> and if it please your Majesty (*Ta* 581).

Visser sums up their history succinctly: 'Not in Old English . . . rather common in Middle English, becoming rarer in early Modern English and nowadays archaic or dialectal' (II § 880 *an*). The proverb 'If ifs and ands were pots and pans, there'd be no need for tinkers' preserves this conjunction, though few modern speakers probably realize that the *ifs* are identical with the *ands*.

30. The conjunction *as* takes the subjunctive:

> He often looks as he were capable of doing us a darker turn (*Ab* 465).

Though very common in Middle English this conjunction, after the sixteenth century, is only found in the phrase *as it were*, an additional *if* after *as* being now usual. Scott re-endowed *as* with its older wider application (see Visser II § 890 *alse*).

VERBS: INFLECTIONS

31. The verb *to be* still preserves in present-day English more inflections than any other English verb; some of the even more numerous older forms were of use to Scott:

(a) *beest*

an thou beest a man (*Iv* 10).

In the sixteenth and seventeenth centuries *beest*, which was properly an indicative form, was used after *if* (and *an*) and *though*, contexts where we would perhaps expect a subjunctive at that period. *Beest* is regularly used by Shakespeare in this context.

(b) *wert*

Wert thou not with me when I said to that same gay Marquis . . . ? (*Ta* 583).

'The modern analogical *wast* has replaced the etymological *were* . . . chiefly under the influence of Tindale and the Bible; the intermediate *wert* (Shakespeare's form) prevailed in literature during the seventeenth and eighteenth centuries and has been used by many nineteenth-century writers' (*OED be* A 6). It is worth noting that this seventeenth- and eighteenth-century form occurs in a novel set in the twelfth century.

(c) *be*

Ye be knaves! Ye lie! (*Iv* 449).

Here we be (*Ta* 583).

The use of *be* for the present plural, where we would now say *are*, became archaic except in dialectal uses by the end of the seventeenth century. The Middle English forms were actually *beth* (Southern) or *ben* (East Midland) so that on either count Scott's use of *be* in his two Richard Cœur-de-Lion novels is only an approximation to historical fact. It is very probable that the dialectal survival influenced Scott here and certain that he was aware of the usage as an acknowledged poeticism:

> Wisdom, Justic, Love, and Peace,
> When they struggle to increase,
> Are to us as soft winds be
> To shepherd boys . . .
> (Shelley, *Prometheus Unbound*, I 796–9).

32. The *-st* inflection of the second person singular has already been discussed in the section on pronouns under *thou* (§ 2). The other important inflection lost since early Modern English is the *-th* ending in the third person singular. The ascendancy of the *-s* inflection over the *-th* inflection was established by the end of the sixteenth century though the latter clung to a precarious existence for some time. In later times it could always be called into service where it served the stylistic or prosodic aims of the author (Franz, § 154). The *-th* inflection is largely reserved by Scott for characters whose consciousness is strongly religious, and where it occurs the surrounding language is often markedly Biblical in style:

> he hath broken his own word, and hath violated my safe-conduct – and judge you also, my reverend brethren, he hath put his hand forth upon a preacher of the gospel, and perchance may sell his blood to the worshippers of Anti-Christ! (*Mo* 495).

The reason for this is not hard to find; the scholars who prepared the Authorized Version in the early seventeenth century took over from Tyndale's much older version the already obsolescent *-th* ending which thus became predominantly associated in Englishmen's minds with Biblical usage. Henry Warden's sermon gives us *includeth*, *doth* (*Ab* 61) and *hath* (*Ab* 63). This Biblically inspired language also extends to the Jews and the Moslems. Isaac the Jew has *cometh* (*Iv* 74), *grieveth* (*Iv* 366) and *giveth* (*Iv* 367), his daughter Rebecca *hath* (*Iv* 294) and *becometh* (*Iv* 366). Saladin, in the guise of El Hakim the physician, favours *-th* endings with proverbial sayings:

> It is written . . . 'abuse not the steed which hath borne thee from the battle!' (*Ta* 750).

> When the rich carpet is soiled the fool pointeth to the stain – the wise man covers it with his mantle (*Ta* 753).

Though often found in religious contexts *hath* and *doth* also occur without Biblical usage in mind. Ivanhoe (*Iv* 393), Sir Piercie Shafton (*Mo* 364), Queen Elizabeth (*K* 544) and Lord Hunsdon (*K* 545) are amongst those who use *hath* in non-religious contexts, while *doth* occurs in Scott's narrative (probably with a slightly comic intention) in his wry comment on Giles Gosling, the innkeeper: 'even the sight of gold made less impression on the honest gentleman than it usually doth on one of his calling' (*K* 9). This may have something to do with the fact that *hath* and *doth* were particularly long-lasting as spelling conventions. There is evidence that in the seventeenth century *-th* spellings were intended to be read as *-s* and in the case of these two common verbs this convention lasted into the eighteenth century well after the *-s* pronunciation was universal (Strang, § 89). There can be no doubt however that by Scott's time the use of *-th* endings (including *hath* and *doth*) was a deliberate archaism and not a spelling convention. The Biblical effect of the *-th* ending carries over into the narrative even to the extent of ousting the original verb form in a quotation from the Scriptures: 'He was generous,' says Scott of Prior Aymer, 'and charity, as it is well known, covereth a multitude of sins, in another sense than that in which it is said to do so in scripture' (*Iv* 20). The original Biblical text reads: 'Charity shall cover the multitude of sins' (1 *Pet* iv 8).

33. Various past participle forms occur in Scott which are for us obsolete:

over whose tombs minsters have been builded (*Iv* 358).

those ... who had not gotten to horse (*Iv* 430; narrative).

the field must be foughten in our presence (*Iv* 536).

now that you have stricken short of your aim (*Mo* 515).

there is more to be gotten by oppressing his feudatories (*Ta* 582).

and bluff King Henry, who builded that wing (*Wk* 55).

I have known a merry gentleman's bones broke for such a smile as you wear just now (*Wk* 460-1).

Not all these were obsolete in Scott's time. The *OED* points out that *broke* was very common in the seventeenth and eighteenth centuries 'and still recognized in verse' (*OED break* v). *Gotten* was barely archaic; it occurs in Scott's narrative and is still used in America and also in British English in the fossilized phrase 'ill-gotten gains'. More probably archaic was *stricken*, now only attributive not participial, and certainly archaic *builded*. *Foughten*, however, is a different case. Scott draws on the stock phrase *foughten field*, found in Elizabethan literature and up to Hobbes and then picked up again by Keats (*Otho*, I iii 44) though only in a posthumously published work which would not have been known to Scott.

VERBS: TENSES

34. In Modern English the simple tenses have been in many cases superseded by an expanded or progressive form. Examination of Jane Austen's careful usage shows that this process had not in her time progressed as far as it has now. Present-day usage demands a continuative form of the present where an event currently taking place is described, but Jane Austen could write:

> 'I walk. I prefer walking.'
> 'But it rains.' (*Persuasion*, p. 177).

(see Phillipps, p. 116). So too in Scott we find:

> What! treason! treason! – ho! – Dan – Jasper – Martin – the villain escapes (*Mo* 392).

> But hush, the Hamako comes – it is to warn us to rest (*Ta* 544).

VERBS: AUXILIARIES

35. Jane Austen and Scott also both use the simple present tense in negative statements where we would now require the auxiliary *do*. With a few exceptions (*e.g.*, with *know*, *mistake*, *matter*) the simpler construction is found less and less from the beginning of the eighteenth century (Jespersen, *MEG* V 23.1.3). Jane Austen preserves the earlier usage with *know* but with other verbs the negative without *do* seems to be reserved for dramatic and elevated contexts (Phillipps, p. 118). Probably Scott's usage added more to the drama of the passage than to its archaic flavour:

> '... let us flee! – Here is thy staff, why wilt thou tarry?'
> 'I tarry not,' said the Pilgrim, giving way to the urgency of his companion (*Iv* 76).

But Rebecca was already busied in carrying her charitable purposes into effect, and listed not what he said (*Iv* 366).

36. Another construction without the modern use of the auxiliary *do* – the original form of the interrogative with subject and verb simply inverted – only survives in a few formulaic phrases. In Scott's time it was scarcely less restricted in use than now; apart from with *say* and *come* Jane Austen uses the inverted interrogative 'with other verbs, very occasionally, in dramatic passages' (Phillipps, p. 118). Instances in Scott do not share this dramatic tone and seem to be archaisms:

How looked he? (*Iv* 70).

Why tarries the Lady Rowena? (*Iv* 37).

Believe you, father, in the high powers which she claims? (*Pi* 419).

what thinks your majesty of the Master? (*Ta* 582).

37. In present-day English the negative imperative likewise cannot be expressed without the aid of the auxiliary *do*. The auxiliary was established in this position by the beginning of the eighteenth century (see A. Ellegård, *The Auxiliary Do*, Göteborg, 1935, p. 161). We can therefore assume with some confidence that the use of the old form of the negative imperative without the auxiliary in Scott is a deliberate archaism:

Trouble not yourself for that (*AG* 259).

Blaspheme not the holy saints, Sir Reginald (*Iv* 363).

Disturb me not with further questions (*Ta* 616).

38. A notable characteristic of late Middle and early Modern English is the use of what to present-day ears seems a periphrastic *do* in positive non-emphatic statements, as in the Authorized Version's: 'He is risen from the dead; therefore mighty works do shew forth themselves in him' (*Mat* xiv 2). There is no doubt that this was out-of-date usage by Scott's day: in the English grammar prefixed to his dictionary Johnson wrote: '*Do* is sometimes used superfluously, as, I do *love*, I did *love*; simply for I *love*, or I *loved*;

but this is considered a vitious mode of speech' (*A Dictionary of the English Language*, London, 1755, I 8):

> O, it is a rich abbey-stede, and they do live upon the fat, and drink the sweet wines upon the lees, these good fathers of Jourvaulx (*Iv* 457).

> for the cruel hand of your people has been red with the blood of the servants of the Lord, and therefore do we come hither in plate and mail, with sword and lance, to open the road to the Holy Sepulchre (*Ta* 511).

39. In his use of *will* and *shall* as auxiliaries Scott for the most part conforms with Standard English usage. However there are some exceptions to this:

> he will change you his purposes as often as the trimmings of his doublet and you shall never be able to guess the hue of his inmost vestments from their outward colours (*Ta* 583).

> Yet it is comfort to think that we leave behind us on earth those who shall be as wretched as ourselves (*Iv* 304-5).

For the use of *shall* in these two quotations following second and third person pronouns no specific explanation can be offered; they are contrary to the normal Standard English usage of Scott's time. Perhaps they are vague archaisms based on the greater frequency of *shall* in earlier English without being related to any particular usage. Equally we could apply to Scott what Jespersen says of another Scotsman: 'The frequent use in Carlyle's works of *shall*, where *will* would nowadays be more natural, is probably due to biblical reminiscences ... of prophetic *shall*, combined, perhaps, with a reaction against the native tendency of a Scotchman to use *will* in many cases where *shall* is considered more correct' (*MEG*, IV 18.12).

Except in legal use (see *OED will* v 3b), the verb *will* only rarely appears in present-day English other than as an auxiliary. Its original force of meaning has been largely lost since the beginning of the eighteenth century. However the more pregnant use in the sense of 'desire' occurs occasionally in Scott:

> we will your daughter remains here (*K* 88).

As used here, with an object clause, *will* in this sense is not attested in the *OED* after the seventeenth century, while Shakespeare is the last author the *OED* records for the use of *will* with a negative meaning 'have no desire for' or 'refuse'

I will none but Hector (*T & C* V v 47).

However it is found in Scott, clearly in conscious imitation:

I will none of thy intercession (*Mo* 524).

VERBS: IMPERATIVE

40. In earlier English it was possible to distinguish a singular and a plural imperative by following it with the appropriate personal pronoun. This was a usage Scott copied:

get ye to your guard again (*Ta* 808).

know thou that I exercise my Christian freedom (*Ta* 505).

Get you into order (*Ta* 895).

stay you here and attend to Miss Wardour (*An* 94).

With the development of the all-purpose second person *you* this was no longer possible and in any case when a need is felt to distinguish the object of the command the tendency has been from about 1700, as Jespersen noted (*MEG* III 11.8.42), to bring the imperative into line with other forms of the verb by placing the pronoun before the verb. All the same the post-placed pronoun appears sporadically after 1700. Its use by that rather formal young man Lovel in *The Antiquary* (the fourth quotation above) may mean that the usage was obsolescent rather than obsolete, but archaisms are not unknown in the language of characters in Scott's more contemporary novels. After Scott, Jespersen quotes only Ruskin, whose works reveal a persistent love of archaisms, and two examples from Shaw's *Saint Joan* 'here evidently to give an archaic colouring to the style' (*MEG*, III 11.8.41). As often happens, the older usage, in this case the placing of the pronoun after the imperative verb, lingers in fossilized phrases. Of these Scott, along with other writers of the period, has his share. The most common is *look you* (*AG* 27, *Be* 413), also found as *look ye* (*Ta* 801) – 'in representations of vulgar speech written *look'ee*' (*OED look* 4a). With the same sense as *look you* we find *see you* (*K* 346) which showed equally little sign of dying out in the early

Period Grammar

nineteenth century. Lastly there is *hark you* (*Be* 415) which appears, in the more normal form *hark ye* (otherwise *hark'ee*), last in Lytton. In the main the use of these set phrases in the earlier nineteenth century seems to be dialectal or substandard rather than archaic.

41. This construction is also found with the pronoun *we*:

wend we to the tent of this sick squire (*Ta* 612).

Ave Maria! be we thankful (*Ta* 506).

Leave we this to the mollahs and the imaums (*Ta* 529).

The mood here is a matter of question – Franz includes it under both the subjunctive and the imperative (§§ 637, 649) and cites Shakespeare's 'Join we together for the public good' (2 *HVI* I i 200), amongst other instances. It is likely that Scott was influenced by the frequent use of this construction in romances, so frequent as to be formulaic:

> Leve we here of this Sqyer wight
> And speke we of that lady bryght
> (*The Squire of Low Degree*, ll. 669–70).

> turne we unto kynge Arthure and leve we sir
> Launcelot in the ermyntayge
> (Malory, *Works*, Vinaver ed., London, 1954, p. 766).

> speke we of the Fayre Maydyn of Astolat
> (Malory, p. 779).

42. Another form of the imperative involves using the auxiliary *do*:

do thou begone to thy quarters (*QD* 202).

Do you, gracious ladies, ride forward (*QD* 243).

do thou, good brother of Salisbury, go to our consort's tent (*Ta* 877).

Jespersen cites examples of this construction from Scott, Dickens, Carlyle and Hardy for the nineteenth century and from Shaw for the twentieth century (*MEG* III 11.8.43). The construction still flourishes in its negative form: 'don't you do that again' but Jespersen's examples make it doubtful if the positive use is normal after the eighteenth century. One Shaw example is highly formal (it is addressed to a prisoner), the other occurs alongside undoubted archaisms. The context of the Carlyle example is likewise clearly archaic. Possibly once again Scott is being old-fashioned but not strongly archaic.

VERBS: SUBJUNCTIVE

43. For some two centuries now the fate of the subjunctive in English has been hanging in the balance. In the early eighteenth century the subjunctive had seemed well set on its way to extinction yet in the second half of that century the resurgence of interest in the language, and the grammars it led to, had to some extent reversed this trend. Careful use of the subjunctive had been set up as a principal aim for those who wished to strive after 'correctness'.* Something similar has happened in our own time. By the start of the twentieth century, despite the efforts of grammarians and school-teachers, the subjunctive was once again on the decline, yet in the post-war period, as Brian Foster points out (*The Changing English Language*, Penguin edn., pp. 220–2), the example of American usage has brought the subjunctive back into partial favour. This unsteady position of the subjunctive, combined with its unfortunate association with 'correctness' of style, makes it very difficult for us to assess how archaic Scott's subjunctives were for his time.

As K. C. Phillipps points out with reference to Jane Austen, a ' "correct" use of the subjunctive was something to which she clearly aspired' (Phillipps, p. 155). Did Scott also aspire to correctness in this matter? There is some evidence to the contrary: Jane Austen and the grammarians she followed (and incidentally, some prescriptive grammarians today) were particularly concerned that the subjunctive should be used after *if* and *whether*, so that she went so far as to replace the indicative of the first edition with the subjunctive in later editions of some of her books. Yet in this construction about which 'correct' writers show so much concern, Scott prefers the indicative even after *an*, the archaic equivalent of *if*. The following examples of this frequent construction are drawn from *Ivanhoe*; in no case is a subjunctive used in the verb: 'an thou hadst', 'an thou canst', 'an thou wert' (*Iv* 451), 'an

---

* This subject is admirably dealt with by S. A. Leonard in his study *The Doctrine of Correctness in English Usage 1700–1800* (New York, 1962). The subjunctive in particular is dealt with on pp. 201ff.

thou gibest' (*Iv* 452), 'If thou hast' (*Iv* 467), 'an thou thinkest', 'an thou hast' (*Iv* 468), 'if no champion appears' (*Iv* 561). On the other hand when the conditional clause is introduced by *so, so that* or *so be that* which were still in use in Scott's time, the mood is usually, but not always, subjunctive; we find:

> It is safe with me . . . so be that this thy scroll produce the sum therein nominated and set down (*Iv* 469).
>
> Within thirty hours – so he have not crossed the Lothian firth (*Mo* 482).
>
> king-like will I answer her so she bring no request unworthy herself or me (*Ta* 741).
>
> let him have all liberty so that he leave not the camp (*Ta* 808).

but also:

> That is but reason . . . so that your betters are served before you (*K* 123).

It is easy to be over-subtle on this matter; probably Scott did not use the subjunctive after *an* in the examples quoted above where *thou* is used because the *-est* ending provided enough archaism for his purposes, while, in the absence of *thou*, the familiar *so that* could be made a little old-fashioned with a subjunctive.

To us the subjunctive sounds strangest in main clauses in hypothetical statements like these from Scott:

> Our union were contrary to the laws (*Iv* 309).
>
> The presence of the mother of God were no protection (*Iv* 305).
>
> This . . . were indeed a perilous and fatal breach (*Ab* 127).
>
> were we not better cease to struggle (*Ab* 491).
>
> An honourable death . . . were the only comfort . . . (*Wk* 24).
>
> Were not your excellency better adjourn (*AG* 262).

Perhaps Scott's original readers felt much the same as we do about this. A comparison with Jane Austen is again helpful: Phillipps points out that this construction is given in her works to pretentious speakers like Sir Edward Denham in *Sanditon* and Mr Collins in *Pride and Prejudice* (Phillipps, p. 155). Perhaps it sounded less strange or pompous when combined with a subordinate clause also in the subjunctive:

> I were worthy that harp and horn rung out shame on me, should I listen to thee (*AG* 608).
>
> Were I capable of such criminal weakness, Markham Everard were the first to despise me (*Wk* 29).

However Visser's quotations (II § 861) suggest that after the Elizabethan period even this construction was limited to consciously literary writers (Walpole, Carlyle).

The subjunctive also appears in the main clause in optative statements:

> Be thou defied (*AG* 10).
>
> be it known to thee (*Ta* 506).

In both cases the situation is dramatic, and it is drama rather than archaism that the reader feels in the language. Archaism has always been drawn on to heighten dramatic language. Modern speakers still use this construction though it has been infrequent since the eighteenth century and limited to fewer and fewer phrases; perhaps the most common in Modern English is: 'far be it from me to . . .'

IMPERSONAL VERBS

44. Originally impersonal verbs had no apparent subject; thus *seems* rather than *it seems*. Impersonal verbs after Middle English tended to die out and with those which remained the *it* subject appears: 'It boots not to complain' (*RII* III iv 18). In some fossilized phrases the verb remained without an apparent subject. The phrases *please you, please your highness* and so on survive into seventeenth-century English. Scott resuscitates this usage:

> and please you (*Ta* 625).
>
> please your highness (*Ta* 625).

(*And* here means 'if'). *Methinks*, one of Scott's most common archaisms (*e.g. Ta* 449, 509, 513, 518, 544, 580, 629, 819), is the only remnant in Modern English of the very common Old English verb *þyncan* (meaning not 'think' but 'seem'). As such its syntax was not easily intelligible; hence the appearance of nonsense forms like *methoughts*. It was kept alive as an archaism but was not normal in Scott's time.

VERBS: INFINITIVE

45.

> I have thought on his passado ever since, and I believe, were it to try again, I know a feat would control it (*Wk* 317).

For a long time a distinct passive form of the infinitive was unknown in English. Where nowadays we would say: 'were it to be tried again' we would have said: 'were it to try again' like Sir Henry Lee. The passive infinitive seems to have largely taken over in this field by the mid-eighteenth century, except in fossilized phrases like 'a house to let', 'I am to blame' or 'they are to seek'.

CHANGES OF USAGES IN CERTAIN VERBS

46.

(a) *Shame* is much less common now as a verb than as a noun, many of its senses as a verb being taken over by the phrase *to be ashamed*. This already applied in Scott's time and his use of *shame* as a verb revived usages long obsolete:

> Rise, rise, De Lacy, and shame thee of thy petition (*Be* 433).

In the *OED* this reflexive use of *shame* is recorded from the thirteenth century to the early sixteenth century and thereafter only here in Scott. Also unfamiliar to us is the following transitive use of *shame*:

> I shame that traitors should have the power to move me thus (*Ab* 337).

Instances of this usage cease with the seventeenth century (except in dialectal use) only to reappear in the nineteenth century after the period of Scott's writing.

(b) On the other hand the verb *warrant* while not now very common – especially since one of its main senses has been more or less taken over by the cognate *guarantee* – was frequent enough in Scott's time. The phrase 'I('ll) warrant you', common as it is in Scott's medieval and renaissance novels, both in the regular form:

> I warrant you the dame will not stoop her crest (*K* 64).

and in the substandard form (imitated from Scots):

> I'se warrant ye (*Wk* 181).

is not archaic for his period (*OED warrant* v 5). However the reflexive phrase 'I warrant me' is a different case. Used with the sense 'I'll be bound' – 'I warrant me thou wouldst have another in requital' (*Ta* 748) – the usage is described as 'originally quasi-archaic' by the *OED*. Scott is the first to use it and is followed only by Disraeli. Disraeli, incidentally, followed Scott in the use of other innovations – for instance he uses Scott's phrase 'masquerade it' (see § 7). This reflexive of *warrant* and the phrases 'masquerade it' and 'brusque it' are the only examples I have found of Scott making any innovations in grammar in order to create archaisms, or apparent archaisms. This is to be contrasted with his frequent creation of psuedo-archaic vocabulary. We may notice while we are on the subject of *warrant* that Scott also revived an obsolete sense of *warrant* 'to promise or predict as certain':

> 'My son,' replied the astrologer, 'let me remind you, I warranted not his death' (*K* 312).

According to the *OED* this sense of the verb had been obsolete since the seventeenth century. Scott perhaps remembered Shakespeare:

> my fainting words do warrant death (1 *HVI* II v 95).

ELLIPSIS OF VERBS

47. A verb of motion is sometimes omitted in English after *let* and *will*:

> let us on (*Ab* 161).
>
> let us back together (*Wk* 85).

The *OED* notes this omission as common in Shakespeare (e.g. *C of E* III i 95); it also seems to have survived in poetry though no example is given for it after Shelley.

> 'Thither will I then,' said the Constable (*Be* 416).

The use of the verb *will* with ellipsis of a verb of motion is attested from Old English but may well have been a poeticism in Scott's time. After the early eighteenth century the *OED* cites only Byron, Scott (here), and Bridges as using the construction.

Chapter 5

INTRODUCTION TO SCOTTISH LANGUAGE

IN INTRODUCING SCOTS into the dialogue of his novels Scott was attempting something quite different from his use of period language. His period language was an artificial creation. It is not a copy of the language of any period but a culling of items from many periods combined with creations of Scott's own, all added to a base of contemporary Standard English. The Scots on the other hand is an attempt at imitating a real language of a particular time, in fact Scott's own time. Furthermore Scott had direct personal access to spoken Scots as well as a substantial body of written Scots, whereas with the period language he had to rely on written sources alone. Of course the Scots dialogue is, like any literary imitation of real speech, a literary artifact and not a transcript of real-life conversation, but there is a basis in reality. It is obvious that Scott was not interested in using dialect just as a bit of artistic colouring, playing up supposed idiosyncracies and peculiarities of Scots. In discussing his aims in writing *Waverley* he says:

> It has been my object to describe these persons, not by a caricatured and exaggerated use of the national dialect, but by their habits, manners, and feelings, so as in some distant degree to emulate the admirable Irish portraits drawn by Miss Edgeworth, so different from the 'Teagues' and 'dear joys' who so long, with the most perfect family resemblance to each other, occupied the drama and the novel (*Wa* 649–50).

Rather, so far as it is possible in a novel, his work is a serious attempt to provide a natural and faithful representation of Scots as it was spoken by many different people. The emphasis of this section of the book is therefore quite different from that of the period language section. Instead of looking at an invented language we are (through the medium of Scott's writing) examining a real language, Scots. The enormous amount of Scots spread over the Waverley Novels justifies us in taking it as, to a large degree, representative of early nineteenth-century spoken Scots in general and not just the Scots of one man.

Yet while there are differences from the period language, still many things remain the same, particularly in Scott's attitudes and approaches to the introduction of language which is not in general currency amongst at least parts of his audience. There is still the same feeling of interest in language for its own sake and the same need and concern for rendering the language intelligible to the audience. When Scott first wanted to write a novel, James Ballantyne was sceptical both about his powers as a novelist and about his decision to introduce a lot of Scots into the dialogue. The reception of *Waverley* proved him wrong and Scott said to him:

> Well, I really thought you were wrong about the Scotch. Why, Burns, by his poetry, had already attracted universal attention to every thing Scottish, and I confess I couldn't see why I should not be able to keep the flame alive, merely because I wrote Scotch in prose, and he in rhyme (*Life*, III 297).

Nevertheless his attention continues to be given to maintaining the interest of the non-Scot, the first step towards which must be making the Scots dialogue intelligible. This attention to the English reader shows itself in many ways, in particular in the spelling, in the choice of a diction which, while Scottish, still has much in common with English and in the introduction, sometimes covert and ingenious, sometimes overt and direct, of explanations of unfamiliar words. This aspect of Scott's art has been given special attention in this section of this study as it was in the period-language section.

Before we discuss the Scottish element in the language of the Waverley Novels we need to answer a question deceptively simple in appearance: what is Scots? There are two obvious answers. Firstly we might consider Scots as being only those elements of lexis, syntax and pronunciation which distinguish English in Scotland from other varieties of English and in particular Standard English. Alternatively it may be defined as any form of English written or spoken in Scotland. The first of these definitions is at times of some practical usefulness but is generally too narrow. It is the fate of local dialects, and Scots is now more of a dialect than a separate language, to be seen as only existing where they differ from the standard or predominant dialect of the language. Yet any dialect will share many features with other dialects of the same language and these are as much part of that dialect as features peculiar to it. We must include in our view of Scots many words which are identical even in form as well as meaning with Standard English words. All the same this narrow definition can be practically useful in studies such as this one – for example, in discussing the foreign sources of Scots vocabulary I have limited myself to discussing only words not found in Standard English. The other definition – Scots as all forms of English found in Scotland – is clearly too broad. No purpose is served by considering Standard English with RP as Scots. And, although we could call Standard English with a Scottish accent Scots, it is best to keep it distinct from forms of the language which also include distinctively Scottish syntax and morphology.

Scots is perhaps best defined historically, as the descendant of the national language of pre-Union Scotland – called, interestingly, *Inglis* in the fifteenth century by the great makars. But we must allow it to include new terms borrowed from English and elsewhere since that period and used freely in situations where dialect is spoken. Yet in the end there can be no hard and fast defining of what we can call Scots. As always where a standard and a non-standard form of a language co-exist in one community, dialects appear in a mixed form far more often than they appear in any 'pure' form. The range of mixture will extend from nothing more than the occasional use of pronunciations taken from the rival variety through to a thorough mixture of pronunciations, vocabulary and syntactic forms. Standard English and Scots and all the mixtures in between belong, then, to a broad continuum. It depends on the speaker and the situation – on education, class, the degree of formality – which mix will be chosen on any one occasion. Recent study of class dialects in England and America has given us a picture broadly similar to that in Scott's novels (except that Scott overemphasizes the uniformity of the upper class dialect, Standard English). The class dialects are not discrete entities. Middle-class dialects show a preponderance of standard forms and working-class dialects a preponderance of non-standard forms but neither dialect exclusively uses one set of forms. There is always a mixture, however slight. In other words each variety is perhaps best thought of, not as having a set of fixed characteristics, but as having a tendency to exhibit such characteristics most of the time. So in Scott we find many speakers of English who occasionally use Scottish pronunciation, grammar or vocabulary and many Scots-speakers who include Standard English items in their speech. Scots then must be seen as existing where Scottish forms very largely predominate – this I will refer to as *full Scots*. Many speakers use Scots much less than this – I will call their language *mixed Scots-English* or *Anglo-Scots*. The question of what may be called Scots in the novels is considered at some length in chapter eight.

Scott's attitudes towards his native dialect were rather mixed. His very use of the English terms *Scotch* (FM 14, An 370n, Wa 348, 359, Re 33) and *Scottish* (FM 14, CC 450, RR 522) in his narrative distances him somewhat from it. We notice that the dialect speakers themselves generally use the native word *Scots* (HM 270, RR 380), although Bartoline Saddletree speaks of *Scotch* (HM 56) as does Nicol Jarvie (RR 356). Scott does not endorse the English Colonel Talbot's prejudiced view that 'even the Lowlanders talk a kind of English little better than the negroes in Jamaica' (Wa 499) even if he probably shared then current attitudes to Black English or Creole, and he will countenance no suggestion that Scots is inferior to the English dialects or even merely equal to them, saying of Jeanie Deans' experiences on her walk to London that 'her accent and language drew down on her ... many jests and gibes, couched in a worse *patois* by far than her own' (HM 411–12). All the same he himself (Wa 359), or his narrators in passages where there is little sense of a narrator's persona distinct from the author (CC 450, RR 522), speaks of the 'vulgarity' attached to Scots or describes it as 'broader and harsher' than English (FM 225). Yet he had pride in the Scottish language. In his *Journal* he writes 'Thomson is superintending a capital edition of Sir James Mellville's Memoirs. It is brave to see how he wags his Scots tongue and what a difference there is in the force and firmness of the language compared to the mincing English edition in which he has hitherto been alone known' (*Journal*, 10 March 1827), and his pride shows too in the extensive use of Scots in the novels by, at some time or other, all classes of people, including King James. But he also seems to have shared the view of many of his contemporaries that, at least since the Scottish king no longer spoke Scots and the old court Scots had died out (see the last two sections of this chapter), English was the 'purer and more classical' tongue (*Letters*, VII 83) even if it was not necessarily the more lively and interesting. All this must be seen in the context of Scott's firm commitment to both the necessity of the Union of England and Scotland and the belief that Scotland could preserve a strong national identity (part of which would be its language) inside the Union. And, despite the confinement of Scots almost totally to the dialogue, Scott provides us with a wider and more varied picture of the Scottish language than any writer since the great age of Scottish poetry at the time of the 'makars'.

The remainder of this chapter provides a background to Scott's use of Scottish language by covering the position of Scots in the early nineteenth century. The following chapters discuss the characteristics of early nineteenth-century Scots as portrayed in Scott's novels. To a lesser extent they relate the state of the language then to what it is now. The final chapter discusses the relationship of Scots and English in Scott's time through an examination of the areas for which Scots is used in the novels.

SPOKEN SCOTS IN THE EARLY NINETEENTH CENTURY

When Scott was born, an educated Scotsman could still speak Scots in public even if many of his contemporaries, especially of the younger generation, cultivated an English accent and diction. For example, in the years around Scott's birth, Boswell's distinguished father, Lord Auchinleck, 'spoke broad Scots from the bench' (F. A. Pottle, *James Boswell: The Earlier Years*, London, 1966, p. 11). Lord Cockburn, born in 1779, and thus only a few years younger than Scott, remembered the older generation who had surrounded him in his youth and recalled that Dr John Erskine's 'language (like that of his colleague, Principal Robertson) was good honest natural Scotch' (*Memorials of his Time*, Edinburgh, 1910, pp. 49–50) and further recalled a number of ladies from his early days who belonged to good society in Edinburgh but whose language was 'like their habits, entirely Scotch, but without any other vulgarity than what perfect naturalness is sometimes mistaken for' (*Memorials*, p. 53).

Cockburn does not say much about the kind of Scots these ladies used; his anecdotes concerning them record their speech

The Language of Walter Scott

which seems to be normal Scots, as far as we can tell from just a few sentences (*Memorials*, pp. 57, 61). Scott however also remembered these ladies and writes at length about their language. He describes it as a special variety of upper class Scots. In *Chronicles of the Canongate* Scott has Chrystal Croftangry describe the speech of Mrs Bethune Baliol:

> It was Scottish, decidedly Scottish, often containing phrases and words little used in the present day. But then her tone and mode of pronunciation were as different from the usual accent of the ordinary Scotch *patois* as the accent of St James's is from that of Billingsgate. The vowels were not pronounced much broader than in the Italian language and there was none of the disagreeable drawl which is so offensive to Southern ears. In short, it seemed to be the Scottish as spoken by the ancient court of Scotland to which no idea of vulgarity could be attached (*CC* 450).

Scott was undoubtedly drawing here on his personal memories of the generation before his own, in particular his own relatives. In 1822 he wrote to Constable:

> Scotch was a language which we have heard spoken by the learnd and the wise & witty & the accomplishd and which had not a trace of vulgarity in it but on the contrary sounded rather graceful and genteel. You remember how well Mrs Murray Keith – the late Lady Dumfries – my poor mother & other ladies of that day spoke their native language – it was different from the English as the Venetian is from the Tuscan dialect of Italy but it never occurd to any one that the Scottish any more than the Venetian was more vulgar than those who spoke the purer and more classical – But that is all gone and the remembrance will be drownd with us the elders of this existing generation (*Letters*, VII 83).

And Lockhart referring to the *Chronicles of the Canongate* passage makes the same point about Scott's aunt; indeed the point is probably taken from Scott's own comments:

> The poet's aunt spoke her native language pure and undiluted, but without the slightest tincture of that vulgarity which now seems almost unavoidable in the oral use of a dialect so long banished from Courts, and which has not been avoided by any modern writer who has ventured to introduce it, with the exception of Scott, and I may add, speaking generally, of Burns. Lady Raeburn, as she was universally styled, may be numbered with those friends of early days whom her nephew has alluded to in one of his prefaces as preserving what we might fancy to have been the old Scotch of Holyrood (*Life*, I 75).

What this court Scots was is not at all clear: Scott has Mrs Bethune Balliot speak *English* in her short appearances in the *Chronicles* and none of the other novels presents us with upper class ladies whose Scots is noticeably different from lower class Scots. Clearly the vocabulary was Scots not English. As for the accent, Scott's description of the 'vowels ... not much broader than in the Italian language' is not very specific. Probably this 'court' accent was old-fashioned, as upper class accents tend to be, and had not undergone some of the more recent changes in Edinburgh pronunciation, such as that from [y] to [i] in words like *guid*. Sir James Wilson speculates that this sound 'probably survived to some extent in the Lothians ... in Allan Ramsay's day' (*The Dialects of Central Scotland*, Oxford, 1926, p. 201) and it may well have survived with some speakers into the time of Scott's childhood. On the other hand it is probably significant that the standard by which this court Scots is judged in all three of these passages is notoriously subjective – the degree of 'vulgarity'. It may be that the upper classes had a distinctive pronunciation; on the other hand the fact that it was common and accepted for Scots to be spoken by upper class people in itself insured that this Scots would not be considered 'vulgar'; vulgar is by definition lower class. But when upper class people stopped speaking Scots and for it substituted English, Scots would then inevitably be associated with lower class 'vulgarity'. It would now seem vulgar even if it had not changed at all. Lockhart's comment half accepts this.

Indeed Scott illustrates this point himself when he has the Duke of Argyle describe Effie Deans (now Lady Staunton) as speaking the old 'court' Scots when in fact what he is noticing is the traces of the common Scots which she learnt in the house of her father, the dairyman Davie Deans:

'She is a Scotchwoman, and speaks with a Scotch accent, and now and then a provincial word drops out so prettily, that it is quite Doric, Mr Butler.'

'I should have thought,' said the clergyman, 'that would have sounded vulgar in the great city.'

'Not at all,' replied the Duke; 'you must suppose it is not the broad coarse Scotch that is spoken in the Cowgate of Edinburgh, or in the Gorbals. This lady has been very little in Scotland, in fact – she was educated in a convent abroad, and speaks that pure court-Scotch, which was common in my younger days; but it is so generally disused now, that it sounds like a different dialect, entirely distinct from our modern *patois*.'

Notwithstanding her anxiety, Jeanie could not help admiring within herself, how the most correct judges of life and manners can be imposed on by their own preconceptions (*HM* 702).

It is true that Effie may have made an effort to assume an upper class accent, but Scott's last sentence suggests another explanation. Effie's pronunciation may not have changed very much at all but what would be 'broad coarse Scotch' in Effie as a dairyman's (or, to use the Scots term, cow-feeder's) daughter has become 'pure court-Scotch' in Effie as a grand lady. The accent is judged, not on its actual sounds, but by the manner and social status of the speaker. It may well be that Scott, looking back when attitudes and circumstances had changed, wanted to find objective criteria by which his aunt's and mother's Scots might be considered free from vulgarity where in fact the most important considerations were subjective ones – changes of attitude rather than changes of pronunciation. (It is interesting to note that Scott, in having the Duke make this comment, seems to have forgotten that the Duke is supposedly speaking in 1737. If the court-Scots was nearly extinct at this period it would not have survived until Scott's childhood some forty years later. The Duke has been endowed with Scott's own historical viewpoint of 1818, the year of the novel's publication. In fact, as we shall see in chapter eight, the novels regularly tend to reflect the linguistic situation of the time of publication rather than the time at which they are set.)

Whatever this court-Scots was, and the differences from normal Scots in pronunciation may not have been as great as Scott felt, it had, according to his testimony, disappeared by the time the novels were written. So too had the use of normal Scots by educated people in public. The process of replacing Scots with English in all but the more informal conversations had been already well under way in Scott's childhood. Dr Johnson, passing through Edinburgh as the starting point of his journey to the Hebrides with Boswell, noted:

> The conversation of the *Scots* grows every day less unpleasing to the *English*; their peculiarities wear fast away; their dialect is likely to become in half a century provincial and rustick, even to themselves. The great, the learned, the ambitious, and the vain, all cultivate the

Introduction to Scottish Language

English phrase, and the *English* pronunciation, and in splendid companies Scotch is not much heard, except now and then from an old Lady (*Johnson: Prose and Poetry*, London, 1963, p. 788).

and Boswell himself was in 1761 one of the three hundred Scottish gentlemen who took lessons in the correct English pronunciation from the Irishman Thomas Sheridan, father of the playwright (Pottle, *James Boswell: The Earlier Years*, p. 65). James Beattie, who published in 1787 a book called *Scoticisms, Arranged in Alphabetical Order; Designed to Correct Improprieties of Speech and Writing* so that Scotsmen would be able to eradicate traces of Scots from their spoken and written usage and who became famous for his poem in English called *The Minstrel*, describes with pride how his own son was induced by his education to abandon his native speech:

> At home, from his Mother and me, he learned to read and write. His pronunciation was not correct, as may well be supposed: but it was deliberate and significant, free from provincial peculiarities, and such as an Englishman would have understood; and afterwards, when he had passed a few summers in England, it became more elegant than what is commonly heard in North Britain. He was early warned against the use of Scotch words and other similar improprieties; and his dislike to them was such, that he soon learned to avoid them; and, after he grew up, could never endure to read what was written in any of the vulgar dialects of Scotland. He looked at Mr Allan Ramsay's poems, but he did not relish them (quoted in D. Daiches, *Robert Burns*, London, 1966, p. 32).

Scots slowly became acceptable in society and in 1803 Galt would write that:

> In polite companies a Scotsman is prohibited, by the imputation of vulgarity, from using the common language of the country, in which he expresses himself with most ease and vivacity, and, clothed in which, his earliest and most distinctive impressions always arise to his mind. He uses a species of translation, which checks the versatility of fancy, and restrains the genuine and spontaneous flow of his conceptions (from an essay on John Wilson in *Scottish Descriptive Poems*, Leyden ed., Edinburgh, 1803, pp. 13–14).

One thing that Galt's comment makes clear is that Scotsmen could still speak Scots. It was still the natural language for expressing emotion and therefore the language of intimate, colloquial talk. But the more public and formal the occasion was, the more Scots would yield to English. The same separation between English for formal contexts and Scots for informal ones no doubt also lies behind Edwin Muir's much later epigram that 'Scotsmen feel in one language and think in another' (*Scott and Scotland*, London, 1935, p. 21). Scotsmen then had a command of *both* languages. Lockhart recognized Scott's ability to speak Scots as well as Scottish English but, significantly, he mentions it as evidence of his powers of mimicry rather than seeing it as a natural command of another variety of the language:

> He had strong powers of mimicry – could talk with a peasant quite in his own style, and frequently in general society introduced rustic *patois*, northern, southern, or midland, with great truth and effect; but these things were inlaid dramatically, or playfully, upon his narrative. His exquisite taste in this matter was not less remarkable in his conversation than in the prose of his Scotch novels (*Life*, I 88–89).

To Lockhart, Scots is an inferior language to be mimicked rather than spoken.

But though English had become established as the language of 'polite companies' as Galt calls it, there too Scots had some place. There is first of all the matter of pronunciation. In a situation such as we have described with Scots and English in competition there must have been a wide variety of accents, from something close to the RP of the time through to a very broad Scots accent even where the diction and grammar were English. Cockburn, for example, comments on Scott's 'Scotch accent and stories and sayings' but contrasts him with 'Jeffrey, his twin star' who 'was sharp English' (*Memorials*, p. 259). In the same passage he further talks of the 'burr in the throat', the 'Berwickshire *burr*' which Scott, in a letter to Joanna Baillie, claims was 'literally and lineally handed down' to him from a Swinton ancestor (*Letters*, VII 63). This feature of his speech, calling as it does for special mention, was unusual for an Edinburgh man of his class but otherwise there is no reason why we may not see him as typical of many Scotsmen of his time in his pronunciation of English. This is how Lockhart describes his accent:

> If at this early period he had acquired anything which could be justly described as an English accent, he soon lost, and never again recovered, what he had thus gained from his short residence in Bath. In after life his pronunciation of words, considered separately,

Introduction to Scottish Language

was seldom much different from that of a well educated Englishman of his time; but he used many words in a sense which belonged to Scotland not to England, and the tone and accent remained broadly Scotch, though, unless in the *burr*, which no doubt smacked of the country bordering on Northumberland, there was no *provincial* peculiarity about his utterance (*Life*, I 88).

Lockhart's comment is a little confusing as it is hard to know exactly what is meant by 'tone' and 'accent'. Bearing in mind that he probably wanted to avoid any suggestion that Scott had a 'vulgar' accent, it seems that what Lockhart means is that Scott spoke English with a pronunciation closer to a London one than broad Scots but still decidedly Scottish. His comment that there was no 'provincial peculiarity' in his speech seems to mean that Scott had an Edinburgh-Lothian accent, or an accepted Standard Scots accent.

So much for pronunciation. Scott's spoken English also included, so it seems, many Scottish words and phrases. He shows a certain consciousness that some of his contemporaries may not have approved, confiding to his *Journal* that 'I write grammar as I speak, to make my meaning known, and a solecism in point of composition like a Scotch word in speaking is indifferent to me' (*Journal*, 22 April 1826). Scott cannot have been the only speaker of his time to interlard his English with Scots.

Lockhart's comment on Scott's powers of mimicry illustrates another way in which Scots mixed with English in conversation; Scots could be introduced to enliven and add realism to anecdotes. Thomas Carlyle in his *Reminiscences* recalls that same Lord Jeffrey whom Cockburn talks of as speaking 'sharp English' in company, occasionally using Scots:

> I used to find in him a finer talent than any he has evidenced in writing: this was chiefly when he got to speak Scotch, and gave me anecdotes of old Scotch *Braxfields*, and vernacular (often enough, but not always, *cynical*) curiosities of that type. Which he did with a greatness of gusto quite peculiar to the topic; ... not to speak of the perfection of the mimicry, which itself was something (Everyman edn., p. 340).

The craze for repeating Scots proverbs as a parlour game described by David Craig (*Scottish Literature and the Scottish People 1680–1830*, London, 1961, p. 24) would also have brought Scots words into polite conversation. Indeed Scots seems to have been felt to possess a certain natural pungency and directness of a kind appropriate to proverbs. In an earlier period, Boswell, who rarely writes Scots, feels that only Scots can truly convey the tartness of his home-thrust at Rousseau; he informs Rousseau that the Scots would say:

> 'Poh! Jean Jacques, why do you allow yourself all these fantasies? You're a pretty man to put forward such claims. Come, come, settle down in society like other people.' And they would say it to you with a sourness which I am quite unable to imitate for you.'
> ROUSSEAU. 'Ah, that's bad.'
> There he felt the thistle, when it was applied to himself on the tender part. It was just as if I had said, 'Hoot, Johnnie Rousseau man, what for hae ye sae mony figmagairies? Ye're a bonny man indeed to mauk siccan a wark; set ye up. Canna ye just live like ither fowk?' It was the best idea could be given in the polite French language of the rude Scots sarcastical vivacity (*Boswell on the Grand Tour: Germany and Switzerland*, London, 1953, pp. 253-4; in the first paragraph Boswell's original French has been translated into English).

This sense of Scots as vigorous and hard-hitting clearly informs Bradwardine's (and, through him, Scott's) delight in the translation of Horace into the vernacular:

> the Baron ... observed ... he was 'the very Achilles of Horatius Flaccus, –
>
> > Impiger, iracundus, inexorabilis, acer.
>
> Which,' he continued, 'has been thus rendered (vernacularly) by Struan Robertson, –
>
> > A fiery etter-cap, a fractious chiel,
> > As het as ginger and as stieve as steel' (*Wa* 577).

To summarize, then, the position of Scots as a spoken language in the 1820s. Scots remains the normal spoken language of the uneducated. Many educated people also know it and can use it in intimate and informal situations but are unwilling, to varying degrees, to use it in society where the norm is considered to be English, but English spoken in many cases with a Scottish accent, strong or weak according to the speaker. Some Scots terms however do come into the language of some educated Scottish speakers of English, and Scots also plays a subsidiary part in polite conversation as the medium of funny stories or for incidental illustration. The situation has changed considerably since Scott's childhood when Scots, spoken in some cases with a more 'refined' upper class accent, was apparently quite acceptable in the best society even if the move towards using English in conversation had already started.

WRITTEN SCOTS IN THE EARLY NINETEENTH CENTURY

The written language had yielded to the dominance of English at a much earlier stage. Even as early as the sixteenth century Knox in his *History of the Reformation* writes in a language close to London English, though with a Scottish spelling and some Scots diction. By the eighteenth century English had taken over completely in prose. Scoticisms were few and the spelling was wholly as in England. David Hume, although he spoke with a broad Scots accent, wanted to write Standard English and considered that Scotsmen 'are unhappy, in our Accent & Pronunciation [and] speak a very corrupt Dialect of the Tongue which we make use of' (*Letters*, Greig ed., Oxford, 1932, I 255). He so much wished to avoid the impurity of Scots idioms that he had his works checked for Scoticisms before they were published and compiled a list of Scoticisms to be avoided which was in fact printed and bound in with many copies of his *Political Discourses*. The difficulty of laying down absolute rules on such matters is made clear in his comment on the proper way of expressing the verb after *hinder*: '*Hinder to do*, is Scotch. The *English* phrase is, *hinder from doing*. Yet Milton says, *Hindered not Satan to pervert the mind*. Book IX' (from *Scotticisms* in *Essays, Moral, Political, and Literary*, London, 1882, II 462). The difficulties of establishing what was English usage did not hinder him from taking exception to other writers' Scoticisms. He writes, to Henry Home that Home's 'Stile is ... very good; correct & nervous, and very pure, only a few Scotticisms as conform for comfortable; which I remarkt' (*New Letters*, Oxford, 1952, p. 27). Hume's obsession with the subject was not unique and illustrates how far English had taken over as the accepted language of prose.

Fortunately the eighteenth century saw by contrast a revival of Scots verse, led by Allan Ramsay and carried on by Fergusson and Burns. Ramsay succeeded in giving Scots a secure, if limited, place in poetry. Yet even so he wrote more English verse than

Scots. Moreover his Scots verse frequently has an interlarding of English terms, or it may be more accurate to say that he often wrote a mixed language. Even where Scots is used, the spelling reflects the dominance of English with spellings like *down* for *doun*, *poor* for *puir* and *should* for *sud* mixed with more traditional Scots spellings. (These were the spelling conventions Scott adopted and they will be discussed in more detail below.) Moreover although Ramsay occasionally wrote seriously in Scots, most of his Scots poetry is informal and comic. As with speech, it is in the most informal contexts that Scots flourishes. The poet talks to his friends rather than 'addresses an audience'. As Kinghorn and Law point out 'what should strike the reader is the very colloquial bias of Ramsay's (as of Fergusson's) literary Scots' (*Poems by Allan Ramsay and Robert Fergusson*, Edinburgh, 1974, p. xvi).

Fergusson and Burns largely follow in Ramsay's footsteps in the use of Scots. They mostly confine it to the more informal genres such as song and satire (which is often, though not necessarily, informal in tone). Both wrote some poetry in English, but Fergusson was less interested than Burns in using the mixed, Anglo-Scots language, even if he occasionally resorts to an English pronunciation for his rhymes. Neither poet adheres to a spelling consistently Scottish in its conventions.

By the end of the eighteenth century, then, Scots had won a place for itself in verse, but a limited place. It was used almost wholly in informal contexts. Moreover it was frequently intermixed with English and even when unmixed Scots was used its identity was disguised by the continual though not continuous use of English spelling.

This was the situation when Scott began to put together his earliest significant work, *The Ministrelsy of the Scottish Border*. In this he continued the tradition of Ramsay and Burns who had combined their own writing of poetry with the editing (and often rewriting) of old Scottish songs. However Scott's own verse, including most of his imitations of the ballads, was written in English. It was only with the novels that he made any change to the existing situation. What the novels did was give Scots a significant place in prose. In introducing Scots into the dialogue and using it so extensively and in so many novels, Scott provided a model which was immensely influential in the nineteenth century and which is still copied today. No earlier prose writer had given Scots such an extensive part to play since the time when English became the standard written language. The position was all the same achieved at a cost. By limiting Scots to dialogue, Scott restricted its range – dialogue is for example, on the whole, more informal than narrative and tends to deal more with the everyday than with the universal. He also finally determined its position as a local dialect rather than a national language. If Scots is not used for all purposes whereas English is (Scott uses English in dialogue as well as narrative) then, however interesting it is, it must *appear* as inferior.

Chapter 6

SCOTTISH SOUNDS, SPELLING AND VOCABULARY

PRONUNCIATION

THE THING WHICH most basically and consistently separates Scots and English is pronunciation. Starting from the same base as Standard English, Scots has developed along a very different phonological path beginning with the separate development of Old Northumbrian in the Old English period. There are a few major differences which affect a large number of words and many small differences with less individual effect but all adding up to make Scots very different from English. During the Old English and earlier Middle English period, Scots developed phonologically as part of the northern dialect of English but later became a distinct dialect or indeed a distinct language. As Scots spread from the region south of the Forth throughout the Lowland areas, it began itself to break up into dialects each with its own distinctive pronunciation. The slight introduction of these dialects into Scott's novels is discussed further on; otherwise, as we have seen, Scott uses Standard Scots to which the following comments apply. These comments are also intended to explain the Scottish pronunciations made evident by Scott's spelling rather than to provide a complete phonological picture of Scots.

Certain variations between Scots and English go back indeed to the earliest stages of the language and dialectal differences which developed in the Old English period. For example, Northumbrian, the ultimate ancestor of Scots, had a 'hard' *g* [g] where West Saxon had a 'soft' *g* [j]. One of the words so affected was *græfa* meaning 'a governor of an area or town'. From this developed Scots *grieve*, used of an official of rather less importance, a farm overseer (RR 195). The West Saxon form was *geréfa*; here the unaccented first syllable was lost and the result is *reeve*.

Scottish Sounds, Spelling and Vocabulary

The biggest differences between Scots and English arise from the separate development of some of the Old English long vowels. In the southern areas of England Old English *ā* becomes *ō* giving the present-day southern English pronunciation of [ou] as in *oak, home, go, ghost, so* and *stone*. In Scots the *ā* persisted and finally developed into an [e:] pronunciation as in *aik-tree* (*An* 91), *hame* (*GM* 199), *gae* (*GM* 5), *ghaist* (*An* 131), *sae* (*Re* 151) and *stane* (*An* 91).* The same pattern applies to foreign words adopted into English before these sound changes took place: Old Norse *frá* gives Scots *frae* and English *fro*, now only found in the phrase *to and fro*. Some of these Scottish forms have penetrated into Standard English. Old English *rād* with its basic meaning of 'riding' developed differently both in form and meaning in English and Scots. In England it came to mean 'what is ridden on', a *road*; in Scotland 'a collective act of riding', a *raid* (*Wa* 128n). Due probably to Scott it is now used in Standard English and has moved even further away from its origins in the compound *air-raid*. (Naturally the same sound development has overtaken *rade* (*GM* 6) the past tense of the verb *ride*). Another relatively recent import into Standard English is *kale* (*Wa* 62, *HM* 68, *BL* 174, *BD* 332) a name used for a kind of curly leaved cabbage. Since Scott's time when it was restricted to Scotland, it has almost totally ousted its English cousin *cole*, derived like it from Old Norse *kál*; even the compound *borecole* which has the same meaning as *kale* is not from the English *cole* but from the Dutch *boerenkool* meaning 'peasants' cabbage'. With the Old English combination *āw*, Standard English follows the same development to [ou] but with the loss of the *w*. In Scots this *āw* follows a separate path from the other *ā* words leading to an [ɑ:] or, in Scott's Edinburgh dialect, [ɔ:] pronunciation as in *Lawland* 'Lowland' (*RR* 380) and *snaw* 'snow' (*HM* 110). In the Scottish dialects south of the Forth, an initial *ā* was often diphthongized, leading eventually to such forms as *yill* (*Re* 554) for *ale* and *yince* (*SRW* 476) for *once*. This initial [j] also developed in some words in Scots which had a diphthong in Old English. For example *earn* 'curdle' appears as *yearn* (*HM* 577) and *earl* appears as *yerl* (*An* 363). As the *SND* notes this 'prefixing of *y* seems to be regarded by many writers as giving a very distinct archaic or dialectal flavour to a word' (*PLD* § 74.1). For this reason we find

---

* In this section I have generally only given one reference as most of these pronunciations are illustrated throughout the Scots dialogue of the novels.

it attached, probably inaccurately, to words which have no diphthong in their history, giving us Cuddie Headrigg's and Richie Moniplies's *yestate* (*OM* 488, *FN* 62) for *estate* and one of Dominie Sampson's few Scoticisms, *yepistle* (*GM* 471) for *epistle*. Indeed we find *E* itself called *Ye* by Edie Ochiltree (*An* 262).

Old English *ō*, by contrast to *ā*, developed in present-day Standard English in a number of directions. It has moved to [u:] in *moon*, to [u] in *good* and *book*, to [ɔ:] in *moor*, to [ʌ] in *blood* and to [au] in *plough*. In Scots a very common development was to [y], a sound close to that in French *lune*. Often this further developed into [i]. This change happened in Scott's own dialect but it is not apparent in his spelling which is the Standard Scots *u-e* or *ui* inherited from Middle Scots. Thus we get *blude* 'blood' (*RR* 353), or *bluid* (*Wa* 336), *dune* 'done' (*FN* 86), *gude* 'good' (*RR* 344), *stude* 'stood' (*RR* 368) and *sune* 'soon' (*An* 97). The same sound change has also overtaken the French borrowing *fool*, yielding *fule* (*FN* 86). Before a back consonant the development is to [ju:] in such words as *heuck* 'hook' (*Re* 302), *heugh* 'crag or steep bank' (*GM* 229, *An* 358) and *pleugh* 'plough' (*OM* 501). (*Heugh*, from Old English *hōh* 'a projecting ridge', corresponds to the English place-name element *Hoo* or *Hoe*.) The *eu* spelling is used to represent this sound. Before [r] the sound which developed was [ø] like *eu* in French *peu*. Here the spelling is usually *ui* as in *puir* 'poor' (*RR* 349) and *muir* 'moor' (*OM* 139) although we also find the alternative *u-e* is used in Cuddie's reference to 'bastards o' the hure o' Babylon' (*OM* 201).

The last important Old English long vowel is *ū* which in Scots has kept its original value as [u:] but in English has become [au]. The traditional Scots spelling of this sound is *ou* as in *doun* 'down' (*RR* 351) and, as we shall see in the discussion of Scott's spelling, he rarely uses the English alternative *oo*.

In Scots as in English there have been fewer changes in the Old English short vowels than in the long ones. Scots has followed Standard English in one of the major changes from Old English, that from [u] to present-day [ʌ] in words like *nut*; in this respect Scots and southern English differ from the Northern and West Midland dialects of England which lie between them and which have retained the [u]. However Scots differs from English in some small particulars – before a nasal consonant Scots replaces [ʌ] with [i] giving *rin* 'run' (*An* 87) and *hinny* 'honey' (*OM* 501). The same variation occurs before other consonants like [z] in *hizzie* 'hussy' (*GM* 140) and *dizzen* 'dozen' (*GM* 223), while a *stickit stibbler* 'a trained but not ordained Presbyterian minister who finds occasional employment giving sermons' (*GM* 467) is metaphorically a gleaner, one who collects grain from amongst the stubble (Scots, *stibble*), who has 'stickit' (failed) in his job. Exactly the opposite sound-change takes place in words like *will* and *wish*: after [w] Scots has [ʌ] for English [i] hence Scots *wunna* 'will not, won't' (*RR* 344) and *wuss* (*RR* 231) – *wuss* is the same word as English *wish* but often means 'want' or 'hope'. The [ʌ] sound may also be found in a number of cases where English had [au]: *hund* 'hound' (*GM* 22), *munt* 'mount' (*Wa* 360), *pund* 'pound' (*OM* 39), *unce* 'ounce' (*FN* 92).

But if Scots parallels English in the change from Old English [u] to [ʌ] it has not followed it in the change of Old English [ɑ] to [ɔ] in closed syllables before [n] and [ng] in words like *long* and *wrong*, which in Scots keep their Old English forms *lang* (*RR* 353) and *wrang* (*RR* 348). The same *a/o* relationship between Scots and English occurs before [m], [p], [b] and [f] but for a quite different reason. Here Scots has unrounded to [ɑ] producing *aff* 'off' (*An* 369), *drap* 'drop' (*An* 270), *tap* 'top' (*OM* 489) and *Tammy Norie* 'a puffin' (*An* 94) where *Tammy* is the proper name corresponding to English *Tommy*. Few non-Scots can be totally unaware of this vowel change since it affects another common name and gives us 'Rabbie' Burns. The [ɑ] sound further appears where English has [ei] in *tak* 'take' (*An* 91) and *mak* 'make' (*An* 88). The vowel was originally short in English but was lengthened in Middle English as being in the first, open syllable of a disyllabic word. In Scots and northern English the early loss of the infinitive ending -*en* had reduced the words to a closed monosyllable so the lengthening did not take place.

In three cases Scots has an [i:] sound where English has [ai]. Two of these arise from different developments of Old English diphthongs: for Old English *ea* before [ç] or [x] Scots has [i:]. Thus Scots has *Hieland* (*RR* 380), pronounced [hilən], where English has *Highland*. Before [g] Old English *ēo* gives [i:] in Scots, producing *fleeing* (*OM* 490) as the Scottish equivalent of *flying* and also *dree* 'endure' (*RR* 491) from Old English *drēogan* a word which is obsolete in Standard English. The other appearance of Scots [i:] for English [ai] is in words of Romance origin, where the foreign [i:] sound was retained in words adopted after earlier changes of [iː] to [ai]: in this group we have *preceesely* (RR 365) and *particulareeze* (An 114).

Amongst the consonants, Scots retained some older English sounds which had been lost in Standard English. The [ç] and [x] of Old English persisted in Scots. Traces of this sound survive in the *written* form of Standard English words where the spelling *gh* indicates its former presence. The older Scots spelling was *ch* but *gh* has often been used from at least the fifteenth century. Because *gh* represents either no sound at all or [f] in English the non-Scottish reader is rarely aware of the sound's presence in Scots. One or other of these closely related sounds is to be found in Scots words like *cleugh* [kluːx] 'a narrow gorge' (OM 200), *flichter* [fliçtər] 'flutter' (SRW 36), *loch* [lɔx] (FM 503) and *quaigh* [kweːç] 'a shallow drinking cup' (OM 102). [ç] occurs initially and [x] finally in *heugh* [çjuːx] 'a crag' (FN 164). However the sound also occurs in quite English-looking words like *might* [miçt] and *thought* [θoxt]. The spelling, which is discussed in more detail further on, disguises the difference from English. Other differences between the two forms of the language hidden by the spelling are: the Scottish trilled [r], the fact that medial *ng* is always to be pronounced [ŋ] as in *singer* and not [ŋg] as in *finger*, the retention of [w] before [r] in words like *write* where the [w] has long been silent in English and the pronunciation of *wh* as [ʍ] and not [w] so that, for example, *whilk* 'which' is pronounced [ʍilk] not [wilk].

The main differences in the pronunciation of consonants which influence Scott's spelling are: the loss or vocalization of certain consonants, the interchange of [s] and [ʃ] and [d] and [ð], metathesis, and certain Norse 'hard' sounds. The most frequently lost sound is [v] (sometimes [f]) making forms like the following very characteristic of Scott's dialogue: *doo* 'dove' (HM 300), *dooket* 'dovecot' (GM 198), *forgie* 'forgive' (OM 328), *gie* 'give' (OM 39), *ill-fa'ard* 'ill-favoured, bad-looking' (RR 253), *loes* 'loves' (An 151), *ower* 'over' (FN 87), *shules* 'shovels' (An 313), *siller*, 'silver, money' (FN 93) and *twalmonth* 'year' (RR 362). This same loss of [v] gives us the exclamation *sirs* (An 357, GM 474) which looks like an addressive but is actually a reduced form of *(God pre)serve us* and the loss of [f] gave Scott as Sheriff of Selkirkshire his local designation of *the Shirra* (see also An 262). In Scots *harvest* has both lost its [v] and extended its meaning so that the *hairst* that Peter Peebles talks of a 'wench quean' running away from (*Re* 302) is 'an engagement to work in the harvest'. A little less common is the loss of [ð] or [θ] although it happens in two very common words: *wi'* 'with' (*RR* 349) and *unco*, a form of *uncouth* meaning 'unknown' (*OM* 534) or 'unusual' (*SRW* 104) but generally used as an intensifying adjective (*RR* 359) or adverb (*An* 328). The change also affected the relative and demonstrative pronoun *that* but, like most Scots writers since the medieval period, Scott prefers for such a crucial word to use the English *that*. The use of '*at* in *Old Mortality* (*OM* 137) is most unusual.

Other sounds are lost through the simplification of certain consonantal clusters. This has happened in English too but spelling disguises the fact. English has lost the [t] in *wrestle* but keeps it in the spelling as Scott does in his spelling of the metathetic Scottish equivalent *warstle* on one of the occasions when he uses it (*HM* 151). In another place he acknowledges the loss with the spelling *warsle* (*HM* 662). In Scots a [d] is often lost either after [l] as in *mouls* 'broken up earth, mould' (*RR* 81; in Scots this word is usually in the plural) or after [n] as in *wanle* 'supple, agile' (*An* 328), which appears in the northern English dialects as *wandle*, or in *Cannlemas* 'Candlemas' (*RR* 80) and *thunner* 'thunder' (*BL* 162).

When preceded by a back vowel, [l] is not lost but vocalized. From this process we get, after *a*, [ɑː] or [ɔː] – finally in *fit-ba'* 'football' (*OM* 205), *ha'* 'hall' (*BL* 157) and *sma'* 'small' (*GM* 199) and medially in *hause* 'neck' (*OM* 131), from the obsolete English *halse*, and *maut* 'malt' (*OM* 488). After *o* the diphthong [au] results, found in: *fowk* 'folk' (*GM* 21), *gowd* 'gold' (*An* 103) and *gowff-ba'* 'golf-ball' (*Re* 220). After *u* the outcome is [uː] as in *fu'* 'full' (*BL* 161) which is also spelt *fou* (*GM* 468), *ou* being the traditional Scots spelling for this sound.

The 'Norse' consonants may not be necessarily due to Norse influence but they follow the pattern of differentiation between Norse and Old English. English [tʃ] is often [k]: *bink* 'bench, frame for holding plates' (*Re* 47), *breeks* 'breeches, trousers' (*RR* 425), *kist* 'chest' (*An* 337), *muckle* 'much, big' (*HM* 428; *much* is from Middle English *muchel*), *open-steek* 'open-stitch' (*RR* 264), *sic* 'such' (*OM* 206) and *thack* 'thatch' (*GM* 512). English [dʒ] is often [g] as in *brigg* 'bridge' (*OM* 489) although in the case of *paitrick* meaning 'partridge' (*HM* 178) the [g] has apparently been further affected and devoiced to [k]; and English [ʃ] is often [sk]: *skirl* 'shrill talk, shriek' (*An* 457) and *skriegh* 'shriek' (*An* 94), pronounced [skri:ç] or [skri:k] although in this latter case English has both *shriek* and *screech* as well as the obsolete or rare *screak*. *Skyte* has the same variation from its English equivalent. When Nicol Jarvie describes Andrew Fairservice as a 'gabbling skyte' (*RR* 378) he is using the Scottish cognate of English *shit* borrowed from Old Norse. It may be more politely interpreted as from the noun *skyte* 'squirt' which may be why such an unusually strong term is acceptable to Scott. Interestingly English also uses *squirt* as a term of abuse. [sk] also appears before [l] where English has [sl], hence *sclate-stane* 'a piece of slate' (*SRW* 147).

English [ʃ] may also appear as [s]. A final [ʃ] becomes [s] in *wuss* 'wish', already mentioned for its change of [i] to [ʌ], and in the national names *Erse* (*An* 114), a form of *Irish* used into the nineteenth century but now replaced by *Gaelic*, *Inglis*, now only found as a surname, and *Scots* (earlier *Scottis*). *Pouss* (*OM* 206) is of French origin and preserves the sound of French *pousser* where English has moved to the palatalized *push*. [ʃ] changes to [s] initially in *sall* 'shall' (*RR* 367) and *sud* 'should' (*OM* 87) due to the weaker stress falling on these auxiliary verbs. A change in the opposite direction, from [s] to [ʃ], happens in some words of Romance origin like *condeshend* (*An* 489) and *veshell* (*An* 476). The same interchange of sounds is found with [ð] and [d]. *Farder* (*HM* 576) is English *farther*, while *woodie* 'a halter' (*RR* 487, *BL* 223) is the Scots equivalent of *withy* since, as Scott explains, 'Twigs of willow, such as bind faggots, were often used for halters in Scotland and Ireland, being a sage economy of hemp' (*RR* 487n). On the other hand *shouthers* 'shoulders' (*HM* 171) and *sowther* 'solder' (*HM* 688) have [ð] for English [d] as well as illustrating the vocalization of [l]. Scott also has *sowder* (*An* 328).

We have already noticed one example of metathesis: *warsle* (*HM* 662) for *wrestle*. To this may be added *girdle* 'griddle' (*HM* 437), *scart* 'scratch' (*GM* 210) or 'a mark with a pen, a scribble' (*HM* 124), and *Southron* 'an Englishman' (*RR* 194), a form of *southern*. *Brod* 'a collection plate' (*GM* 55) is a meta-thesized form of *board*. *Curpel* 'crupper' (*HM* 57) and *girnel* 'granary' (*Wa* 65) each show a very similar development. Not only have both been influenced by metathesis but also in each an [r] has been changed into an [l]. Scottish *lavrock* (*FN* 45) evolved from Old English *lāferce* by metathesis; English *lark* is a reduced form of the same word.

Sound changes usually affect a whole series of words. But where the change is due to the workings of popular etymology the change is by its nature usually confined to individual words. The French *portmanteau* is a simple compound indicating its function derived from *porter* 'carry' and *manteau* 'coat, cloak'. Sometimes the word was partially anglicized as *portmantle* (*SRW* 16). But to those ignorant of French the word would be differently explained. The first element was thought of as *pock* or *poke* a word meaning 'bag'. Add to this the Scoticizing of the second element as *manty* 'a loose flowing robe' (*HM* 539) and we get Andrew Fairservice's *pokmanty* (*RR* 194). A further misunderstanding or, more probably, a mispronunciation produces *pockmanky* (*GM* 457). *Mankie* is a sort of material and just possibly it was thought of as the second part of this word. Folk etymology has likewise affected *necessity* which often appears as *needcessity* (*HM* 318, *Re* 152) and, less strikingly, *ballad* where the *-ad* ending has been mistaken for the better-known *-ant* giving us *ballant* (*GM* 457).

Scots and English have not always been in line with their treatment of foreign loan words, providing another source of variation in pronunciation between them. Old Scots had a sound – the so-called *l mouillé* – which was unknown to English though found in French. According to Murray this sound, represented by the digraph *lz*, survived into the nineteenth century (*DSCS* 124), but it has now become a simple [l] or an [l] followed by a [j] sound (*PLD* §108). Having this sound in their phonetic system, the Scots, when they borrowed from French, retained it whereas in English it was lost. This accounts for triads like: French *assoil, assoille* (from the verb *assoudre*), English *assoil*, Scots *assoilzie* (*An* 357, *FM* 426). As it happens, both Scots and English have lost this word which was already archaic when Scott used it (except in Scottish legal use); it has been replaced by *absolve*, found in English from the sixteenth century, a direct borrowing from the Latin *absolvere* the ultimate origin of French *assoudre*. Following the same pattern we have: French *brouiller*, English *broil*, Scots *bruilzie* 'brawl' (*Wa* 386, *HM* 233); French *espuille, espoille*, English *spoil*, Scots *spulzie* 'plundering' (*Wa* 130); and French *touiller*, English *toil*, Scots *tuilzie* 'quarrel' (noun: *Wa* 563, *GM* 292, *Mo* 486; verb: *RR* 349). Clearly the meanings as well as the forms have diverged in Scots and English. The history of *ulyie* 'oil' (*An* 129) is slightly different.

Middle English abandoned the Old English borrowing *ele* and took both northern French *olie* and central French *oile*. After the thirteenth century, however, the *olie* forms are found only in the north especially Scotland. Forms like Scots *ulyie* may be influenced by later French forms such as *huile* and *uille*.

Scots also had the sound of French *gn* in *digne* [ɲ] spelt *nʒ*, *nz* or *ny*. As the *SND* notes (*PLD* §110) Murray gave this pronunciation as still current in the nineteenth century in the words *gaberlunzie* 'professional beggar' (*An* 90, *Re* 59) and *cunzie* (*Wa* 167). The spelling suggests that it may have also been present in *menzie* (*Ab* 488) or *menyie* (*Re* 136) which corresponds to the obsolete English *menie* and means 'a retinue'. *Cunzie* 'coin, money' preserves the sound of Old French *cuigne* not present in its English cousins *coin*, *quoin* and *coign* which are also based on the slightly different French variant *coing*. The [ɲ] sound developed into [ŋ] giving, for example, the older pronunciation of *Menzies* as *Mingies*. However, as in English, spelling pronunciations have become very common with the advance of literacy: *Menzies* is pronounced as it is written and an unhistoric [z] has also appeared in *gaberlunzie*. *Menzie* and *cunzie* present no problem as they are obsolete.

Other foreign words which have taken different forms in English and Scots are French *carte* which for some unexplained reason has become *card* in English though in Scotland it kept its original form (*An* 185), Latin *dirige*, the first word of an antiphon sung for the dead, which in English becomes *dirge* but in Scots *dirgie* (*BL* 323) or the metathesized *drigie* (*BL* 331) and has there the different meaning of 'funeral feast', and *procurator* which has been adopted in its full form by both forms of the language but in Scotland has been shortened to the trisyllabic *prokitor* (*HM* 239) while in England it has been further reduced to *proctor*. *Procurator* is almost obsolete in English but in Scots, though virtually obsolete in the sense 'solicitor' (*HM* 107), it still survives in the compound *procurator-fiscal* 'the public prosecutor in a sheriff court' (*SRW* 212) and in other senses.

Parallels to *oil/ulyie* where English adopted two forms of a foreign word, and a different one survived in each country, can be found in *bailie/bailiff* and *remeed/remedy*. English adopted both the earlier *bailif*, the object case of *baillis*, and the later French *bailli*. However, although *bailie* can be found in English until the mid-eighteenth century, after that the present situation obtained where Scots uses *baillie* and English *bailiff*. Of course over the last six centuries there has been plenty of chance for separate development of meaning: in England a *bailiff* was by Scott's time a rather lowly official, a steward or one who serves writs and makes arrests, while in Scotland a *baillie* could be a considerable figure, like Bailie Nicol Jarvie, the equivalent of an English alderman with some magisterial powers as well. The recent changes to local government have rendered the term obsolete in Scotland. Anglo-French gave English *remedy* while Central French gave it *remeed*. The latter is, from the fifteenth century, only Scottish (RR 197; BL 209). An interesting case is *lamour/amber*. When Arabic words have been adopted into a European language it has sometimes been with the definite article retained as in *algebra*, sometimes with it omitted as in *imam*. In the case of Arabic *al-anbar* both possibilities were adopted giving in Latin both *ambra* and the aphetic *lambra*. In French we have *ambre* and *lambre* both of which were adopted into English but *lammer* (BL 176) or *lamour* (HM 188) became the Scots form and *amber* the English one.

In certain cases it is quite clear that the Scots and English borrowings were and remained quite separate processes. Scots took from French the form *must*, a variant of *musc* from which English gets *musk*. The form *must* for this word has never been accepted into standard English. In Scots it developed the general sense of 'powder'; it is used in Scott as a verb (*moust, An* 129; *muist, Re* 143). Scots *carvy* used in the compound *carvy-seed* (*An* 183) is from French, Italian or Spanish *carvi* while English *caraway* is from Mediaeval Latin *carui*, and Scots *shabble* 'a curved sword' (RR 358, FN 87) whatever its origin, comes from a different immediate source to English *sabre*, although the ultimate origin must be the same, possibly an oriental one.

Anglo-Norman forms of French words generally entered English in the earlier Middle English period before Central French had come to be the prestige variety in England. In these circumstances the use in Scotland of a Central French form where English adopted and retained an Anglo-Norman form seems to indicate a later, direct influence of French on Scots rather than an influence through English. For example the endings *-arie* and *-orie* in Anglo-Norman appear as *-aire* and *-oire* in Central French. Thus Scots has *ordinar* (RR 43, HM 275) and English *ordinary*, Scots *inventar* (GM 295), earlier found as *inventour*, and English *inventory*. Both *contrair* (BL 146) and *contrary* were found in earlier English but *contrair* was later limited to the north. With *cruells* (SRW 33) and *scrofula* two languages (Latin and French) rather than two dialects provide the sources. This disease, known in England also as the King's Evil as it was thought the English kings could cure it with their touch, was called *scrofulae* in Latin giving, through the medium of popular Latin *scrofellae, French *escrouelles* from which comes *cruells* as Scott's note points out (SRW 33n). No doubt folk etymology associated the word with the adjective *cruel* but we also find it spelt *crewels* in *The Heart of Midlothian* (HM 687). So too with *paragraph* and *paraffle*; the original Greek and Latin word denoted the sign used at the beginning of a paragraph. In French it was shortened to *parafe* and applied to a flourish added to a signature. Scots adopted the French, gave it the frequentative form *para(f)fle*, and applied it figuratively to ostentatious display (An 276, Re 69).

A variation in the form of a word between Scots and English can also be explained by borrowing from Old Norse. Scots *nowte* 'cattle' (HM 683) is not a form of archaic English *neat* but a borrowing of Norse *naut*, while Scots *loup* (FN 619, BL 247), from Old Norse *hlaupa*, is found alongside its English synonym and cognate *leap*. In Scotland itself the origin of *nowt* was misunderstood and the [au] diphthong was taken to represent an earlier [ol] with the familiar sound-change of the vocalization of [l]. Hence the appearance, from as early as the fifteenth century, of the form *nolt* (Wa 137). Similarly *stern* (HM 256) is from the Norse cognate of English *star* and *raun* (Re 83) is from the Norse cognate of English (*fish*) *roe*.

SPELLING

Before we discuss the spelling of Scots in the novels, we must decide to what extent Scott is responsible for it. Except on a few occasions when he was sick and dictated to an amanuensis Scott wrote his novels out himself. His manuscripts are scantily and unconventionally punctuated – he was fond of using dashes – and his spelling was, in the case of some words, rather idiosyncratic. Since he was attempting to preserve his anonymity he did not want his handwriting to be on show at the printers where it could be seen by visitors. His manuscripts were therefore transcribed and the transcript sent to the printer. The transcriber

Scottish Sounds, Spelling and Vocabulary

filled out the punctuation, made the spelling a little more consistent and brought it into line with standard practice in such matters as the past participle termination – spellings like *chilld* and *helpd* became *chilled* and *helped*. The proofs were returned to Scott who then made further corrections which were themselves transcribed onto a fresh set of proofs from which the page was finally corrected and set up. The spelling was thus subject to change by Scott's transcriber and printer. In fact the transcriber does not seem to have made a lot of changes to Scott's spelling and the author always had a chance to approve, or even amend, the results of the transcription. In the circumstances it seems reasonable to talk of the spelling as Scott's own.

We should note, by the way, that there was a further stage. Some of the spelling conventions were changed again when the Collected Edition was prepared. These changes will be discussed later. For the moment what is said applies to the spelling in the Collected Edition and other editions, like the Border Edition, based on it.

Three rather contradictory aims influence the spelling of Scots in the novels. They are: to indicate the relationship of a Scots word to an English one, to use the traditional spelling of Scots, and to attempt some kind of phonetic reproduction of Scottish pronunciation. The simplest way to establish a relationship with English is to use the spelling of the related English word. As we have seen Scott did this very extensively; a great part of the Scots dialogue is spelt in the English way. But less drastic means could work towards the same end. One of the worst ways is the unhappy compromise of using a more or less phonetic spelling but indicating the variation from the cognate English by including apostrophes. This is a bad method because it has bad side-effects. Though an English reader may find this helpful, it supports the prejudice that Scots is a corrupt dialect, a perversion of the true English caused by the vulgar habit of dropping consonants. This was especially true in view of a growing eighteenth- and nineteenth-century tendency to see the true English as the standard *written* language. (One result of this has been that most of the main changes in English in the last hundred years or more have been towards bringing spelling and pronunciation closer together: *herb* and *hospital* have gained an [h] in pronunciation which was never there before, the [t] has been restored to *often* and so on.) Deviations in pronunciation from the written norm were rapidly being categorized as illiterate. When Scots writers by using apostrophes drew special attention to such deviations (which in fact also existed and still exist in the received pronunciation of Standard English) it was very easy for the idea to arise that Scots was by its very nature an illiterate, non-literary language. So the relegation of Scots to a secondary position as a literary language, already evident in the limitation of subjects for which it is used, is further reinforced by this practice.

Scott spells relatively few words with apostrophes but his page is nevertheless dotted with them because these words include some very common ones, in particular *a'* 'all', *o'* 'of' and *wi'* 'with'. (In a few rare cases *a'* is replaced by *aw* (e.g. *FN* 75, 78) but as both spellings occur in the one speech of Meg Dodds (*SRW* 14) it would seem that the same pronunciation, namely [ɔː], is indicated in both cases). Associated with these are some common contractions like *o't* 'of it' and *wi't* 'with it'. After this the most common use of the apostrophe is to indicate a corresponding final *l* in English. Here the apostrophe may, in fact, be considered as having a phonetic value since, as we have seen above, the vocalization of [l] generally leads to lengthening of the preceding vowel. Some of these words, like *all* itself, end in *-all* in English: *gowff-ba'*, 'golf-ball' (*Re* 220), *snaw-ba'* 'snow-ball' (*RR* 349), *ca'* 'call' (*GM* 201) and *fa'an* 'fallen' (*BL* 159). Others end in English in *full* or *ful*: *fu'* 'full' (*BL* 161), *awfu'* (*GM* 200), *poorfu'* 'powerful' (*HM* 117), and *shamefu'* (*BL* 178). Occasionally the apostrophe indicates the disappearance of an earlier [v] but most of these are exceptional cases for Scott – *bra'* (*Re* 563, *Wa* 405) is usually *braw* (the word is a form of English *brave*); *gi'en* (*An* 186) is more frequently *gien*; *ha'* 'have' (*Wa* 434) is usually *hae* (*ha'* normally corresponds to English *hall*); *ha'arst* 'harvest, a harvest job' (*OM* 447) is elsewhere *harst* (*RR* 356) or *hairst* (*Re* 302); *lo'es* (*OM* 392) is paralleled by *loes* (*An* 151). Scott's inconsistency here blossoms in the spellings of the words which in English would be *ill-favoured* and *well-favoured*, that is 'bad-looking' and 'good-looking': *ill-fa'ard* (*RR* 253), *ill-faur'd* (*OM* 207), *ill-fa'red* (*Pi* 64), *ill-fard* (*OM* 117), *weel-far'd* (*Wa* 386), *weel-fa'rd* (*Wa* 563) and *weel-faurd* (*HM* 456).

Another compromise which reflects both the English cognate and the Scottish pronunciation is a partially phonetic spelling which also retains elements of the English spelling. Two interesting cases are *wad* and *sud*, the Scots equivalents of *would* and *should*. In English the *l* of both *would* and *should* is of course silent and likewise in Scots *wad* is pronounced [wɑd] and *sud* amongst its many pronunciations [suːd, sʌd, søf, sid] has none which includes [l]. Yet *suld* is Scott's normal form (e.g. RR 349) and much more frequent than *sud* (OM 87). The *l*, though silent in English as well as Scots, is included to make the word *look* more like the English one. On the other hand *wald* (FN 49) is very rare in Scott compared to *wad*, Scott's normal form (e.g. Re 152). Ironically the word he always spells the English way is *could* even though, once again, there is no [l] in either the English or Scots pronunciation. In fact the *l* in the English spelling is unhistorical having been introduced on the analogy of *would* and *should* in which an [l] was present in Old English. In the same combination of consonants in *chield* (Re 358) it is the *d* rather than the *l* which is not needed; but *chield* is more common in Scott than *chiel* (Re 152) even though the normal meaning in Scots is 'fellow' rather than that of English *child*. In the speech of Scotsmen Scott often employs the English spelling *behoved* (Wa 166, FN 28, RR 264, OM 488) and, less often, indicates the Scots vowel by the spellings *behuved* (An 546, OM 555) and *behooved* (GM 105). He does not however proceed to indicate the frequent loss of the *v* in Scots which, combined with some further contraction, gives forms like *bude*; evidently the pronunciations with *v* and without existed side by side but, even with the broadest speakers, Scott chooses to use only the form more easily recognizable by his southern readers. Perhaps because with a noun the context can give a clearer idea of the meaning he is, by contrast, willing to use both *claithes* (FN 44, SRW 34) or *claiths* (HM 239) and *claes* (OM 89) or *claise* (HM 241). Another compromise between English and Scots is evident in compounds where one element is anglicized, the other not, as in *downfa'* (GM 200) and *gae-down* 'go-down, i.e. a drinking bout' (GM 197, An 44) which could have been *dounfa'* and *gae-doun*.

Sometimes the relationship with English indicated by the spelling is a spurious one. The reproducer of dialect is generally more than usually aware of the discrepancy between speech and writing. The result is often 'eye-dialect' where the spelling varies from the English one, which suggests a difference in pronunciation, whereas in fact the pronunciation is the same as in English – an example is 'honest Mrs Blower's' *imitashion* (SRW 354). Mrs Blower is good-hearted but badly educated; however even

Lady Penelope Penfeather could not object to her pronunciation of this word. The spelling conveys the impression of poor education, but actually indicates a Standard English pronunciation. So too with Andrew Fairservice's *sum* (RR 195) for *some*. Likewise the spellings *Lonnun* (FN 576) *Lon'on* (FN 461) and *Lonon* (Re 151) indicate a pronunciation of *London* without the [d] which was Standard English until the middle of the last century (see Strang, § 50) and Englishmen still use the pronunciations of *Edinburgh* which are indicated by the spellings *Embro'* (*Wa* 282) and *Edinbro'* (*Wa* 563) even though Scott confines these spellings to speakers of Scots. *Faut* (RR 358) or *fau't* (OM 206) is a more doubtful case. English *fault* derives from French *faute* and the usual Middle English spelling, used to the seventeenth century, is *faut*. From the fifteenth century an etymological *l* was often inserted in the spelling. With the eighteenth century a movement begins to include the *l* of the spelling in the pronunciation yet still in 1755 Johnson noted that the normal pronunciation was the historical one without the [l]. By Scott's time however Walker was writing that the [l] 'is sometimes suppressed in *fault* but this suppression is become vulgar' (John Walker, *A Critical Pronouncing Dictionary*, London, 1864, 'Principles of English Pronunciation', § 404). Scott no doubt had heard it but apparently took it to be a Scoticism. *Vault* has a similar history to *fault* though the OED remarks that 'it is not clear at what date the *l* finally established itself in this word': in Caleb's speech it appears as *vau't* (BL 349).

The Standard English participal ending *-ing* actually develops from the Old English gerund ending *-ung*. In Scots the original Old English participal ending *-and* was retained. However in Scots the final [d] of *and* had been lost and in both English and Scots the final consonants of *ing* had been changed from [ŋg], the Middle English pronunciation, to [n]. As a result in both Scots and English the participle and gerund ended in [n]. But the general eighteenth-century movement towards 'correctness' in Standard English which included, amongst other things, pronouncing words as they were spelt, overtook the participal ending and people began to pronounce it with a final [ŋ]. The [n] was nevertheless tenacious and the process of change to [ŋ] has only really been completed in this century. In Scott's time the matter was very much undecided. Walker writes: 'If my observations do not greatly fail me, I can assert, that our best speakers do not invariably pronounce the participal *ing*, so as to rhyme with *sing*, *king* and *ring*' (Walker, § 410). Clearly usage still sanctioned an [n] pronunciation even if Walker himself thought 'the participal *ing*, therefore ought always to have its ringing sound', that is [ŋ], 'except in those words formed from verbs in this termination'. (The exception is to avoid 'disgusting repetition' which has 'a very bad effect on the ear'.) Now that the [ŋ] pronunciation has become normal in Standard English, some Scottish writers have used the spelling *-an* to indicate the different pronunciation (and derivation) of the Scots participle. Scott may well have thought this unnecessary if he took the normal English pronunciation of the participle and gerund to be with a final [n]. Certainly he almost invariably uses *ing* and only very rarely *in* or *in'*. The few appearances of these spellings are perhaps to be considered as 'eye-dialect' such as *creepin'* (*OM* 534), *kickin* (*HM* 361), and *pooin'* 'pulling' (*Re* 612). In some of these cases the context may have drawn Scott's particular attention to the spelling and pronunciation. *Rinnin* 'running' occurs in *Waverley* in the phrase 'a rinnin ring' (*Wa* 434); perhaps Scott became particularly conscious of the [n] in the unstressed inflection when he found it right beside [ŋ] in the stressed *ring*. In the same passage we also find *burning* and *flinging*. In *The Heart of Midlothian* Scott is making a special point of emphasizing the difference between the English-speaking magistrate and the Scots-speaking thief, Ratcliffe. The magistrate says *whipping-post* and Ratcliffe *whuppin-post* (*HM* 200). Phonetics is not so important here as the maintenance of the distinction between the two speeches. This effect is achieved, even if the spelling does overstate the difference in pronunciation.

When we turn away from those spellings where the main impulse is to make a connection with English, we find Scott still encountering a basic problem – what spelling conventions should he use? It may well be argued that, so long as no special local dialect of Scotland is intended, the spelling does not really matter. The silent reader recognizes that Scots is being spoken so long as the spelling of a number of words differs in any way at all from the Standard English one. The reader who wishes to read aloud with a Scots pronunciation will either have to bring his own knowledge of Scots to bear or will need a phonetic transcription far more thorough than Scott could have provided in the pages of a novel. The important thing is to indicate that dialect is being used – the details of pronunciation must be dealt with by the reader. This is the extreme view yet has some justification. But although Scott was not willing to proceed to a fully phonetic spelling, or even to give up using English spellings for a lot of words, we may reasonably assume he wanted his spelling to give the reader some help with pronunciation. The question was whether to use the traditional Scots spelling or to use English spelling conventions to make the phonetic value clear to the English reader. Scott's answer was characteristically an inconsistent use of both conventions. This was also the way most of his eighteenth-century predecessors had settled the question.

Needless to say, not all the conventions of Scottish spelling were foreign to English readers. Some of the more exotic Scottish spellings had long been abandoned. The Old Scots spellings *sch* for English *sh* and *quh* for English *wh* survived in documents into the eighteenth century but were then replaced by their English equivalents. Apart from an archaic passage in *Chronicles of the Canongate* (*CC* 379–80) the only survival of *quh* in Scott is, as we might expect, in the legal term *umquhile* '(the) late' (*FN* 577, *OM* 33, *GM* 571) and even this is often spelt *umwhile* (*GM* 23, *Wa* 81). The problem is that *wh* in Scots represents the voiceless sound [ʍ] whereas in English it usually represents [w]. The loss of *quh* took away a useful method of differentiating the two sounds. The Old Scots spelling *ch* for [ç] or [x] had not been lost but from the late Middle Ages *gh*, the English equivalent, had been a strong rival. Scott, like Ramsay, preferred the *gh* spelling. Unfortunately, though the sounds have disappeared from English, the spelling survives in words which once had the pronunciation, being either silent as in *night, might, though* or [f] as in *enough, laugh*. To spell the Scottish [miçt] as *might* does not convey the difference in pronunciation from English [mait]. The alternative is equally unsatisfactory: *ch* will be given its normal English value and *micht* will look like [mitʃt]. So the spelling is of little help unless the reader already knows something about the Scottish phonetic system. The most that is achieved is that the non-Scot becomes aware that the word is not pronounced as in English. The Antiquary's pedantry allows one exceptional case. Scots retains in its form *sealgh* [selx] the final sound of Old English *sealh* whereas Standard English has lost it in *seal*, in this case with no trace left in the spelling. Jonathon Oldbuck tells

Scottish Sounds, Spelling and Vocabulary

how he saw Hector 'engaged in an animated contest with a *phoca*, or seal (*sealgh*, our people more properly call them, retaining the Gothic guttural *gh*)' (*An* 462). But this is exceptional – no such comment can be attached to other appearances of the word (*Re* 352, *RR* 509). Scott occasionally uses *ch* but rarely has it in words found also in English; *eneuch* (*RR* 381) is rare beside *eneugh* (*GM* 199) or *aneugh* (*Re* 152) or the fully English *enough*. *Ch* is more frequent in Scots words but even there *gh* is usually an alternative. At least once we find *cleuch* 'a narrow gorge' (*Re* 41) but there is also *cleugh* (*OM* 200, *SRW* 550). Words of Gaelic origin tend to be spelt with *ch* like *do(u)rlach* 'a quiver for arrows' (*FM* 331) or 'a portmanteau' (*Wa* 405), *loch* (*Wa* 159) and *spleuchan* 'a tobacco pouch' (*HM* 310, *GM* 524). Yet Scott seems to have originated the *gh* spelling in *spreagh* 'stolen cattle' (*RR* 356, *Letters* II 235) where the [ç] is actually a Scots development of the final aspirate in Gaelic *spreidh*. *Gh* can also be a problem when omitted. The Scots form of the English word *neighbour* had also lost the sound which gave rise to the English *gh* spelling. But because the *gh* is silent in English, *neibor* (*HM* 124) looks like mere 'eye-dialect'. In fact *ei* represents an [i:] sound, as we can see in the alternative spelling *neebor* (*Re* 143).

The digraphs *lʒ* and *nʒ* might also cause confusion. As we saw before, the sounds [lj] and [nj] they represent are developments from French sounds not adopted into Standard English. To an Englishman and increasingly to Scots the *ʒ* seems to represent [z] not [j]; hence the present pronunciation of *Menzies* as [menzi:z]. The problem can be avoided by the substitution of *y*, as Scott has done in *Mackenyie* (*Wa* 599), but he prefers to retain the traditional Scots spellings like *assoilʒie* (*FM* 426), *bruilʒie* (*Wa* 386), *chainʒie* (*OM* 80) and *spuilʒie* (*Wa* 436).

Turning to vowels, the short vowels present relatively few problems but still conceal a few traps. The spellings *het* 'hot' (*HM* 110), *rubbit* 'robbed' (*HM* 53) and *simmer* 'summer' (*An* 315) represent much the same sound as an Englishman would expect them to but *sangs* 'songs' (*Wa* 288) is deceptive. Scots does not have the [a] sound which *a* usually represents in English, as in *sang* the past tense of *sing*. The sound is nearer to that in English *father* but shorter: [ɑ].

The long vowels are more complicated. When, by a sound change, the spelling *ai*, which had represented a separate diphthong in Middle English, came to have the same sound as the spelling *a* used for a long vowel, a new way of representing the length of the vowel came into being. In Middle Scots this convention was applied to *e*, *u* and *o* as well so that a following *i* or *y* became a standard indication of a long vowel. Thus Scots *moyn* had the same vowel sound as English *mone* 'moon'. The combination *ai* is of course familiar in English though its value is slightly different; in Standard English *ai* is the diphthong [ei], in Scots it is the single vowel [e:]. The Scots form of *whole* can thus be spelt *haill* (RR 83) or *hale* (CC 583). However in English *ei* is much less common and *ui* rare. (*Oi*, as a way of indicating that an *o* was to be pronounced long, had by Scott's time dropped out of use in Scots.) In the relatively few words it appears in English *ei* generally represents [i:] as in *receive*. So too in Scots *neist* 'next' (RR 212), *reik* 'a trick' (RR 361) and *reive* 'plunder' (RR 356). For the same sound Scots also uses *ie* and, like English, *ee* and many words alternate between these three spellings: *remeed* (RR 197) and *remeid* (FN 28); *speel* 'climb' (*An* 91) and *spiel* (HM 309); *skeily* 'skilled' (OM 491) and *skeely* (HM 414). In Standard English *ie*, when found in a single syllable word ending in the vowel, always represents [ai] as in *pie* and *die*. This also applies where such words are compounded as in *piecrust*. As a result *Hieland* (RR 380) might puzzle an English reader as being an unnecessary alternative to *Highland*. In fact by Scottish rules it represents the pronunciation [hi:land]. The *ee* spelling is the normal one with those Scots words which retain a Romance [i:] not found in English, for instance *ceeveleesed* (*Re* 552) and *preceese* (*Wa* 286). It is interesting to note that the spelling used for such words is one shared with English so that the phonetic value is unambiguous. Perhaps Scott wanted to make sure his audience would recognize a well-known feature of Scottish speech – its elimination is one of the first of Walker's 'Rules to be observed by the Natives of Scotland for attaining a just Pronunciation of English' (*A Critical Pronouncing Dictionary*, p. 9).

The few occurrences in Standard English of *ui* in words like *guide* and *build* are no help in recognizing the sound represented by Scots *ui*. It indicates, as we have seen, either [y] or [i] in words like *bluid* (*Wa* 336), [y] or [ø] in words like *muir* (OM 139), [ju] or [jʌ] in words like *story-buick* (*An* 502). A common alternative is *u-e* as in *blude* (RR 353) and *buke* (*An* 355) and, for the [ju] or [jʌ] sound, *eu* as in *heuck* 'hook' (*Re* 302). Occasionally the [y] sound was represented in eighteenth-century Scots by *oo*. This gave rise to the spelling *loot* for *luit*, the past tense of *lat* 'let'. The currency of this spelling, used by Scott (*HM* 630), had given rise to the unhistorical pronunciation [lu:t]. On the other hand *aboon* (*HM* 415; *Wa* 274) probably arises from an earlier variant form in *ū* existing alongside the *ō* form which would give rise to the more common form and spelling *abune* (*An* 186).

The traditional Scots spelling of [u:] is *ou*. Scott much prefers this to the English alternative *oo* which was increasingly used in the nineteenth century for this sound because *ou* to non-Scots reads as [au]. For Stevenson too the historical associations of the *ou* spelling were too great for him to happily replace it with *oo*. He explains his feelings in the 'Note' to Book II of *Underwoods*:

> the Scots tongue has an orthography of its own, lacking neither 'authority nor author'. Yet the temptation is great to lend a little guidance to the bewildered Englishman. Some simple phonetic artifice might defend your verses from barbarous mishandling, and yet not injure any vested interest. So it seems at first: but there are rocks ahead. Thus, if I wish the diphthong *ou* to have its proper value, I may write *oor* instead of *our*: many have done so and lived, and the pillars of the universe remained unshaken. But if I did so, and came presently to *doun*, which is the classical Scots spelling of the English *down*, I should begin to feel uneasy; and if I went a little farther, and came to a classical Scots word, like *stour* or *dour* or *clour*, I should know precisely where I was – that is to say, that I was out of sight of land on those high seas of spelling reform in which so many strong swimmers have toiled vainly. To some the situation is exhilarating; as for me, I give one bubbling cry and sink. The compromise at which I have arrived is indefensible, and I have no thought of trying to defend it. As I have stuck for the most part to the proper spelling, I append a table of some common vowel sounds which no one need consult; and just to prove that I belong to my age and have in me the stuff of a reformer, I have used modification marks throughout (*Works*, New York, 1921–23, VIII 152–3).

The difficulty is that while *ou* can be substituted for *ow* in a number of words – *doun* (*RR* 351), *toun* (*Wa* 74), *tour* 'tower' (*HM* 579) – which at least makes it clear there is a difference from English (though what difference is not so clear) there is no substitute then available where the English spelling is also *ou*. *Oo* may be used but Scott did not like it. Thus spellings like *hoose* (*HM* 611) and *aboot* (*RR* 83) in words which already have *ou* are rare, while spellings like *doun* and *toun* in words which have *ow* in English are common. The use of *dooted* 'doubted' in *Redgauntlet* is conditioned by Darsie/Scott's desire to make a special point of the pronunciation: 'it might be *dooted*, as our old Professor used to say, whether the Justice was anything more than an ass' (*Re* 288). Rarest of all is the substitution of *oo* for *ow* which Scott nevertheless resorted to in *poorful* 'powerful' (*HM* 117) to avoid confusion with the verb *pour*. *Doon* (*Wa* 73) as an alternative to *doun* is very unusual for Scott.

On the whole then we may say that, with Scott's spelling, phonetic reproduction is his least interest. Occasionally he uses English spellings like *oo* or prefers spellings shared by Scots and English like *ee* which make the phonetic value clear but generally he is more influenced by the two other aims, to indicate the relationship with English and to use the Old Scots spelling. The resultant mixture is a nice reflection of Scott's mixed feelings about Scottish versus British nationalism. On the one hand he is eager to preserve the traditions (including the spelling) of the Old Scottish national literary language even though the effect may be to make the pronunciation very unclear to English readers; yet at the same time he strives so hard to accommodate the audience of Scotland's 'sister-kingdom' that many of the words in any passage of his Scots are given the spelling of their English cognates. The Scottish nationalist and the British nationalist exist side by side.

A further note needs to be added. To judge by the work of G. A. M. Wood on *Redgauntlet* ('Scott's Continuing Revision: The Printed Texts of *Redgauntlet*', *Bibliotheck*, VI (1971–73), 121–198) and my own collation of a number of passages in *The Heart of Midlothian* the conventions of spelling were varied considerably in certain particulars between the first and Collected editions. Especially, a number of apostrophes were regularly removed where the apostrophe represents a *v* in the corresponding English word. *De'il* regularly changes to *deil*, *gi'e* to *gie*, *gi'en* to *gien* and *lo'e* to *loe*. A few cases were missed, leaving the occasional spellings already noted like *lo'es* (*OM* 392). In less common words the change was less thoroughly carried out – *ha'rst* (*Re* 1st edn II 140) was changed to *hairst* (*Re* 302)* in *Redgauntlet* but *ha'arst* remains in *Old Mortality* (*OM* 447). The apostrophe

---

* References are here given to the Border edition but the spellings here mentioned are identical with those in the Collected Edition.

is also generally removed in *an'* 'if' and *awa'* and in *kenn'd*, which usually becomes *kend*. Yet we may also find the retention of *kenn'd* in, for example, *Guy Mannering* (*GM* 565). The inconsistency of Scott's own spelling is reflected in the fact that in two cases in *Wandering Willie's Tale* this change to *kend* represents a return to the original manuscript spelling (*Re* 165, twice) while in another the manuscript had the third variant *ken'd* (*Re* 151). A different kind of change is the replacement of the Scottish termination *-ie* with the English equivalent *-y*. This particularly affects the word *bonny* which is usually *bonnie* in the first editions although it does occur as *bonny* in at least one case, in the first edition of *The Heart of Midlothian* (II 94). On the other hand even in the Collected Edition we find an alternation between *hinny* (*An* 5, *OM* 40), *hinnie* (*OM* 90, *HM* 243), and even *hinney* (*GM* 208), and, contrary to the usual trend, the first edition's *hinny* was at least once changed to *hinnie* (*Re* 192). The *-ie* spellings may have been removed because they looked archaic; certainly in other cases old-fashioned spellings are replaced by newer ones: *chuse* becomes *choose* and *burthen* and *murther* become *burden* and *murder*. One rather puzzling change is that, while in *The Heart of Midlothian Scots* is often changed to *Scotch*, yet in *Redgauntlet Scotch* itself is more than once changed to *Scottish*. The treatment of *frith* or *firth* meaning 'an estuary' is also inconsistent and interesting. The various editions all hesitate between the two forms, the final result being that both *firth* (RR 351) and *frith* (*An* 1, *HM* 617, 731, *Re* 414) are found in the Collected Edition. Wood's work on the text of *Redgauntlet* allows us to see that this confusion began right from the first handling of Scott's manuscript. Twice Scott himself wrote *firth*; once the first edition retained it and once, only a few pages later on, changed it to *frith*. The Collected Edition here achieves uniformity; it changes the first case as well to *frith*. Curiously the Border Edition keeps *this* change but reverts to the original manuscript spelling in the second case.

The situation is thus:

MS	1st edn	Collected edn	Border edn
firth	firth (II 311)	frith (XXXVI 132)	frith (Re 414)
firth	frith (II 320)	frith (XXXVI 139)	firth (Re 420)

This attempt at regularization extended to *The Heart of Midlothian* as well, where the first edition's *firth* (IV 93) is changed to *frith*

(*HM* 617) while *frith*, where it is used in the first edition (IV 291, 349) is retained (*HM* 731, 764). Both *frith* and *firth* had been in Standard English since the seventeenth century but the quotations in the *OED* (*firth* sb², *frith* sb³) suggest that *frith* (now less common in Standard English) was in the seventeenth and eighteenth centuries the more likely choice in non-Scottish contexts. Perhaps therefore, Scott, or his publisher, saw *frith* as English and *firth* as Scottish. If so, this may have been an influence on him since many of the uses of *frith* are in narrative where Scott is less likely to use Scottish forms.

How far all these changes were Scott's responsibility is hard to say – the interleaved copy of his works, on which he made the corrections for the Collected Edition text and which would make clear who was responsible for what, was last heard of in 1939 and its whereabouts are now unknown. Perhaps the regular changes were the printer's responsibility and some at least of the changes to more unusual words, Scott's responsibility. Whoever was responsible, the main change is a desirable one – the loss of a number of apostrophe spellings.

SCOTTISH SENSES OF WORDS ALSO IN STANDARD ENGLISH

Differences in pronunciation are not the only differences between words common to Scots and English. There are also many differences of usage and meaning. Sometimes Scottish usage varies only very slightly from English. For example in English one would certainly talk of 'putting on clothes' but would not use the verbal phrase intransitively and it would be impossible to say as Madge Wildfire does that 'ane maybe is a thought bonnier and better put-on than their neighbours' (*HM* 449) where *put-on* means 'dressed'. In other cases there has been a more radical development in Scots where a word has come to be used as a different part of speech. For a verb used as a noun we may cite the example of *vex* which in Scots means 'an annoyance, a vexation' (*SRW* 36, *GM* 352, *OM* 488); according to both the *OED* and the *SND* Scott is the first to record this usage. Meg Dodd's adjectival use of *woe/wae* in speaking of her 'wae and bitter heart' (*SRW* 215) is paralleled in earlier English but by Scott's time was archaic or dialectal; so too with the noun *mettle* as an adjective: 'That's a mettle beast of yours' (*Re* 163; also *RR* 489,

HM 473). On the other hand such usages as 'this is gey like a place for them' (*An* 277) and 'the plaids were gay canny' (*Wa* 535) do not appear and have never appeared in Standard English where *gay* does not function as an adverb. In Scots, however, it can mean, as here, 'rather, very, pretty'. This is probably a development from distinctively Scottish adjectival senses of *gay* where it has a vaguer sense than English and can mean, when referring to quantity, 'considerable' or 'large':

> Kippletringan was distant at first 'a gey bit', then the 'gey bit' was more accurately described as 'ablins three mile', then the 'three mile' diminished into 'like a mile and a bittock', then extended themselves into 'four mile or thereawa' (*GM* 2-3).

All of which is to say, as Guy Mannering's last informant told him 'It was a weary lang gate yet to Kippletringan' (*GM* 3). The other element in the initial assessment of distance, *bit*, is also often used in Scots quite differently to the way it is used in English. As well as Scottish senses parallel to the sense of English *bite* 'a mouthful' giving rise to proverbial phrases like *the bit and the buffet* (*BL* 280) – i.e. 'food and blows', which is what the hanger-on Craigengelt can expect from his patron Bucklaw – and *bit and sup* 'food and drink' (*BL* 376), the English senses appear but with different grammatical usages. The English use of *bit* in deprecatory phrases like 'the man's a bit of a fool' can be found in Scots but with the additional non-English use in the plural as in 'three bits of English birkies' (*BL* 282), the force of which is hard to convey in English. (A *birkie* (*FN* 620, *HM* 250, *Re* 200) is a smart fellow.) Moreover Scots has developed a quasi-adjectival use of *bit* from the omission of *of* and we find 'this bit job' (*RR* 194), 'my puir bit doggie' (*HM* 453), 'a bit chack of dinner' (*Re* 128) and 'a bit book or maybe a bit letter' (*OM* 91).

The meaning of a word can be extended by redefining its boundaries. English usage confines the term *mittens* to the kind of gloves which have either no special parts for each finger or a special part for the thumb only. In Scots *mittens* can be applied to any kind of glove. As it happens Scott's note of explanation in *The Heart of Midlothian* does not make this clear; he merely says: 'a kind of worsted glove used by the lower classes' (*HM* 313n). Standard English has extended the word *silver* to cover firstly money made of silver and, more recently, money made of the various alloys used to imitate silver. In Scots the extension was even greater: *siller* came to mean any kind of money (*RR* 276, *OM* 40, *Re* 160). When Effie Deans, now Lady Staunton, meets, but does not recognize, her long-lost child their conversation makes this general meaning very clear, since he calls gold coins by implication 'siller':

> More might have passed, but Lady Staunton stepped between them with her purse in her hand, and, taking out a guinea, of which it contained several, visible through the net-work, as well as some silver in the opposite end, offered it the caird.
> 'The white siller, lady – the white siller,' said the young savage, to whom the value of gold was probably unknown.
> Lady Staunton poured what silver she had into his hand, and the juvenile savage snatched it greedily (*HM* 737).

Another way of spreading the application of a word is by its transference to something associated with the thing it denotes. For example the word *hairst*, a form of the word found in Standard English as *harvest*, is applied to a job taken during the harvest (*Re* 302). A snack or, frequently, a drink of strong spirits taken in the mid-morning – 'a matutinal dram' as Scott defines it (*Wa* 405) – has by association itself come to be called a *morning* (*Wa* 162, 405, *RR* 252). Perhaps a desire for a euphemism aided this development – certainly a euphemism suits the lips of Andrew Fairservice, who maintained 'I . . . never could find the way unless I had taen my morning' (*RR* 252). *Wame*, the Scottish cognate of English *womb*, has, by that vagueness about anatomy which often characterizes ordinary speech, come in Scotland to be used for the stomach (*An* 272). From that point it has developed a figurative sense identifying it with the seat of a man's emotions (*RR* 82), as has happened to so many anatomical terms: *belly, head, heart, guts, stomach*. In another figurative development it comes to mean 'hollow, cavity': 'in the wame of a wave' (*An* 90).

Verbs too have extended their meaning. From the sense 'arrange in groups, classify' the verb *sort* easily came to mean in Scots 'to tidy' (*OM* 539). Perhaps the meaning of 'scold, punish' (*Mo* 37) is a figurative extension of this sense. It is also applied to looking after somebody's needs (*BL* 363) or, more particularly, to feeding an animal (*OM* 493). Scots further retains the obsolete sense 'choose' (*HM* 318).

Scottish Sounds, Spelling and Vocabulary

Words have as well developed specific senses unknown to English. In Scots *like* can mean specifically 'love' as when Jeanie rejects Dumbiedikes's marriage proposal with 'I like another man better than you, and I canna marry ye' (*HM* 388). *Ride* can have the particular sense 'go out on a raid' which we find in the 'popular saying' quoted by Scott in *The Minstrelsy of the Scottish Border*: 'Elliotts and Armstrongs ride thieves all' (*Minstrelsy*, 1802, I 36). Derivatives carry this same meaning: *riding* (*Re* 162) is 'going on raids', *the riding days* (*Re* 152) is the period of the Border wars and raids, and *riders* (*LLM* IV xi, *Letters* I 330) are those who go out on such raids, or, to use another of Scott's words for them, *reivers*, (*RR* 356, *Wa* 131).

WORDS OBSOLETE IN STANDARD ENGLISH

Different parts of the vocabulary of Old English have survived in the different English dialects. Scots, like any other dialect, preserves a number of words not found in Standard English. While, on the whole, such survivals may be a matter of accident, occasionally we can suggest an explanation. Perhaps the Old English *fæge* 'fated to die' disappeared from Standard English because it represents the language of the educated and presumably less superstitious. Certainly the word fits in well with folk beliefs or superstitions in Scotland, where it appears in the forms *fey* and *fie*. A belief that those who are about to die show the fact in their behaviour influences its meaning in Scots. Scott's own explanations make this clear:

> 'I think,' said the old gardener . . . , 'the gauger's *fie*,' – by which word the common people express those violent spirits which they think a presage of death (*GM* 78).

> His step was irregular, his voice hollow and broken, his countenance pale, his eyes staring and wild, his speech imperfect and confused, and his whole appearance so disordered, that many remarked he seemed to be *fey*, a Scottish expression, meaning the state of those who are driven on to their impending fate by the strong impulse of some irresistible necessity (*HM* 40).

In *The Fair Maid of Perth* Oliver Proudfute who will soon after be mistaken for Henry Smith and murdered by Bonthron – a startling and unexpected event to overtake the centre of the novel's comic relief – comes on Fastern's E'en (Shrovetide) to the house of Simon Glover:

> 'Canst thou not be serious for a moment, neighbour Proudfute?' said the Glover. 'I want a word of conversation with you.'
> 'Serious?' answered his visitor. 'Why, I have been serious all this day – I can hardly open my mouth, but something comes out about death, a burial, or suchlike – the most serious subjects that I wot of.'
> 'St John, man!' said the Glover, 'art thou fey?' (*FM* 297).

With a culture embodying such folk beliefs in fate it is very appropriate that the Old English word *wyrd*, used so often in Anglo-Saxon poetry to express the idea of the predestined order of things, should have survived in Scotland. It is found in the phrase *dree one's weird* 'suffer one's fate' which also preserves another English word (*drēogan* 'suffer, endure') which, like *wyrd*, disappeared from Standard English after the Middle Ages. Meg Merrilies, a great believer in fate who only on the next page dies with the words 'I kenn'd it would be this way' (*GM* 565), uses the phrase in talking of Harry Bertram: 'did I not say he would come back when he had dree'd his weird in foreign land till his twenty-first year?' (*GM* 564). It also appears in *The Fair Maid* (*FM* 225) and the variant 'he drees the doom he ettled for me' in *Rob Roy* (*RR* 491–2). (For *dree* see also *An* 111 and *LLM* II v – there spelt *drie* – and for *weird* see also *GM* 391.)

Other Old English words surviving in Scots include the three important verbs *dow* 'be able' (*OE dugan*; *GM* 392, *An* 315, *HM* 337, *OM* 491, *SRW* 101, *RR* 396), *gang* 'to go' (*OE gangan*; *HM* 185, *GM* 2, *OM* 40) and *kythe* 'to reveal' (*OE cȳðan*; *RR* 503, *FN* 86) though *kythe* in Scots developed the further sense 'appear, seem' (*HM* 167). Amongst nouns there are *lave* 'the remainder' (*OE lāf*; *An* 586, *RR* 79, *OM* 376) and *snood* (*OE snōd*; *Wa* 160, *Mo* 155). In Scott can be found *kinrick* (*RR* 197), the descendant of Old English *cyningrice* 'kingdom', containing an element which Standard English has only in the obsolescent *bishopric*. For some reason English has lost the original word *bear* found still in Scots (*Mo* 3) and replaced it by *barley*, in origin apparently an adjectival derivative. Scots distinguishes between *bear* 'or bigg, a coarse kind of barley' (*Mo* 3n) – *bigg* is from Old Norse – and *barley* which is superior in quality but less hardy. Butler's husbandry is little advanced when he 'read Virgil's "Georgics" till he did not know bear from barley' (*HM* 117).

Gloaming 'twilight' (*Wa* 641, *An* 45, *Journal*, 4 May 1826) provides a clear example of the inadequacy of written texts as a record of the language. It is obviously the same word as Old English *glomung* yet no record of its use has been found in written texts between Old English and the fifteenth century. Due possibly to the poetic suggestiveness of its similarity to *glow*, it has since the nineteenth century re-entered English literary use.

In some cases the Old English word has survived but changed its meaning. In Old English *gedæfte* meant 'meek' but in Middle English its meaning degenerated into 'stupid, foolish'. This sense survives in Scots *daft* (*HM* 181, *BD* 330), and Nicol Jarvie uses it when he admits that 'the Hieland blude o' me warms at thae daft tales' (*RR* 361). In the same speech, moreover, he uses the word in two other closely related and exclusively Scottish senses: 'frivolous, giddy' – 'many a daft reik [trick] he has played' (also *RR* 282, *An* 271) – and 'merry and frivolous' in the phrase *the Daft Days* used of the Christmas Season: 'sic as folks tell ower at a winter-ingle in the daft days'. The English now use *daft* to mean 'foolish' but they have not accepted the word in its strongest Scottish sense, 'mad, insane' (*OM* 87, *Re* 117). The original meaning of Old English *byldu* has been similarly lost. In Old English the word, related to our *bold*, means 'boldness' but since boldness may provide protection and shelter the meaning came to be that. In Scots it survives in the form *bield* and is used of 'a place of shelter' (*GM* 72, *An* 44). The verb shows a similar development of meaning: 'fed, clad and bielded me' (*FM* 223). In *sweer* (*An* 187) or *swear* (*LM* 42) meaning 'reluctant' the development is from the Old English sense 'lazy'. One of the more interesting changes of meaning comes in *haugh* 'level ground on the bank of a river' (*Wa* 69, *Re* 42) or simply 'level plain' (*OM* 19). The Old English *h(e)alh* means 'a corner' and the same meaning attaches to its Middle English derivative *hale*. The *OED* suggests that the Scottish sense may have developed from the meandering of a northern stream in a narrow valley forming triangles or 'corners' of level alluvial soil on each side of the stream.

Standard English has of course also deviated from Old English. However in some cases the original meaning, lost in Standard English, has remained in Scots. The basic meaning of Old English *tūn* is enclosure. From here it naturally develops to cover an enclosed farmyard and its buildings and then the farm homestead; from being applied to the group of buildings on a farm it is applied to a group of independent buildings, a hamlet, and then to a larger unit the modern 'town'. Standard English retains only the end-product of this line of development but Scots still uses the word to describe a farm especially its buildings (*Wa* 74, *GM* 211) and, like Australian English in which the words *village* and *hamlet* are unknown, retains the word to describe a small group of houses (*Mo* 3). Scots also has its own meaning for the derivative *township*, as Scott explains: 'the land belonging to the various families by whom the Town [i.e. hamlet] was inhabited, was called the Township' (*Mo* 3).

In two cases, relevant to us here, Southern English discarded Old English terms and then reformed them later. Present-day English *day's work* is a new combination of the elements making up Old English *dægweorc*. Scots, unlike Standard English, retained the earlier creation as *dawerk*, *daurk*, *daurg*, *darg* which appears with a number of spellings in Scott: *darg* (*HM* 415), *daurg* (*Re* 302) and *dargue* (*FM* 445). The early Modern English verb *meat* meaning 'to feed' was formed from the noun to fill the place of Old English *metian* which was by then obsolete in all forms of English. As a verb *meat* disappeared again in the eighteenth century except in dialects, including Scots. Scott's use of the word in *The Monastery* (*Mo* 164) is thus both dialectal and period.

Certain of the Scots words in the novels were not entire strangers to the literary English of the period. While obsolescent, they were not obsolete, and survived as poetic words or in certain limited contexts. By 1700 the Old English verb *bide* had passed out of normal use in English. For the eighteenth century the *OED* cites only Coleridge's *Rime of the Ancient Mariner* and Thomson's *Castle of Indolence* both avowedly archaic in their diction. In the nineteenth century the word seems to have returned to more general literary currency, perhaps aided by Scott's use of it. In Scots the word remained colloquial and it figures in Scott's dialogue (*An* 184, *RR* 286). *Trow* 'believe' had become obsolete in literary English by the eighteenth century except in the catch-phrase *I trow* appended parenthetically to a sentence. Even this usage was perhaps an archaism; it too appears in *The Ancient Mariner*. Again the verb was normal colloquial Scots, as is clear from its frequent appearance in the novels (*An* 286, *HM* 426, *RR* 349, *BL* 187). Judging by the *OED* the old English verb *reave* 'to steal, plunder, take away, deprive' had almost disappeared from literary English except in the archaic use of the participle *reft* such as we find in Scott's own poetry:

> A wild resemblance we can trace,
> Though reft of every softer grace (*BT* III Introd. i).

Scottish usage retained all parts of the verb, usually spelt *reive* (*RR* 356), as well as the derivative adjective *reiving* (*RR* 310, *OM* 39, *FM* 53) and noun *reiver* 'robber, bandit' (*Wa* 131, *RR* 356). Scott's fondness for *reiver* revived it as a Standard English word but it seems to have fallen out of use again. The survival of *wife* in the original broader sense of 'woman' (*GM* 391, *An* 353, *Re* 563) is of a different kind. From probably the seventeenth century it has been restricted to dialect except in describing a woman selling some commodity, like Keats's *gingerbread wife* ('Dawlish Fair', l.3). In Scots *wife* often carries a somewhat disparaging tone (e.g. *GM* 391).

Passing to foreign loan words, the earliest sense of *danger* in English is 'power of a lord or master' especially 'power to harm'. Yet again Scots preserves the root sense obsolete in English since the seventeenth century. In 'Wandering Willie's Tale' (*Re* 154) the word may be slightly old-fashioned – this sense seems to be fairly rare in Modern Scots – and this may also be the case in *The Pirate* (*Pi* 161). In *The Betrothed* with its twelfth-century setting, it is clearly an archaism recalling Middle English usage (*Be* 412). Perhaps different habits of worship or Presbyterian conservatism explain the Scottish survival of the older meanings of *exercise*: 'family worship' (*HM* 137, 212, *Re* 397) and 'an expounding of the Scripture'. The latter sense is represented in Scott by the verb: 'the unhappy lass who danced off the head of John the Baptist, upon which chapter I will exercise this night for your further instruction' (*HM* 141). Noun and verb became obsolete in English at the end of the seventeenth century. From the early sixteenth century we find *jealous* used in English to mean 'suspicious' but the latest *OED* example for an English text is dated 1755 (*OED jealous* 5). In Scots the usage continued throughout the nineteenth century and appears in Scott (*GM* 379, *Re* 62). A related sense 'suspiciously vigilant' perhaps still survives in English in the phrase 'to keep a jealous eye on someone' although it is probably now often intended and taken as meaning 'envious'. English also borrowed from the French the equivalent verb *jalouse* 'suspect' and this too is found in Scott (*An* 194, *OM* 39).

Words as well as senses of words have followed this pattern. The Old Norse loan *ware* 'to spend' is unknown in literary English by Scott's time but has flourished in Scots up to the present day. Its frequency in Scott suggests full life; it appears even in the *Journal* amongst its relatively infrequent Scoticisms (*Journal*, 8 June 1826, *An* 546, *HM* 227, *BL* 383, *BD* 437, *CC* 422). *Mense*, a word of wide meaning: 'dignity, respect, recompense, common sense, tact', and probably in *Rob Roy* identical in meaning with the 'discretion' Andrew Fairservice also claims for the Scots (*RR* 79), is also from Old Norse. *Mense* is a modification of the Middle English form *mensk* from Old Norse *mennska* 'humanity, kindness' which is found only in Middle English. The same goes for the derivative *menskful* which readers of *Sir Gawain and the Green Knight* will remember (l.555) and which appears in Scots as *menseful* (*Mo* 389, *Pi* 375), more phonetically spelt *mensefu'* (*HM* 435, *OM* 79).

From French, as Scott himself suspected (*RR* 436n), English took *gabare* 'barge' found in Scots as *gabbart* (*RR* 436, *FM* 302), but only sixteenth- and seventeenth-century English texts use the word whereas it has survived in Scotland to the twentieth century meaning 'a kind of lighter used in the Clyde' (*RR* 436n). *Spence* 'a pantry' (*Wa* 152, *Mo* 16) is an aphetic form of the Middle English borrowing of French *dispense*. It becomes dialectal in England in the eighteenth century but in Scots survives and adds another sense, as Scott describes, in 'a sort of interior apartment in which the family ate their meals in the summer season' (*Mo* 36). *Douce* occurs in English from the Middle Ages until the early seventeenth century but has remained firmly entrenched in Scots and is now thought of as a wholly Scots word. It is, of course, a borrowing from French *doux* (feminine, *douce*) 'sweet' but in Scotland has developed the meaning 'sober, respectable, sedate, quiet' (*GM* 292, *An* 183, *RR* 357, *HM* 386, *OM* 38). Other French loans which are dialectal or archaic in England from the eighteenth century are *tass* 'cup, goblet' (*GM* 21, *RR* 252, *Re* 156) and *ratton* or *rotten* 'a rat' (*GM* 197).

To list all of these words lost in English and retained in Scots is to give the impression of a conservative dialect. The impression may not be correct. It seems likely that Scots lost words which English retained – unfortunately a writer like Scott whose Scots

Scottish Sounds, Spelling and Vocabulary

is regularly intermixed with English expressions provides no guide on this score. Moreover it is always harder to prove a word was not in use than that it was. Perhaps Scots was conservative, a dialect beginning to die and lose its power of independent creation and rejection of words: we cannot say. There is at least some evidence to the contrary in the appearance of new senses of words like *spence* and the independent borrowing of foreign words not found in English like *rokelay*. Despite some conservative elements, Scots in the early nineteenth century still appears to some extent as a living language, dynamically open to change.

NEW WORDS CREATED IN SCOTS

Two of the simplest and most productive ways of creating new words in the various forms of English have been by combinations and by the addition of suitable affixes. Scots is no exception. Often the elements in such combinations are found in Standard English but the particular combination is not. This is the case with *burn-the-wind* 'an old cant name for blacksmith' (*FM* 38), *change-house* 'a small inn' (*Wa* 87, *FN* 460), *cow-feeder* 'a dairy-farmer' (*HM* 129), *ground officer* 'manager of an estate' (*An* 151, *GM* 63; *grund-officer* (*Re* 154)), *gutter-blood* corresponding to English *gutter-snipe* (*HM* 270) but with the extra meaning of 'a native of a particular town' (*FN* 119), *kill-cow* 'swashbuckler' (*RR* 146) and *single house* 'a house "having only one room occupying its whole depth from back to front"' (*HM* 377). When Ellen's song in *The Lady of the Lake* contains the lines

> Weird women we! by dale and down
> We dwell, afar from tower and town.
> We stem the flood, we ride the blast,
> On wandering knights our spells we cast (*LL* I xxx)

we naturally take *weird women* as made up of the familiar adjective *weird* and *women*. In fact *weird* here is a use of the noun *weird* 'fate' (*GM* 391, 564) in combination with *woman* to mean 'fortune-teller, witch'. Scottish retained the Old English *wyrd* but it was lost in Southern English so that when Holinshed in his story of Macbeth picked up the phrase *weird sisters* meaning 'the Fates' from Wyntoun and Shakespeare followed him, Englishmen supplied a meaning for *weird* which seemed to fit the circumstances of Macbeth's encounter. With the help especially of

Shelley, *weird* came into present-day English meaning 'strange' or 'uncanny'. At other times the familiarity of the elements is obscured by the Scottish form of one or more of them: the first element in both *laigh-house* (HM 400) and *laigh-shop* (*An* 1) corresponds to English *low*. Even if he did recognize this the non-Scott would probably need the explanations which Scott offers, 'inferior tenement' (HM 400) and 'cellar' (*An* 1). Scott is also helpful with the Scots phrase *Borrowing Days* (HM 415) providing the note: 'The last three days of March, old style, are called the Borrowing Days; for as they are remarked to be unusually stormy, it is feigned that March had borrowed them from April, to extend the sphere of his rougher sway. The rhyme on the subject is quoted in Leyden's edition of the Complaynt of Scotland.' The rhyme in question was supplied for the reader in the 1833 Glossary:

> March borrowed frae Aprile
> Three days, an' they were ill:
> The first o' them was wind and weet,
> The second o' them was snaw and sleet,
> The third o' them was sic a freeze,
> That the birds' legs stack to the trees.

We often think of regional varieties of English as being made up of everyday terms and forget that, especially as the language of all English-speaking countries draws closer together, many of the principal differences are in words which are far from being household ones, such as those used to describe the machinery of government and the law. One simple example is Scotland's separate legal system. Its special institutions are given names made up of elements found in English but not so combined. Members of the supreme civil court make up the *College of Justice* (*Re* 6); formally some of them are known as *Lords of Council and Session*, less formally *Lords of Session* (HM 57) and even less formally, in a now obsolete phrase, *Lords of Seat* (HM 57n). Phrases of this kind make up much of the distinctive regional language of countries like Australia and New Zealand where the difference in everyday vocabulary is more limited.

Naturally other compounds make use of Scottish elements. The Scottish *claik-goose* or *clack-goose* (HM 653) corresponds exactly to English *barnacle-goose*. *Claik* means 'a barnacle' and in both countries it was believed this kind of wild goose was hatched from barnacles. Both *back-spaul* 'the back part of the shoulder' (*Pi* 118) and *spule-blade* 'shoulder-blade' (*Re* 165) include one element known in English – the other element is *spaul* which Scots borrowed from French *espaule* (Modern French *épaule*). *Hand-waled* 'hand-picked' (*HM* 151) includes the Old Norse borrowing *wale*. *Wean* 'child' (*HM* 58, *RR* 81, *HM* 238) in written form does not at first look like a compound but is actually a reduced form, of *wee* and *ane* 'small one' and, as the *SND* notes, outside Mid Scots where it is common, *wean* 'is still thought of as two distinct words'.

Phrasal compounds are common and expressive: 'to blaw in one's lug' (*OM* 60, *Re* 191), that is 'to blow in one's ear', means 'to flatter' and so a flatterer is a *blaw-in-my-lug* (*SRW* 24). The *wuddy* is a hangman's noose; a rogue is described as *cheat-the-wuddy* (*RR* 310) although Scott sometimes uses the anglicized *cheat-the-gallows* (*HM* 677). There is also a jocular reference to the time 'when ye played Cheat-the-woodie' (*Re* 370). A wild and unreliable person is described as *loup-the-dike* 'leap the wall' (*Re* 615) or *loup-the-tether* 'escape the tether' (*Re* 557). *Loup-the-dike* provides a suggestive surname for a minor character in *The Bride of Lammermoor*. The corresponding nouns *dike-louper* (*FN* 579) and *fence-louper* (*FN* 544) express a stronger condemnation when used in Scott; they denote 'a person of loose sexual morals'. *Fence-louper* is very unjustly applied to Margaret Ramsay by the harsh-tongued Sir Mungo (*FN* 544) and *dike-louper* very deservedly applied to Buckingham by King James (*FN* 579). (The *SND* defines the meaning of *fence-louper* here as 'a jumper of fences, a trespasser' (*SND lowp* v 1) but a meaning similar to the one it gives to *dike-louper* (*SND dyke* n 1) seems, in view of the rest of what Sir Mungo says, more likely on this occasion.) *Rin-there-out* (*HM* 68, *Wa* 509) and *gang-there-out* (*RR* 311, *GM* 5) correspond roughly to English *gadabout*, *rin* being the Scots form of *run*, but they are rather stronger in tone, meaning usually 'vagabond', whether as a noun or as an adjective. Our picture of the character of Jenny Rinthcrout in *The Antiquary* is thus supplemented by her name. Incidentally Scott provides the first *OED* citation for *gadabout* (*Letters* IV 420). This combination of verb and adverb to provide a noun or adjective, like *gadabout*, naturally appears also in Scots. In *ca'throw* (*HM* 237) or *ca'through* (*An* 328) meaning 'a disturbance' and *gae-down* (*An* 44, *GM* 197) meaning 'a spree, a drinking match' some familiar elements – *call*, *through*, *go* and *down* – are combined to furnish quite new words and meanings.

Several Scottish compounds are the same as English ones but their quite different senses suggest that they were independent creations in Scotland. For example in earlier Scots the verb *upset* does not mean 'overturn' but rather corresponds to English *set up*; the 'upsetting of the mass' (*Ab* 392) means its establishment. This usage is now obsolete, perhaps due to the possible ambiguity, but Scots still has *the upset price* 'the price from which bidding must start at an auction' (*GM* 135) and the adjective *upsetting* meaning, not 'disturbing one's emotional calm', but 'presumptuous' (*RR* 535). *Outcast* had in Scots the meaning 'quarrel' and the associated verb is *cast out*. Jeanie tells her father:

> 'Reuben never sleeps weel . . . when you and he hae had ony bit outcast.'
> 'Nae outcast, Jeanie; God forbid I suld cast out wi' thee, or aught that is dear to thee' (*HM* 689).

This older style of English verb-adverb compound with the adverb prefixed is common in Scots, but not all such verbs are of Scottish creation. For instance the meaning 'intoxicated' for *owerta'en* (*SRW* 16) or *overtaken* is a survival of an obsolete Standard English usage as can be seen from Shakespeare in Polonius's 'There was a' gaming; there o'ertook in's rouse' (*Ham* II i 58). *Uptake* 'understanding' (*OM* 89) is now Standard English – 'he's quick on the uptake' we say, following exactly the sense of Cuddie's comment to his mother: 'Everybody's no sae gleg [keen] at the uptake as ye are yoursell' (*OM* 89). Originally it is a Scottish creation and is included in the 1833 Glossary as being unknown to English readers. The equally familiar *outlay* 'expenditure' (*An* 165) is likewise first found in Scots. But other Scots creations like *outshot* 'a projecting part of a building' (*OM* 493, *Mo* 379), *upgang* 'ascent' (*HM* 426) and *upgive* 'relinquish' (*Letters* II 148) have not been accepted into English.

One area where Scots has been particularly fertile in new words is family relationships. At least two words have been created for grandfather: *luckie-dad* (*HM* 689) and *gudesire* (*Re* 153, *HM* 531, *BD* 399, *BL* 333) anglicized, as often happens in *Waverley*, as *goodsire* (*Wa* 164). A great-grandfather will naturally be a *great-gudesire* (*FN* 640). *Lucky-dad* extends from the use of *Lucky* in addressing an elderly woman, either by itself (*BL* 179) or in conjunction with her Christian name – 'Luckie Elspeth' (*An* 357) – or her surname – 'Luckie Mucklebackit' (*An* 358). *Lucky* is applied especially to a grandmother. Unfortunately, by a careless oversight that was perpetuated even in the revised Collected Edition, *gudesire* appears to the reader of *Redgauntlet* to mean 'father'. Scott at first intended Wandering Willie's story to apply to Willie's father. Then, realizing, as Mary Lascelles suggests ('Scott and the Art of Revision' in *Imagined Worlds*, London, 1968, p. 151), that the time scheme of the generations fitted very badly with the historical events mentioned, Scott decided, in the process of actually writing the tale, to change the protagonist into Willie's grandfather, his 'gudesire'. Typically he left his printer to sort out this minor detail and only changed a few of the incidences of *father* to *gudesire*. The transcriber who prepared the text for the printer failed to correct all appearances of *father* and even though further correction was made at proof stage (see the facsimile page in Mary Lascelles' article for an example) one instance of *father* survives, to the confusion of the readers, in later editions (see *Re* 168).

Gude supplied in Scots the place of English *-in-law* so sister-in-law is *gude-sister* (*OM* 548), daughter-in-law is *gude-daughter* (*An* 522) and mother-in-law is *gudemither* (*An* 356). Of course *gude* cannot carry this meaning in *gudeman* and *gudewife*. These two terms were not originally confined to Scotland but had by Scott's time ceased to be used in Standard English. *Gudeman*, sometimes spelt in the English way as *goodman*, means 'husband' (*HM* 125, *Re* 191, *An* 143, *OM* 487) or 'the head of the household' (*HM* 120, *Wa* 290). It can also be an addressive (*FM* 26). The use of *gudeman* to denote the tenant of a small farm – 'the Goodman (the tenant, that is) of Ballengiech' (*TG* 252) – is an exclusively Scottish usage as is the very similar use of *gudewife* of a mistress of a farm – 'the gudewife o' Bell's-moor' (*OM* 39). The other senses of *gudewife* also correspond to senses of *gudeman*: they are 'wife' (*BL* 183) and 'mistress of a household' (*GM* 218) as well as its use as an addressive (*Re* 145).

From Gaelic the Scots took *oe* (*An* 523, *HM* 58) or *oye* (*Re* 173) for 'grandchild' and from Old and Middle English they retained the word for 'uncle', *eme* (*HM* 182). The Scottish form of English *nephew* is *nevoy* (*Re* 200, *OM* 75, *An* 475), while the childish versions of *mither* 'mother' and *sister* were *minnie* (*HM* 275, *Re* 150, *An* 353) and *tittie* (*HM* 65, *OM* 365). A brother is a *billy* (*BD* 426), a term which can also mean 'fellow' (*FN* 46, *GM* 223).

Words like *minnie* and *tittie* remind us by their endings of the Scottish fondness for diminutives such as Burns has illustrated in relation to his role as poet with his *bardie* and *musie*. Many diminutives are, like *musie* in Burns, nonce-words created for the occasion. Richie Moniplies talks of David Ramsay the clockmaker, 'Watchie Ramsay' as he is called elsewhere (*FN* 545), 'scribbling in his bit bookie' (*FN* 31), and Provost Crosbie had hoped to get 'some bit postie' (*Re* 357) to give his son an income. Others were more permanently established, like Meg Murdockson's *naggie* addressed to her horse (*HM* 427), as well as *lassie* (*FN* 104, *SRW* 36, *HM* 301) and *laddie* (*SRW* 30) which are chiefly Scottish even though *lass* and *lad* are used in England. *Doggie* was perhaps in origin a Scots rather than an English creation – Scott's use of it in *Waverley* slightly predates the *OED*'s earliest citation – and even if it has been accepted into southern usage, it remains there a word to be used to or by children or in addressing a dog itself. English adults would not be likely to use it unselfconsciously in conversation with other adults in the way we find it in Scott (*Wa* 337, *Re* 357).

Other diminutives develop from words unknown in present-day English. *Sunk* 'a seat made of turf' gives rise to *sunkie* 'a little bench' (*GM* 201). James VI's cook considers he would appreciate 'a curn or two of Greek' (*FN* 278; cf *Re* 413) – *curn* is the Scots form of *corn* and means 'grain'. From it come both the diminutive *curney* with the sense in Scott of 'a small group' (*QD* 545) and the adjective *curney* 'grainy': Niel Blane complains that wheat-flour is 'far from being sae hearty or kindly to a Scotchman's stomach as the curney aitmeal is' (*OM* 280). Scott was perhaps aware that *kemp* 'a champion', a word found in Old and Middle English but by his time only lingering in Scottish ballads (*Minstrelsy*, 1802, II 339), was of Germanic origin. Certainly he likes to use it of the northern Germanic peoples writing in his introduction to Burt's *Letters* of 'Viga-Glum and other celebrated Kemps and homicides of the North' (Burt's *Letters*, 1818, I 62) and in *The Pirate* using *kempies* (*Pi* 434), the diminutive of *kemp* or a derivative of the verb *kemp*, to refer to 'Norse champions' as the 1833 Glossary has it. A more complicated example of a diminutive formed in *-ie* is *haddie* 'haddock' (*An* 54) where the *-ock* of *haddock* has been mistaken for the diminutive ending found in, for example, *hillock* and has been replaced by the more common equivalent *-ie*. The *-ock* ending gives us Scots *lassock* (*OM* 60), an alternative to *lassie*, and *bittock* 'a little bit' (*OM* 147, *RR* 246, *GM* 3). *Window* has been changed to *winnock* (*OM* 344) following the same process as that which changed Middle English *warlow* into Scots *warlock* (*BL* 331) but with the difference that *warlock* has become the accepted English form of the word while *winnock* remains confined to Scots. A third diminutive ending is *-et*; *nick-nack* and *pie* 'a magpie' become *nick-nacket* (*Ab* 267) and *pyot* (*SRW* 123) while *biggin* 'a linen cap' (*FM* 331, *Ta* 580), a word now unknown to us but possibly still in use then, gives us *biggonet*, usually found in the plural (*HM* 361, *BL* 183).

The *-ie* ending can also be added to adjectives often making little difference to the meaning: *swankie* means much the same as *swank* 'agile, active-looking'. From this derives the noun *swankie* 'a strapping young fellow' (*Mo* 497). Or it can be added to verbs, as both Scotland and America did with *cook* – the Scottish *cookie* is not however the same as the now familiar American one, being a bun rather than a flat cake very like a biscuit. Other combinations not found in southern English are with the noun *skeel* (*skill*) and the verb *fend*. *Skeely* means 'skilled' (*An* 549, *OM* 491) sometimes specifically in medicine (*SRW* 603) and *fendy* means 'able to fend for oneself' (*Wa* 163). We remember that the unflattering nickname of the hero of *The Fair Maid* was 'the Gow Chrom'. *Gow* (*gobha*) means 'smith', *chrom* (*crom*) 'crooked' or, as here, 'bandy-legged'. The second word was borrowed into Scots and when the suffix *-ie* is added we get a name for 'a cow with crooked horns', *crummie* (*Re* 15) or *crombie* (*Letters* VI 147).

Many of the compounds in Scots are, like many of the diminutives, nonce-words. *Body* is used in Scots to mean 'a human being' or 'a person' in idioms not found in Standard English. It may express sympathy – 'a poor body' (*Wa* 276) – or some degree of contempt – Jeanie 'irreverently termed the landed proprietor' (Dumbiedikes) 'the "body" ' (*HM* 133). This carries over to the freely formed compounds of *body* and another noun. Contempt is manifest in:

that droghling coghling bailie body (*Wa* 387)

the auld doited whig body's daughter (*HM* 433)

that fool-body's debts (*GM* 390)

while sympathy shows in:

> it was an awkward thing for a woman-body (*HM* 143)
>
> these poor rebel bodies (*Re* 372).

Lad is also used in compounds with both feelings possible: Miss Damahoy is not at all sympathetic towards the *writer-lads* and *prentice-lads* who come 'traiking after' her servant-girls (*HM* 359), while Edie Ochiltree probably has mixed feelings, but mainly sympathetic, towards the *captain-lad*, M'Intyre (*An* 272).

The addition of *like* as a suffix to an adjective provides us with further occasional compounds. The *SND* remarks that it corresponds more or less to the English suffix *-ish*; it seems in Scott to be useful in expressing irony or understatement. Peter Peebles in his dissatisfaction with the English legal system exclaims angrily:

> A bonny like justice I am like to get amang ye (*Re* 303)

and Lady Singleside means that it is a *very* odd thing when she asks:

> Is not it an odd like thing that ilka waf carle [every insignificant churl] in the country has a son and heir, and that the house of Ellangowan is without male succession? (*GM* 390–1; the gloss is provided by Scott in a footnote).

No words could be more distinctly Scottish in origin than those based on Scottish place-names. The vigorous dance the *strathspey* (*Wa* 163, *Re* 178, *LL* II xi) may have originated in the town of that name in Moray but whether it did or not the town's name has become attached to it. The *Lochaber axe* (*Wa* 143, *HM* 37) described by Scott as 'an ancient weapon, ... a long pole, namely with an axe at the extremity, and a hook at the back of the hatchet' (*HM* 37) has somehow become associated with the district in the south of Invernesshire. The small Scottish coin called a *bawbee* was originally worth six Scots pennies but its value was later lowered to three Scots pennies. The name is reminiscent of *bauble* which also often signifies something of trifling value but it is probably a shortened form of *Sillebawbe* recalling a sixteenth-century Master of the Mint, Alexander Orrok of Sillebawbe. A less flattering derivative is *Fifish*, which means 'crazy' or 'eccentric'. Apparently their neighbours had a low opinion of the inhabitants of Fife as Bryce Snailsfoot points out in *The Pirate*: 'He will be as wowf as ever his father was ...

very, very Fifish, as the east-country fisher-folk say' (*Pi* 144). *Wowf* has the same meaning as Fifish; in *Redgauntlet*, *Fifish* is offered by Peter Peebles as an alternative to both *daft* and *wowf*:

'Ou, he is just a wud harum-scarum creature, that wad never take to his studies; daft, sir, clean daft.'
'Deft!' said the [English] justice, 'what d'ye mean by deft – eh!'
'Just Fifish . . . wowf – a wee bit by the East Nook or sae.'
(*Re* 304–5).

The reference to the East Nook is merely a further elaboration of *Fifish* since the kingdom of Fife stretches, as Andrew Fairservice grandly informs Frank, 'frae Culross to the East Nuik' (*RR* 196). Who the Andrea Ferrara was who gave his name to fine Scottish broad-swords is a mystery. Tradition alone tells anything about him and that tradition is summarized by Scott himself in a note to *Waverley*: 'it is in general believed that Andrea de Ferrara was a Spanish or Italian artificer brought over by James IV. or V. to instruct the Scots in the manufacture of sword blades' (*Wa* Note XXI). The novels exhibit the usual variety of Scott's spelling of unusual words, with the Christian name Italian in *Andrea Ferrara* (*Wa* 374), English in *Andrew Ferrara* (*SRW* 86, *FN* 586, *Wa* 451) and Scottish in *Andra-Ferrara* (*RR* 314) and *Andro Ferrara* (*HM* 361).

Amongst all these words originating from Scotland, Scott's own creations should not be forgotten. They are fairly few in number: his major contribution to the language was in bringing old or dialect words into the literary language, not in creating new ones. He did all the same add a few creations of his own, like *free-lance* and *red-handed*, and amongst them are some to do with Scotland. As far as we can tell it was Scott who first used *clansman* (*LL* II xviii, *FM* 504, *Wa* 212, *CC* 455), a word which has proved useful to later writers. His word for a Highlander, *trewsman* (*LM* 40), has on the other hand not been taken up. It is both less frequent in Scott than *clansman* and less in line with our stereotype picture of the Highlands. The word *kiltman*, had Scott used it, might have had more success. Scott is also the first who is recorded as using the term *bonnet-laird* (*An* 40, *SRW* 9) but this may well be accidental and his note gives no hint of its being a new creation: 'A "bonnet-laird" signifies a petty proprietor, wearing the dress, along with the habits, of a yeoman' (*An* 40n). A bonnet is, in English terms, a cap. It had not always been the distinctive dress of the farmer: a coin of James V was called a *bonnet-piece* (*Mo* 305, *An* 302) because the king was portrayed on it wearing one. Scott was often innovative in the use of *bonnet*; by metonymy he applies it (*FM* 238) and the more specific *blue-bonnet* (*RR* 359, *OM* 43) to a man, or more particularly to a Scotsman, or more particularly still to a Covenanter. *Gang-there-out* and *loup-the-tether*, already mentioned as alternatives to *rin-there-out* and *loup-the-dike* (p. 215) may possibly be Scott's own creations as he provides the earliest *SND* quotations for them and *fence-louper* (*FN* 544) is only found in Scott.

In *hellicat(e)* Scott so far remoulded an earlier word as virtually to form a new one. It is his respelling of *hallockit*, a participal form of the verb *hallock* 'to behave in a crazy, boisterous way', which means 'giddy, flighty, irresponsible, violent, crazy'. The spelling was clearly suggested to Scott by the similarity of *hellcat* and it may well be a case of mistaken etymology. Scott uses it both as a noun (*BD* 420) and as an adjective (*Re* 351, *SRW* 23, *OM* 202, *HM* 274, *An* 516). *Dargle* too seems to be a mistake. Wandering Willie tells how 'Glen, nor dargle, nor mountain, nor cave could hide the puir hill-folk when Redgauntlet was out' (*Re* 151). The Dryburgh edition suggests that *dargle* is a mistake (on the part of the transcriber?) for *dingle*. This would fit with Scott's habit of linking synonyms with *or* but the *SND* has a more interesting explanation: 'The district on the banks of the River Dargle, which flows into the sea near Bray, is known as The Dargle and is a beauty spot popular with Dublin people. Perhaps Scott had heard of this spot and used the name as a general name for a river valley'. Whatever the explanation, the word, unlike *hellicat*, has not found favour with later writers and remains limited to this one appearance in Scott.

LOAN WORDS

All historians of the English language find food for comment in the paucity of loan words from the Celtic languages in Standard English. There are a number of words of disputed origin, so no exact figure is possible, but it is clear that when the Anglo-Saxons came to Britain they borrowed no more than a handful of Celtic words from its inhabitants as well as a few Latin loan words. This is much less than their descendants were to borrow from the natives of countries like America and Australia, although in

Scottish Sounds, Spelling and Vocabulary

those countries, especially Australia, the need to name unfamiliar flora and fauna helps to explain many of the borrowings. In all these countries contact with the original inhabitants was often hostile. In England the Celtic speaking areas for a long time existed as separate political and social entities and, by the time the largest of these, Wales, had been incorporated into the English kingdom, the East Midland dialect – the one furthest away from and least open to Celtic influence – had begun to establish itself as the standard. Later on a few words creep in mainly through the English contact with Ireland. English thus gains *skene* 'a dagger' (later to re-enter with Scott) and *glen*, with its alternative form *glin*, used by Spenser in his *View of the Present State of Ireland*. Only with the eighteenth-century discovery of Scotland as a land of romantic scenery do Scottish Gaelic words enter English and then it is via Scots, a fact which reflects the declining importance of the Celtic languages. Travel-writers like Burt and Boswell brought *loch* into Standard English and the poets (including Collins and Cowper) gave *glen*, which had been misinterpreted as 'a country hamlet' by Spenser's E.K. and hence by Spenser's imitators, its correct meaning and a secure place in the language, so much so that Jane Austen used it in *Pride and Prejudice* (p. 253, see *OED glen, loch*). Even here, everyday English stopped short of Scots which has adopted other Gaelic geographical terms like *strath* 'a valley' (*Wa* 112, *LM* 82, *LL* III iv) and *corr(e)i* 'a hollow in a hillside' (*Wa* 145, *LL* III xvi) from *coire* 'a cauldron' (although *corri* has been adopted as a specialist geographical term in attributive use with relation to glaciation).

By contrast with England's relation with Celtic speakers, in Scotland Celtic and English speakers were united in a kingdom where Celtic speakers for a long time played a major role – a role they never had in the English kingdom – and where the main centres of the English speaking population were much closer to the Celtic speaking areas. A number of Gaelic words for ordinary, everyday things bears testimony to this close relationship. The Gaelic word for a crab, *partan*, found its way into Scots from at least the fifteenth century and succeeded in limiting the use of the English word *crab* to describing the edible varieties. From Gaelic too are *oe* (*An* 523) or *oye* (*Re* 173, *HM* 58) meaning 'a grandson' and *clachan* 'a village, usually with a church' (*Wa* 404, *Wa* Note V, *HM* 667). The Gaelic *sonas* 'prosperity, good luck' gives the Scots *sonse* with the same meaning. Scott makes quite frequent use of the derivative *sonsy* although, as commonly happens with derivatives, the adjective has moved away in meaning from the original loan word. In Scott it means 'engaging' – 'a sonsy, merry companion' (*Re* 357) – with perhaps a slightly different emphasis in the description of Jeanie Deans as a 'good comely sonsy lass' (*HM* 582). It can even be applied to a periwig (*An* 54) though here the word indicates little more than a sense of approval.

Partan and *oe* were borrowed at least as early as the fifteenth century while *clachan* did not come into general Scots use until the later nineteenth century; this lengthy period of borrowing and the kind of words adopted bespeak a long and close association of the two languages. At the same time neither language has succeeded in impregnating the other in the way French did English in the Middle Ages, and as the *SND* notes 'the interchange of vocabulary, while considerable in both directions, has been moderate if we consider the closeness of contact' (*PLD* § 11). Another group of words reflects a less healthy relation of the two language groups. Only when Highland society (and with it Gaelic) was well into its decline did Lowlanders become greatly interested in preserving the outward signs of Highland life such as the Highland dress. Scott of course made great use of Highland dress in the ceremonial surrounding the visit of George IV to Edinburgh in 1824, no doubt seeing in it something distinctively Scottish. It is due to this sort of interest, which began in the later eighteenth century, that present-day Scots has a place for words like *sporran* 'a Highlander's pouch' (*RR* 312, *FM* 97) and *skene-dhu* 'a black-hilted knife "now commonly worn in the stocking with the hilt protruding"' (*SND skean*). Scott in one of his letters provides the first *SND* citation for this word in Scots (*Letters* III 37) and uses it also in *The Two Drovers* (*CC* 564). Significantly the name of the decorative *skene-dhu* has survived while the name of the functional *skene-occle* (*Wa* 278, *FM* 42) meaning 'a knife concealed in the sleeve' from Gaelic *sgian achlais* 'armpit knife', was not retained by writers after Scott. It is cited in the *SND* only from Burt's *Letters from a Gentleman in the North of Scotland* (from which Scott clearly took it) and from Scott himself. Also obsolete is the simple *skene* 'dagger' (*FN* 486) without qualification. As we noted before this word also entered English from Irish in the sixteenth century and appropriately it is used in *Kenilworth* with reference to Irishmen (K 291). Another word which came into the English-speaking parts of Britain from both directions is *trousers* or *trews*. Middle English adopted *trouse* from Irish although a plural form *trousers* finally established itself in English. In Scotland the form *trews* was borrowed to denote the close-fitting Highland tartan trousers. By this time the Great Vowel Shift had changed the English vowel from [u:] to [au] and Scott has to explain the unfamiliar looking *trews* as 'close trousers' (*Wa* 170) or 'close pantaloons' (RR 389) for the benefit of his southern readers. But though these Gaelic names have become attached in Scots to these elements of Highland dress the most distinctive of all – the *kilt* – is called in Scots and English by that Norse-derived name. Scott did introduce into his novels the Gaelic *philabeg* (HM 654) but its use is now rare. Literally it means 'little kilt' since what we call the kilt was formed by cutting off the plaid at the beltline thus making a separate skirt.

The reluctance with which the English have borrowed from the conquered Celts is in stark contrast with the eagerness with which they borrowed from the peoples who conquered them – the Danes and the Norman-French. In Scotland too the Norsemen – in this case Norwegians rather than Danes – were conquerors and succeeded in establishing themselves along the northern coast and the Western Isles. Though these settlements were for a time powerful they were eventually absorbed into the Celtic speaking Highlands or supplanted by Scots, although in the Northern Islands which were not until later politically a part of Scotland, a Norse dialect called *Norn* survived until the eighteenth century. They also settled extensively in the South-West (Galloway and Dumfriesshire). In both these areas they were surrounded by Celtic-speakers and it may be significant that at least one Norse word entered Scots via Gaelic – the Scots *berlin* (GM 402) or *berling* (GM 45) represents the Gaelic *birlinn*, an adaptation of Norse *byrðingr* 'a ship of burden'. The amount of Norse settlement in the Scots-speaking areas is an unsettled question but place-name evidence suggests that it was sparse and took place, if at all, in the South-East (see W. F. N. Nicolaisen, *Scottish Place-Names*, London, 1976, p. 113). The direct influence of Norse speakers was probably less important than transmission through Northern English. For a long time Scots was virtually identical with Northern English, and in a large part of the area covered by that dialect there was considerable Norse settlement.

Norse influence in the Northern English dialects is high, and no doubt many Norse words entered Scots via Northern English. In at least one case a Norse word seems to have come into Scots from even further south – *or* 'before' is a southern English form of Old Norse *ar*, the Norse cognate of English *ere*. This is a special case; generally the Norse influence in Scots exceeds that in Standard English. Comparisons of the content of the everyday normal vocabulary of dialects is in fact difficult, but what is beyond dispute is that there are a number of Norse words in Scots not found in Standard English.

The Norsemen, unlike the Normans, settled in these parts of England as ordinary farmers and fishers not as a ruling class and many homely words have been borrowed from them: *carl* 'man' (*GM* 391, *An* 45, *HM* 652, *OM* 153), *carlin(e)* 'woman' (*An* 353, *Re* 150), *eilding* 'fuel' (*An* 143, *GM* 454, *BD* 419), *hoast* 'cough' (*An* 71, *OM* 59), *kittle* 'tickle' (*Wa* 278, *BL* 185, *Re* 139, *SRW* 226), *sark* 'shirt, chemise' (*GM* 18, *RR* 231, *OM* 326, *HM* 53). The useful word *gar* 'make, cause to do' which is very common in Scott (*An* 113, *GM* 215, *OM* 366, *FN* 257) is from *gera*, an equally common word in Old Norse. Other useful, if not quite so common, verbs are *big* 'build' (*An* 274, *GM* 22, *OM* 263), *ettle* 'plan, aim' (*RR* 492, *Mo* 225) and *wale* 'choose' (*Re* 176, *HM* 282).

It is a universal phenomenon that when a new people with a new language move into an area they may borrow very few common nouns and yet borrow a great many proper nouns, especially place-names, from the existing inhabitants. For reasons which are obviously connected with this phenomenon the few borrowings of common nouns often include geographical terms. From the earlier inhabitants the Greeks took words like *thalassa* 'sea' and *nesos* 'island' which are foreign to Indo-European. The English picked up Celtic *coombe* 'valley'. The English in Australia borrowed the aboriginal *billabong*. The Scots, though not conquerors in the same way, picked up, as we have seen, *strath* 'valley', *glen* 'narrow mountain valley', *corri* 'hollow in hillside' and *loch* 'lake, inlet of sea' from Gaelic and from Norse they took *slack* 'a hollow in the land, often waterlogged' (*GM* 208, 222) and *scaur* 'crag, precipice' (*OM* 148, *Ma* V xii). Another Old Norse word is *firth* 'an estuary' (*RR* 351), or, in its metathesized form, *frith* (*An* 1, *GM* 400, *HM* 764, *Re* 414). It was borrowed into Standard English in the seventeenth century as was its

Norwegian counterpart *fjord*. But since 'firths' in Norway are usually surrounded by sharply rising cliffs or banks, the application of *fjord* in English has come to be confined to estuaries of such a kind. Names of fauna and flora are also often borrowed from other inhabitants of a country and another prominent grouping of Old Norse words in Scots is the names of birds: *gled* 'a kite' (*Wa* 387, *Mo* 320) *lungie* 'a common guillemot' (*An* 91) and *solan* 'a gannet' (*An* 68, *Ma* III iii).

Many of these words are also, as we would expect, found in the northern English dialects. *Eilding, gar, hoast* and *slack* are examples. Other Norse words in Scots were earlier on used still further south in the Southern English dialects – these have been considered in the section on words obsolete in English.

A number of words of French origin found in Scots but not in English – words like *ashet* 'a dish', from the French *assiette* – are often cited as reflecting the special relationship between France and Scotland during the period of the 'auld alliance'. The best known of these is perhaps the spurious one *petticoat-tails* (*BL* 357) which is often explained as a corruption of *petits-gâteaux*. This is incorrect; these biscuits were so called simply because the rounded edge looked like the scalloped edge of a petticoat. The 'auld alliance' may indeed have something to do with the appearance in Scots of words which are either very rare or unknown in present or past Southern English; a word like *cummer* (*An* 361, *BL* 325, *Mo* 87, *HM* 255) or *kimmer* (*FN* 248, *An* 432) both had the same original meaning as *gossip*, 'a godmother', and has followed *gossip* in its modern development of meaning. Other words in the same category are *corbie* 'a raven' (*RR* 331, *FM* 422, *SRW* 603), *dour* 'severe, obstinate, sullen', (*An* 328, *RR* 311, *HM* 677, *OM* 108, *Pi* 54), *fash* 'trouble' found both as a noun (*HM* 459, *OM* 39) and as a verb (*RR* 197, *Re* 164, *FN* 245, *BD* 331) and its derivatives *fasherie* with the same meaning (*Re* 160, *Mo* 39) and *fasheous* or *fashious* 'troublesome' (*GM* 525, *An* 274, *RR* 81) and *falset* 'falsehood' (*FN* 27). These are relatively early borrowings from French – *corbie* and *fash* from the fifteenth century, *dour* and *falset* from the fourteenth century. All are thus evidence of the independence of Scots from English when the Scottish kingdom was a separate entity. Yet even after the Union it seems Scots still had an independent existence. English does not have the term *rokelay*, given to a short cloak worn by women in the eighteenth century. It is used accurately by Scott in his novels of that period (*Wa* 89, *HM* 242, *Pi* 121) but also anachronistically in *The Monastery* (*Mo* 487). Derived from French it is a corruption of *roquelaure* named after the Duc de Roquelaure (1656-1738), since in France a similar garment was worn by men in the later seventeenth century. Also in the eighteenth century the Scots, renowned as gardeners, borrowed the French name for a jargonelle pear, *cuisse-madame* or 'lady's thighs', so named from its shape. In Scots it has the form *queez-maddam* and it is fittingly given to Scott's representative of the breed of Scottish gardeners, Andrew Fairservice (*RR* 282). Of course not all French words found in Scots are independent borrowings. Some of them, even if they are now unfamiliar to Englishmen, were in normal English use for some time though now obsolete. Like Norse words with a similar history these words have been dealt with earlier.

Other languages have contributed to Scots vocabulary especially Dutch and German: from Low German comes *grue* (*SRW* 434) or *grew* (*RR* 511) meaning 'to shudder', also used of the blood – 'to run cold' ('these stories make one's very blood grew,' *FN* 652) – and of the flesh – 'to creep' (*Re* 162). It is from *grue* that Scots developed *gruesome* now used in English. From Low German and/or Dutch comes *howff* meaning 'a haunt, a place of resort' (*HM* 236, *FN* 612, *SRW* 40) and hence applied to a pub (*OM* 38) while from the Dutch alone come *fozy* 'spongy' (applied to vegetables, *RR* 198) and *toy* 'a woman's cap or head-dress with flaps down to the shoulders' (*Wa* 89, *OM* 529).

The most exotic of all the foreign loan words which find their way into the Scots of the novels is one which clearly intrigued Scott himself: *massymore* 'a dungeon'. He uses the word as early as the *Minstrelsy* and constantly plays around with the spelling though generally preferring unetymological forms incorporating *massy* (*Ab* 518, *An* 433, *Minstrelsy*, 1802, *I* 79, *Ma* IV xi, *FM* 322n) to less suggestive forms like *Massamore* (*FM* 322n). He correctly identifies the word as of Arabic origin, though he does not seem to realize that it came to Scots via Spanish, and, perhaps struck by the appearance of such a word in Scots but not English, he feels compelled to comment on how it got there: '*Massamora*, an ancient name for a dungeon, derived from the Moorish language, – perhaps as far back as the time of the Crusaders' (*An* 433). The etymology is repeated in a footnote in *The Fair Maid of Perth* where Scott cites Jamieson as his source.

Scottish Sounds, Spelling and Vocabulary

CHANGES IN ENGLISH AND SCOTS SINCE SCOTT'S TIME

Just as English has changed over the last 150 years, so has Scots. However, with Scots one is more conscious of losses than of gains. This is partly because Scots terms have in fact in many cases yielded ground to English ones but even more perhaps because Scots is generally defined as the specifically Scottish elements of the language used in Scotland. These have certainly declined in number. However if we were to define it as 'the English used in Scotland' we would have to say that Scots has gained a number of words which have also entered English over the last century and a half. My *Scotsman* of today (31 August 1977) has in its main front page article alone *unemployment* (first OED citation 1888), *stabilise* (OED first citation used of a ship 1861, general sense 1875; not in OED used, as here, intransitively) and *reflation* (OED Suppl first citation, 1932). These words are clearly now in normal literary use in Scotland. Nor of course has Scots been without accessions of words of purely Scottish use providing an addition to 'Scots' in the normal, narrower sense. The same front page in another article supplies the relatively new term *Regional Council* denoting a local government body of a kind not found in England or Wales. All the same, additions like these have probably not equalled losses of specifically Scottish terms. Moreover, in a study of this kind only the losses show up, since the additions are by definition not part of Scott's language. We should further not forget that there have been losses as well to Scott's English.

Many of the losses reflect changes in society or its customs. It is no longer usual to hire mourners at a funeral and the name for them, *saulie* (*GM* 365, *An* 347) has disappeared, along with the, to us, distasteful custom. The hair-styles called *cockernony* (*HM* 368, *OM* 61, *BL* 176, *SRW* 214) and *cock-up* (*HM* 368) went out of fashion. Fashions often return but not necessarily with the same name and these names are long since dead. *Cock-up* is interesting, partly because its demise in this sense has left room for the modern colloquial sense 'a state of affairs confused by mismanagement' – quite misleading if read into Mrs Saddletree's condemnation of her servant's 'cockups and ... fallal duds' (*HM* 368), a scolding further obscured for us by the disappearance of *fallal* 'gaudy trippery'. Its other interest is the fact that it may be an anachronism. This is the *SND*'s first citation but Patrick Walker, on whom Scott drew very heavily indeed in *The Heart of Midlothian*, writing in 1728 recalls the time 'about Thirty Years ago, when Cockups were in Fashion' (*Remarkable Passages in the Life of Alexander Peden*, Edinburgh, 1728, p. 145). The novel is, however, set in 1736. To take another example, The Court of Session is no longer made up of fifteen judges; in fact it was reduced to thirteen in Scott's own time (in 1830) – a move he supported although he had objected to other changes to the legal system – so that it has for a long time been inappropriate to refer to them as *The F(e)ifteen*, a popular name found in *Guy Mannering* and *The Antiquary* (*An* 13, *GM* 308).

Where institutions or customs passed away the terms used to describe them did not always disappear – sometimes they have a half-life in history-books or they have extended or transferred their meaning to other things. A historian might well speak of a Highland chief's *following* as Scott does (*Wa* 134) thus using it in its earlier sense of 'a band of retainers'. However his readers on the other hand will probably see it as a use of the word in its more extended current sense 'a band of adherents of any kind to any person'. As it happens, not only the sense but the currency of the word has been extended: it is clear from Scott's footnote in *Waverley* ('*Scottice* for followers'; *Wa* 417n) and the way in *Old Mortality* he speaks of the Duke of Monmouth's 'numerous following, as it was called' (*OM* 359), that the word was then exclusively Scottish though now used in other areas of English. Along with the chief's following have gone most of his male attendants or *gillies* (*Wa* 173, *RR* 340, *HM* 736) though the name for them had not disappeared entirely, being used for a sportsman's attendant (*SRW* 394), nowadays generally an angler's attendant. On the other hand some of the terms describing the more violent side of Highland life had totally disappeared – probably even by Scott's time *cateran* or *catheran*, a name for the Highland marauders, and something of a favourite word with him (*Wa* 64, *RR* 448, *OM* 68, *FM* 41), was really only used in history-books and novels. Such marauders had been eliminated when the English imposed peace on the Highlands after the 1745 rebellion.

Place-names and other proper names are often more conservative than the language in general. Sometimes a word has been superseded as a common noun but lingers on where it has been attached as a proper name to some still-existing object. A tollbooth was naturally enough a place where tolls were collected; sometimes it was, or also became, the town hall though equally often it was demoted to the role of a prison (*RR* 289, *GM* 21, *HM* 11). All these senses of *tollbooth* are now obsolete and the word has gone out of use except that there is still, for example, a building called the Canongate Tollbooth. However the tollbooth of which the nickname provides the title of *The Heart of Midlothian* was demolished in 1817 (see *HM* Note II). Similarly, a granary is no longer called a *girnel* (*Wa* 65) but we still find the word as a farm-name and though the gates of cities (where indeed they survive at all) are not now known as *ports* (*HM* 74; *Re* 350) we will encounter such street-names as Bristo Port.

Social history may influence some changes in the vocabulary but for other changes no such obvious explanation can be supplied. Bad and good human qualities have remained, conceit and eagerness are still with us, but the terms *flory* 'conceited' (*Re* 192) and *frack* 'bold, eager, ready' (*An* 545) are obsolete. *Fleshers* (*FN* 27) without changing their occupation have become *butchers*. Another occupational name which has changed is *wabster* (*RR* 353), the Scottish form of English *webster* which dropped out of English usage (except as a surname) in the seventeenth century and is now in both countries in ordinary speech and writing replaced by the new agent noun *weaver* with its more obvious connection with the verb. In Scotland this change may well have something to do with the near-disappearance of the trade – the less common a practice is, the more it needs a self-descriptive name so outsiders will understand what it is. It seems a pity that *Pace* (*Re* 164), an old name for Easter found in Middle English and of course in Modern French *Pâques* and going back, ultimately, through Greek and Latin, to the Hebrew name for the Passover, should not remain alongside the equally interesting *Easter* which derives from Germanic, non-Christian backgrounds. *Pace* is now however obsolescent though the etymological spelling *Pasch*, which perhaps owes more to knowledge of Latin than of early Scots, has some life as a literary usage – it appears in George Mackay Brown's *Magnus* (Quartet Books, 1977, p. 123) but in a clearly archaic passage.

Some words in falling out of use in present-day Scots have merely followed a path they had already taken in English – either a long time ago, like *frack* (*Ab* 545) which is from the Old

English *fræc* 'bold, greedy' but disappears in England from the late Middle Ages, or quite recently, like *decay* 'a decline in a sickness' (*HM* 282) obsolete in Standard English only since the mid-eighteenth century and now obsolete in Scots. *Forfairn* 'exhausted' (*An* 270, 352) or 'ruined', also now obsolete, was on the way out in Scott's time. The old verb *forfare* 'to go amiss, ruin', which is of Old English origin but not known in Modern English, by the time he was writing only appears, as here, in the past participle.

The increasing influence of English is very obvious where distinctive Scottish variants have been replaced by the English equivalent. *Coin* has replaced *cunzie* (*Wa* 167), a separate Scottish development from Old French *cuigne* 'wedge, die for stamping money'. English *coin* derives from the French variant *coing* from which we also get *quoin* 'wedge, cornerstone' and the Shakespearean phrase *coign of vantage* 'useful projecting corner, observation point' which Scott picked up and brought into nineteenth-century English (*HM* 72, *QD* 331). *Examiner* 'one who conducts an exam' has replaced *examinator* (*Re* 124), a form found in English but more common and long-lasting in Scots. In other cases words of purely Scottish creation have been replaced by quite unrelated words: *bankrupt* has replaced *dyvour* (*Re* 162, 168, 561).

However, if English expressions have replaced some native Scottish ones there has been a perhaps surprising amount of movement the other way. Some of these words are generally recognized as of Scottish origin by non-Scots speakers insofar as they are thought of as particularly appropriate to Scottish contexts. The stereotype Scotsman is expected to be *dour* 'dogged, humourless', *canny* 'shrewd' and *pawkie* 'wily'. Not really endearing characteristics and hardly compensated for by allowing the women to be *bonny*. *Pawkie* (*HM* 181) is very rare outside Scottish contexts and *bonny* (*An* 129, *Re* 113, *GM* 197, *RR* 276; ironically *HM* 177, *Re* 620) is not much more common, but *canny* and *dour* have come to be used more generally. There could hardly be any people whose stereotype is further from the Scots' than the Spanish, but a writer in *The Sunday Times* (28 August 1977, p. 8) can write of the Spanish Communist leader 'Carillo appears as one of the most sober and canny politicians around'. Even here the expression may be felt to have gained some force from its slightly unusual application. But the English in adopting these words have not taken on all the Scottish meanings. To non-Scots *dour* means 'obstinate, stubborn' (*HM* 677, *OM* 108) or, more often, 'humourless' (a sense I have not found in Scott) but not 'hard, stern, severe', as in *The Antiquary* (*An* 328; spelt *dure*, *An* 287) nor do they apply it to land (*Pi* 54). *Canny* has been adopted meaning 'shrewd, knowing' (*Wa* 132) but not 'skilful' (*OM* 61) or 'lucky' (*Wa* 599) or 'comfortable' (*An* 143).

While Englishmen may not recognize *brownie* 'a household sprite' (*RR* 212) and *bogle* 'a ghost' (*An* 358, *GM* 7, *RR* 212) as Scottish words, they will nevertheless probably not be surprised to discover that they too were unknown in Standard English before Scott's time. However much they have now been accepted into English use, their meanings insure that an air of the folk hangs about them so that an origin in Scots dialect does not go against expectations. As it happens, English has adopted only one of the two Scottish senses of *bogle*, the one which is most common in Scott. The other, 'scarecrow', we find in the combinations *pease-bogle* (*FN* 89) and *potato-bogle* (*Re* 202), or *potatoe bogle* as Scott privately spells it (*Journal*, 3 February 1826), for scarecrows in fields of peas or potatoes.

More significant in terms of the influence of Scots in nineteenth- and twentieth-century English are the number of words which few people would ever suspect of having entered, or in some cases re-entered, English from Scots. They have become thoroughly acclimatized and have no lingering associations with Scotland. The glossary at the end of the Magnum Opus edition, prepared, as Scott's novels were written, with the English as well as the Scottish audience in mind, includes definitions of *aw(e)some* (*An* 355, *GM* 108, *Re* 153), *glamour* (*GM* 458, *Pi* 84, *LM* III ix), *grewsome* (*HM* 302, *RR* 423, *OM* 545, *BD* 432), *kith* (as in *kith and kin*; *Wa* 133, *RR* 283), *uncanny* (*An* 274, 356, *Wa* 593, *GM* 554), *slogan* (*FM* 58, *Ma* V iv) and *winsome* (*An* 88, *OM* 89). All of these before Scott's time were Scottish terms only or, like *kith* and *winsome*, had been found in earlier English but had died out in the south. Two more Scots terms for which glosses were provided and which are now used in English are *wizzent* (glossed 'withered'; *HM* 271) and *guffá* 'a loud laugh', though the modern reader may not recognize in them *wizened* and *guffaw*. In fact we also find the forms *wizzened* (*SRW* 311) and *wizen'd* (*OM* 118). Naturally the meanings of words have not always remained the same after the transition to English. *Glamour* which the glossary interprets as 'magical deception of sight' (e.g. *LLM* III ix) but which Scott also uses less specifically to describe any kind of magic (e.g. *GM* 467) has changed its meaning considerably, simply by being now used only figuratively. The modern metaphorical sense has carried the word even further from its source as a corruption of *grammar*. Nor have all the Scottish senses necessarily transferred to English. In English, for example, *uncanny* does not mean 'dangerous' (*An* 274).

Not all of the Scots words current in present-day English are listed in the glossary of the Collected Edition which is by no means complete in its coverage of either Scots or archaic language *Forbear* 'ancestor' (*BL* 326), *outlay* (verb, *Wa* 49; noun, *An* 165) *raid* (*Wa* 128n, *LLM* V xxviii) and *scantly* (*Ma* III xiv, *LLM* II xvii) are not included in the glossary (perhaps because their meaning is easily deducible) but none of these was used in the literature of England during the century before Scott. All have entered, or like *scantly* re-entered, Standard English since he wrote.

Scotland's contribution to sport, Saunders Fairford's beloved *golf* (see *Re* 199), had by Scott's time spread to England but it is only since then that it has become one of the most popular games in English-speaking countries and brought into familiar English use a number of terms of Scottish origin. Many of these words appear in Scott in other senses since a lot of the technical language of golf was provided from the resources of Scots by the simple expedients of specialization or transfer of meaning although the term *golf* itself is *probably* – its origin is much disputed – derived from Middle Dutch *kolf* 'a club'. Scott had his say on this matter writing to John Cundall, who had written a pamphlet about the history of golf, that he doubted if 'the word *Golf* is derived from the verb to gowff or strike hard. On the contrary I conceive the verb itself is derived from the game and that to gowff is to strike sharp and strong as in that amusement' (*Letters* VIII 296; cf *SND gowf* n^1 v^1, n^2 v^2). Scott did not apparently share the elder Fairford's passion for the game, and basic golfing terms like *links*, *bunker* and *caddie* are more useful to Scott in their wider meaning from which the golfing senses had developed. Darsie, the Englishman, writing to Alan, the Scotsman, describes how he found himself in an area of 'sandy knolls, covered with short herbage, which you call Links, and we English, Downs' (*Re* 34). *Link*, a word found in Old English meaning 'a ridge of bank' but afterwards dying out in England except in dialect, came in Scotland to be used (in the plural) of land near the seashore, sandy, gently rolling and covered with coarse grass. Such land provided the first golf-courses, and still provides them where available, but the term came to be associated not so much with the kind of land as with the purpose it served and *links* is now applied in many countries to golf-courses far from sea-shores and where any sand has had to be carefully imported. Funnily enough, the term which Scott chooses as an English equivalent to *links* is less help now to the non-Scots reader than the indirect aid given by golf-courses, since the word *down* is no longer applied to sand-hills as it was in Scott's time (*OED down* sb^{1}3) having been replaced by the late eighteenth-century import *dune*, itself a borrowing of a Middle Dutch word cognate with *down*.

Bunker 'a sand pit' (*Re* 136) was likewise a general term given a specific sense in golf. Like *links* it no longer applies simply to naturally occurring features but also to carefully constructed artificial obstructions on golf-courses. Indeed after a narrowing of meaning it has now widened out again to cover anything providing an obstruction for golfers (*OED Suppl bunker* 4). *Bunker*, in origin the same word as English *bunk* and derived from Scandinavian sources, appeared first in Scottish and did not enter English until the nineteenth century. In fact its use in English is not confined to the golfing term. The word first meant a chest or box, and various senses involving the idea of a receptacle developed from this, including the meaning 'store-place for coal'. Writing in the nineteenth century, the *OED* editors noted that in English use it applied only to storing places in ships, whereas the Scots used it also of storing places on land. Burchfield's *Supplement* to the *OED* has had to withdraw this note since *bunker* is now also in England applied to the place where the household's supply of coal is kept. The bunker or chest was often used as a seat so that the Laird of Dumbiedikes found that 'no seat accommodated him so well as the "bunker" at Woodend' (*HM* 131).

In Scott *caddie*, known to us as the name for a golfer's attendant, is still applied to someone providing a rather wider range of similar services. In the eighteenth century a large body of men or boys, forming an organized group, lived by running errands for citizens in Edinburgh and other large Scottish towns. They figure therefore in those of Scott's novels which touch on the life of the well-to-do citizen in Edinburgh of that time: *Guy Mannering* (*GM* 343), *The Heart of Midlothian* (*HM* 315) and *Redgauntlet* (*Re* 120). The usual spelling in Scott's novels is *cadie*.

The *OED* quotations suggest that the word *stance* in the general sense 'standing-place, position' after being used in the sixteenth and seventeenth centuries became obsolete in Standard English in the eighteenth century. In Scots it did not go out of use and is still current. From the general sense developed the special golfing sense 'the position of the player's feet as he prepares to strike the ball' which has now entered Standard English and is used of players in other games as well. In Scott, however, we find the word used in its general sense (*An* 43, *HD* V xii) and in another specialized sense 'a site for building on' (*PP* 172; note also *building-stance*, *SRW* 50).

It is hardly through Scott's influence that these golfing terms which help us in reading him have been introduced into Standard English, but his enormous influence on nineteenth-century literature may well have played a part in bringing many of the other words into use. The best discussion of this subject is Paul Roberts' 'Sir Walter Scott's Contribution to the English Vocabulary' (*PMLA*, LXVII, (1953), 189–210). It is noticeable that some of them are words which he used a lot, though not I think overused, like *bonny* and *dour*. Others have to do with some of his favourite themes like the supernatural *bogle*, *brownie*, *glamour*, and, one not mentioned before, *wraith* 'a ghost or the spectral appearance of a living person' (*Ma* VI Introd. 146). Indirectly too, Scott may have helped Scoticisms enter English by providing an encouraging example for later writers like Stevenson who also had large English audiences. Nothing can be proved, but the probability is certainly strong that Scott's influence had much to do with this strong influx of Scoticisms. Certainly it would seem likely that Scott, who always has half an eye on English readers, would have a greater effect in this regard than a writer like Burns who writes more exclusively for Scotsmen, even if we did not have to take into account Scott's greater popularity with non-Scots readers. Scott's careful mixture of Scots-cum-English dialogue is bound to transfer some knowledge of Scottish terms to non-Scots readers.

I have left to this point two interesting words because in this case there is little doubt that Scott had nothing to do with their coming into English. They have not entered English from Scots but in slightly different form or with different meaning have been adopted from American usage. From Americans some Englishmen and, for that matter, Australians and others have picked up the habit of addressing those close to them as *honey*. This is Scott's universal addressive *hinny* (*An* 5, *OM* 40, *Re* 261, *HM* 300) presented in a more recognizable form. By contrast the original of the Scottish word *sculduddery* is obscure. It first appears in Mrs Centlivre's play *Wonder* (See *SND*) and in Scots has the meaning 'lewd behaviour' (*HM* 231) or, more mildly, 'obscenity of language' (*Re* 165). It can also be used as an adjective (*Re* 155). In the late nineteenth century what is clearly the same word, though with a different form and meaning, *sculduggery*, 'fraud', appears in America. It is this US form and meaning which have been taken into present-day British English.

College in the sense of 'university' has not been adopted into Standard British English but books and films have made this idiom well-known outside North America. The established universities in England consisted of a number of colleges so that the terms *college* and *university* remained separate. In Scotland and the United States however, the universities often consisted of only one college. So in Scotland in the nineteenth century we find universities, including Edinburgh (*Re* 4, *HM* 108n) and Glasgow (*RR* 231), referred to as 'the College'. Since this time English usage has prevailed in Scotland and it is now rare for *college* to be so used while in the US *college* seems to be yielding ground in colloquial use to *school*. But although they use *college* in this way the Americans do not seem to have adopted for a university student the Scots term *collegeaner* (*HM* 108). Secondary institutions were also differently named in Scotland. The Edinburgh High School, founded in 1519, was the first to use this name which later spread to schools in other Scottish burghs. In England the term has been used much less commonly but in the US it appears frequently from the 1820s and in Australia it is the normal term for the state-run secondary school. So terms which Scott's original English readers may have found strange will be familiar to many of his present readers. Even where a reader does not use the word himself it may still be familiar due to the widespread exposure of other parts of the English-speaking world to American idiom.

The Language of Walter Scott

SOME SPECIALIST LANGUAGES

Of all the specialist languages or jargons found in Scots the most important is the terminology of Scottish law and the Scottish legal system. We have the names of courts such as *The High Court of Justiciary* (HM 318) and judges such as the *Lords of Session* (HM 176). We find that solicitors are called *writers* (BL 170) and barristers are called *advocates* (Re 330, HM 177). There are crimes with archaic-sounding names like *hamesucken* 'assaulting someone in his own house' (Re 209, FN 455), *spu(i)lzie* 'open seizure of another's goods' (Wa 130, Re 310) and *stouthrief* 'robbery with violence' (FM 48, Re 310, BL 172) and names of legal actions like *multiplepoinding* (SRW 158, BL 214, Re 206). And so on. This is hardly surprising in a man who was himself a lawyer and court official and who loved all manifestations of the Scottish national identity, of which the separate Scottish legal system is one of the most important. However the language of Scottish law is simply too large a subject to be taken up here. Instead I will look briefly at just one aspect of the law which was of particular interest to Scott and then at a few other selected specialist languages.

In his autobiographical fragment Scott notes how in his time at the University of Edinburgh:

> the Scotch law lectures were those of Mr David Hume. . . . I can never sufficiently admire the penetration and clearness of perception which were necessary to the arrangement of the fabric of law, formed originally under the strictest influence of feudal principles, and innovated, altered, and broken in upon by the change of times, of habits and of manners, until it resembles some ancient castle, partly entire, partly ruinous, partly dilapidated, patched and altered during the succession of ages by a thousand additions and combinations, yet still exhibiting, with the marks of its antiquity, symptoms of the skill and wisdom of its founders, and capable of being analyzed and made the subject of a methodical plan by an architect who can understand the various styles of the different ages in which it was subjected to alteration (*Life* I 58).

One of the appeals Scots law had for Scott, then, was as a modern descendant of the laws of the medieval feudal state which he represented so often in his novels. The most basic element of feudalism is the system of land tenure. It is no wonder that the novels show an interest in Scottish land tenure, the origin and terminology of which we so easily recognize as feudal. Indeed the interest seems to have been inherited: according to Scott his father took 'a pleasure in analyzing the abstruse feudal doctrines connected with conveyancing' (*Life* I 7). Scott makes this feudal element quite explicit in his note on 'Building-Feus in Scotland':

> Every alienation or sale of landed property must be made in the shape of a feudal conveyance, and the party who acquires it holds thereby an absolute and perfect right of property in the fief, while he discharges the stipulations of the vassal, and, above all, pays the feu-duties (*SRW* Note I).

The word *feu*, related to the English *fee*, *fief*, and *feudal*, is used for both the form of tenure: 'a speculative builder took land in feu' (*SRW* 14) and the piece of land so held, 'her own incapacity ... to manage the feu' (*Mo* 130), and also as a verb meaning 'to grant land in feu' (*SRW* 35). The feu is granted to a *feuar* (*BL* 171, *SRW* 426), by a *feu-charter* (*BL* 170) giving *feu-rights* (*BL* 167) and requiring *feu-duties* (*Mo* 386).

Continuing this interest in the feudal system Scott, in *Waverley*, takes pleasure in using the word *baron* in its Scottish sense of 'the owner of a freehold estate erected into a barony by the Crown and held direct from the Crown'. Contrary to the general usage of his time Mr Bradwardine in *Waverley* is called 'the Baron' (*Wa* 80, 97, 383, 593, 635) even in informal contexts and on more formal occasions 'the Baron of Bradwardine' (*Wa* 78, 141, 381) or even, exceptionally, by Evan Dhu at his most ceremonious, 'Baron of Bradwardine and Tully-Veolan' (*Wa* 141). Though *Baron* is the correct legal term the normal designation at the time would have been 'the laird of Bradwardine' which is the way the 'Baron' himself talks about his neighbours:

> There was the young Laird of Balmawhapple, a Falconer by surname, of the house of Glenfarquhar, given right much to field-sports – *gaudet equis et canibus*, – but a very discreet young gentleman. Then there was the Laird of Killancureit, who had devoted his leisure *until* tillage and agriculture (*Wa* 80).

An alternative would be 'Mr Bradwardine' (*Wa* 640) or, more formally, 'Mr Cosmo Comyne Bradwardine, of Bradwardine and Tully-Veolan' (*Wa* 93) as this same laird of Balmawhapple calls him. The most familiar way of referring to a laird is simply by calling him by the name of his estate in the way Meg Merrilees calls the elder Bertram 'Ellangowan' (*GM* 20) and Meiklewham calls Mowbray 'St Ronan's' (*SRW* 155). The heir to an estate may also be called by its name just as Cuddie addresses Henry Morton as 'Milnwood' (*OM* 203) though Morton's uncle is still in possession of the estate. This informal usage is not dignified enough for Scott's picture of the Baron. In spite of the author's informing us that 'his intimates, from his place of residence, used to denominate him Tully-Veolan, or, more familiarly, Tully' (*Wa* 47) there is little evidence of this in the dialogue. When the person concerned was a woman, either the actual possessor or the laird's wife, the title *Lady* was prefixed to the name of the estate. This usage is now nearly obsolete and was probably equally uncommon in Scott's time: Hogg in 1828 and Carlyle in 1860 refer to it as a custom of the past (see *SND lady* 1(2)). It was probably still current in the early eighteenth century and appears in two novels set at that period: Bucklaw's grand-aunt is called 'Lady Girnington' (*BL* 95) and on his inheritance of her estate at her death he becomes Laird of Girnington (*BL* 279) while Davie Deans' second wife hopes that Jeanie will become 'Lady Dumbiedikes' (*HM* 121) by marrying the Laird of Dumbiedikes. By the period, later in the same century, at which *Guy Mannering* is set the custom was evidently dying out, if Scott's usage is to be accepted as a guide. The owner of the estate of Singleside is generally called 'Mrs Margaret Bertram' (*GM* 334, 371) but Dandie Dinmont, either because he is countrified and old-fashioned or because it increases his own self-consequence in being remotely related to her, refers to her as 'Lady Singleside' (*GM* 378). Her father was, of course, talked of as 'Singleside' (*GM* 334, 352).

Scott's use of the term *baron* rather than the usual *laird*, is deliberate. He wants us to see Bradwardine as, like Mowbray's ancestor, 'a grave Scottish baron, of "auld lang syne" ' (*SRW* 8), an interesting and imposing relic of the feudal past, even if occasionally a little ridiculous. He went on in later novels to deal with such feudal barons of the past – men like Julian Avenel, 'Baron of Avenel' in *The Monastery* (*Mo* 317) and Sir Patrick Charteris, 'Baron of Kinfauns' in *The Fair Maid* (*FM* 127). Indeed, since *Waverley* is set before the abolition of heritable jurisdictions which followed on the 1745 rebellion, Bradwardine's title had some meaning; a Baron had certain judicial powers inside his barony. Bradwardine shows no great inclination to

Scottish Sounds, Spelling and Vocabulary

exercise his powers outlined in the charter of David the First which created the barony of Bradwardine and Tully-Veolan and which he loved to recite (*Wa* 77), but in other cases such powers were used. This led to the *baron-court* (*HM* 106), where the baron acted through his deputy or *baron-baillie* (*HM* 408, *Wa* 48, *SRW* 424), also known simply as a *baillie* (*Re* 161, *Wa* 391).

A more important scene of local justice was the *Sheriff-Court* (*Re* 208). Until the abolition of heritable jurisdictions in 1747 the administration of justice in the counties was in the hands of a *Sheriff* (*OM* 19) whose position was generally hereditary, a system which Scott called 'contrary alike to common sense and the free and impartial administration of justice' (*TG* 1179). The sheriff's appointed deputy was called the *Sheriff-Depute*, 'so called as deputed by the Crown' (*TG* 1179), and after 1747 he took over the powers of the former hereditary sheriffs (see *GM* 88, *Re* 351). This was the position Scott himself held in Selkirkshire. The Sheriff-Depute was generally known simply as the *Sheriff* (*SRW* 212, *Re* 361) or, to give it the common spoken form, the *Shirra* (*An* 262), a title by which Scott delighted to be known. The Sheriff-Depute had deputies called *Sheriff-Substitutes* (*Re* 351, *GM* 113) who could carry out most of his duties, though Scott himself wanted to hand over as little of the work as was consistent with his other interests. The sheriff was also helped by other officials: the *Sheriff-Clerk* (*SRW* 17), clerk of the Sheriff-Court, and the *Sheriff-Officer* (*RR* 342) or *Shirra'-officer* (*An* 273) who carried out the Sheriff's warrants. In some counties the equivalent of the Sheriff was called a *Stewart* and the county was called a *stewartry* giving rise to the phrase 'neither county nor stewartry' (*Re* 352).

In local government as well the institutions and nomenclature were different from those of England. An English *mayor* was a Scottish *provost* (*HM* 19, *Re* 349) who was assisted by *bailies* (*HM* 19, *RR* 411, *FM* 110). The town council also at one stage included the heads of the Incorporated Trades called *deacons* (*HM* 19, *FM* 110). A town with a municipal government like this was called a *burgh* (*Re* 350, *OM* 527, *FM* 113) and, if its charter derived direct from the Crown, a *royal burgh* (*Re* 396). *Burgh* is normally pronounced like the English *borough* although since the seventeenth century the two countries have preferred to use different spellings of the same word.

Scottish money deserves a mention both because it figures a

lot in the novels and because it can be confusing. The Scottish pound – a money of account not a coin – was originally equal to the English pound but by the seventeenth century it had devalued to 1s 8d English or one twelfth of an English pound. It was officially abolished at the time of the Union but seems to have survived in unofficial use in the eighteenth century. The devalued Scottish pound provided material for John Bull's contempt of his northern neighbour, Sawney. In *Redgauntlet* Peter Peebles provokes the amused scorn of the English landlord by asking:

> 'Then ye will have nae breakfast that will come within the compass of a shilling Scots?'
> 'Which is a penny sterling,' answered Crackenthorp, with a sneer. 'Why, no, Sawney, I can't say as we have – we can't afford it; but you shall have a bellyful for love, as we say in the bull-ring' (*Re* 552).

Elsewhere Scott quotes the couplet:

> How can the rogues pretend to sense?
> Their pound is only twenty pence (*Wa* 169n).

No wonder then that Bailie Macwheeble found the sum of £294.13.6 frightening when expressed in 'its original form of Scotch pounds, shillings and pence' (*Wa* 48). References in *Old Mortality* (*OM* 39) and *Waverley* (*Wa* 48, 168) to pounds Scots are accurate but a similar reference is anachronistic in the fourteenth-century setting of *The Fair Maid* (*FM* 496) since at that stage a Scots pound was equal to an English one. It follows from the value of a Scots pound that a Scots shilling is worth one English penny. Ailie's parsimony shows in her worrying about Morton 'gieing maybe the feck [most part] o' twal shillings Scots for your supper' (*OM* 542) and Caleb, playing, as always, his role of defender of the dignity of the house of Ravenswood, is able to sound very grand as he hands over a single penny while talking to the recipient of giving him 'twal pennies' (*BL* 181; 'Monetae Scoticae, scilicet' says Scott's note). Similarly since the English mark was worth 13s 4d the Scottish merk was worth one twelfth of this, that is 1s 1½d or one eighteenth of an English pound. This obscure detail is unlikely to be known to the modern reader who will not recognize the full richness of the blend of self-importance with a pretence of modesty, so perfectly appropriate to the Cameronian Gilfillan, when he tells how 'my sma' means, whilk are not aboon twenty thousand merk, have had the blessing of increase, but the pride of my heart has not increased with them' (*Wa* 335). He calls a solid sum of about £1100 'small' but in his next breath contradicts the effect and makes it sound far grander than it is by choosing to express it in Scottish merks.

Before the Union with England there had been a number of small Scottish coins in use. A *plack* (*RR* 254, *Wa* 442, *OM* 208, *BL* 223, *FN* 567) was four pence Scots, a *bawbee* (*An* 492, *RR* 254, *FN* 103, *HM* 141) six pence, but was later lowered to three pence, and a *bodle* (*An* 47) or *boddle* (*FN* 566, *GM* 129, *RR* 254) was valued at two pence. In English terms this gives, of course, respective values of one-third of a penny, a half-penny or a farthing and one-sixth of a penny. The minting of these coins had stopped long before Scott's time, though some may still have been in circulation, so that it seems probable that the words were used, not in relation to specific coins, but as general terms for very small amounts of money. This is certainly how they are used in Scott. Meg Dodds' usage, where the only precisely significant money term is the English pound, is typical:

> They wad hae seen my father's roof-tree fa' down and smoor me before they wad hae gien me a boddle a-piece to have propped it up – but they could a' link out their fifty pounds ower head to bigg a hottle at the Well yonder. And muckle they hae made o't – the bankrupt body, Sandie Lawson, hasna paid them a bawbee of four terms' rent (*SRW* 32).

Other phrases like 'without paying you a bawbee' (*HM* 583) and 'he wasna a plack the waur' (*Wa* 442) are equally unspecific, while the phrase 'plack and bawbee' (*FN* 567, *RR* 254, 317) is equivalent to 'every penny of it' or 'every cent'; Rob Roy assures Bailie Jarvie: 'I'll pay up your thousan pund Scots, plack and bawbee' (*RR* 317). According to the 1833 Glossary 'two and plack' means 'two bodles and a plack' but Caleb is not being so precise when he says of the disreputable Craigengelt:

> the loon has woodie [gallows] written on his very visnomy, and I wad wager twa and a plack that hemp plaits his cravat yet (*BL* 223).

Lastly we may note the combination with other nouns. Henry Smith's armour deflects 'steel lances as if they were boddle prins' (i.e. 'pins worth a boddle'; *FM* 624) and Peter Peebles' poverty is well illustrated when, in the scene already mentioned, he begins by asking for a *plack-pie*, that is a pie costing a plack. Ignorant of the Scots *plack*, the landlord takes him to be asking for 'black pies, as you call them, . . . made of sheep's head' (*Re* 552).

The Scotsman had his revenge for the Englishman's scorn of his money in the size of his liquid measures:

> The Scottish pint of liquid measure comprehends four English measures of the same denomination. The jest is well known of my poor countryman, who, driven to extremity by the raillery of the Southern, on the small denomination of the Scottish coin, at length answered, 'Ay, ay! But the deil tak them that has the least pint-stoup' (*Re* 413n).

In fact a Scots pint, officially abolished in 1826, was 3.001 English pints and the *SND* notes that it is 'hard to explain' the frequent assertion by Scott and others that the Scots pint was equal to four English pints. To drink a *pint-stoup* of liquor (*GM* 457, *Re* 413), then, was to consume a considerable quantity. (*Stoup* is a name applied to a drinking vessel or container for liquid (*HM* 111) but was originally applied to a bucket.) A half of a Scots pint was called a *chappin* (*RR* 408, *OM* 41) while a quarter of a Scots pint was called a *mutchkin* (*Re* 162, *HM* 414). The latter Scott, by his incorrect computation, sees as nearly the equivalent of an English pint: Jeanie Deans, when in England, writes of 'ane pint, as they ca't, of yill, whilk is a dribble in comparison of our gawsie Scots pint, and hardly a mutchkin' (*HM* 414). These measures gradually fell out of use, though they did survive their official abolition. On the other hand, *magnum*, a name given to a half gallon bottle (*SRW* 16, *An* 19) has not only survived but has also, since Scott's time, been accepted into Standard English usage.

Turning to another area, we realize why the Waverley Novels give the feeling of such a rich texture of Scottish life when we stop to take note how often a little thing like Scottish food is mentioned. (Indeed in all the novels, whether Scottish or not, there must be few subjects which are mentioned so consistently as food.) For example we find reference to three different soups made from a chicken, or *chucky* as Provost Crosbie calls it (*Re* 351). They are: *cock-bree* (*SRW* 43), *friar's chicken* (*GM* 294, *OM* 324) which is made of veal, chicken and beaten eggs, and *cock-a-leeky* (*SRW* 10), this last being now well known outside Scotland. Add to this a *brandered fowl* (*SRW* 434) which is just a grilled

Scottish Sounds, Spelling and Vocabulary

fowl under another name, as *brander* is the Scottish name for a gridiron (see *GM* 218). A relatively poor society where nothing is wasted is reflected in dishes like the well known *haggis* (*RR* 341, *Mo* 151) and the less well known *powsoudie* 'sheep's-head broth' (*An* 457), and *crappit-heads* 'stuffed haddock-heads' (*GM* 294) as well as the use of *braxy mutton* 'mutton from a sheep which has died of disease' (*Re* 378) and the making of *brose*, which Scott describes as 'the fat broth ... in which salted beef has been boiled, poured upon highly toasted oatmeal, a dish which even now is not ungrateful to simple old-fashioned Scottish palates' (*FM* 294; see also *Re* 379). Other far from extravagant dishes are *crowdie* 'oatmeal and cold water, eaten raw' (*RR* 341) and a *bannock* (*Re* 379) described by the *SND* as 'a round, flat, thickish, cake of oatmeal, barley, pease or flour, baked on a girdle'. In some areas salmon provided some variety in this rather poor diet. After the 'salmon-hunting' by Dandie Dinmont and his friends,

> The best were selected for the use of the principal farmers, the others divided among their shepherds, cottars, dependants, and others of inferior rank who attended. These fish, dried in the turf-smoke of their cabins, or shealings, formed a savoury addition to the mess of potatoes, mixed with onions, which was the principal part of their winter food. In the meanwhile a liberal distribution of ale and whiskey was made among them, besides what was called 'a kettle of fish,' – two or three salmon, namely, plunged into a cauldron and boiled for their supper (*GM* 232).

Quite different company enjoy this same 'kettle of fish' in *St Ronan's Well*. At a picnic, or *fête champêtre* as Scott calls it (*SRW* 187), Lady Penelope Penfeather and the society from the spa eat freshly caught salmon cooked in this way by the riverside. Even in the eighteenth century English writers like Fielding had adopted the phrase, but only in a figurative sense; a 'pretty kettle of fish' is 'a mess, a muddle, an embarrassing state of affairs'. Interestingly the only other place where Standard English preserves this older meaning of *kettle*, where it is not limited to a vessel with a spout, is the non-figurative parallel compound *fish-kettle*, meaning a large oval-shaped saucepan for boiling fish.

ADDRESSIVES, EXCLAMATIONS AND OATHS

Scots, like English needs addressives. The different Scots addressives are worth some attention because they play such a big part in establishing the feel of the Scots discourse in the novels. One of the most important is the simple word *man* (*An* 359, *GM* 5, *RR* 365) which can be used in Standard English but which has in Scots, as in other varieties of English like Black English and South African English, a wider currency. It can be doubled for emphasis as when Mrs Macleuchar, 'overwhelmed' by Oldbuck's protests at the non-arrival of the coach, cries out, 'Oh, man, man!... take back your three shillings, and mak me quit o' ye' (*An* 7). It can even be addressed to a horse (*HM* 427) or, in the phrase *my bonnie man*, to a dog (*GM* 493). Similarly *lass* or *lassie* cannot only be used in addressing a girl (*HM* 301) but also in speaking to an older woman (*An* 179, *SRW* 43), and a boy or a young man can be *lad* (*An* 359). Some of the Scots addressives are common English words though disguised by their Scottish form. The Scots variant of English *joy* gives *my jo* (*HM* 299, *OM* 91), also used in talking of a third person to refer to a boyfriend (*Mo* 41, *HM* 241, *OM* 89, *GM* 379). *Honey* is used in the English form by Sir Mungo Malagrowther in speaking to Margaret Ramsay (*FN* 104) who is hardly impressed by his unusual politeness, but more often it has its Scots form *hinny* with the usual Scots change of *u* to *i*. Again it figures both as an addressive (*An* 358, *OM* 90, *Re* 261, *HM* 300, *GM* 208) and in ordinary use with reference to a third person (*Re* 261). *Dove*, likewise used in its English form as an addressive in *Nigel* (*FN* 460), undergoes another common Scottish sound-change (the loss of *v*) and is found as *doo* (*GM* 198) or *dow* (*OM* 80). It often combines, like other addressives with *bonny*, to give *my bonny dow* (*Wa* 387) or *my bonny doo* (*HM* 300). The familiar English addressive *sir* is corrupted to *stir* (*OM* 92) and it is probably the old term of abuse *sirrah* which, in similar fashion, has given rise to the milder Scottish *stirra* (*An* 190, 270). One word totally unknown to English is *cummer*. It is, as mentioned earlier, borrowed from the French and like the English equivalent *gossip*, was often used as an addressive (*HM* 225, *An* 361). Finally there are the Scottish names used for indicating various family and other relationships (see pp. 216–18) which can be used in addressing the person concerned as they would be in English:

> 'Oh, what was it, grannie?' – and 'What was it, gudemither?' – and 'What was it Luckie Elspeth?' asked the children, the mother, and the visitor in one breath (*An* 356–7).

Scottish Sounds, Spelling and Vocabulary

In particular *gudeman* (*An* 363) and *gudewife* (*Wa* 288) may be used as respectful forms of address even where the person addressed is not, as these words generally imply, the male or female head of the household.

Waverley on his first day at Tully-Veolan managed to deduce from the conversation of the inhabitants that 'in Scotland a single house was called a "town" and a natural fool an "innocent"' (*Wa* 74). However by the end of the day he was presumably still puzzled that 'two bare-legged damsels' should on his first appearance, alone, apparently use a plural addressive in a shrill exclamation of 'Eh, sirs!' (*Wa* 69). In fact *sirs* is not an addressive but an exclamation being a much shortened form of (*God pre*)*serve us* with the Scottish loss of *v* in *serve* as in *doo/dove*. So when one of Mrs Mailsetter's gossips exclaims 'Eh, preserve us, sirs' (*An* 179) she is actually repeating the phrase in two different forms. *Sirs* is very often combined with *eh* (*Wa* 128, *BL* 178) or with *hech* or *hegh*, 'an exclamation, akin to a sigh, generally expressive of sorrow, fatigue, pain, surprise or contempt' (*SND hech* I; see *GM* 474, *Re* 190, *An* 582, *OM* 59). A subject is supplied in *dear sirs* (*An* 345) where *dear* is elliptical for *dear Lord*. Other exclamatory sounds are *Ow* (*GM* 5) or *Ou* (*An* 359, *BL* 331), roughly equivalent to English *oh* or *ooh*, sometimes combined with *ay* to mean 'yes, indeed' (*Wa* 359), and *hout*, which is used to express some sense of disagreement or annoyance with the speaker. Though used alone (*HM* 303, *An* 180), *hout* is particularly likely to appear in combinations: *hout awa* (*An* 129, *SRW* 123, *RR* 254) means 'nonsense!' as does *hout tout* (*RR* 254), although sometimes the latter might be translated as 'not so fast!' (*BL* 179, *HM* 305). *Hout fye* expresses disapproval (*An* 182) or disagreement (*SRW* 123, *Re* 379). *Hout na* (*GM* 6) or *hoot no* (*SRW* 36) is a strong negative and even *hout ay* (*RR* 255) is only a reluctant assent and seems to involve as much disagreement as agreement with the other speaker. *Aweel* (*OM* 60, *BL* 180, *FN* 50, *An* 47) is a weakened form of *ah well* and the Scottish equivalent of *Sssh* is *whisht* (*Wa* 288, *An* 356, *RR* 312, *FN* 564).

As always in oaths and exclamations both God and the Devil may be called on, but in Scotland it is often by names which Englishmen may not recognize. In Scott's time, however, many of his southern readers would have recognized the, to them, obsolescent clipping of *God* to *Odd* (*An* 97, *BL* 187, *GM* 494). This aphetic form was used in Standard English up to the later eighteenth century and figures in other Scott novels as an archaism; it is probably now obsolete in Scotland as well. The Collected Edition glossary explains it rather coyly as 'a minced oath, omitting one letter'. A different way to avoid the divinity's name is to replace it with *Good* or rather *Gude* (*GM* 200, *An* 6, *RR* 361). The devil is *deevil* (*BD* 340) or, more frequently, *deil* (*BD* 342, *FN* 455, *Re* 152, *An* 4). An alternative is *fient* (*GM* 554). More indirectly, a reference to the Devil can be disguised by using euphemisms like *sorrow*, *ne'er* and *gudeman*. *Sorrow* can be used in both imprecations – 'Sorrow be in your thrapple [throat] then' (*GM* 5) – and addressives – 'Get out o' the gate, ye little sorrow' (*An* 349). The word is sometimes more equivalent to *plague* – 'sorrow fa' the brood o' bishops and their rents' (*RR* 349) – as a prim note in the Border Edition glossary acknowledges: 'A term unwarrantably used in imprecations or strong asseverations equivalent to English "plague" &c'. The English *devil a bit* appears accordingly as *sorra a bit* (*BL* 337); an alternative is *deil haet* (*HM* 331, *FN* 46, *RR* 332, *An* 579). Originally this was *Deil hae it* (*Devil have it*) but the elements of the contraction were not easy to recognize and *haet* was sometimes taken as a noun with the result that an indefinite article was included: 'fient a haet care I' (*GM* 554). For *sorrow* meaning 'plague' the alternative is *weary*: 'Weary on Lunnon, and a' that e'er came out o't' (*HM* 53; also *BL* 183, *OM* 533).

Ne'er means 'the devil' in phrases like 'the ne'er be in me' (*Wa* 509) meaning 'devil take me': 'ne'er be in me if they arena killing every ane of the wounded and prisoners' exclaims Cuddie after the fight at Drumclog (*OM* 248). *Ne'er* apparently has the same meaning in the phrasal compound *ne'er-be-licket* which means 'devil a bit':

> Weel, I was at the search that our gudesire ... made wi' auld Rab Tull's assistance; but ne'er-be-licket could they find that was to their purpose (*An* 113).

The way in which the phrase is made up is rather obscure; the 1833 Glossary offers this explanation: 'nothing which could be licked up, by dog or cat; absolutely nothing'.

In the novels I have not noted *gudeman* in oaths and exclamations but it is effectively used by Madge Wildfire in speaking of her 'auld ne'er-do-weel deevil's buckie o' a mither' (*HM* 274; for *deevil's buckie* see also *Re* 621, *Wa* 510):

Scottish Sounds, Spelling and Vocabulary

Our minnie's sair mis-set, after her ordinar, sir – She'll hae had some quarrel wi' her auld gudeman – that's Satan, ye ken, sirs. . . . The gudeman and her disna aye gree weel, and then I maun pay the piper; but my back's broad eneugh to bear't a' (*HM* 275).

The effectiveness of this lies in the coalescence of *gudeman's* euphemistic meaning 'the Devil' and its more ordinary meaning 'husband'. There is consequently the tragic implication that Madge herself now has no father other than the Devil.

LOCAL DIALECTS

With three exceptions – the speech of men from Aberdeenshire, from the Highlands and from Shetland – all Scots speakers in the novels are made to speak in the same dialect, Standard Scots.* Though Scott might, for example, have given Dandie Dinmont, who is from Liddesdale on the border of England and Scotland, the distinctive Southern Scots accent, he did not choose to do so. Indeed only a few writers have attempted to imitate any particular Scottish dialect faithfully. Instead most use the standard form of the language as developed by Ramsay, Fergusson and Burns in the poetry of the eighteenth century. This was a descendant of the old court Scots which was basically the Scots of sixteenth-century Edinburgh and, although some of the more distinctive old Scots spellings like *quh* for *wh* and *sch* for *sh* had been dropped, this Standard Scots had not in its spelling caught up with all recent changes in Edinburgh Scots. This is evident in poetry in the rhymes. The *SND* (*PLD* § 93.1) quotes a couplet from Burns' 'O Guid Ale Comes':

> I sell'd them a' ane by ane –
> Guid ale keeps the heart abune.

The spelling represents an older stage of Scots; Burns, whether using an Ayr or an Edinburgh pronunciation, would have rhymed the two words perfectly as [jin] and [əbin]. In fact *ale* and *guid* also underwent the same sound changes as *ane* and *abune* respectively and would have been pronounced [jil] and [gid]. This has been hidden, with *guid*, by the traditional Scottish

---

* The Shetland dialect is somewhat out of the mainstream of Scottish dialects as it is heavily influenced by the pre-existing Scandinavian language Norn which died out in the eighteenth century. Amongst Scott's novels it occurs only in *The Pirate* and it is not dealt with in this study.

spelling and, with *ale*, by the English spelling. Just occasionally the poets will drop into a spelling influenced by local dialect. Mackie notes that the 'Lothian "yae" occurs in Fergusson's "Ode from Horace", and "yence" in several poems, "Hame Content" and the "Eclogues" among them, but he also uses "anes" – the Standard Scots word for "once", often spelt "ance" or "aince"' (A. D. Mackie, 'Fergusson's Language: Braid Scots Then and Now' in *Robert Fergusson 1750–1774*, S. G. Smith ed., Edinburgh, 1952, p. 136).

Scott in all this follows the pattern of his predecessors. His spelling is generally Standard Scots and not a reproduction of Edinburgh Scots (his own dialect) or any other dialect. For instance, like Burns, he uses *abune* (*An* 186) or *aboon* (*Wa* 274) and *gude* (*GM* 200) and not *abin* and *gid*. Local forms do occasionally appear but are not used consistently. Peter Peebles tells Joshua Geddes:

> twa mutchkins o' yill between twa folk is a drappie ower little measure. What say ye to anither pot? or shall we cry in a blithe Scots pint at ance? – The yill is no amiss (*Re* 554).

If Peter, an Edinburgh man, says *yill* he should also say *yince* and not the Standard Scots *ance*. Furthermore the Edinburgh form of *twa* is *twae* [twe:]. Scott does use *yince* (e.g. *SRW* 476) but makes no attempt to give it consistently or even very frequently to all speakers from south of the Forth where it is now, and probably was then, the normal form. His usual form is *ance* or sometimes the more archaic *anes* (e.g. *RR* 357). *Yin* for *ane* (the English pronoun *one*) is also very infrequent – I have noticed no example in Scott though it does appear in the 1883 Glossary. Another mark of Edinburgh speech in our time is the pronunciation [ʍe:] where the rest of Scotland has [ʍɑ:] or [ʍɔ:] for *wha* 'who'. But if Scott intended the spelling *whae* to represent this sound it is curious that the only instances I have noticed are with speakers from Glasgow or Lanarkshire where the pronunciation was not used: they are Cuddie Headrigg (*OM* 89) and Nicol Jarvie (*RR* 364). Likewise the form *whare* for Standard English *where* and Standard Scots *whar* may represent [ʍe:r] found in East Mid-Scots south of the Forth and in Southern Scots as opposed to the [ʍɑ:r] or [ʍɔ:r] of other areas. However Scott seems to prefer the spellings *whar* or *where*. *Whare* for [ʍe:r] would be accurate for Jeanie Deans (*HM* 138) but it is possibly wrong in being assigned to Nithsdale men (*Re* 177). Very likely Scott and others who use the spelling *whare*, like Burns, Fergusson and Lockhart (see *SND whar*), did not intend it to have any precise phonetic value but merely saw it as a compromise between English *where* and Scots *whar*. In the long run it would be wrong to put too much weight on spelling, especially in view of the way Scott's spelling could be, and was, altered by his printer's transcriber. His erratic mixture of English and Scottish spellings shows us anyway that his interest was not primarily in phonetics. And there are other considerations which might influence the spelling. The old Scots equivalent of the English adjective *own* is, as we would expect, *awn*. But in the early eighteenth century *ain* appears, possibly a development from a cognate Old Norse word, and it has become the standard form in modern Scots. Scott's occasional use of *awn* (RR 314, Mo 28) is thus not an indication of local pronunciation but an archaism of spelling. The same may also apply to *aw* which is used in the speech of James I in *The Fortunes of Nigel*; as a spelling to indicate the word *all* with vocalized *l*, *aw* is much earlier used than *a'*, the spelling Scott almost always has for this very common word.

Outside the cases of Aberdeenshire and Highland Scots, indications of local non-standard pronunciations are few and far between. Even the Shetland dialect is represented only by its vocabulary and not by its pronunciation. There are however a few cases. When Wandering Willie arrives with Darsie at the dance where he is to play the fiddle, the Nithsdale men ask 'And wha is't tou's gotten, Wullie, lad?' (*Re* 177). The change of *i* to *u* after *w* (as in *Wullie*) is widespread in Scots but *tou* for *thou* is a feature of pronunciation in Renfrewshire and Ayrshire. Scott's example is the only one in the *SND* attributing the form to the west Dumfriesshire area but it may well have extended that far south.

The setting of *Guy Mannering* does not conform to geographical fact as is so often the case with Scott's settings. Ellangowan Castle, around which most of the action takes place, is based on Caerlaverock Castle in west Dumfriesshire (see *GM* 35n), but the country described as surrounding it seems to be more like the Kirkcudbrightshire coast of Wigtown Bay. Lost after nightfall somewhere in this region Mannering is told to 'gae back as far as the Whaap' (*GM* 5). Scott adds a useful but also misleading footnote: 'The Hope, often pronounced "Whaap", is the sheltered part, or hollow, of the hill. "Hoff", "howff", "haaf" and "haven" are all modifications of the same word'. His first sentence is accurate; in Southern Scots *h* before *o* becomes [ʍ], spelt *wh*, so this is a genuine Southern Scots variant pronunciation of *hope*. Mannering is perhaps a little too far to the west to encounter this pronunciation but it would have been used in more easterly parts of Dumfriesshire where for example we find Dandie Dinmont's farm *Charlies-hope* in the name of which the same word appears in its standard Scottish form. The second sentence of Scott's note spreads confusion everywhere. *Howff* or *hoff* meaning 'an enclosed yard', 'a haunt' (*HM* 236, *SRW* 40) or 'a tavern' (*FN* 612, *OM* 48) is derived from German *Hof* 'an enclosed space'. *Haaf* 'the deep sea' (*Pi* 91), a word used in the Shetland dialect, is from Old Norse *haf* 'the ocean'. *Haven* is from Old English, ultimately perhaps from *haf* but more probably from another source. None of the three words is therefore related to *hope* (or *whaap*) which derives from Old English *hop* 'a piece of enclosed land'. As if to further confound the reader a second noun *hope*, derived from *hóp*, an Old Norse word for 'a land-locked bay', also exists in Scots. It too appears in a place-name – the name of the small village near the Master of Ravenswood's refuge, Wolf's Crag: 'It was a little hamlet which straggled along the side of a creek formed by the discharge of a small brook into the sea ... It was called Wolf's-hope (i.e. Wolf's Haven)' (*BL* 167). It was perhaps because of the similarity in *meaning* of this *hope* to *haven*, which itself is similar in *form* to *haaf* and *howff*, that Scott thought all these words were derived from the same source. Returning to *whaap*, it is at least possible, but unlikely, that Scott was correct in giving this pronunciation to someone living near 'Ellangowan' which could be near the Southern Scots area to which this sound change is now confined; it is certainly inappropriate to ascribe a form arising from the same sound change to the Midlothian-born Jeanie Deans when she writes to her father about a *whorn* 'horn' (*HM* 414).

Two of the few other indications of local dialect belong also to Southern Scots. As I have remarked, Dandie Dinmont is not given a Southern Scots accent; but he is given at least one local word. After being attacked by thieves he urges his rescuer Brown to escape with him as 'I see some folk coming through the slack yonder' (*GM* 208). The *SND* takes this as an example of *slack* in its widespread Scottish sense of 'a hollow or declivity' (*SND slack* n² 1), but the context makes it clear that the word appears here with a sense which Scott himself explains when he uses the word again a few pages later on: 'a deep morass, termed in that country a slack' (*GM* 222; this is the *SND*'s sense 3 under which this quotation is cited). The word *country* here means 'district' as it did in Standard English at the time and this meaning of the word seems only to be found in Southern Scots. That the word means 'marsh' or 'bog' is clear in the wider context of the first example but the immediate context is confusing to the modern reader. When Dandie points out the men coming across the 'slack' Brown sees 'five or six men . . . coming across the moss' (*GM* 208). The word *moss* makes us think of moss-covered ground but in this context *moss* has its Scottish sense 'marshy ground, bog' and is equivalent to *slack*. The other Southern Scots word is given to Meg Dodds in *St Ronan's Well*. The site of her Cleikum Inn is rather indeterminate as Scott describes it but it must be in or near the Southern Scots area which includes Roxburghshire. If her guests are recalcitrant she rebukes them, or gives them 'what in her country is called a *sloan*' (*SRW* 18). This is the only *SND* quotation for *sloan* 'a retort, a snub' which is otherwise only known in dictionaries, where it is marked as a Roxburghshire word. Incidentally the use of *country* to mean 'area' is well illustrated in Darsie's conversation with Wandering Willie:

> I asked him if he was of this country.
> '*This* country!' replied the blind man – 'I am of every country in broad Scotland, and a wee bit of England to the boot' (*Re* 139).

Twice Scott mentions another word as being a local one. In *The Antiquary* he writes of 'dells, glens, or as they are provincially termed, *dens*' (*An* 210) and in *Redgauntlet* Darsie, writing very much in Scott's style of course, describes 'a deep dell or dingle, such as they call in some parts of Scotland a den, and in others a cleuch, or narrow glen' (*Re* 41). The *SND* quotations are from most parts of the country for *den* and, for that matter for *cleuch*, so if Scott was right in thinking of the two words as local dialect we cannot now trace their distribution. *Cleugh* appears in other novels (with this alternative spelling; *SRW* 550, *OM* 200, *BD* 338) but Scott does not add any further comment.

Fergusson, like Scott later, only imitated the pronunciation of two non-standard varieties of Scots: the Aberdeenshire dialect and the Scots of Gaelic speakers. The reason is no doubt the same with both authors – both of these varieties of Scots have sharp distinguishing features occurring in a number of important words making them easy to imitate in short passages. No major character in the novels speaks either. The Aberdeenshire, or, more generally, the North-Eastern, dialect is represented in *The Antiquary* by Francie Macraw from Inverurie, Edie Ochiltree's companion in his soldiering days (*An* 369–72, 384), and, very briefly, in *The Bride of Lammermoor* by Davie Dingwall 'the writer, that's come frae the North' (*BL* 170). Davie who elsewhere speaks English drops into his native accent when trying to establish a tone of intimacy with Caleb (*BL* 355). Two major sound changes differentiate this dialect from Standard Scots. Firstly, words which elsewhere developed from earlier English *ō* or from French *u* to the various sounds represented by the Standard Scots spellings *ui* and *u-e* developed in the North-East into [iː], usually written *ee*. Compare *puir* 'poor' (*RR* 349) with *peer* (*An* 369, *BL* 355) and *fule* (*FN* 86) and *fule-body* (*GM* 468) with *feel* (*An* 384) and *feel-body* (*An* 369). Also affected by this change are *dee* 'do' (*An* 369), *jeedge* 'judge' (*An* 371), *jeest* 'just' (*An* 384) and *seere* 'sure' (*An* 371). Secondly, *wh* [ʌ] becomes *f*. This change is particularly useful to the author in establishing the Aberdeen accent in a short passage of dialogue as it affects common words like *fan* 'when' (*An* 371) and *fat* 'what' (*An* 369, *BL* 355). *Wha* 'who' similarly becomes *fa*, but not *fae*, the incorrect form Scott gives it (*An* 371). Other *wh* words are similarly affected, like *fite* 'white' (*An* 372). Working by analogy Scott also used *Fusht* (*An* 369) as the supposed North-Eastern form of *Whisht* 'Hush' (*Wa* 288, *An* 356). The word is otherwise unrecorded and we might well doubt, along with the *SND*, if it ever really existed. Indeed the shortness of the passages concerned, the presence of such mistakes and the absence of other dialect markers besides these two sound changes makes clear Scott's marginal interest in, and slight acquaintance with, this dialect.

The *f* for *wh* is possibly due to the influence of Gaelic. The same change took place where English speakers were surrounded by Celtic speakers in Ireland but, as the *SND* remarks, it is 'curious that old Gaelic areas like Fife and Galloway do not present this phenomenon' (*PLD* § 134). Be that as it may, the Scots given to Gaelic speakers in the novels includes this feature. *Fa* is used for *wha* (*RR* 290) and *fat* for *what* (*LM* 34).

Scottish Sounds, Spelling and Vocabulary

This language given to Highlanders is a highly developed literary convention and as such can often be remote from reality. The use of *she* as a general-purpose pronoun for Highlanders can be found in literary sources as far back as the fifteenth century but it seems to have no basis in reality. It is an unfortunate convention since it tends inevitably to make the speaker a figure of fun. Our prejudices about illiterate speech operate with double vigour when we find both the pronouns themselves and the cases confounded. *She* is generally subjective for *I* (*GM* 342, *RR* 293), *you* (*FM* 625, *LM* 34), *he* (*RR* 294, *Wa* 228) or *it* (*Wa* 405) and *her* generally objective, for *me* (*RR* 293), *you* (*LM* 34, *RR* 295) and *it* (*Wa* 422) or possessive for *my* (*FM* 624) or *your* (*RR* 408). However the potential confusion forces the writer into using, for example, *her* as a subject:

> She had better speak nae mair about her culter, or, by G—, her will gar her eat her words (*RR* 408).

This translates as:

> You had better speak no more about your culter, or, by G—, I will gar you eat your words.

'Her will gar' and not 'she will gar' must replace 'I will gar' because *she* has already been used for *you*. Similarly a Highlander was thought to refer to himself as *her nainsell* 'her own self': 'I have eaten the town bread' becomes 'Her nainsell has eaten the town pread' (*RR* 394). Again this usage exists only in the Lowlander's imagination though perhaps it is 'intended to translate the common Gaelic emphatic pronoun adjuncts *-se*, *-sa* and *fhein*, self' (*SND nain*). So well established was this as a literary convention that *Her Nainsell* became a jocular name for a Highlander.

The quotation about 'the town pread' illustrates another feature of this pseudo-Highland Scots: the substitution, especially initially, of one consonant for another to represent Gaelic-influenced pronunciation. The voiceless Gaelic *b* is signalled by the use of *p* as in *ped* 'bed' (*RR* 301) and *pegged* 'begged' (*HM* 720), and the unvoiced *d* by *t*: *matam* 'madam' (*HM* 721), *Tavie* 'Davie' (*HM* 767), *teil* 'deil' (*LM* 34). *T* also replaces *th* initially, a position where it is not found in Gaelic: *ta* 'the' (*Wa* 148), *tat* 'that' (*RR* 290, *Wa* 148), *tem* 'them' (*Wa* 273), *tree* 'three' (*Wa* 148). Other sounds not found initially in Gaelic are [dʒ] and [tʃ] so that we have *shentleman* (RR 301, HM 725) for *gentleman*, *Sharvie* (RR 394) for *Jarvie*, *shase* (RR 407) for *chase*, and *sharge* (HM 727) for *charge*. This Highland Scots appears frequently in Scott – with Fergus' clansmen in *Waverley* (*Wa* 148, 228, 273 &c), with the caddie in *Guy Mannering* (*GM* 342-3), with Conachar's foster brother in *The Fair Maid of Perth* (*FM* 623-5), with Rob Roy's distant relative and follower (RR 290-301, 394) and on a number of other occasions. In line with the author's treatment of ordinary Scots, the various Gaelic-influenced pronunciations are not used consistently: *deil* (*Wa* 273) is, for instance, used close to *teil* (*Wa* 278) and *ta* only rarely replaces *the*. No doubt these consonantal substitutions do not provide us with a very accurate impression of a Gaelic accent. Furthermore they tend to give the impression that Highlanders are speaking an even more corrupt form of what many readers in Scott's time would have seen as an already sufficiently corrupt dialect of English. His Highlanders tend as a result to look ignorant and foolish; only the chieftains and leading men of the clan, who like the upper class Lowlanders are made to speak English, escape this.

CHRISTIAN NAMES

Fashions in christian names have always been different in Scotland from England.* There are of course the obvious Highland names like *Callum* (*Wa* 170), *Dougal* (RR 293), *Duncan* (HM 651) and *Fergus* (*Wa* 170). *Eachin* is another; it is the name adopted by Conachar in *The Fair Maid of Perth* when he returns to his clan to be its chief. It was often anglicized as Hector, hence the giving of that name to the Highlander Hector M'Intyre in *The Antiquary*. But even the Lowlanders differed from the English in their fashions in the choice of names. Names which were more common in Scotland than in England in Scott's time are: *Adam* (*An* 262), *Alexander* (*Re* 126), *Alison* (*M* 59), *Andrew* (RR 80), *David* (HM 106), *Euphemia* (HM 321), *Gilbert* (*GM* 136), *Griselda* (*An* 64) or *Grizel* (*Hm* 53) – 'I present to you ... my most discreet sister Griselda, – who disdains the simplicity as well as patience annexed to the poor old name of Grizel' says Oldbuck to Lovel (*An* 64) – *Janet* (*Wa* 348), *Jean* (*GM* 352), *Marion* (BL 178) and *Nigel*, (FN 37). Some of these names like *Adam*, *Alison*, *Janet* and

* For information about the popularity of christian names I have drawn particularly on the frequency charts in L. A. Dunkling's *First Names First* (London, 1977).

Nigel have since become popular in England and *David*, which had always been quite common in England but not as common as in Scotland, has become a very popular English name. Many of these names had distinctive Scottish forms and diminutives. The diminutive of *Adam* is *Edie* (*An* 43) – not to be confused with English *Eddie* for *Edward*. *Alexander* gives birth to a host of names; the name itself is changed to *Elshender* (*BD* 367) and to *Saunders* (*An* 443) and these give rise to diminutives *Elshie* (*BD* 367), *Sandie* (*SRW* 32, *RR* 367) and *Sawney*, a nickname used by Englishmen in addressing Scots (*Re* 502). (Charles Churchill's vitriolic anti-Scots poem 'The Prophecy of Famine: A Scots Pastoral' (1763) includes a dialogue between two Scots called *Jockey* and *Sawney*.) *Alison* has two diminutives, *Ailsie* (*BL* 326) and *Ailie* (*GM* 214); in a moment of joy at the return of her beloved Henry Morton 'Mrs Alison Wilson' the housekeeper allows herself to be called *Ailie* (*OM* 533). *Andrew* has the Scots form *Andro* (*RR* 364) and as a diminutive is *Dandie* (*GM* 197) or *Dand* (*GM* 224), so that Andrew Wilson's nickname was *Handie Dandie* (*HM* 340). *Davie* is the diminutive of *David* and is applied, with the greater freedom in using diminutives characteristic of Scots, to the serious Davie Deans (*HM* 113) and the poet Sir David Lindsay (*An* 65) as well as to the mad Davie Gellatley (*Wa* 73). *Euphemia* is actually Effie Deans' real name and was also given to her sister Jeanie's daughter but, perhaps with Effie's seduction in mind, 'the child was never distinguished by the name of Effie, but by the abbreviation of Femie which in Scotland is equally commonly applied to persons called Euphemia' (*HM* 685). When Effie comes to visit Jeanie there is a touching moment when Femie is presented to her aunt who is now the grand Lady Staunton and cannot acknowledge openly her relationship to the children and Jeanie:

> 'Come here, Femie', said Mrs Butler, 'and hold your head up.'
> 'What is your daughter's name, madam?' said the lady.
> 'Euphemia, madam,' answered Mrs Butler.
> 'I thought the ordinary Scottish contraction of the name had been Effie' replied the stranger, in a tone which went to Jeanie's heart (*HM* 723).

The diminutives of *Gilbert*, *Griselda* and *Janet* are *Gibbie* (*BL* 184), *Grizzie* (*An* 18) and *Jenny* (*OM* 132). Gilbert Glossin's pretensions to gentility are nicely deflated by Meg Merrilies' derisive exclamation 'Gibbie Glossin! that I have carried in my creels a hundred times, for his mother wasna muckle better than mysell' (*GM* 200). *Jeanie* (*HM* 113) and *Menie* (*SD* 657), diminutives of *Jean* and *Marion*, provide the names of heroines of *The Heart of Midlothian* and *The Surgeon's Daughter*. The popularity of *Halbert*, a form of *Albert*, was confined not just to Scotland but to a particular part of Scotland. E. G. Withycombe notes in *The Oxford Dictionary of English Christian Names* that it is 'still common on the Scottish Borders' (*s.v. Albert*) and the narrative of *The Black Dwarf* opens with these words: 'In one of the most remote districts of the south of Scotland, where an ideal line, drawn along the tops of lofty and bleak mountains, separates that land from her sister kingdom, a young man, called Halbert, or Hobbie Elliot . . . was on his return from deer-stalking' (*BD* 336).

There are other names which, though used in both countries, have distinctive diminutives in Scotland. When young servant girls are addressed as *Babie* (*BL* 52, *An* 185) this is not a use of the common noun *baby* as an endearment (as in present-day English) but a diminutive of *Barbara*. Where English has *Larry* and *Georgie*, Scots has *Lawrie* (*FN* 47) and *Geordie* (*HM* 455), the latter being part of King James' name for George Heriot, the goldsmith: *Jingling Geordie* (*FN* 45). *Jamie* (*Wa* 360), the diminutive of James, has in the 1960s and 1970s come into English use as a full name and not just as a diminutive, but it was originally Scots. *Stephen* followed many other Scots words in the loss of *v*, giving us *Steen* and the surname *Steenson* (*Re* 152, *RR* 367) with the diminutive *Steenie*, the name of the hero of 'Wandering Willie's Tale' (*Re* 152) and Steenie Mucklebackit, the young fisherman drowned in *The Antiquary* (*An* 97). *Antony* also changes quite considerably with the addition of an initial consonant to yield *Nanty* (*Re* 410) as does *Tibb* (*Mo* 22) or *Tibbie* (*Re* 162) for *Isabella*. Even more drastic is the change of *Mary*, via *Mall* (English *Moll*), to the now obsolete *Mause* (*OM* 83) and of *Elizabeth* to *Elspeth* (*An* 356, *Mo* 15) or *Elspat* (*CC* 473), of which the diminutive is *Eppie* (*HM* 58). Occasionally, of course, English people will be addressed or talked of by the Scots forms of their names: Jock Jabos, whose own name has the Scots *Jock* (*GM* 199, 296, *HM* 58, 111, *An* 487) where English has *Jack*, speaks of Julia as 'Miss Jowlia Mannering' (*GM* 296) and Meg Dodds – again notice *Meg* (*SRW* 9, *GM* 19) for English *Mag(gie)* – calls Francis Tyrrell 'Francie Tirl' (*SRW* 25).

Scottish Sounds, Spelling and Vocabulary

Amongst these names some have become common nouns. *Jock* in its diminutive form *jockie* comes to mean 'a pedlar, a gipsy' – Scott speaks of 'gypsies, jockies, or cairds' (*GM* 59) with *caird* being another word for such a person (*HM* 706). The sense 'a horse-dealer' was perhaps an English development (it is first cited in the *OED* from Brome) but survived later in Scots than in English and appears in Scott (*HM* 197, *Re* 95) as does the sense 'courier' (*Re* 493) from which develops the modern Standard English sense 'a professional rider at horse-races'. A *jockey-coat* – the word is a Scottish creation – is 'a heavy overcoat suitable for horse-dealers and postillions' (*GM* 222, *HM* 197). *Jock* also combines with *leg* to give *joctaleg* 'a large pocket knife' (*RR* 461). A *Tammy Norie* (*An* 94) is a puffin, the first element being the diminutive of *Tam* (*OM* 379, *GM* 197), the Scottish equivalent of *Tom*. *Billy*, though not exclusively Scottish as a diminutive for *William*, has nevertheless taken on a number of special senses in Scotland, including 'brother' (*BD* 426) and 'fellow, chap' (*GM* 223, *FN* 46) while *cuddie* meaning 'a donkey' (*GM* 21, *HM* 116) is probably the same word as the one used as a diminutive in Scotland for *Cuthbert* and given to Cuddie Headrigg in *Old Mortality* (*OM* 81).

This last example brings us to the dumb animals which have special Scottish affectionate names too. A cat was called *baudrons*; according to Grizel Oldbuck her ancestor's ghost had whiskers 'as long as baudron's' (*An* 114; the misprint for *baudrons*' is corrected in the Dryburgh edition). A dog was often named *Bawty* (*Wa* 338, *HM* 270); King James' dogs are called *Bash* and *Battie* (*FN* 481). The word *crummie* meaning 'a cow with a crooked horn', which we have already considered in another context, can further be used as the cow's name (*Mo* 23) – one of the rocks Lovel must fasten his rope around in coming down the cliff is called 'Crummie's horn' (*An* 91). A cow with a white face is called *Hawkie* or *Hackie* (*OM* 364), a development from the adjective *hawkit* (*HM* 622) or *hackit* (*Ab* 245) 'having a white face'. Warrack gives the cow's name *Grizzy* (*Mo* 23) as a use of the diminutive of *Grizel* or *Griselda*, though it is tempting to associate it with Spenser's word *grisy* 'grey' (*FQ* I ix 25).

THE PROBLEM OF INTELLIGIBILITY

Much of what has been said about how Scott solved the problem of intelligibility with period language applies with equal force to Scottish language, although the reader at a disadvantage is different – a non-Scot rather than a non-scholar. Here too we find the full gamut from the obvious intrusion of a footnote to the subtle manipulation of the context to provide an explanation. Most of the footnotes were added in the Collected Edition and they still remain relatively few in number. In *Redgauntlet* Scott added, amongst others, notes on *bink* (*Re* 47), *braxy mutton* (*Re* 378), *hallan* (*Re* 43), *multiplepoinding* (*Re* 206) and *pokes* (*Re* 200). A bink is, to use Scott's gloss, 'the frame of wooden shelves placed in a Scottish kitchen for holding plates' (*Re* 47n). Scott's decision to add a note here is a little surprising, especially considering how few notes he added; the main text reads:

> The *bink*, with its usual arrangement of pewter and earthenware, which was most strictly and critically clean, glanced back the flame of the lamp merrily from one side of the apartment (*Re* 46–7).

The context seems to have been arranged to provide the reader with a reasonable chance of guessing what a bink is, and in many other cases in the novels Scott was content to do no more. In fact the addition of footnote glosses in the Collected Edition is on the whole rather haphazard. When *bink* appears in the narrative of *The Fair Maid* it is glossed by the much more common method of including an explanation in the main text: 'a range of shelves like those of a beauffet, popularly called *the bink*' (*FM* 32). Elsewhere (*SRW* 21, *HM* 210) *bink* must rely simply on what the reader can deduce from the context with an element of confusion added by the definition in the Collected Edition's glossary: 'bench, bank, acclivity'. This does not work very well in *The Heart of Midlothian* where the surrounding context is full of words unfamiliar to a non-Scot. Davie Deans is determined not to show his emotions over Effie's situation and, turning to Jeanie:

> He even chid his daughter for having neglected, in the distress of the morning, some trifling domestic duties which fell under her department.
> 'Why, what meaneth this, Jeanie?' said the old man – 'The brown four-year-auld's milk is not seiled yet, nor the bowies put up on the bink' (*HM* 210).

With *bink* plus *seil* meaning 'strain' and *bowie* meaning 'bowl'

Scottish Sounds, Spelling and Vocabulary

the reader may well not follow the precise meaning. On the other hand the main purpose of the passage is still served; we have no trouble in understanding that Davie is trying to forget this sorrow in the everyday concerns of his dairy. The general sense is also sufficient with Dandie Dinmont's description of how he trains his hunting dogs:

> I have six terriers at hame, forbye twa couple of slow-hunds, five grews, and a wheen other dogs. There's auld Pepper and auld Mustard, and young Pepper and young Mustard, and little Pepper and little Mustard – I had them a' regularly entered, first wi' rottens, then wi' stots or weasels, and then wi' the tods and brocks; and now they fear naething that ever cam wi' a hairy skin on't (*GM* 197).

Lots of these words would be unfamiliar to English readers. *Slow-hound* (*An* 32, *FM* 418), a name for a kind of blood-hound, was a Scottish term though its unelided form *sleuth-hound* 'so called from *slot* or *sleut*, a word which signifies the scent left by an animal of chase' (*TG* 72, *An* 267) especially when shortened to *sleuth* is now known in English, probably due to Scott's use of it. *Grew* is also a shortening like *sleuth*; it is from *grew-hound* the Scottish form of *greyhound*. *Rotten*, according to the *SND* a form used north of the Forth but here given to a southern Scot, is a variant of *ratton* 'a rat', a dialect word in England since the eighteenth century. *Stot* may not be immediately recognizable as a form of *stoat* and is not to be confused with *stot* 'a steer' (*RR* 358, *Wa* 89). *Tod* is a Scots word for 'fox' and *brock* a general dialect word for 'badger'. But the reader probably picks up the general idea that the dogs are gradually accustomed to bigger and bigger animals.

Terms of abuse or of endearment are by their nature rarely of any precise meaning. They are likely to be supported by redundant adjectives, but this is a realistic reflection of actual speech. No one is likely to seriously mistake the sense of 'ta filthy, gutty hallions' (*RR* 293), even out of context. (*Gutty* 'gross'; *hallion* 'rascal, idler).'

A closely related practice is Scott's habit of explaining one Scots word with another Scots word. Here too the precise sense is less important than the chance to introduce local colour in the form of unfamiliar words. In *Redgauntlet* Scott talks of a 'a *haugh*, or *holm*' (*Re* 42) and redundantly in *Old Mortality* of 'haugh and holme' (*OM* 106). Both words mean a stretch of low-lying land beside a river. By Scott's time *haugh* was exclusively Scots and *holm*, in this sense, limited to Scotland and the north of England. It is possible that Scott did not realize that *holm* was not Standard English. Or perhaps he stuck to *holm* because of the absence of any exact English synonym; his other explanations of *haugh* are inadequate: the 'narrow meadow' of *Waverley* (*Wa* 69) and the 'level plain' of *Old Mortality* (*OM* 19) both lie beside brooks but this is not an obvious part of the definition. A more extended example has already been mentioned in another context. Darsie describes:

> a deep dell or dingle, such as they call in some parts of Scotland a den, and in others a cleuch, or narrow glen (*Re* 41).

Here we have no less than two English synonyms (*dell, dingle*) and three Scots ones (*den, cleuch, glen*).

Occasionally, but not often considering how much new vocabulary he had to deal with, Scott falls into redundancy in trying to fit in an explanation. In *The Fair Maid* he talks of the Highlanders' 'knives called skenes' (*FM* 520) but on other occasions in the same novel he speaks redundantly of 'skenes and dirks' (*FM* 42) and 'knives and skeans' (*FM* 242). Or again Joshua Geddes describes himself to Darsie as 'a tacksman or lessee of some valuable salmon fisheries' (*Re* 82). A tacksman is a lessee and the latter term can only have been introduced for the sake of the reader.

Most of what has been said so far also applies to period language. Some features of the handling of Scots are however less closely parallel. One situation Scott found useful, but which he could not exploit with period language, is the confrontation of a Scots-speaker with an English-speaker. His first novel offered him the advantages of this situation with its English hero and, almost as soon as Waverley arrives at Tully-Veolan, we read of his reactions to the vocabulary of Scots. He is informed that the Baron is 'with the folk who are getting doon the dark hag' (*Wa* 73). The phrase is mysterious but when he talks to Rose all is explained:

> The first greetings past, Edward learned from her that the *dark hag*, which had somewhat puzzled him in the butler's account of his master's avocations, had nothing to do with either a black cat or a broomstick, but was simply a portion of oak copse which was to be felled that day (*Wa* 76).

Scottish Sounds, Spelling and Vocabulary

Town 'a house' and *innocent* 'an idiot' are commented on in the same way (*Wa* 73-4). There is also an English protagonist in *Rob Roy*, Frank Osbaldistone, to whom Nicol Jarvie explains the term *blackmail* (RR 359) and Andrew Fairservice the terms *fley* 'frighten' and *bogle* 'ghost' (RR 245) while Frank himself, as narrator, notes that Andrew calls beehives *skeps* (RR 231) and remarks later on 'I only heard the monotonous and plaintive cries of the lapwing and curlew which my companions denominated the peasweep and whaup' (RR 376). Perhaps the best confrontation of the two languages in that novel is another between Frank and the provoking Andrew. Andrew tells how:

> 'I was doun at the Trinlay-knowe ... about a wee bit business o' my ain wi' Mattie Simpson ... and when we were at the thrangest of our bargain, wha suld come in but Pate Macready the travelling merchant?'
> 'Pedlar, I suppose you mean?'
> 'E'en as your honour likes to ca' him' (RR 193).

Frank's ill-advised interruption allows Andrew to draw out further his long-winded account until he finally gets his revenge when Frank prompts him with:

> 'And after all, Andrew, what are these London news you had from your kinsman, the travelling merchant?'
> 'The pedlar, your honour means?' retorted Andrew, – 'but ca' him what ye wull' (RR 196).

Travelling and *traveller* are still used in Scotland to avoid derogatory terms like *gipsy* and *tinker*; even as late as 1971 HMSO issued a book entitled *Scotland's Travelling People*. Scott would possibly have been surprised at the euphemism's survival since he has Peter Pattieson comment on:

> those modest itinerants whom the scrupulous civility of our ancestors denominated travelling merchants, but whom, of late, accommodating ourselves, in this as in more material particulars, to the feelings and sentiments of our more wealthy neighbours, we have learned to call packmen or pedlars (OM 14).

Interesting as the interchange of English and Scots speakers on their respective idioms can be it is surely carried a bit far, as we have remarked before, when Darsie Latimer, who left England before his teens, plays the role of English commentator on Scottish speech (e.g. *Re* 34, 46).

It is particularly since Scott wrote that Scottish terms have entered Standard English but this process had begun in his time and some words no longer needed glossing. *Clan* (*Wa* 139, *RR* 356, *FM* 505), a Scots word from Gaelic, was used in eighteenth-century English texts, allowing Scott to introduce his own creation *clansman* (*Wa* 212, *CC* 455, *FM* 504) without any problems in its being understood. Englishmen visiting Scotland or Scotsmen writing for the English had used *glen* (*Wa* 112), *kilt* (*Wa* 140) and *loch* (*Wa* 159). But, surprisingly, while *plaid* was already used in England for tartan material as well as for the piece of clothing (*HM* 535, *Wa* 140, *OM* 112), the now more common word *tartan* (*HM* 535, *FM* 119) seems, on the evidence of the *OED*, to have entered Standard English only in the nineteenth century. Scots words might also be known to English readers from their use as archaisms in English literature. The verb *trow*, for example, was well established in eighteenth-century English as an archaism and was so used by Scott in his medieval and renaissance novels. In Scots it was still in normal use (*RR* 349, *HM* 426). *Sain* 'to bless' is found as an archaism in Byron (*Don Juan*, XVI, 'Beware, Beware' vi) but, though now archaic in Scotland, was then apparently quite usual, especially in the phrase *God sain* (*An* 328, *HM* 426).

Other words, while not used in English, are sufficiently close to English words for the reader to recognize them. *Sponsible* (*RR* 283, *OM* 115) will immediately be associated with *responsible*, *contrair* (*BL* 146, *HM* 279) with *contrary*. It is also possible to guess the meaning of words like *awesome* (*GM* 108) which are derivatives of words in English. Moreover the basic sound changes which separate English and Scots can quickly be deduced; our love of seeing patterns soon alerts us to groups of pairs like *aits/oats, hame/home, rape/rope* and *good/gude, blood/blude, moon/mune* and we can apply the analogy to new words as they come along. Frequency is here an important factor and some words will be understood simply because they occur so often in Scott: important verbs like *ken* 'know', *maun* 'must' and *speer* 'ask' and prepositions like *anent* 'concerning' and *forby* 'except' are not glossed but are quickly understood.

Sometimes the similarity to English can be a hindrance rather than a help. When Rob Roy tells Nicol Jarvie 'The only drap o' gentle bluid that's in your body was our great grand-uncle's that was justified at Dumbarton' (*RR* 317) his pride in his ancestor may seem well placed until we realize that *justified* in Scots means 'executed' as when Evan makes his bid to save Fergus MacIvor by offering 'that ony six o' the very best of his clan will be willing to be justified in his stead' (*Wa* 610).

As we have already seen in our discussion of spelling one of Scott's most important ways of keeping his Scots intelligible is the use of English spelling. This has already been discussed in detail. It may be added that this process sometimes extends to words not found themselves in English but which can be partially anglicized. Scott has a word *fusionless* (RR 267, SRW 510), *fizzenless* (RR 195) or *fissenless* (Om 54) meaning 'without sap, pith, or strength'. It derives from the Scots word *fushion*, the English equivalent of which, by a separate development from French was *foison*. *Foison*, which meant 'plenty' or 'power', became obsolete in English by the end of the seventeenth century but Scott would have come across it in Shakespeare, even, indeed, in a reference to Scotland: Macduff assures Malcolm that 'Scotland hath foisons to fill up your will' (*Mac* IV iii 88). Perhaps remembering Shakespeare, Scott at least once anglicizes Scottish *fusionless* as *foisonless* (OM 225) but *foisonless* was not an English word and only appears in English texts after Scott. Somewhat similar treatment is given to the Scots word *burrows-town* 'a borough' (*An* 350, FN 87) which is at times replaced in the Scots dialogue by the archaic English *borough-town* (GM 77, OM 267). English *causeway* is a development by way of the compound *causey-way* from the earlier *causey*. In Scotland *causey* remained in use and developed a sense not found in England, 'a paved road in a town' (*An* 273, FN 44); sometimes we find the English form *causeway* used for this Scottish sense (Re 350, FN 455, SRW 209). But of all the anglicizations the most extreme is *hellicat*, Scott's already discussed remodelling of *hallockit*. *Hellicat* makes sense to the English reader, being so near to *hellcat*, but etymologically *hallockit* has no relation to *hell* or to *cat*.

All of these devices leave some words unclear to the English reader. As I have suggested, Scott was probably not greatly worried as long as the general sense came over. And, just as with period language, he may at times have been happy that more prudish readers could not penetrate the full meaning of a Scots word. That the boy Godfrey, born to a girl that 'did not live far from hereabouts' (GM 18), is his own illegitimate son is a fact discernible amongst the jumble of details in Godfrey Bertram's narrative, but the level of indirectness in conveying this information is sustained by the use of the Scottish term *come o' will* meaning 'bastard' (*GM* 19). The reader may easily glide over the details without picking up the full sense while the later reference to this old scandal (*GM* 544) can be dismissed as mere malicious gossip on the part of Sir Robert Hazlewood. In fact the little detail of the illegitimate son fills out nicely Godfrey Bertram's kindly but weak character. In *The Monastery* the full violence of Julian Avenel's reproach to his mistress 'thou foolish callet' (*Mo* 334) is masked by this Scots term for 'strumpet'. In this case a reader of Shakespeare will be able to recognize a word found in *The Winter's Tale* (II iii 90) which survived, in Scotland, its disappearance in post seventeenth-century Standard English. Similarly Effie's having lived with her seducer, George Robertson, is not made very prominent in Sharpitlaw's question 'Where was't that Robertson and you were used to howff thegither?' (*HM* 248) owing to the use of the Scots verb *howff* 'dwell, lodge'. Excrement is another thing not generally mentioned in the polite society of Scott's time and he makes no effort to explain *skyte*, a word of Norse origin cognate with English *shit* – 'this gabbling skyte' is how Nicol Jarvie describes Andrew Fairservice (*RR* 378). Another of the Bailie's comments might also have caused offence if written in plain English instead of 'braid Scots'. Meaning that Rob Roy is in danger of being hanged he says 'his craig wad ken the weight o' his hurdies if they could get haud o' Rob' (*RR* 360). *Craig* means 'neck' and *hurdies* 'buttocks'.

Some sly jokes of a similar nature are hidden in some of the personal names used in the novels. Saunders Fairford has an elderly client 'Lady Bedrooket, who calls ten times a year for the quarterly payment of her jointure of four hundred merks' (*Re* 113). *Drook* or *drouk* means, 'drench' and Mary M'Intyre is described as 'sair droukit' (*An* 107) after being out in stormy weather. The Scots term conceals a rather poor joke at the old lady's expense.

Chapter 7

SCOTTISH GRAMMAR

INTRODUCTION

THE DIFFERENCES BETWEEN Scots and English in grammar are not enormous. A few elements of Scots grammar appear on almost every page of Scots dialogue, in particular the use of the pronoun *ye* and the enclitic negative *-na*. Other elements are more thinly spread. As usual Scott does not maintain consistency. The use of the *-it* termination for weak past tenses and participles (see § 29) is widespread but perhaps half the time or more it yields to English *-ed*. The Scottish use, in certain circumstances, of *-s* inflections of the verb with all persons in the present tense (see § 28) mostly gives way to the Standard English restriction of *-s* to the third person singular. All the same, there are enough elements which occur regularly – like *ye*, *-na* and *thae* 'those' – to insure that a passage of Scots dialogue always has a strong element of Scots grammar.

Just as in its vocabulary, Scots is in its grammar sometimes more innovative than English; sometimes more conservative. For example it has produced new or simpler weak past tenses like *gied* 'gave' and *sleepit* 'slept' (see § 29) but also retained, in the form *leugh*, the Old English strong past tense of *laugh*, lost in Standard English (see § 30). Whereas English has taken up *those*, which used to be the plural of *this*, as the plural of *that*, Scots has kept the old plural as *thae* (see § 8).

Because the dialect is conservative in some ways, the Scots grammar in the novels coincides at certain points with Scott's period grammar. The relative pronoun can, in Scots as in the period language, be omitted where it is the subject of the clause (see § 11). *Thou*, the commonest of Scott's archaisms in the medieval and renaissance novels, appears also in the Scots dialogue, but its use is very much on the decline by his time and it is rare compared to *ye* (see § 4), the reverse of the situation in the period language.

The Language of Walter Scott

One of the disadvantages the dialects labour under as literary languages is that they all have features which are known to speakers of the standard language as 'substandard', the usage of 'vulgar' speakers. Standard English had rejected adverbial *that* meaning 'so' and *as* used as a relative, but these were still Scottish usages (see §§ 22, 10). Moreover speakers of the standard form of the language tend, with small justification, to feel their language is more logical. Hence the use of *ane* (one) with a following *they* or *their* (see § 7) would have condemned Scots in their eyes as illogical and therefore inferior. Yet this usage had been acceptable in earlier English.

Dialogue in novels is never like a transcript of real-life conversation, nor should it be. No doubt Scott was influenced in the presentation of Scottish dialogue by written Scots as well as spoken Scots. The models closest to him in time were the eighteenth-century poets who, fortunately for him, very often wrote in a colloquial, speech-based style. All the same we must not label any variation from the most colloquial idioms as 'literary' or the result of English influence and thus inaccurate as a record of speech. As I argue below in relation to *wha* (see § 9), the literary language and the spoken language are not separate entities; they interact with each other and literary usages naturally enter into even slightly formal speech.

NOUNS

1. The most common nominative plural in Old English was *-as*, given to many masculine words, but another large group of words had their plural in *-an*. These two give us present-day *-(e)s* and *-en*. In southern Middle English the *-en* plurals remained very common and only in the Modern English period was the *-(e)s* plural established as the norm. In northern Middle English on the other hand the *-en* plural very early became rare. Two of the few northern *-en* plurals of this period survive in Scott. They are *shoon* (Re 58, An 128) or *shune* (OM 539) for 'shoes' and *een* (HM 188, An 350) for 'eyes'. Standard English retains *oxen* which appears in Scots as *owsen* (OM 76, RR 355). From their rarity *-en* plurals become confusing, the result being the formation of double plurals like *breekens* (HM 763) alongside the regular plural *breeks* (FN 621, OM 489). The word is the same one as English *breeches* with Scottish *k* for *ch*. The singular of *owsen, owse*, is, like

the alternative *nowte*, not common; *nowte* remains unchanged in the plural (*HM* 683). Scots also preserves the unmarked plural of *pound* (*pund*) after a numeral, found in earlier English:

> ten pund Scots (*OM* 39).
>
> your thousan pund Scots (*RR* 317).

This applies to other money terms:

> twenty thousand merk (*Wa* 335).

and to measurements:

> thirty mile (*An* 186).

The plural of *year* can also be uninflected:

> they didna 'gree at 'a for twa or three year (*GM* 390).

On the other hand the *s* of *corpse* was taken as a plural inflection and the new singular *corp* is formed:

> they would nicker, and laugh, and giggle if their best friend was lying a corp (*BD* 426).

Finally we should note that the noun *parritch* 'porridge' is treated as a plural in Scots:

> They're gude parritch eneugh (*OM* 75).
>
> keep your ain breath to cool your ain porridge, – ye'll find them scalding hot, I promise you (*OM* 469).

PERSONAL PRONOUNS

2. The first person singular pronoun in Scots is in its stressed form [ɑ:] or in its unstressed form [ə]. The English [ai] is also used but is reserved, according to the *SND*, 'for very dignified or emphatic expression' (*SND a*). We must therefore assume that where Scott writes *I* in broad Scots dialogue one of the first two pronunciations is intended. I have only found one case where Scott uses a distinctive spelling to suggest the Scottish pronunciation:

> Am trenching up the sparry-grass, and am gaun to saw sum Misegun beans (*RR* 195).

Rather than the pronoun being omitted here, *am* is presumably for *a'm* with the *a* representing [ɑ] or [ə].

3. As well as the unemphatic *us* Scots has the emphatic pronoun *huz* which Murray calls 'the only Scotch word which aspirates an originally simple vowel' (*DSCS* 188). The emphasis comes out in the following:

> '... He hasna settled his account wi' my gudeman, the deacon for this twalmonth ...'
> 'Nor wi' huz for sax months' (*An* 182–3).

> Sudna ye hae come faster up yoursells, instead of flyting at huz? (*OM* 248).

> Thae are bonny writer words, – amaist like the language o' huz gardeners and other learned men (*RR* 254).

The tone of the last quotation extends to Scott's note in his journal:

> Hogg came to breakfast this morning, having taken and brought for his companion the Galashiels bard David Thompson as to a meeting of huzz Tividale poets (*Journal* 12 December 1825).

4. The normal second person pronoun in the Scottish dialogue, whether addressed to one person or more, is *ye* or *you*. *Ye* is the more frequent but is regularly intermixed with *you*, which occurs up to a third of the time. The distinction between *ye* as nominative and *you* as accusative has long been lost and both *ye* and *you* are used as subject and object and with prepositions:

> Ye ken little about it – little about it ... I could tell ye something about that.... But this that I am gaun to tell you was a thing that befell in our ain house in my father's time ... and I tell it to you that it may be a lesson to you, that are but a young thoughtless chap, wha ye draw up wi' on a lonely road (*Re* 150).

> O, if ye had spoken a word, ... if I were free to swear that ye had said but ae word of how it stude wi' ye, they couldna hae touched your life this day (*HM* 303).

> you tauld him ... that ye wadna hear o' coming between me and the death that I am to die (*HM* 307).

Scottish Grammar

The possessive pronoun is usually *your* but this sometimes takes the Scottish forms *yer* (*Wa* 282, 288, 289) or *yere* (*Wa* 404, *An* 186).

Thou and *thee*, so frequent as archaisms in Scott, are very rare in the Scottish dialogue. The *SND* notes that they 'survived in colloquial use until the mid-nineteenth century in most places, being particularly frequent in West Mid-Scots, as recorded especially by Galt'. Murray, writing in 1873, says that 'the second person singular pronoun has quite disappeared from the spoken dialect' (*DSCS* 188). In Scott this pronoun has already been largely replaced by *ye* or *you*, and the appearance of *thou* and *thee* is relatively rare. As in the continental languages and earlier English usage, *thou* could be used both in affection and in contempt and was used by parents to children and superiors to inferiors. One of the characters who does use it is Mause Headrigg in *Old Mortality*; she uses it affectionately in addressing her son, Cuddie (*OM* 89, 99), and contemptuously in addressing Claverhouse (*OM* 245). However when she uses it in addressing Mr Kettledrummle, the minister, her language is very biblical and it seems to be this biblical influence more than Scots idiom which leads to the choice of *thou*:

> I say, what ails thee now, that thou art blacker than a coal, that thy beauty is departed, and thy loveliness withered like a dry potsherd (*OM* 241).

We might note the use of biblical English *thou art* rather than Scots *thou is* (see § 28). Most of the time, nevertheless, Mause uses *ye* and *you*. Other English-speaking characters use *thou* and *thee* in this novel but with them it is either an archaism (the novel is set in the seventeenth century) or again, in the speech of the Cameronians, biblical usage.

The relatively frequent use of *thou* in this novel may reflect the fact that it is almost the earliest-set of the Scottish novels but we also find it in later-set novels like *The Heart of Midlothian* where Meg Murdockson, whom, perhaps, Scott wanted to show as having a particularly broad dialect speech (see § 33), uses *thou* briefly in castigating her daughter Madge Wildfire. Even with her it proves to be only a temporary variation from *ye*:

> What signifies what we were, ye street-raking limmer .... I'se tell thee what thou is now – thou's a crazed hellicat Bess o'Bedlam, that sall taste naething but bread and water for a fortnight, to serve ye for the plague ye hae gien me – and ower gude for ye, ye idle taupie! (*HM* 274-5).

We see that the change back to *ye* is made without any change in tone; even the continuing strong terms of contempt are not sufficient to maintain the use of *thou*. The opposite feeling, deep love, comes out in Steenie Mucklebackit's mother's mourning over his dead body in *The Antiquary*:

> O my bairn, my bairn, my bairn! what for is thou lying there, and eh! what for am I left to greet for ye! (*An* 414).

For a last example, Wandering Willie when he arrives at the Brokenburn-foot dance is greeted with *tou* (a local form? see above) and *thee* (*Re* 177, 179) although generally addressed as *ye* on this occasion. Most of these examples come from speakers of the lowest social classes and they are perhaps to be seen as old-fashioned usages, which always survive most strongly with the highest and lowest classes of society.

As in *Old Mortality*, so in the other Scottish novels *thou* also appears in the dialogue of English-speakers. There are a variety of reasons for this. With Joshua Geddes in *Redgauntlet* it is the well-known usage of the Quakers (*Re* 252-4). With Jonathan Oldbuck (e.g. *An* 70), the Antiquary living in the 1790s, it may be either an old-fashioned English usage, since *thou* survived into the eighteenth century in colloquial speech, or one of his archaistic affectations. In the letters between Darsie Latimer and Alan Fairford they address each other, not consistently, as *thou*; this too may be a slight affectation between close friends. Finally, in his last words before dying, the elder Bertram in *Guy Mannering* berates his enemy Glossin:

> Out of my sight, ye viper, – ye frozen viper, that I warmed till ye stung me! Art thou not afraid that the walls of my father's dwelling should fall and crush thee limb and bone? (*GM* 128).

Though Bertram elsewhere speaks Scots he here speaks English. Rather than being either period language or Scots idiom, *thou* here seems to me to be part of a more high-flown language adopted as being suited to the seriousness of the occasion.

5. The periphrastic alternative to the possessive pronoun, *of thee* for *thy* and so on, appears in Scott both as an archaism (see chapter 4, § 12) and as a Scoticism:

> the Hieland blude o' me warms at thae daft tales (*RR* 361).

6. The use of the *-self* pronouns as the independent subject of a sentence and not merely in apposition to another pronoun which we have seen to be an archaism in the medieval and renaissance novels seems, like the preceding usage, to survive in Scots:

> Mysell am not clear to trinquet and traffic wi' courts o' justice, as they are now constituted (*HM* 283).

In *Old Mortality* however the usage, occurring in the *English* speech of Balfour, is period:

> thyself shall vote and judge (*OM* 307).

In keeping with the use of *she* for *I* in pseudo-Highland speech discussed previously, the Highlanders are made to use *hersell* in the same way for *I*. Guy Mannering's guide in Edinburgh, a Highlander, says of himself:

> Hersell could have tell'd ye that; but she thought ye wanted to see his house (*GM* 342).

Various emphatic alternatives to the *-self* pronouns are found in Scots. A periphrastic form with *o'* may be used:

> I ken nae friend he has in the world that's been sae like a father to him as the sell o' ye (*HM* 124).

> Kirkcaldy, the sell o't, is langer than ony town in England (*RR* 196).

or *ain* 'own' may be included:

> is this your ainsell in blood and bane (*Re* 305).

> I'll be your wife my ainsell (*GM* 235).

Nain (*An* 384), the product of the mistaken division of *mine ain* and *my nain*, gives us *her nainsell* which like *hersell* is given to Highlanders:

> her nainsell will never bid thee less (*FM* 625).

7. The indefinite personal pronoun *ane* is followed by the plural pronouns *they* and *their*:

> ane would take care o' him if they could (*HM* 68).

> ane maybe is a thought bonnier... than their neighbours (*HM* 449).

> where ane may sleep... till they hear the lavrock singing up in the air (*FN* 45).

This was once acceptable usage in Standard English (*OED one* 21) but now *one/one's* is expected in Britain and *he/his* in the US. It will be interesting to see whether the pressure for non-sexist pronouns will take US usage back to the old *they/their* or bring it into conformity with British *one/one's*. Scots also retained another usage with *ane* obsolete in Standard English – *ane* meaning 'someone':

> there's ane coming down the crag e'en now (*An* 91).

> there's ane frae Cumberland been waiting here for ye (*BD* 426).

The last *OED* citation for this meaning of *one* is dated 1759 (*OED one* 20a).

DEMONSTRATIVE PRONOUNS

8. Besides the English demonstratives *this* and *that* Scots has a third demonstrative *yon* used of something distanced in time or space. The form is the same for singular and plural:

> to say something to yon folks (*HM* 306).

> What think ye o' yon bonny hill yonder, lifting its brow to the moon? Trow ye yon's the gate to heaven . . . ? (*HM* 426).

As for *this* and *that*, they have plurals different in Scots to English. The plural of *that* is *thae*, the regular development of Old English *þā* where Standard English has adopted the plural of Old English 'þis': thus we have 'thae fearless follies' (*OM* 28), 'thae cattle' (*RR* 244), 'thae cockle-brained callants' (*SRW* 16) and 'Thae are bonny writer words' (*RR* 254). The plural of *this* is *thir*, the origin of which is much disputed; we find: 'thir cauld nights' (*GM* 443), 'thir ridings' (*OM* 84) and 'thir kittle times' (*OM* 280). Occasionally Scots uses *that* where English uses *this*:

> I will say that for the English . . . that they are a ceeveleesed people (*Re* 552).

This usage may be found in Old English (*OED that* dem. pron. 1c).

The pronunciation in Scotland was often reduced to [ɑːt] or [ət] but it is very rare for Scott to show this in his spelling:

> ye should think shame o' yoursell, 'at should ye (*OM* 137).

This is the only example of this form that I have noticed.

RELATIVE PRONOUNS

9. In Scots before the sixteenth century as in English the normal relative pronoun was *that* or, in its reduced Scottish form, *at*. From the sixteenth century *whilk* and *wha* begin to be used in literature but, just as in Standard English *that* has remained more common in speech than in writing, so in Scots speech *that* (or *at*) apparently retained in colloquial speech its position as the normal relative, so much so that Murray firmly asserts that *wha* 'is not used as a relative in the spoken Scotch' while *whilk* he only mentions as used 'when the antecedent is a sentence or clause' (*DSCS* 196). In spite of this we find *wha(e)* used in ordinary speech in Scott's novels:

> the Hieland lairds whae hae deil a boddle o' siller (*RR* 364).
>
> the Argyle family, wha stand for the present model of government (*RR* 365).
>
> a lawfu' king, wha wishes to reign in luve (*FN* 87).

Only some cases conform to the comment of Grant and Dixon that *wha* is used 'in rhetorical prose and poetry' (*MMS* 102):

> the accused Titus, wha was made the instrument of burning the holy Temple (*HM* 181).

Wha may also be used as an indefinite pronoun meaning 'whoever':

> She may marry whae she likes now, for I'm clean dung ower (*OM* 89).

We also find the oblique cases but they are much rarer in Scott than *wha* itself:

> Wae betide ye! ... and cut the houghs of the creature whase fleetness ye trust in (*OM* 245).
>
> there's Ane abune whase command I maun obey before your leddyship's (*OM* 85).

It is probably not coincidental that both these passages are very religious in tone and the first very rhetorical.

Similarly *whilk* occurs freely as a relative, a usage which the *SND* describes as 'literary'. Some cases have, following Murray's rule, a clause as an antecedent:

in Bailie Mac-Candlish's time (honest man) we keepit the kirk, whilk was most seemly in his station, as having office (*GM* 292).

but many others have simple nouns as antecedents:

the breath of man whilk is in his nostrils (*An* 272).

In fact Murray's firm assertion is hard to accept unless we apply it only to very informal speech. With the example of written Scots and English before them it is surely likely that Scots-speakers, even in only slightly formal speech, would occasionally use *wha* and *whilk*. Rather than seeing Scott's use of these pronouns in dialogue as a literary convention, we might see them as a realistic representation of the tendency of the spoken and written forms of the language to interact and influence each other, especially in any speech which has even a small degree of formality.

All the same there is some reflection of the preference for *that* in speech in its use where Standard English would nowadays prefer *who* or *which*. In modern literary English *that* is generally restricted to clauses which have a defining function. Not so in the novels:

When Sanders Aikwood, that was forester in thae days, ... was gaun a daundering about the wood (*An* 271).

that it may be a lesson to you, that are but a young thoughtless chap, wha ye draw up wi' on a lonely road (*Re* 150).

As to the form of the word, I have not found an example of *at* as a relative though there is an example of it used as a demonstrative (see § 6).

10. *As* has a long history as a relative pronoun going back to Middle English (see *OED as* adv 24) but by the nineteenth century it was considered to be non-standard. It is characteristic of the speech of the uneducated Jo in *Bleak House*. Asked how he comes to possess two half-crowns he answers:

They're wot's left ... out of a sov-ring as was give me by a lady in a wale as sed she was a servant and as come to my crossin one night and asked to be showd this 'ere ouse (Penguin edn, p. 321).

The usage also survived in dialect including Scots though the *SND* notes it as rare. In *Waverley* it is given to the horse-dealer

Scottish Grammar

Jinker who is described as speaking 'broad Scotch of the most vulgar description' (*Wa* 359):

> the aits will be got bravely in ... and the cornmongers will make the auld price gude against them as has horses till keep (*Wa* 360).

11. The omission of the relative as subject, already dealt with as an archaism (see chapter 4, § 15), is also a feature of Scots. Modern English usage would not allow the following sentences which are perfectly idiomatic Scots:

> it was a' about a bit grey cowt, wasna worth ten punds sterling (*HM* 369).

> I'll gie him a tass o' whiskey shall mak the blue low [flame] come out at his mouth (*OM* 280).

> her house was taen up wi' them wadna like to be intruded on wi' strangers (*RR* 388).

INTERROGATIVE PRONOUNS

12. While in Standard English we can replace 'why did he do it' with 'what did he do it for', we cannot use the Scots construction where *what* and *for* are not separated but together open the clause:

> If the law canna protect my barn and byre, whatfor suld I no engage wi' a Hieland gentleman that can (*RR* 360).

> I fear nae man – what for suld I? (*RR* 353).

Why not thus becomes *what for no*, a phrase liberally used by Scott's characters:

> 'I don't understand driving the plough.'
> 'And what for no?' (*OM* 76).

> What for no tak Guse Gibbie? (*OM* 24).

> and then to bed, wi' God bless ye – and what for no? (*SRW* 16).

> and wha sae happy as they – And what for no? (*SRW* 37).

ARTICLES

13. *The* before a numeral means 'the year'. Lord Auchinleck writes to his son James Boswell in Holland:

we are pretty well supplied with the classics, and now they are put up in the library room, they make a good show. However if you fall on any of the very old editions before the 1500, and get them cheap, it is worthwhile to take them (in *Boswell in Holland*, F. A. Pottle ed., London, 1952, p. 106).

In Scott we usually encounter the idiom in reference to the two main Jacobite rebellions of the eighteenth century where it has now become a name for the uprisings themselves; when Mr Foxley refers to Redgauntlet's involvement in the more serious of the two rebellions, he retorts:

> And is it so singular that a man should have been out in the forty-five?... your father, I think, Mr Foxley, was out with Derwentwater in the fifteen (*Re* 308).

It is nevertheless applied by Scott to other years. Wandering Willie tells of Redgauntlet's ancestor that 'he was in the hills wi' Glencairn in the saxteen hundred and fifty-twa' (*Re* 151), while Gudyill, the butler, speaks of 'the Burgundy that came ower in the thirty-nine' (*OM* 131). *The Fifteen*, meaning 'the 1715 rebellion', should not be confused with the popular name for the judges of the Court of Session also called *the F(e)ifteen* (*An* 13, *GM* 308) or, rather irreverently in *Waverley*, *the auld Fifteen* (*Wa* 360).

14. In early Scots we find *the* prefixed to family names in the Lowland areas to distinguish the most important person of that name. *The Bruce* and *the Douglas* are well-known examples. We find the idiom, which probably originated in the translation of French *le* or the transformation of French *de*, in Scott's *Lady of the Lake*:

> Can I not frame a fever'd dream,
> But still the Douglas is the theme? (*LL* I xxxv).

However Scott went further and applied the idiom to Highland names, so that the wife of Rob Roy, head of the outlawed MacGregor clan, refers to him as 'the MacGregor' (*RR* 442). This usage, incorrect when applied to a Highlander, was picked up by Scott's readers and is now regularly employed to denote the chief of a Scottish clan. It is ironical that the modern usage should originate in its unhistorical application to the chief of a disbanded clan.

Scottish Grammar

15. In certain cases the English prefix *to-* is replaced in Scots by *the*. *The night* means 'tonight', *the day* 'today':

> And div ye think ... that my man and my sons are to gae to the sea in weather like yestreen and the day, ... and get naething for their fish (*An* 142).

> I'll try to gar her lie down and take a sleep after dinner, for deil a ee she'll close the night (*HM* 310).

As in Middle English *morn* means 'the following day' and *the morn* means 'tomorrow':

> to dance a' night ... and no to be fit to walk your tae's-length the morn (*Re* 144).

and *tomorrow morning* is *the morn's morning*:

> He'll ken himself better the morn's morning (*BL* 146).

16. In Scott the use of *ane* as an indefinite article is a deliberate archaism. As the *SND* notes '*Ane* had become the conventional literary form for the indefinite article in Middle Scots, and this usage survived (alongside of *a*, *an*) in formal prose until the early eighteenth century, rarely later'. We find it, appropriately in Jeanie Deans' letters, being one of the few features which identify them as early eighteenth-century:

> the ransom of her, whilk is ane pardon or reprieve (*HM* 577).

It is also used in the legal document with which Saddletree tortures Davie Deans:

> he the said defender not being ane qualified person (*HM* 178).

as well as in Davie's own rather formal speech:

> one of the ... warldly-wise men that stude up to prevent ane general owning of the cause (*HM* 181).

This usage was sometimes found in Middle English with *one*.

17. In colloquial Scots the indefinite article *a* often retains that form, rather than changing to *an*, before a vowel but, as the *SND* and Grant and Dixon (*MMS* 76) note, this usage rarely appears in literary texts and I have found only one example in Scott:

deil a ee she'll close the night [devil an eye will she close tonight] (*HM* 310).

This case may well arise from *deil a* being considered as almost a compound adjective and thus not inflectable.

ADJECTIVES

18.

> a braw time of night, and a bonny (*OM* 59).
>
> a creditable calling and a gainfu' (*RR* 193).

This way of arranging two adjectives qualifying the one noun is yet another archaism which survives as ordinary usage in Scots. It has already been discussed as part of the medieval and renaissance novels' period language (chapter 4, § 18). At the same time the modern usage with the prop-word *one* can be found in the Scottish dialogue as well:

> Ye are a bonny young leddy, and a gude ane, and maybe a weel-tochered ane (*An* 151).

19. With the numeral for 'one' Scots makes a distinction between *ae* (used before a noun) and *ane* (when the word stands alone). The distinction is well illustrated in Davie Deans' answer to Bailie Middleburgh's query 'You have two daughters, I think, Mr Deans?':

> Ae daughter, sir – only ane (*HM* 281).

Less succinctly the distinction is illustrated here too:

> But I will enlarge on this farther as we pass along, gin ye list to bid your twa lazy loons of porters there lift up your little kist between them, whilk ae true Scotsman might carry under his arm. Let me tell you, mistress, ye will soon make a toom pock-end of it in Lon'on, if you hire twa knaves to do the work of ane (*FN* 461).

Middle English similarly had both *o* and *oon* but used *o* before a consonant and *oon* before a vowel or *h*:

> O flessh they been, and o fleesh, as I gesse,
> Hath but oon herte, in wele and in distresse
> (*CT* IV 1335–6).

Scottish Grammar

The distinction in Scots carries through to *the tae* and *the tane* which are in origin misdivisions of *that ae* and *that ane*. Compare

> the tae half of thae puir creatures (*RR* 354).
>
> the tae way or the tither (*RR* 372).

with

> what is the tane but a waefu' bunch o' cauldrife professors (*HM* 176)
>
> it was the tane or the tither o' them (*HM* 186).

Both English and Scots maintain the distinction with *no/none, nae/nane*. English:

> I have no books.
> I have none.

Scots:

> I name nae names (*GM* 104).
>
> he's nane o' your great grandees (*RR* 357).

20. The ordinal numbers in Scots end in *-t* rather than English *-th*:

> an ill-mumbled mass, as it was weel termed by James the Sext (*HM* 587).

Alternatively the cardinal can be used for the ordinal:

> it was a blessed day, being the nineteen of September, of all days in the year (*FN* 156).
>
> it was accounted a backsliding even in godly Hezekiah that he complied with Sennacherib, giving him money, and offering to bear that which was put upon him (see the saame Second Kings, aughteen chapter, fourteen and feifteen verses) (*OM* 113).

INTERROGATIVE ADJECTIVES

21. The interrogative adjective *whaten* is a reduced form of *what kind*. Sometimes an article is added to it giving *whatna*:

> whatna wife's this. . . ? [what sort of woman is this] (*An* 515).

Whaten can also be used in dependent clauses; Jeanie, with all the bookshops of London before her, writes to Reuben Butler:

I wish I had whaten books ye wanted [I wish I knew what sort of books you wanted] (*HM* 579).

ADVERBS

22. Adverbs of place include some which will be dealt with as prepositions, such as *ahint* 'behind' (*GM* 391) and *ben* 'inside' (*An* 274). *Ben* sometimes had the particular meaning 'into the inner room':

> Baby, bring ben the tea-water (*An* 185).

giving rise to the noun *ben*:

> the *ben*, or parlour end of the house (*BL* 176).

To certain adverbs of place Scots adds *by* where English would use the adverb plus *there* or, in the case of *in*, here:

> he ... lives upby at the Cleikum (*SRW* 476).
>
> their newfangled ordinary down-by yonder (*SRW* 29).
>
> outby yonder at the Bass (*BL* 355).
>
> Come in by – in by (*Re* 400).

In the following case English would simply have *by* for Scots *ower by*:

> Jock was sorting him up as I came ower by (*An* 186).

Note too the addition of *awa'*:

> 'The limes,' he assured us, 'were from his own little farm yonder-awa,' indicating the West Indies with a knowing shrug of his shoulders (*RR* 347).

Awa' can also be added to place-names particularly in the compound *Aberdeen-awa* or *Aberdeen-a-way* as Scott spells it (*Wa* 276) meaning 'from the area around Aberdeen'.

The use of *gay* and *unco* 'uncouth', as adverbs is not known in English. They are some of Scott's commonest intensive adverbs: 'unco brave' (*An* 328), 'unco wild' (*OM* 147), 'unca soon' (*Re* 189), 'gay well' (*SRW* 437), 'gay sure' (*HM* 177), 'gay thick in the head' (*OM* 91). *Clean* does function as an adverb in English but, though the *SND* does not list it, there seems to be some evidence that *clean* as an intensive with an adjective was a Scoticism in the early nineteenth century, though Scott's use of it may have popularized it in literary English later in the century. The *OED* has no examples of this usage from the earlier eighteenth century until it is picked up by Charlotte Brontë in the phrase ' "clean daft" ' (placed by her or Mrs Gaskell in inverted commas). Combined with the Scots *daft*, this is almost certainly picked up from a Scottish writer, very probably Scott. Examples for later in the century suggest that *clean* so used had re-entered Standard English (*OED clean* adv 5d). It seems however to have gone out of use again.

As an adjective *ill* has a much wider use in Scots than in English, and so too as an adverb:

> he wad hae liked ill to hae come in ahint them (*RR* 534).
>
> if I didna see the bogle, I could as ill see the hen, for it's pit-murk (*BL* 106).
>
> the fishing comes on no that ill (*An* 515).

The last quotation also illustrates the use of *that* as an adverb. Except with an adverb or adjective of quantity, this was apparently by Scott's time considered substandard and is so used in Dickens (see G. L. Brook, *The Language of Dickens*, London, 1970, p. 247 and *OED that* III for examples).

> she'll hae a hantle siller, if she's no that bonny (*RR* 276).
>
> Elshie's no that bad a chield (*BD* 432).
>
> the roads are no that ill for boot-hose (*HM* 133).

Two adverbial usages discussed before as archaisms are encountered in the Scottish novels as Scoticisms; these are the use of *something* as an adverb (see c.4, § 20) and some special uses of *e'en* or *even*. *Something* is common as an adverb in the Scots of our author's contemporaries (see *SND some* adj 1(9)(ii)) which may account for Scott's fondness for it. In fact it is not clear whether it was obsolete or merely obsolescent in Standard English usage in Scott's time. In *Redgauntlet* Alan is said by Thomas Trumbull to be 'going on a something particular journey' (*Re* 414). The use of *e'en* referred to is that before a verb where English would now use *just* (see c.4, § 19).

> they e'en gae him leg-bail (*RR* 198).
>
> I'll e'en hirple [hobble] awa there wi' the wean (*An* 190).

E'en, of course, provides the first element of the Scots temporal adverb *e'enow* or *eenoo*. Here too it sometimes takes the place of *just* where *e'enow* corresponds to English *just now* (*An* 286) but at other times *e'enow* means 'shortly' (*OM* 109). Scott typically uses a range of spellings from the very anglicized *even now* (*An* 286) through *e'enow* (*RR* 231, *OM* 109) to *enow* (*An* 326) but does not use the *oo* spelling to represent the word's [uː] pronunciation.

PREPOSITIONS

23. Many of the distinctive Scottish prepositions are easily recognizable as closely related to words in English: *abune* 'above' (*An* 186), *ahint* 'behind' (*HM* 427), *ayont* 'beyond, on the other side of' (*An* 271), *sin* 'since' (*RR* 258). *Ben* 'inside' (*GM* 211) has no close relative in present-day English though descended from Old English *binnan*, while *forby* 'besides' (*OM* 147) combines two prepositions found only separately in English. *Anent* 'concerning' (*HM* 177) is the northern form of a word which appeared in Southern English until the seventeenth century as *anenst*. It derives from Old English *on efn* 'on even (ground with)'.

A more important group are the prepositions shared with English but used differently. *Till* is in Standard English now limited to temporal senses, though in Middle English it extended also to local and dative senses such as survived in Scotland:

Speak till him (*RR* 276).

I selled her till him (*Wa* 361).

to gang in till't to see the wark (*An* 186).

The use of *till* with the infinitive has always been northern or Scottish:

them as has horses till keep (*Wa* 360).

That's as muckle as till say (*HM* 270).

Till here takes the place of English *to*, and *into* is in Scots *intill* (*HM* 280). *By* can in Scots mean, like *forby*, 'besides, except':

Few folks ken o' this place, . . . there's just twa living by mysell (*An* 270).

Apart from these distinctly different senses the choice of prepositions in Scots is not always the same as in English. *O'* (a reduced form of both *of* and *on*), *of* and *on* themselves, *to* and *wi'* 'with' occur where English would choose differently:

> Ye'll no be the waur o' something to eat, I trow (English, *for*; *GM* 451).
>
> It's a queer thing o' me, gentlemen (English, *about*; *RR* 361).
>
> I hope your honour will think on what I am saying (English, *about*; *OM* 205).
>
> unless mony lees [lies] is made on them (English, *about*; *An* 274).
>
> take it all to yoursell, Captain, and meikle ye are likely to make on't (English, *of*; *SRW* 132).
>
> came hame ... with the creel full of caller trouts, and had them to their dinner (English, *for*; *SRW* 16).
>
> I might have looked for some bit postie to him (English, *for*; *Re* 357).
>
> some can clink verses, wi' their tale, as weel as Rob Burns or Allan Ramsay (English, *according to*, *by*; *SRW* 34).

Similarly the English phrase *at all* in Scots is *of all* which becomes *ava'*:

> I hae nae right to be here ava' (*OM* 198).

Finally, *again*. This is now only an adverb in Standard English, the prepositional uses, now largely catered for by *against*, having become obsolete early in the seventeenth century. In Scots *again* could still be a preposition:

> Sae the law gaed again the leddies at last (*OM* 495).

24. *Of* is omitted after nouns of quantity like *bit*, *hantle* 'a considerable quantity', *pickle* 'a small quantity' and *wheen* 'a small number':

> their bit cauld meat (*SRW* 16).
>
> a hantle bogles (*GM* 7).
>
> a pickle ait-meal (*An* 270).
>
> the wee pickle sense he had (*OM* 92).
>
> a wheen duddie bairns (*HM* 449).

CONJUNCTIONS

25. The conjunction *and* or *an* meaning 'if', archaic in English (see chapter 4, § 29), still flourished in Scotland in Scott's day. It can be used as a conditional or to introduce an indirect question. Sometimes *if* is introduced as well:

> an he sleeps in this damp hole, he'll maybe wauken nae mair (*An* 272).

> And if ye are deaf, what needs ye ... keep folk scraughin' [screeching] t'ye this gate? (*HM* 271).

> Ye speered at [asked] me when we locked up and if we locked up earlier on account of Porteous (*HM* 193).

The Scots form of *if* was *gif*, though it comes up much less often in Scott than *if*. It is now nearly obsolete in Scots:

> and gif that ye could airt [direct] it my way, I sall be thankful, man (*BL* 355).

An alternative to *an* and *gif* is *gin* which is probably a reduced form of *gien* 'given', no doubt influenced by the idea that *gif* was connected with *gie* 'give' (see *SND gin* conj[2]).

> I daur say my cousin Rob could get at it gin he liked (*RR* 364).

26. *Without* used as a conjunction is one of the idioms which James Beattie in his *Scoticisms* (Edinburgh, 1787, p. 101) pointed out as a pitfall to be avoided by the Scot aiming to speak Standard English:

> thae corbies dinna gather without they smell carrion (*RR* 255).

27. Though found in Middle English the use of *as* as a conjunction after a comparative has long been confined to dialect. English now uses *than*:

> she doesna value a Cawmil mair as a Cowan (*RR* 406).

The present-day English meaning of *as* here will not fit the context.

VERBS: INFLECTIONS

28. In the present tense, where the verb is immediately adjacent

to its pronoun, the inflections are the same as in present-day English except that the second person singular takes the same form as the third person singular; the *-st* forms are not found in Middle Scots or in Modern Scots. We have already noticed the comparative rarity of *thou* compared to *ye* in the Scottish dialogue of the novels; nevertheless the few examples of *thou* illustrate the Scottish inflections:

> thou kensna about thae things (*OM* 89).
>
> what for is thou lying there (*An* 414).
>
> I'se tell thee what thou is now ... thou's a crazed hellicat Bess o' Bedlam (*HM* 274).

However, when the subject is something other than a personal pronoun (e.g. a noun, adjective, interrogative or relative), or when the pronoun is separated from the verb, the third person singular form may be used for all persons. We thus find it with the first person singular:

> Ye'll no teach me law, I think, neighbour – me that has four gaun pleas (*HM* 747).
>
> I keep the straight road ... and answers naebody with the tong but women of mine ain sect (*HM* 414).
>
> It's gude ale, though I shouldna say sae that brews it (*OM* 487–8).

and with plural subjects:

> against them as has horses till keep (*Wa* 360).
>
> so there's hope Plainstanes may be hanged, as many has for a less matter (*Re* 209).
>
> that will be when the deil's blind; and his een's no sair yet (*GM* 199).
>
> they were queer hands, the monks, unless mony lees is made on them (*An* 274).

The *-s* inflection of the third person is however used in all cases, even with the pronoun adjacent to the verb, when the tense is the historic present used for the past:

> Ou, sir, that's what I said to the gardener; but he says he saw them turn down by the Mussel-craig. 'In troth,' says I to him, 'an that be the case, Davie, I am misdoubting – ' (*An* 81).

So at last they were clean aff thegither. And then some of the company at Gilsland tells her that the estate was to be sell'd (*GM* 390).

(This second quotation can alternatively be explained as the use of *some* to mean 'someone' for which the last *OED* quotation is dated 1729 (*OED some* A 1) but which may have survived later in Scotland.)

Sometimes we find the *-th* inflections used in the midst of passages of Scots dialogue. These are not examples of Scottish inflections; Scots already had the *-s* inflection for the third person singular when *-th* was still normal in Southern English. They rather show the strong influence of biblical language, even on the uneducated, and are often allusions to particular biblical passages as when Edie Ochiltree exclaims:

> There's naebody chasing us, . . . we're e'en like the wicked, that flee when no one pursueth (*An* 358).

Compare the Authorized Version's

> The wicked shall flee when no man pursueth: but the righteous are as bold as a lion (*Prov* xxviii 1).

The verb *do* is unusual in having a form in the present tense unknown in any position to English. When the verb is used emphatically, especially in interrogative sentences, the form used is *div*:

> Div ye ken what's hanging ower the house of Knockwinnock (*An* 545).

> Div I ken onything o' Lord Evandale? Div I no? (*OM* 491).

The third person singular of the verb *to be* is normally *is* as in present-day English but on at least one occasion Scott uses *be's*, a form found in Middle Scots:

> What trade be's that, man? (*Re* 178).

29. The normal ending for the past tense and past participle of weak verbs is [it] or [t], but, according to the rules laid down by Murray (*DSCS* 199), after a monosyllable (or an accented syllable) ending in a vowel or in a liquid or nasal consonant (except where it is part of a consonantal cluster), [t] becomes [d]: *belanged* (*SRW* 104), *caa'd* 'called' (*SRW* 236), *gaed* 'went' (*Re* 164), *gar'd* 'caused'

(BL 182), *kamed* 'combed' (HM 712), *kend* 'knew' (RR 246), *sell'd* 'sold' (GM 200) and *speired* 'asked' (GM 201). The rules given by Murray however are not as strict as he would make them out to be and as well as these forms we find *gar't* (OM 199), *kent* (RR 347) and *selt* (CC 589). In addition we find other verbs with the same final consonants but with the standard Scottish ending [it] like *hangit* (HM 763). The full [it] is only retained after a plosive as in: *cookit* (Wa 641), *cuttit* (OM 328), *likeit* (An 286), otherwise spelt *liket* (RR 363) or *likit* (RR 346), *rubbit* 'robbed' (GM 199), *ruggit* 'pulled' (RR 199), *sleepit* (FN 46), *stoppit* (GM 199), *tuggit* (RR 199) and *walkit* (BL 186).

According to Murray in all cases not so far covered, the [it] is reduced to [t]. In Scott we find the occasional form like *catcht* (GM 45) as well as *gart*, *kent* and *selt* which, we have already seen, do not conform to Murray's other rules and are anyway far less common in Scott than *gar'd*, *kend* and *sell'd*. Nevertheless in general Scott seems to avoid the [t] forms despite the frequency in his works of the [it] forms. For instance he chooses to use the English *-ed* spelling between two [it] forms in the phrase 'tuggit and rived and ruggit' (RR 199) in a case where, at least by Murray's rules, [t] would be the expected ending. In fact the *SND*, which of course only reflects written Scots, gives both forms for this verb, which means 'tear' or 'pull'. It is possible that Scott was dissuaded from using the [t] forms in cases like *rive* by the difficulty of choosing a suitable and unambiguous spelling; *rivet* suggests the full *-it* pronunciation, *rivt* changes the vowel and *rive't* may be mistaken for *rive it*. Be that as it may, the use of the English spelling suggesting a [d] ending in cases where [t] might be expected is in keeping with his overall practice of mixing English and Scots spellings of past tenses and participles. To choose two simple examples, Edie Ochiltree uses *likeit* and *liked* on the same page (An 286) while Richie on the one page has *craw'd*, *banged*, *crammed* and *grippit* which conform to Murray's rules and *mounted*, *minded*, *swarved*, *dirked*, *righted*, *gathered*, *laughed* and *rowted* which do not (FN 49). On the other hand the entries in the *SND* show Scott was not alone in giving most of this second group of words a *written* form in *-ed*.

Some verbs which are strong in English are weak in Scots. *Steal* has the strong past tense *stole* in Standard English but in Scots we find *steal'd* (HM 630), the weak form, as well. *Stickit*, not *stuck*, is the past tense (RR 212) and past participle (GM 16) of *stick*, though in Scots it can mean 'fail' or 'bungle'. The past participle of *gie* (English *give* with the Scots loss of *v* as in *doo* 'dove') is the strong form *gien* (*Wa* 641), also spelt *gi'en* (*SRW* 242), but for the past tense we find both the strong form *gae* (*OM* 199) and the weak *gied* (*GM* 108). So too with the verb *gae* 'go' (*GM* 5), which has the strong past participle *gane* (*Re* 164) or *gaen* (*GM* 292) and the weak past tense *gaed* (*OM* 39). *Gae* can therefore be either the present of the verb meaning 'go' or the past of the verb meaning 'give'. The past forms of *gae* 'go' make up the deficiencies of the verb *gang* which is interchangeable with it in meaning but which only exists in the present tense (*GM* 2, *OM* 40, *HM* 185) and has no past forms of its own. In other cases Scots has formed new and simpler weak forms where English also has weak forms, but ones which are complicated by an additional change in the vowel. The past tense of *sleep* in Standard English is *slept* but in Scots can be *sleepit* (*FN* 46), as can also the past participle (*OM* 500), and the past tense of *seek* can be, not English *sought*, but *seekit* (*An* 177). *Tell* and *sell* have both the new simple forms and the historical, more complex ones. For instance in the past participles we find both *tell'd* (*HM* 306) and *tauld* (*Wa* 434), both *sell'd* (*GM* 200) or *selt* (*CC* 589) and *sauld* (*RR* 380) with a similar range in the preterite: *tell'd* (*GM* 44), *tauld* (*RR* 379), *selled* (*Re* 208), *sauld* (*An* 583). The development in the sound of the historical forms is standard for Scots – compare *auld* (*GM* 199), *bauld* (*SRW* 436) and *cauld* (*OM* 130), corresponding to *old, bold* and *cold*. The verb *catch* is a Middle English borrowing from French and, like almost all new words in English, formed its past with a simple weak form, *catched*. But, because of its similarity in meaning to Old English *læccan*, Middle English *lachen*, it copied the more complicated weak forms of that verb and produced *caught* on the analogy of *laught*. The two forms existed side by side as in Shakespeare's

> I saw him run after a gilded butterfly; and when he caught it, he let it go again; and after it again; and over and over he comes, and up again; catched it again (*Cor* III i 65–9),

but in the nineteenth century *catched* came to be considered non-standard and occurs only in uneducated speech or dialect, such as Scots (*RR* 374).

Various verbs borrowed from Old Norse and not found in Standard English are weak in Scots. We have already looked at the various past tenses and past participles of *gar* and *ken* and the weak past tense of *rive*. *Rive* in fact can also be found as a strong verb with a past tense *rave* (*FN* 49) and a past participle *riven* (*BD* 331). *Tyne* 'lose' (*Re* 351) has a past participle *tint* (*FN* 45, *Wa* 434). Finally *speer* 'ask' (*GM* 5), which is derived from both the Old English weak verb *spyrian* and the Old Norse *spyrja*, has *speired* (*GM* 201) as its past participle.

30. Many Old English strong verbs have become weak in both Scots and English. But some verbs which are now weak in English remain strong in Scots. *Creep* and *leap*, strong verbs in Old English, now form their past tense and past participle in Standard English with the weak forms *crept* and *leapt*. In Scots they remain strong but, though belonging to different classes of strong verbs in Old English, they form their preterite and past participle in the same way: preterite, *crap* (*FN* 45), *lap* (*Re* 164); past participle, *cruppen* (*HM* 58), *luppen* (*OM* 213). The verb *greet* 'weep', obsolete in English by the later eighteenth century and originally of the same class as *creep*, has the same inflections, with a preterite *grat* (*RR* 377) and a past participle (which I have not found in Scott) of *grutten*. The verb *cleek* 'seize, clutch, hook', which is apparently from an unrecorded Old English verb *clǣcan*, has the strong past tense *claught* (*GM* 109). And one of the Old English auxiliaries which Standard English has lost, *dugan* meaning 'to avail, be profitable', survives in Scots with its strong past *dought* (*SRW* 101, *HM* 337) although the weak form *dowed*, even if rare, can be found (*An* 315). In Scots the verb means 'to be able, to be willing'. *Laugh* too was strong in Old English, and Scots, as well as the weak form now used in Standard English, has the preterite *leugh* (*FN* 45). *Pled* as a past tense (*LI* IV xiv) and past participle (*HM* 185) of *plead* is not a strong form but a contracted form of the now normal Standard English *pleaded*. *Pled* was acceptable in seventeenth-century English but thereafter became dialectal. Scott seems to have become aware of this usage being a Scoticism and removed it from *The Fair Maid of Perth*. The first edition reads 'Ramorny . . . pled his knighthood, and demanded the privilege of dying by the sword, and not by the noose' (III 249) where the Collected and Border editions read 'pleaded' (*FM* 613).

The tendency for new verbs in English and Scots to become weak verbs can be counteracted where there exists a prominent and obviously analogous group of strong verbs. There are a number of verbs which have the same inflections as *sing-sang-sung* – for instance *spring* and *ring* – and it is easy to understand why *ding* 'strike, beat', a borrowing probably from Old Norse, came to be a strong verb in Scots with a past tense *dang* (*Re* 170) and a past participle *dung* (*OM* 89). In Scots the verb *fling* also conforms to this regular pattern with the past tense *flang* (*Wa* 594), a form which is found in Standard English until the eighteenth century, but is thereafter replaced by the irregular *flung*.

While English and Scots share many strong verbs derived from Old English, the vowel-patterns are often different in Scots due to its separate phonological development. One of the most basic elements in this is the northern retention of *ā* where Southern English changed to *ō*. This feature of Scots phonology gives us *hame* beside English *home* and in the verbs, *drave* 'drove' (*OM* 39), *rade* 'rode' (*BL* 186) and *raise* 'rose' (*Re* 173). Likewise Old English *ō* remains in Standard English, but in Scots generally becomes [y] or [i], except that before a back vowel it becomes [juː] and before *r* [ø]. The first two sounds are spelt *ui* or *u-e*, the last *eu*. Thus Old English (*ge*)*dōn*, *stōd* and *swōr* yield *dune* (*GM* 455), *stude* (*HM* 307) and *swure* (*GM* 108) and, returning to a verb mentioned before, *lōh* gives us the strong past tense of *laugh*, *leugh*.

Lastly we must note the presence or absence of *-en* in the past participle. Where English has *got*, *held*, *let*, *put* and *stood*, Scots has *gotten* (*SRW* 33), *hadden* (*GM* 5), *letten* (*OM* 201), *putten* (*RR* 374) and *studden* (*An* 583). Furthermore in the case of *let* Scots has also formed a new strong preterite *loot* (*OM* 202). (For *gotten* as an archaism see chapter 4, § 33.)

The converse, in the use of *spoke* where present-day English has *spoken*, is not a case of Scots dialect. Though it appears in a dialect passage (*HM* 452) it was in fact acceptable in early nineteenth-century English and occurs in Scott's narrative as well (*HM* 99).

31. The Scots verb *aught* 'possess, own' is a preterite-present verb twice over. The Old English *āgan* which has the same meaning as its Scots descendant consists of a present tense, which was in origin a preterite, plus a newly formed weak preterite. This new preterite has in both Scots and English itself been adopted as the present of new verbs but, whereas the resultant English verb

ought has changed in meaning, the Scots verb *aught* has maintained the Old English sense:

> let them that aught the mare shoe the mare (*Re* 350).

In Scots the verb can also be used as a past participle in the sense 'possessed of' as we find in the speech of Meg Dodds:

> and a paper about the neck o't to show which of the customers is aught it (*SRW* 29).

The verb *straught* or *straight* meaning 'stretch' is not strictly speaking a preterite-present verb but does derive from the adjectival use of the past participle of the verb *stretch*. This adjectival use is found in English in the common adjective *straight* but in Scots the adjective was used as a verb. Hence we find:

> I am blithe to see you straight your legs on the causeway of our auld borough again (*SRW* 209).

Straught can also be used to mean 'lay out a corpse for burial':

> hand of woman, or of man either, will never straught him – dead-deal will never be laid on his back (*BL* 326).

A new weak past participle is formed:

> if the dead corpse binna straughted, it will girn and thraw [groan and twist] (*BL* 326–7).

Stretch itself appears in Scots in the form *streek* (*An* 270) with the past participle *streekit* (*SRW* 14).

32. The first verbs in English ending in *-ate* were formed from participial adjectives borrowed from the Latin past participle *-atus* forms of first conjugation verbs. The pre-existing adjective naturally served as the past participle of the new verb so that a number of verbs had past participles identical in form with the present tense. This survived late with some verbs like *situate*, where the uninflected past participle is recorded well into the nineteenth century alongside *situated*, but generally after the sixteenth century *-ed* forms take over. In Scots there are some later survivals; we find *distribute* and *educate* used as participles:

> were favour equally distribute, as in the days of the wight Wallace (*HM* 61).

> he's been weel educate (*HM* 237).

This also applies to the verbs *exauctorate* 'to remove from office' and *examinate* 'examine', the first of which was obsolete in English after the eighteenth century and the second always confined to Scots. Examples of these as past participles may be found in Scott (*exauctorate*, HM 57; *examinate*, RR 534).

33. The present participle in Scots derives from the Old English participle ending *-and* and not, as in English, from the gerund ending *-ung*. Nevertheless the participle and gerund both levelled to [ən] or [in] and only in Southern Scots was the distinction between them maintained (*DSCS* 211). Scott makes no distinction in form, and indeed generally spells both of them in the English way with *-ing*. The one regular exception to the English spelling is the participle of *gae* 'go' which has the special form *gaun* and which is used frequently (RR 362, 378, *An* 287, GM 292, 455). Otherwise spellings in *-in* or *-in'* are very rare – I have counted about twenty and though there must be more, they are clearly rare. As I have already argued (see pp. 196–7), such spellings may possibly be mere eye-dialect since [in] was still an acceptable alternative in Standard English to [iŋ]. On the other hand [in] was coming to be considered vulgar and Scott does sometimes seem to use it to represent a particularly broad and 'vulgar' accent. Meg Murdockson who is described as 'an old woman of the lower rank, extremely haggard in look, and wretched in her apparel' (HM 270) is given *in'* three times in one speech: *wantin'*, *tellin'*, *scraughin'* (HM 271). It is also used to point a contrast between the Scots of Ratcliffe and the English of Bailie Middleburgh: *whipping-post*, *whuppin-post* (HM 200; Ratcliffe further has *wunnin* (HM 194) for *winning*), and, rather curiously in her letters, to show up the inadequacies of Jeanie's education (HM 415, 577; see p. 331). But there seems to be little reason for the very occasional appearance of the spelling with other speakers (OM 489, 534, *Wa* 434, Re 612, HM 361, *An* 288, 262, 436).

VERBS: NEGATION

34. The normal negative in Scots is the enclitic *-na*, usually, in Scott, attached to the verb rather than written as a separate word. It occurs particularly with the verb *to be* and with auxiliary verbs: *amna* 'am not' (*An* 333), *arena* 'are not' (BL 184), *binna* 'be not'

(subjunctive, *HM* 367), *binna* 'do not be' (imperative, *RR* 350), *canna* 'cannot' (*FN* 481), *downa* 'cannot' (*RR* 365), and *maunna* 'must not' (*HM* 370). 'Will not' is usually *winna* (*HM* 182), less often *wunna* (*RR* 331) and occasionally *willna* (*OM* 378), while 'would not' is *wadna* (*HM* 271). The negative of other verbs can be formed with the verb *to do* as is normal in English:

I dinna ken (*BL* 182).

I didna see the bogle (*BL* 106).

The gudeman and her disna aye gree weel (*HM* 275).

if he doesna gie him full satisfaction (*OM* 134).

but sometimes the enclitic *na* is added to the verb itself especially with common monosyllabic verbs:

I kenna (*HM* 188).

I carena (*RR* 359).

I doubtna (*RR* 363).

it maksna muckle matter whilk (*HM* 186).

Na serves as the negative particle, often being repeated:

Na, ye needna say a word about it (*RR* 362).

Na, na, . . . he's nane o' your great grandees (*RR* 357).

For a more emphatic negation of the verb *no* is used:

This is no it (*HM* 178).

it's no a Scots tune, but it passes for ane (*Re* 139).

or *nane*:

If you will walk by my advice you will quarrel nane (*Pi* 288).

An even more emphatic negative is supplied by the phrase *at no rate*:

they canna come at no rate (*GM* 103).

As we can see from this last quotation the double negative is allowable in Scots; so also:

I want my bairn, or I want naething frae nane o' ye (*HM* 270).

No is used rather than *na* in various idioms where it is not immediately connected to a verb:

> speaking to him about his soul, when the puir chield hardly kens whether he has ane or no (*OM* 135).

> No but my hinny might have been better if he had liked (*Re* 140).

VERBS: TENSES

35. Scots often employs a continuous tense where Standard English would have a simple tense, particularly in the present with *think* or its equivalent:

> sae me and my mither yielded oursells prisoners. I'm thinking we wad hae been letten slip awa, but Kettledrummle was taen near us (*OM* 201).

> an unco cockernony she had busked on her head at the kirk last Sunday. I am doubting that there will be news o' a' thae braws (*OM* 61).

I'm thinking means much the same as the colloquial English *I imagine* and *I'm doubting* corresponds to *I'm afraid*. (See also *An* 47, *GM* 6, *An* 81, *HM* 193.) The usages occur with other tenses and verbs:

> I canna meddle wi' a friend's business but I aye end wi' making it my ain. Sae, I'll een pit on my boots the morn, and be jogging ower Drymen-Muir wi' Mr Frank here (*RR* 367).

> And ae day at the spaw-well . . . she was seeing a very bonny family o' bairns . . . and she broke out: 'Is not it an odd-like thing that ilka waf carle in the country has a son and heir, and that the house of Ellangowan is without male succession?' (*GM* 390-1).

> ye wad rather hear ae twalpenny clink against another, than have a spring from Rory Dall, if he was coming alive again (*Re* 144).

VERBS: AUXILIARIES

36. Ever since the eighteenth century, grammarians have tried to reduce the use of *shall* and *will* to some ordered pattern in Standard English. The rules however have been so complicated and the distinction, essential to these rules, between simple futurity and

an expression of intention often so difficult to make that they have rarely been strictly followed and, in less regulated forms of English like American English, Australian English and Scots, either *shall* and *will* have been largely interchangeable or *shall* has largely disappeared. Only in Standard English written in England was any regularity achieved, enough for us to recognize where Scott appears to deviate from normal usage (see chapter 4, § 39).

In Scots *shall* takes the form *sall* or the reduced form *'se* while *will* as in English, is often reduced to *'ll*. Distinctions between simple futurity and intention do not seem to govern Scott's use of these verbs. The only discernible pattern is that *'se* is generally confined to use with *I*, *we* and *ye*, particularly *I*:

I'se hae them up (*An* 97).

I'se find ye three men (*RR* 367).

I'se gie you my personal warrandice (*Wa* 593).

we'se try (*OM* 492).

ye'se hear, ye'se hear (*An* 262).

while *sall* and *'ll* can be used with all persons, the latter being much the more frequent:

I sall gang and hear him just the very same (*HM* 593).

He sall no want a good dinner , . . that I'se engage for (*SRW* 26).

Now sall he teach others (*HM* 639).

I'se be silent or [before] thou sall come to ill (*OM* 99).

a bonny stour . . . that sall serve me for fighting a' the days o' my life (*OM* 490).

d'ye think ye'll help them . . . ? (*An* 97).

I'll try to gar her lie down (*HM* 310).

I'll send little Jenny, she'll rin faster (*An* 143).

we'll ding Jock o' Dawston Cleugh now after a' (*GM* 380).

Sall is now obsolete in Scots, except in negative forms like *sanna* which I have not found in Scott, and *'se* is only used, as in Scott, with personal pronouns. Possibly Scott avoided the use of *'se* with he, *she* and *it* because of their potential for confusion with *'s* for *is*.

However, in an exceptional case, the reaction to Sybil Knockwinnock's giving birth to a son, fathered by her lover, four months after her marriage is summarized thus:

> she's be burnt, and he's be slain, was the best words o' their mouths (*An* 328).

The reason for the introduction of this, for Scott, unusual construction is that the phrase 'she's be burnt and he's be slain' is taken from a poem in Ramsay's *Tea-Table Miscellany* about a gaberlunzie (i.e. beggar) man who elopes with the 'gudewife's' daughter (see *Miscellany*, London, 1733, I 86). In Scott it appears, appropriately enough, in the speech of the old gaberlunzie, Edie Ochiltree.

With verbs like *warrant* and *uphaud* 'uphold' *'se* functions as 'a kind of emphatic present' (*SND sall* 2):

> I'se warrant we'll sune heave them on board (*An* 97).

> I'se warrant it was the tae half o' her fee and bountith (*OM* 203).

> I'se uphaud her for ... the bitterest Jacobite in the haill shire (*RR* 83).

Similarly *will* is used for a present tense, often with a continuous form of the verb, in tentative statements or as an indirect way of asking a question:

> Jeanie wad be writing ye something, gudeman? (i.e. 'Has Jeanie written you something?' *HM* 629).

> ye will be the same lad that was for in to see her yestreen? (*HM* 193).

37.

> O Ferguson! thy glorious parts
> Ill suited law's dry, musty arts!
> My curse upon your whunstane hearts,
>   Ye Enbrugh gentry!
> The tythe o' what ye waste at cartes
>   Wad stow'd his pantry.

So Burns in his poem 'To William Simpson, Ochiltree' (ll. 16–20). In the last line *wad* equals English *would* with the typical Scots omission after it of *hae* 'have'. The same idiom appears in Scott:

> ye wad thought Sir Arthur had a pleasure in gaun on wi' them the deeper (*An* 287).

Scottish Grammar

I hae kend the day when less wad ser'd him, the oe of a Campvere skipper (*HM* 270).

I wad likeit weel just to hae come in at the clipping-time (*An* 286).

38. *Should* followed by the present or perfect infinitive was used in earlier English in subordinate clauses reporting another person's statement indirectly. Sometimes it implies that the present speaker is not committing himself as to the truth of the statement. The usage is now obsolete in Standard English and was possibly obsolescent in Scott's day (see *OED shall* v B 15) but was certainly not obsolete in Scots:

> I hae heard, cummer, that some ill-tongue suld hae come between the earl, that's Lord Geraldin, and his young bride (*An* 526).

> John Blower ... used to sing a sang about a dog they ca'd Bingo, that suld hae belanged to a farmer (*SRW* 104).

> They had a braw sport in the presence ... how ye suld have routed a young shopkeeper (*FN* 257).

In the following quotation from 'Wandering Willie's Tale' the indication that the clause is reported speech is implicit. Some such phrase as 'I am told that' should be understood:

> a little lonely change-house, that was keepit then by an ostler-wife, they suld hae caa'd her Tibbie Faw (*Re* 162).

Amongst English writers Shakespeare uses the idiom:

> But didst thou hear without wondering, how thy name should be hanged and carved upon these trees (*AYLI* III ii 182–4).

39. In Scots the verb *can* is used with other auxiliaries especially *will* where English now has to resort to a periphrasis with *be able to*. In earlier English we do find this construction; in Chaucer's *Troilus and Criseyde* the hero laments

> So lost have I myn hele and ek myn hewe,
> Criseyde shal nought konne knowen me (V 1403–4).

In Scott we have:

> ye'll can teach me (*HM* 451).

he'll no can haud down his head to sneeze, for fear o' seeing his shoon (*An* 352).

THE VERB *behove*

40. *Behove* in Scots can be used personally whereas in English it has been restricted to impersonal use since the end of the Middle English period. It means, as in English, 'to be incumbent on' but seems frequently to be used ironically:

> There was a young gentleman on the box, and he behuved to drive; and Tam Sang, that suld hae mair sense, he behuved to let him (*An* 546).

> ae auld hirpling deevil of a potter behoved just to step in my way (*FN* 28).

(Also *Wa* 166, *RR* 264, *GM* 105.)

Chapter 8

THE EXTENT OF SCOTS IN THE NOVELS

SCOTS IN THE DIALOGUE

IT IS IN THE DIALOGUE of the novels that Scots plays its largest part, yet not all of the dialogue is in Scots. There are four main categories of speakers: those who speak English, those who speak English but on special occasions fall into Scots, those whose normal speech is a mixture of Scots and English, and those who speak Scots. Yet although there is no doubt that this is the situation Scott wishes to reflect, his spelling habits cloud the picture a little. As we have noted before, Scott used English spellings a lot of the time in what appear to be passages of Scots. In the case of the eighteenth-century poets, whose practice Scott followed in this respect, the presence of rhyme often makes it clear that Scottish pronunciations are intended where there are English spellings. Of Fergusson, who followed Ramsay and preceded Burns in this practice, Mackie writes:

> 'Creature' he rhymes with 'nature' (craitur and naitur), 'shoulder' with 'powder' (shoother, poother), . . . 'yard' with 'laird' . . . 'dies' with 'sees', 'ground' with 'wind' (grund and wund), . . . 'doubt on' with 'Newton', . . . 'crown' with 'dragoon', . . . 'done' with 'June', . . . 'lies' (noun plural) with 'fees' (Mackie, 'Fergusson's Language', pp. 131-2).

Fergusson's spelling, then, is not a good guide to pronunciation. In the case of Scott's prose there are no rhymes to help us, but there are other indications that here too English spellings must often be read with Scottish pronunciations. Firstly, Scott often makes a comment on the character's dialogue which indicates that he is to be seen as speaking with a broader accent than the spelling suggests. In *Waverley* Jinker is described as speaking 'in broad Scotch of the most vulgar description' (*Wa* 359).

'Vulgar' here clearly refers to his accent and diction not his subject matter, yet this extremely broad Scots-speaker uses on the next page *bravely* for *brawly*, *poor* for *puir* and *sold* for *selled* (*Wa* 360). Similarly, we will see, Jeanie and Effie Deans and Nigel Olifaunt, Lord Glenvarloch are described at various points as having pronunciations more broadly Scotch than the spelling of their speech would indicate. Secondly, in the speech of characters who use Scots as their basic language, the swapping back and forth between English and Scottish spelling is usually too erratic to represent any pattern of usage. Where speakers knew both English and Scots, English pronunciations no doubt did creep into their Scots, especially as English was the more prestigious variety of the language, but it is probably being oversubtle to see these apparently haphazard variations in spelling as intended to indicate this. In the circumstances it seems likely that Scott was following the substantial tradition, provided by eighteenth-century Scottish poetry, of English spellings allied with Scottish sounds. This was after all the only modern model Scott had for the representation of Scots. It therefore seems that we should consider a passage as full Scots when it contains a substantial proportion of Scottish spellings even if some English spellings are also present.

The problem is that the presence of *some* English spellings in *all* passages of Scots makes it impossible for us to decide in some cases whether Scott intends to use a subtle sociolinguistic indicator or is merely inconsistent in his spelling: for example, when Jeanie thinks Butler is losing interest in her because he has not written to her, her thoughts run like this:

> 'It would have cost him sae little fash,' she said to herself; 'for I hae seen his pen gang as fast ower the paper, as ever it did ower the water when it was in the grey goose's wing. Wae's me! maybe he may be badly – but then my father wad likely hae said something about it – Or maybe he may hae taen the rue, and kensna how to let me wot of his change of mind. He needna be at muckle fash about it,' – she went on, drawing herself up, though the tear of honest pride and injured affection gathered in her eye, as she entertained the suspicion, – 'Jeanie Deans is no the lass to pu' him by the sleeve, or put him in mind of what he wishes to forget. I shall wish him weel and happy a' the same; and if he has the luck to get a kirk in our country, I sall gang and hear him just the very same, to show that I bear nae malice' (*HM* 592–3).

The Extent of Scots in the Novels

Here we have a mixture of injured pride and sadness. We might argue that injured pride expresses itself in the more formal English – *would have* for *wad hae*, *he wishes* for *he wusses*, *I shall wish* for *I sall wuss* – while sadness expresses itself in Scots – *I hae seen, he may hae taen, I sall gang*. Surely this is too subtle; besides it fails to explain all details of the spelling. I am much more inclined to see Scott here as simply inconsistent.

We can see the pressures which led Scott to use a mixture of spellings inconsistent with phonetic accuracy. Scott, unlike the eighteenth-century poets, built up a substantial English audience which he could not afford to alienate. The mixed spelling he adopted made the Englishman's task of understanding much easier. And, apart from intelligibility, there is probably another reason why Scott wanted to introduce English spellings. He was interested in presenting his Scots-speaking lower-class characters as dignified human beings and not as ignorant, stupid and laughable fools. Even today some feeling clings to dialect that attributes less intellectual power to its user and laughs at him for it. In *The Heart of Midlothian* it is particularly important that the heroine Jeanie should be above ridicule especially in her great scene with the Queen. Consequently, though Scott pictures the Queen unable to 'help smiling . . . at the first sound of her broad northern accent' Jeanie's first speech, a request for 'her Leddyship to have pity on a poor misguided young creature' (*HM* 558), has English spellings in the two words Scott very frequently spelt as *hae* and *puir*. To make doubly sure no incongruous feelings arise in the reader, he adds that she spoke 'in tones so affecting, that, like the notes of some of her native songs, provincial vulgarity was lost in pathos' (*HM* 559). On the other hand it is important for Scott's picture of Jeanie that we can continue to see her as a simple Scottish girl. At a later stage where a 'provincial' accent and a certain *naïveté* are not in conflict with the total effect of the scene – Jeanie is merely being taken to the Duke of Argyle's estate – Scott goes out of his way to give her a strong Scottish accent. We have seen that he rarely indicates the Scottish [u:] pronunciation by the English spelling *oo*, preferring to use the Scottish but misleading *ou*. Yet Jeanie is made to ask, 'Is yon high castle the Duke's hoose?' (*HM* 611).

The inconsistencies of Scott's spellings make it impossible to distinguish minor variations in the amount of English admixture in his Scots dialogue but major variations are nevertheless clear enough. Before considering which characters use what language we can look at an example of what I take to be full Scots and an example of mixed Anglo-Scots.

In *Rob Roy* Andrew Fairservice in his story of the survival of Glasgow cathedral offers us a piece of sustained Scots as broad as we ever find it in the novels:

> Ah! it's a brave kirk; nane o' yere whigmaleeries and curliewurlies and opensteek hems about it, – a' solid, weel-jointed masonwark, that will stand as lang as the warld, keep hands and gunpowther aff it. It had amaist a douncome lang syne at the Reformation, when they pu'd doun the kirks of St Andrews and Perth, and thereawa', to cleanse them o' papery and idolatry and image worship and surplices, and sic like rags o' the muckle hure that sitteth on seven hills, as if ane wasna braid eneugh for her auld hinder end. Sae the commons o' Renfrew, and o' the Barony, and the Gorbals, and a' about, they behoved to come into Glasgow ae fair morning to try their hand on purging the High Kirk o' popish nicknackets. But the townsmen o' Glasgow, they were feared their auld edifice might slip the girths in gaun through siccan rough physic, sae they rang the common bell, and assembled the train-bands wi' took o' drum, – by good luck, the worthy James Rabat was Dean o' Guild that year (and a gude mason he was himsell, made him the keener to keep up the auld bigging, – and the trades assembled and offered downright battle to the commons, rather than their kirk should coup the crans, as others had done elsewhere. It wasna for luve o' paperie – na, na! nane could ever say that o' the trades o' Glasgow. Sae they sune came to an agreement to take a' the idolatrous statues of sants (sorrow be on them) out o' their neuks. And sae the bits o' stane idols were broken in pieces by Scripture warrant, and flung into the Molendinar burn, and the auld kirk stood as crouse as a cat when the flaes are kaimed aff her, and a'body was alike pleased. And I hae heard wise folk say that if the same had been done in ilka kirk in Scotland, the Reform wad just hae been as pure as it is e'en now, and we wad hae mair Christian-like kirks; for I hae been sae lang in England that naething will drived out o' my head that the dog-kennel at Osbaldistone Hall is better than mony a house o' God in Scotland (RR 264-5).

(*Drived* in the last sentence is the reading in both the Collected and Border editions but it is clearly a mistake for *drive't*, which is the reading in the Dryburgh edition.)

To begin with pronunciation, two things should be borne in mind. Firstly, even if we replaced all the English spellings with

Scottish ones we would not have a phonetic transcript. Neither Scottish nor English spelling is a full reflection of pronunciation. Secondly, in terms both of reading the passage aloud and of the silent reader's apprehension of what language is being spoken, the use of further Scots spellings would make no real difference. Whether we read this aloud or silently the preponderance of Scottish forms is so great that we unhesitatingly identify what we have as broad Scots spoken consistently with a Scottish pronunciation.

There are certain inconsistencies obvious inside the passage itself. We have *doun* and *douncome* but also *downright* as well as *gunpowther* and *townsmen* and *of* alongside *o'*. Other words which are spelt in a Scottish fashion elsewhere in Scott though here given their English form are *brave* (*braw*), *seven* (*seeven*), *behoved* (*behooved*), *good* (*gude*), *done* (*dune*), *should* (*sud* or *suld*), *others* (*ithers*), *came* (*cam*), *take* (*tak*), *stood* (*stude*), *folk* (*fowk*) and *same* (*saam(e)*). The same applies in reverse; all the words here given a Scottish form can be found elsewhere in the Scots dialogue with their English form. We might also expect some use of the *-it* form of the preterite or past participle (see chapter 8, § 29). In fact, according to the rules set out by Murray (*DSCS* 199) *-it* became *-ed* in certain situations including after *r* in a monosyllable, which explains *feared*, and after a vowel in an accented syllable, which gives us, after the loss of the intermediate *v*, the normal Scots *behude* for the word Scott gives us in its English form *behoved*. However, we would still expect *offert* for *offered*, *assemblit* for *assembled* and *pleast* for *pleased*. As it happens Scott, while using the *-it* ending quite frequently, rarely uses it where it has been elided to *-t*, and this may explain the *-ed* forms here. On the other hand, though Scott uses *-it* frequently he is by no means regular or consistent even in the use of that unelided ending, so that the choice of endings here is quite probably accidental rather than carefully thought out.

There are other spellings which Scott might have used but chose not to. The [uː] sound could have been indicated by *oo* especially where the use of *ou* is ineffective as being already the English spelling: so *about*, *out* and *house* could have been *aboot*, *oot* and *hoose*. We have just seen how Scott used *hoose* with Jeanie, but this was a special case and generally, as we know, Scott preferred not to employ these English-based spellings. The need for intelligibility as much as national pride no doubt induced him to use a spelling which, though phonetically misleading to an Englishman, is easily understood by him. In the same way he chooses to use the spelling *ee* for [iː] which Scots shares with English rather than the Scots alternative *ei* which would give *weel* and *keep* further Scottish flavour as *weil* and *keip*. The spelling then is of Scott's usual kind; it is not a phonetic transcription but a combination of words spelt in the Scottish way with other words spelt in the English way.

Vocabulary presents a different problem. Clearly there are a number of Scottish words – *whigmaleeries, curliewurlies, coup, crans, crouse* – and words used in a Scottish way – *sorrow* is here used, as commonly in Scotland (see above), as an oath. Words with Scottish forms in this passage or which appear elsewhere in Scott with Scottish forms are also obviously Scots. But we cannot exclude other words like *idolatry, image, worship, surplices, edifice, agreement, idolatrous* and *statues*. To exclude such words is to limit Scots to whatever is not also found unchanged in English. But English and Scots are a continuum and share many common words. This applies as much to literary words as to colloquial ones; we may see literary words more often in passages of English but this is because written English is more extensive than written Scots. But such literary words are still available, when needed, to be incorporated into a passage of Scots. Indeed Scottish speech was perhaps often more formal than English speech. It often shows the influence of biblical English, represented here by both the diction and the non-Scottish *-eth* ending of the phrase 'the muckle hure that sitteth on seven hills'. This seems to be what Wordsworth refers to in 'Resolution and Independence':

> Choice word and measured phrase, above the reach
> Of ordinary men; a stately speech;
> Such as grave Livers do in Scotland use,
> Religious men, who give to God and men their dues
> (stanza xiv).

This solemn style is here combined with down-to-earth realism. The combination of the colloquial and the literary, the pithy and the stately is typically Scottish.

The vocabulary can therefore be considered as Scottish; the presence of words shared with English does not make the passage English. Where a passage does become English is where the ordinary Scottish terms are replaced by English ones, where, for example *ken* gives way to *know*.

Much the same applies to grammar. On the whole, Scots grammar differs from English in minor particulars – represented here by the Scottish personal use of *behove* where English is confined to the impersonal – with just a few more frequently occurring differences like the *-na* negative (as in *wasna*).

The passage is a good example of broad Scots as it is represented in our novels. It would be spoken with a strong Scottish accent and employs familiar Scottish diction and syntax. It has been influenced by English but only in a way which has enriched rather than superseded the Scots.

Most of the Scots in the novels is like this, but in some passages and with some speakers there is a clear illustration of the increasing tendency in Scott's time of English to displace Scots. Saunders Fairford is in many ways a portrait of Scott's father. We know that Scott remembered his father's generation as speaking Scots in company and Saunders is represented as so doing. His relation to his son, Alan, of how Alan comes to be Peter Peebles' advocate is typical of his speech:

> 'Whisht, Alan! – never interrupt the court – all *that* is managed for ye like a tee'd ball;' (my father sometimes draws his similes from his once favourite game of golf;) – 'you must know, Alan, that Peter's cause was to have been opened by young Dumtoustie – ye may ken the lad, a son of Dumtoustie of that ilk, member of Parliament for the county of ——, and a nephew of the Laird's younger brother, worthy Lord Bladderskate, whilk ye are aware sounds as like being akin to a peatship and a sheriffdom, as a sieve is sib to a riddle. Now, Saunders Drudgeit, my lord's clerk, came to me this morning in the House, like ane bereft of his wits; for it seems that young Dumtoustie is ane of the Poor's Lawyers, and Peter Peebles's process had been remitted to him of course. But so soon as the harebrained goose saw the pokes, (as, indeed, Alan, they are none of the least,) he took fright, called for his nag, lap on, and away to the country is he gone; and so, said Saunders, my lord is at his wit's end wi' vexation and shame, to see his nevoy break off the course at the very starting. "I'll tell you, Saunders," said I, "were I my lord, and a friend or kinsman of mine should leave the town while the court was sitting, that kinsman, or be he what he liked, should never darken my door again." And then, Alan, I thought to turn the ball our own way; and I said that you were a gey sharp birkie, just off the irons, and if it would oblige my lord, and so forth, you would open Peter's cause

on Tuesday, and make handsome apology for the necessary absence of your learned friend, and the loss which your client and the court had sustained, and so forth. Saunders lap at the proposition, like a cock at a grossart; for, he said, the only chance was to get a new hand, that did not ken the charge he was taking upon him; for there was not a lad of two Sessions' standing that was not dead-sick of Peter Peebles and his cause; and he advised me to break the matter gently to you at the first; but I told him you were a good bairn, Alan, and had no will and pleasure in these matters but mine' (Re 199–200).

In several ways this is closer than Andrew Fairservice's speech to English. There are relatively few Scottish forms – *whilk, ane, wi'* and *nevoy* (but also *nephew*) – while at the same time there are many English forms of words which Scott elsewhere gave their Scottish form: *all* (*a'*), *ball* (*ba'*), *have* (*hae*), *soon* (*sune*), *goose* (*guse*), *none* (*nane*), *away* (*awa'*), *gone* (*gane*), *so* (*sae*), *off* (*aff*), *should* (*suld*), *town* (*toun*), *own* (*ain*), *would* (*wad*), *make* (*mak*), *your* (*yere*), and *good* (*gude*). As well as these we find *of* rather than *o'*, usually one of the most frequent Scottish forms in passages of full Scots. In the grammar we find the Scottish use of *gey* (*gay*) as an adverb meaning 'very' and the past tense of *leap* as *lap* not *leapt*. On the other hand *did not* and *was not* appear rather than *didna* and *wasna*, *these* rather than *thir* and *liked* rather than *likeit*. The vocabulary includes a number of Scots terms including *ken, that ilk, laird, peatship, sib, process, poke, birkie, grossart* and *bairn*. But we also find English terms where Scots equivalents were in normal everyday use, like *must* rather than *maun* and *know* instead of *ken* (although *ken* appears twice later in the passage).

English, then, has made deeper inroads here than in Andrew Fairservice's case. Ordinary Scots idioms are being replaced by English ones, and the pronunciation, so the presence of many fewer Scottish forms suggests, is not as broad. The trouble is that the spelling only provides a vague impression rather than specific information. We have seen that in a passage which we have every reason to see as presenting broad Scots there are interspersed many English spellings. The mixture of pronunciations would be totally arbitrary if we took each of these separate English spellings as each indicating an English pronunciation for the word concerned. The overall impression is the most important factor in guiding our pronunciation. So too in this passage, where the fewer Scottish spellings indicate an accent less broad than Andrew's, we still should probably not take the spellings of individual words as phonetically meaningful for each word. The spelling conveys some general impressions – that Saunders aims somewhere between a Scottish and an English pronunciation, that he was 'careful' in his speech (that is, tried more than Andrew to bring pronunciation and accepted spelling into line) – but it is doubtful if Scott wanted us to imagine the individual words as spoken in strict conformity with the spelling. We should not forget too that realism may not have been Scott's only aim. It may be that he avoids Scottish spellings not so much because a lawyer's accent would have been so different from a gardener's as because he does not want to weaken his picture of Saunders as an educated man. In particular this may account for the infrequency of apostrophe spellings like *o'* and *wi'* which are particularly liable to convey the feeling that the speaker is illiterate.

With these passages we can compare, at least as regards spelling, much longer passages of the speech of two individual characters. The first of these is the total dialogue of Mrs Flockhart in *Waverley*. Like Andrew's speech, Mrs Flockhart's dialogue is, in terms of Scott's novels, broad Scots. Words like *ane* 'one' (4), *auld* 'old' (2), *ca'd* 'called' (3), *cam* 'came' (3), *doun* 'down' (2), *mysell* 'myself' (2), *sae* 'so' (3), *sair* 'sore' (3), *ta'en* 'taken' (4), *tak* 'take' (2), *wad* 'would' (3), *weel* 'well' (4) and *wi'* 'with' (4) are consistently given their Scottish form. (The number of occurrences of each word is given in brackets.) The same applies to a number of words which appear only once like *amang* 'among', *bluidy* 'bloody', *ceevil* 'civil', *forgie* 'forgive', *mony* 'many', *shouther* 'shoulder', *thae* 'those' and *wha* 'who'. Yet even in this broad Scots dialogue *poor* (2) is used as well as *puir* (4), *of* (1) as well as *o'* (5) and *very* (3) as well as *vera* (1), while *folk* (2), *have* (1), *lady* (3), *other* (1) and *same* (1) completely oust *fowk*, *hae*, *leddy*, *ither* and *saam(e)*, all of which are common spellings elsewhere in Scott. Needless to say the *oo* spelling for [u:], which Scott did not often use, is not found here – instead we have *house* (1), *our* (1) and *out* (1).

With overall word-counts of this kind it may be possible to make finer distinctions between characters. For example, King James in *The Fortunes of Nigel* appears, at first glance, to speak a Scots as broad as that of Mrs Flockhart, yet a word-count of some of his dialogue (*FN* 81, 84–96) seems to show that English spellings are in fact more prevalent in his dialogue than in hers. The number of words and the size of the overall vocabulary is only a little larger but the picture is slightly different. A number of words have only Scottish forms – *a'* 'all' (1), *auld* 'old' (1), *awa* 'away' (2), *chalmer* 'chamber' (1), *fause* 'false' (1), *fule* 'fool' (3), *haud* 'hold' (2), *lang* 'long' (2), *mair* 'more' (2), *sae* 'so' (2), *sax* 'six' (1), *ta'en* 'taken' (1) and *wha* 'who' (1) – but rather more words than with Mrs Flockhart have both Scots and English forms like *ain* (3) and *own* (1), *dune* (1) and *done* (1), *frae* (3) and *from* (1), *gude* (1) and *good* (1), *luve* (1) and *love* (1), *mak* (1) and *make* (1), *vera* (1) and *very* (3), and *wi'* (5) and *with* (2). Most significant of all, *o'* only appears twice beside twenty occurrences of *of*, probably to avoid giving a learned king 'illiterate' pronunciations. *Brave* (1), *called* (1), *gold* (1), *master* (1), *other* (1), *ourselves* (1) and *wrestled* (1) entirely displace *braw*, *ca'd*, *gowd*, *maister*, *ither*, *oursells* and *warstled*. Overall then, though James speaks a broad Scots, his pronunciation may be a little less broad than Mrs Flockhart's.

Who, then, speaks what? Those who speak English in the Scottish novels include, of course, Englishmen – and, as it happens, quite a few of Scott's heroes are Englishmen (Waverley, Frank Osbaldistone, Francis Tyrrell). Some of his other heroes, though Scottish by birth, have been educated outside Scotland and speak English (Brown-Bertram, Lovel, Fergus MacIvor). But English is not confined to Englishmen by birth or education. Many upper-class Scotsmen speak English, and only English, including members of the peerage and their families, like Lord Evandale and his sister in *Old Mortality* and the Lady Betty mentioned briefly in *Waverley* (*Wa* 487), baronets, like Sir Robert Hazlewood in *Guy Mannering*, and their children and landed gentlemen, like Major Melville in *Waverley* and the lairds of Langcale and Gilbertscleugh in *Old Mortality*. The exclusive use of English is also found with some middle-class characters, like the lawyers Mr Protocol in *Guy Mannering* and Mr Fairbrother in *The Heart of Midlothian*, and with clergymen, like 'the minister of the parish, who had been Charles Hazlewood's tutor' in *Guy Mannering* (*GM* 577) and Mr Morton in *Waverley*. Here the use of English is probably the result of both social class and education. It is noticeable that the younger generation of these classes has a greater tendency than the older to stick to English.

Rose Bradwardine in *Waverley*, Lucy Bertram in *Guy Mannering*, Henry Morton in *Old Mortality*, Alan Fairford in *Redgauntlet* and Mary and Hector M'Intyre in *The Antiquary* all both only use English and also have near relations in the previous generation who use a greater or less amount of Scots. The lowest the exclusive use of English goes in the social scale is to the servants of upper-class people like the Duke of Argyle's servant Archibald, whose dignity and imposing presence is maintained by the use of English, and Isabella Wardour's maid servant (*An* 146).

Scott was aware that the use of English by people in the upper classes is often historically inaccurate, especially for novels set much before his own time. In *The Fortunes of Nigel* the hero, Lord Glenvarloch, speaks pure English except for the Scots colloquialism *barns-breaking* when he is angry and anxious (*FN* 44), the legal term *wadset* (*FN* 66) and his use of *anent* in repeating his servant Richie's words (*FN* 242). Yet Scott has Richie say of Nigel that he has 'a pleasant speech, something leaning to the kindly north-country accentuation, but not much, in respect of his having been resident abroad' (*FN* 459). Earlier on, when Nigel seeks entry to the sanctuary of 'Alsatia', the disreputable parson argues against allowing in 'a beggarly Scot' whose 'speech bewrayeth him' (*FN* 301–2). It seems that we are to take Nigel as speaking with a Scottish accent even though there are no Scottish spellings in his speech. Likewise the mysterious Lady Hermione in the same novel is of Scottish descent on her mother's side; she tells Margaret Ramsay that in Madrid with the Scottish and Irish officers, 'I had perpetual occasion to exercise my mother's native language, which I had learned from my infancy' (*FN* 344). Yet she too speaks always in English. Lady Hermione, who is related to Nigel, and Nigel himself were perhaps thought of by Scott as speaking the old 'court Scots' which, as we know, Scott described his aunt as speaking. Certainly whenever a character is mentioned as speaking court Scots their language in their dialogue is always English. So it is with Mrs Bethune Balliol in *The Chronicles of the Canongate* and with Effie Deans after she has become the fashionable Lady Staunton.

Naturally, alongside those whose language is exclusively English, we find a number of characters of the same social classes who mix a few Scoticisms with their English. This sometimes manifests itself regularly in their speech, sometimes only in moments of strong emotion. Such a slight admixture of Scots can be seen as high up the social scale as the Duke of Argyle in *The Heart of Midlothian*. While the basis of his dialogue is English he sprinkles it with Scots addressives and Scots proverbs. When he first meets Jeanie he calls her 'my bonny lass' making use of 'the encouraging epithet which at once acknowledged the connexion betwixt them as country-folk' (*HM* 528) and later tells her 'ilka man buckles his belt his ain gate – you know our old Scotch proverb' (*HM* 535). His Scots extends beyond this to the use of ordinary terms like *fou* (*full*) meaning 'drunk' (*HM* 567) and his praise of Jeanie's 'canny hamely sense' (*HM* 590). The Scots of another Duke – Lauderdale – is concentrated entirely in addressives; he speaks to Macbriar as *laddie* (*OM* 472), and Lord Huntington's only Scots is the two addressives *man* (*FN* 155) and *laddie* (*FN* 233). Lower down the social scale we have the Antiquary, Jonathan Oldbuck of Monkbarns. His normal speech is English – late eighteenth-century English mixed with a goodly allowance of Latin and phrases from Shakespeare. His fondness for archaisms means he uses a number of words which are both archaic and Scots: *an* 'if' (*An* 110), *dree* 'endure' (*An* 111), *somedele* 'somewhat' (*An* 70). In a moment of emotional stress he comes out with full colloquial Scots:

> 'Ye donnard auld deevil,' answered his guest, his Scottish accent predominating when in anger, though otherwise not particularly remarkable, – 'ye donnard auld crippled idiot . . . ' (*An* 12).

In fact, though Oldbuck uses a sprinkling of Scottish pronunciations like *ta'en* (*An* 11) and *deil* (*An* 103) and Scottish words like *canny* (An 101), *landlouper* 'rascal' (*An* 163) and *sneeshin* 'snuff' (*An* 192), we do not again see him falling into Scots in emotional moments. Scott seems to have forgotten this characteristic. Indeed when Oldbuck is angry not much later in the book he uses English, including *devil* instead of, as in this earlier passage, *deevil* (*An* 44, 47).

For most of the novel Oldbuck's colourful and occasionally Scots speech could not contrast more sharply with the pompous and laboured Standard English of his neighbour and fellow antiquary, Sir Arthur Wardour. But even Sir Arthur, in a moment of violent emotion when his daughter's life is at stake, turns to Scots, the Scotsman's natural language for expressing feeling:

What are ye doing wi' my bairn? What are ye doing? (*An* 99).

Major Bellenden at Charnwood, Edith's uncle in *Old Mortality*, is of similar social rank to Oldbuck and also mixes Scots with his English, though his speech is less entertaining and interesting.

(Oldbuck shows, incidentally, in his general speech that Scott could write interesting *English* dialogue as well as interesting *Scots* dialogue, contrary to what is often asserted). The Major uses *carles* 'fellows' (OM 153), *skinker* 'butler or drunkard' (OM 153), *leasing-making* 'sedition' (OM 157), *hamely* (OM 160) and *biggit wa's* 'stone walls' (OM 263) as well as the anglicized *borough-town* (OM 267; also GM 77) – a form of the word Scott usually less fully anglicizes as *burrows-town* (An 350, FN 87).

Education rather than birth has given Reuben Butler his English speech but he too reverts to Scots in moments of emotion. Trying to explain to the ignorant and foolish Bartoline Saddletree the difference between *quivis* and *cuivis* he finally loses his patience:

> 'Then what the *deevil* d'ye take the nominative and the dative cases to be?' said Butler, hastily, and surprised at once out of his decency of expression and accuracy of pronunciation (HM 64).

Again, when Jeanie unexpectedly produces a large sum of money in £50 bank-notes, his reaction is:

> 'How on earth came ye by that siller, Jeanie? – Why, here is more than a thousand pounds,' said Butler, lifting up and counting the notes (HM 711).

In his surprise he uses the Scottish form – *siller* – and meaning – 'money' – of English *silver*. His only other Scotticism is anglicized – he refers to Davie as the *goodman* (HM 640) not *gudeman*. Dominie Sampson, who has trained for the ministry even if he remains a 'stickit stibbler', speaks English too, but twice when excited or emotional he uses *waur* for *worse* (GM 46, 138) and when he has just drunk a cup of Meg Merrilies' brandy his pompous word for 'letter' becomes *yepistle* (GM 471) with the Scottish addition of initial *y*, which we have discussed above (see pp. 183–4). He also uses the legal term *umwhile* 'late, deceased' (GM 23). Two last cases: Mr MacMorlan, the sheriff-substitute, in *Guy Mannering* always speaks English but in his joy at the possibility of Lucy Bertram inheriting Lady Singleside's estate he turns to Scots. His opinion of her will is that:

> It's as tight as a glove, – naebody could make better wark than Glossin, when he didna let down a steek on purpose. But [his countenance falling] the auld b———, that I should say so, might alter at pleasure (GM 336).

(The bowdlerized term of abuse is another measure of his excitement). Yet even here his Scots is not very broad. The other Lucy, the tragic Lucy Ashton, is another English-speaker, but in her grinning exultation at her attempt to murder her husband, Bucklaw, she says to those who have carried her husband away: 'So, you have ta'en up your bonny bridegroom' (*BL* 441).

With all these characters the amount of Scots they use is relatively limited. In other characters there is a much more considerable intermixing of Scots and English. Some characters speak a mixed language, an Anglo-Scots; others alternate between Scots and English. An interesting case of mixed language is the Baron of Bradwardine. When he first appears he uses a number of Scottish words (as well as archaisms and Latin tags) but there is no hint of a Scottish accent:

> Then there was the Laird of Killancureit, who had devoted his leisure *until* tillage and agriculture, . . . He is, as ye may well suppose from such a tendency, but of yeoman extraction, – *servabit odorem testa diu*; and I believe, between ourselves, his grandsire was from the wrong side of the Border, – one Bullsegg, who came hither as a steward, or bailiff, or ground-officer, or something in that department, to the last Girnigo of Killancureit, who died of an atrophy. After his master's death, sir, – ye would hardly believe such a scandal, – but this Bullsegg, being portly and comely of aspect, intermarried with the lady dowager, who was young and amorous, and possessed himself of the estate, which devolved upon this unhappy woman by a settlement of her umwhile husband, in direct contravention of an unrecorded taillie, and to the prejudice of the disponer's own flesh and blood, in the person of his natural heir and seventh cousin (*Wa* 80–81).

Ground-officer 'steward', *umwhile* 'deceased', *taillie* 'entail' and *disponer* 'disposer' are all Scoticisms. The Baron's language continues to be like this and remains so when he returns to the scene after a gap of 250-odd pages. Then suddenly, a few pages later on, we hear him speak with a Scottish accent. Fergus promises him a good dinner at his quarters in Edinburgh:

> 'And wha the deil doubts it,' quoth the Baron, laughing, 'when ye bring only the cookery, and the gude toun must furnish the materials? Weel, I have some business in the toun too; but I'll join you at three, if the vivers can tarry so long' (*Wa* 384).

His language must now be identified as a mixture of educated

The Extent of Scots in the Novels

Scots and English. *Vivers* is a Scots term which has had some currency in later Standard English 'probably due its frequent occurrence in the Waverley Novels' (*OED vivers*; see also *RR* 79, *FN* 558). On the other hand *maun* has been replaced by the English *must*. A more fully Scots passage might have *hae* for *have* and *sae* for *so* but, as we have seen, in the novels even the passages of broad Scots are not consistent in these particulars. For the rest of the novel the Baron retains his suddenly discovered Scots pronunciation, even if it varies in intensity a little. It is reduced to the one word *sae* when he addresses Prince Charles:

> 'And by my honour, sir . . . the lad can sometimes be as dowff as a sexagenary like myself. If your Royal Highness had seen him dreaming and dozing about the banks of Tully-Veolan like a hypochrondriac person, or as Burton's "Anatomia" hath it, a phrenesiac or lethargic patient, you would wonder where he hath sae suddenly acquired all this fine sprack festivity and jocularity' (*Wa* 402).

Note too the use of more colloquial Scots terms here like *dowff* 'dull' and *sprack* 'lively'. Conversely his accent can be markedly Scots in moments of emotion as when he queries whether Waverley has followed the proper course in wooing his daughter:

> I hope ye hae secured the approbation of your ain friends and allies, particularly of your uncle, who is *in loco parentis*? Ah, we maun tak heed o' that (*Wa* 602).

Why does Scott change the Baron's accent? Realistically there can be no justification, but from the literary point of view we can probably understand how it happened. When we first meet the Baron he is living at home – his accent must not be allowed to interfere with Scott's presentation of him as a dignified man even if a little eccentric. He must not seem to be a mere ignorant countryman. Especially in this, his first novel, Scott may well have doubted how his audience would react to broad Scots speech. When we see him again he is clearly a highly respected officer and counsellor of Prince Charles. At this stage a Scots accent can be usefully employed to contrast with Fergus MacIvor's English speech and heighten our feeling of the unpromising heterogeneity of Prince Charles' division-torn army. Another character who speaks a mixture of English and Scots though tending at times to move towards one or the other, is Sir Mungo Malagrowther in *The Fortunes of Nigel*, while more consistent in his mixed language is Saunders Fairford in *Redgauntlet*.

One of those who oscillates between Scots and English and something in between rather than generally maintaining a mixed language is Lady Margaret Bellenden in *Old Mortality*. This oscillation in her case seems to represent something fundamental to her character. While she likes to play the grand lady and hostess, she has also found pleasure in the past in a good gossip with her ploughman's mother, Mause Headrigg. Perhaps, for all her grand manner, Scots comes easiest to her. When she vents her displeasure at the Guse Gibbie incident on Mause she speaks in Scots; the angrier she gets the more Scots her speech. She begins like this:

> Is it true, Mause, as I am informed by Harrison, Gudyill, and others of my people, that you hae taen it upon you, contrary to the faith you owe to God and the king, and to me, your natural lady and mistress, to keep back your son frae the wappenschaw, held by the order of the sheriff, and to return his armour and abulyiements at a moment when it was impossible to find a suitable delegate in his stead... (*OM* 83).

but, in less formal style, she soon speaks like this:

> Dinna tell me of your son's illness, Muuse! Had he been sincerely unweel, ye would hae been at the Tower by daylight to get something that wad do him gude; there are few ailments that I havena medical recipes for, and that ye ken fu' weel (*OM* 84).

By contrast, when she ceremoniously greets Bothwell on his arrival at Tillietudlem she reverts to English (*OM* 124-129), a pattern of alternation which is continued throughout the novel. To cite another example, Grizzel Oldbuck, a Scots-speaker in general, unlike her brother who no doubt had a fuller education, also moves into English at a formal moment, when she welcomes Lovel to her home:

> My brother... has a humorous way of expressing himself, sir, – nobody thinks anything of what Monkbarns says; so I beg you will not be so confused for the matter of his nonsense. But you must have had a warm walk beneath this broiling sun: would you take ony thing, – a glass of balm wine? (*An* 66).

The Scots accent which shows in *ony* expands, in her complaint at what her brother paid for some fish, into this:

A fair bargain! when ye gied the limmer a full half o' what she seekit! An ye will be a wife-carle, and buy fish at your ain hands, ye suld never bid muckle mair than a quarter. And the impudent quean had the assurance to come up and seek a dram. But I trow, Jenny and I sorted her! (*An* 177).

This distinction between English as the language of formal speech and Scots as that of informal speech comes out particularly sharply with Bailie Middleburgh in *The Heart of Midlothian*. The bailie is described as 'something of a humorist, and rather deficient in general education; but acute, patient and upright' (*HM* 266). We might expect him to speak Scots, like his Glasgow counterpart and near-contemporary Bailie Nicol Jarvie, but when he makes his formal interrogation of Butler he uses English. Indeed in revising the novel for the Collected edition Scott went to the trouble of removing from this passage some slight traces of a Scottish accent; the first edition's *ane* (II 18) and *o'* (II 20) become in the Collected edition *one* (*HM* 197) and *of* (*HM* 198). However, when the bailie returns after an intervening chapter, his language is Scots (*HM* 231-2) as he talks confidentially to the city clerk and procurator-fiscal. In his speech at the end of this informal chat he reverts to English to give his orders but falls back towards Scots as he begins to reflect more informally on the events:

I will speak to the Lord Provost . . . about Ratcliffe's business. Mr Sharpitlaw, you will go with me and receive instructions – something may be made too out of this story of Butler's and his unknown gentleman – I know no business any man has to swagger about in the King's Park, and call himself the devil, to the terror of honest folks, who dinna care to hear mair about the devil than is said from the pulpit on the Sabbath. I cannot think the preacher himsell wad be heading the mob, though the time has been, they hae been as forward in a bruilzie as their neighbours (*HM* 232-3).

Another chapter intervenes and we find him speaking English with a couple of Scoticisms – *suddenty* (*HM* 269) and *gudewife* (*HM* 270). Here the tone is still fairly formal though not as formal at the interrogation of Butler. Finally, apart from the use of the addressive *goodman* (*HM* 282), Bailie Middleburgh maintains his use of English in his attempt to convince Davie Deans that Jeanie should be allowed to testify in court. His use of English enhances his authority in dealing with Davie and from a literary point of view probably supports Scott's presentation of him as the representative of common sense in contrast to Davie's religious bigotry.

Lairds seem to be placed very much on the social dividing line between Scots-speakers and English-speakers. As a result their use of the two languages often reflects their personal characters more than their social status. Silas Morton of Milnwood habitually wanders in the one scene between Scots and English. The alternation seems appropriate to his character; he would like to be a respected country gentleman aspiring to the cultural superiority represented by the use of English but most of the time he is nothing but a narrow-minded rural miser. Godfrey Bertram of Ellangowan similarly slips in and out of English, mirroring in this yet another kind of mixed personality – a man capable of a more 'cultivated' manner but increasingly parochial in his outlook from an indolent love of staying at home.

The unsureness about social rank extends to servants. Their association with the upper classes makes them want to possess for themselves the gentility of speaking English but they naturally belong to the Scots-speaking lower classes. King James's cook Laurie Linklater reveals his social pretensions in speaking English with a few Scoticisms (*FN* 473–8) when berating a tradesman and addressing Nigel, Lord Glenvarloch, but drops into a more mixed Scots-English when talking more informally to Richie Moniplies (*FN* 555–6). Elspeth Mucklebackit, mother of a fisherman but earlier the Countess of Glenallan's servant, was 'weel-educate' according to Edie Ochiltree (*An* 518) who also remarks that sometimes she 'gets to her English, and speaks as if she were a prent buke' (*An* 517). In fact her language varies between English, Scots and a mixture of the two.

George Heriot can consciously change from English to Scots when he wishes to impress Richie (*FN* 27) but generally he prefers English. This may be considered as a realistic touch in a novel set in James I's London where Scotsmen were unpopular and consequently well-advised to shed their native tongue. However there is nothing particularly realistic about having him speak English with occasional Scoticisms when addressing his king and countryman who uses broad Scots (*FN* 84ff). Equally unrealistic is the way Andrew Skirliewhitter learns to speak pure English between the time he copies out a document for Heriot and the time when he receives the redemption money for Nigel's estate, a period of only a few months. Admittedly 'times have changed with him' and he is now on the way to becoming a wealthy lawyer, but we would still expect some trace of his lowlier origins to survive in his speech. Of course we can be over-subtle here; it is very likely that Scott (just like the ordinary reader) was not particularly aware of what language he had given to Andrew some five hundred pages before. What is certain is that in each scene considered separately the choice of language is entirely fitting: the servile scrivener anxious to please Heriot speaks Scots; the lawyer with pretensions to gentility speaks English.

Such considerations regarding the dramatic effect of the scene influence Scott's choice of language on many occasions. Evan Dhu in *Waverley* shows a considerable variety in his choice of language moving from English to Scots to Highland Scots to Gaelic. There seems to be some inconsistency here as well as some historical inaccuracy. There is no good reason why he should sometimes use a Highlands and sometimes a Lowlands pronunciation of Scots. He is not portrayed as having the cunning of Callum Beg who can drop his Highland accent and adopt a Lowlands one when he wants to mislead a too inquisitive innkeeper (*Wa* 276-7). Moreover it seems that Highlanders when they did not speak Gaelic spoke Standard English rather than Scots. Such was Dr Johnson's observation:

> Those Highlanders that can speak English, commonly speak it well, with few of the words, and little of the tone by which a Scotchman is distinguished. Their language seems to have been learned in the army or the navy, or by some communication with those who could give them good examples of accent and pronunciation. By their Lowland neighbours they would not willingly be taught; for they have long considered them as a mean and degenerate race (*A Journey to the Western Islands* in *Johnson: Prose and Poetry*, London, 1963, p. 682).

This may be thought to apply, however, to those Highlanders whose encounter with the language was through education or through contact with English-speakers rather than to those who, like Evan, lived on the edges of the Lowlands and came into direct and fairly frequent personal contact with Scots-speakers. But whether Evan's variability in language is justifiable on historical grounds or not, it is certainly justifiable on artistic grounds. When he first appears it is as the representative of his fosterbrother Fergus carrying a message to Bradwardine. The Baron speaks to him 'with an air of dignity, but without rising, and much, as Edward thought, in the manner of a prince receiving an embassy' (*Wa* 141). It is fitting in these circumstances that the 'ambassador' is endowed with all the formality of speaking 'in good English', even more so as it is an English enlivened with Ossianic imagery. When Evan last appears it is in the moving scene at his trial with Fergus where he offers to find six clansmen to die in Fergus' stead. Scott makes him speak Scots, which fits perfectly with the picture he is drawing; Evan embodies the simple and ordinary Highlander with an innate nobility of nature born of his devotion to his chief, a nobility which rises above such petty markers of social status as dialect. He is thus given the common man's language, Scots, though Scott wisely avoids giving him the Highland pronunciation which had become too replete with comic associations.

Finally we move to those whose language is more or less consistently Scots. Here we find lower-class and uneducated people, people below the dividing line which the lairds straddle. In *Old Mortality*, for example, we have peasants like Cuddie Headrigg, the ploughman, his mother and children and the mad peasant preacher Mucklewrath, servants like Lady Margaret's maid Mysie and her butler Gudyill, Major Bellenden's Pike and Alison (or Ailie) Wilson the housekeeper at Milnwood and lesser middle class like the innkeeper, Niel Blane, and his daughter. *The Antiquary* further adds small shop-keepers like Mrs Mailsetter the postmistress, Mrs Heukbane the butcher's wife and Mrs Shortcake the baker's wife, fishermen like the Mucklebackits, and itinerant beggars, represented by Edie Ochiltree. From *Guy Mannering* we may add farmers like Dandie Dinmont and gipsies like Meg Merrilies (who also uses cant words, but *not* Romany), while from *Rob Roy* we may add substantial merchants, perhaps a little old-fashioned in their ways, like Nicol Jarvie and from *The Heart of Midlothian* members of the underworld like Meg Murdockson, Madge Wildfire and Daddie Ratcliffe. These are the sort of people who speak Scots in the novels.

The one exception is a remarkable one since he is at quite the other extreme of the social scale. This exception is King James in *The Fortunes of Nigel*. James's speech is that of a learned, if somewhat pedantic, man and it may not be quite as broad in some particulars as the speech of peasants but it is still broad Scots. It is a historical fact that James spoke Scots, but this is probably *not* the main reason why Scott gave him such vivid Scots speech. After all, if James speaks Scots, so by all historical considerations should his old companion, Lord Huntinglen, and for that matter his son Charles who was brought up in Scotland and whom we likewise know to have spoken with a Scottish accent. Yet Lord Huntinglen uses a few Scoticisms and Charles none at all. It seems clear that Scott's chief interest in James's language was to create the character of the gossip-scholar-king, as he does so brilliantly, rather than to reflect historical fact. No doubt, too, Scott was happy to use the choice of language to heighten the significant contrast between James and Charles.

It is important to note that, while all of these speakers show an overwhelming preponderance of Scots speech, most of them will on certain occasions move towards speaking English. As we have noted, English tends to be the language of formal speech and it will be adopted where formality is an advantage to the speaker. Edie Ochiltree has a large amount of dialogue in *The Antiquary* and almost all of it is in Scots. However, when he wants to impress Lovel and Hector M'Intyre with the folly of duelling, he turns to a highly biblical English to lend solemnity to his speech, although as he continues he reverts to Scots:

> 'What are ye come here for, young men?' he said, addressing himself to the surprised audience, 'are ye come amongst the most lovely works of God to break his laws? Have ye left the works of man, the houses and the cities that are but clay and dust, like those that built them, and are ye come here among the peaceful hills, and by the quiet waters, that will last whiles aught earthly shall endure, to destroy each other's lives, that will have but an unco short time, by the course of nature, to make up a lang account at the close o't.... Gang hame, gang hame, like gude lads; the French will be ower to harry us ane o' thae days, and ye'll hae feighting eneugh (*An* 264-5).

Such biblical English is also adopted by Davie Deans in *The Heart of Midlothian* at various moments of solemn emotion and there is no doubt that the English Authorized Version provided many Scots with their main example of formal language as well as being deeply tied up with their religious feelings. Even in the midst of his very secular concerns, Nicol Jarvie expresses his strong sense of the value of what he might achieve by a biblical allusion:

> they wad do weel, and deserve weel baith o' the state and o' humanity, that wad save three or four honest Hieland gentleman frae louping

heads ower heels into destruction, wi' a' their puir sackless followers, ... and save your father's credit, – and my ain gude siller that Osbaldistone and Tresham awes me into the bargain, – I say if ane could manage a' this, I think it suld be done and said unto him, even if he were a puir ca'-the-shuttle body, as unto one whom the king delighteth to honour (RR 366).

The Bailie moves easily from his Scots into idioms, like *unto* and the *-eth* ending, foreign to Scots but found in the king's question to Haman 'What shall be done unto the man whom the king delighteth to honour' (*Esth* vi 6).

The formality of English may also be used for less noble purposes. When Oldbuck tries to complain to Mrs Macleuchar about the non-arrival of her coach an interesting linguistic situation develops. The usually English-speaking Oldbuck in his anger uses the Scots word *doited* meaning 'in her dotage' while the Scots-speaking Mrs Macleuchar, making an attempt to bolster her shaky position by shifting the grounds of argument, temporarily turns to English for the tones of righteous indignation but, failing in her attempt, sinks back into the known security of Scots where she can pretend she knows nothing about it at all:

'Mrs Macleucher, good woman,' with an elevated voice; then apart, 'Old doited hag, she's as deaf as a post, – I say, Mrs Macleucher!'

'I am just serving a customer. – Indeed hinny, it will no be a bodle cheaper than I tell ye.'

'Woman,' reiterated the traveller, 'do you think we can stand here all day till you have cheated that poor servant wench out of her half-year's fee and bountith?'

'Cheated!' retorted Mrs Macleuchar, eager to take up the quarrel upon a defensible ground. 'I scorn your words, sir; you are an uncivil person, and I desire you will not stand there to slander me at my ain stairhead.'

'The woman,' said the senior, looking with an arch glance at his destined travelling companion, 'does not understand the words of action. – Woman,' again turning to the vault, 'I arraign not thy character, but I desire to know what is become of thy coach.'

'What's your wull?' answered Mrs Macleuchar, relapsing into deafness.

'We have taken places, ma'am,' said the young stranger, 'in your diligence for Queensferry – '

> 'Which should have been half-way on the road before now,' continued the elder and more impatient traveller, rising in wrath as he spoke...
> 'The coach? Gude guide us, gentlemen, is it no on the stand yet?' answered the old lady, her shrill tone of expostulation sinking into a kind of apologetic whine. 'Is it the coach ye hae been waiting for?' (*An* 4-5).

Thus the Scots-speaking characters may all on occasions turn to English but their normal speech is broad Scots.

What has been said applies to all the novels with seventeenth-, eighteenth- and nineteenth-century settings. In the novels with earlier settings the amount of Scots is greatly reduced, allowing prominence to be given to the use of period language, including some obsolete Scottish words which have been discussed earlier (see pp. 30-2). In *The Fair Maid of Perth*, for example, Scott has Chrystal Croftangry, the supposed author, tell us that

> I have not placed in the mouth of the characters the Lowland Scotch dialect now spoken, because unquestionably the Scottish of that day resembled very closely the Anglo-Saxon, with a sprinkling of French or Norman to enrich it. Those who wish to investigate the subject may consult the 'Chronicles of Winton', and the 'History of Bruce', by Archdeacon Barbour. But supposing my own skill in the ancient Scottish were sufficient to invest the dialogue with its peculiarities, a translation must have been necessary for the benefit of the general reader. The Scottish dialect may be therefore considered as laid aside, unless where the use of peculiar words may add emphasis or vivacity to the composition (*FM* 14).

Though Scott's description of late fourteenth-century Scots as close to Old English may not strike us as very accurate, the passage does describe very precisely his own practice in the novel. The use of Scots is, as usual, largely confined to the lower and middle classes (that is mainly the townsmen like Henry Smith and Simon Glover and their servants like Luckie Shoolbred) but, in this novel, it also extends to the lower edges of the upper classes, represented by Sir Patrick Charteris. However, contrary to Scott's usual practice, with all these characters the Scots appears only as isolated words in otherwise English speech. Indeed some of the Scoticisms blend into the period English since words like *an* 'if' (*FM* 56), *dree* 'endure' (*FM* 225) and *remede* 'remedy' (*FM* 478) are both Scots and also archaic English. The upper classes, including the royal family and the Highlander Conachar-Eachin, all speak English. In *The Monastery* the limitation on Scots is achieved in a different way. While the servants Tibb and Martin speak Scots, and the church-vassal Elspeth Glendinning varies between Scots and English, other people of similar class like Elspeth's sons and the miller's daughter Mysie are made to speak English. So too does the Lady of Avenel (whose husband corresponds in rank to a laird in the later-set novels) and her daughter as well as the monks who are such important characters in the novel. In other words, the use of Scots is limited by bringing English somewhat lower down the social scale than we might expect from our experience of the other novels.

Returning to the novels of the seventeenth century and after, it will be clear by now that Scott did not in his novels aim to reflect the historical realities of the use of Scots and English by Scotsmen at the various periods. Only in the novels with settings contemporary with Scott's own lifetime like *Guy Mannering*, *The Antiquary* and *St Ronan's Well* and possibly to some extent with the slightly earlier setting of *Waverley* does the distribution of Scots and English reflect historical fact. This is because the situation in the novels is roughly that of Scott's own time. This is clearest in the consistent picture of the younger generation speaking English where the older generation speaks Scots. This is accurate enough in *The Antiquary* with Mary and Hector M'Intyre's English compared to their aunt Griselda Oldbuck's Scots, but is quite misleading in *Old Mortality*, set in the later seventeenth century, where Henry Morton and Edith Bellenden speak English and his uncle and her grandmother speak Scots or a mixed Scots-English. In the seventeenth century, Scotsmen of all ranks spoke Scots. The historical inaccuracy becomes particularly obvious in *The Fortunes of Nigel* with King James himself speaking Scots while Scottish nobles like Nigel speak English. As we have seen, the discrepancy is so glaring that Scott feels obliged to try and correct it but can only resort to further complicating the issue by having other characters identify Nigel's speech as Scots in glaring contradiction to the fact that all his speeches are given in English.

The discrepancy between fact and fiction also comes out in one of Scott's notes to *The Heart of Midlothian*. As we have seen Bailie Middleburgh is made to alternate between Scots and English. His English shows no sign of a Scots accent; yet the real life town-councillors of the time, indeed no less a person than the Provost himself, seem to have spoken with a strong Scots accent when they came before the House of Lords to be questioned about the Porteous Riots, at least according to Scott's anecdote.

> The magistrates were closely interrogated before the House of Peers, concerning the particulars of the Mob, and the *patois* in which these functionaries made their answers, sounded strange in the ears of the Southern nobles. The Duke of Newcastle having demanded to know with what kind of shot the guard which Porteous commanded had loaded their muskets, was answered naively, 'Ow, just sic as ane shoots *dukes and fools* with.' This reply was considered as a contempt of the House of Lords, and the Provost would have suffered accordingly, but that the Duke of Argyle explained, that the expression, properly rendered into English, meant *ducks and waterfowl* (HM 278n).

(In Scots the two words are pronounced [dju:k] and [fu:l] and Scott elsewhere uses the spelling, *deuke*, for the Scots equivalent of both *duck* (*An* 183) and *duke* (*GM* 197) though the latter may be merely eye-dialect.)

In summary; we may take the novels set after the sixteenth century as more or less reflecting the situation in Scott's own time with regard to the use of Scots and English. This means that for the novels set from the mid-eighteenth century onwards the linguistic situation is more or less historically accurate and that, for those set before, the further back we go the more inaccurate any representation of English speech for Scotsmen will be, until it reaches the point where it is quite inappropriate. Nevertheless, it would be unfair to Scott to end on this note. Despite the historical inaccuracies the novels provide an interesting sociolinguistic study of the interaction of two dialects of the same language, one standard, one local, in a wide number of different situations.

SCOTS IN THE NARRATIVE

Although Scott's major innovation in the use of Scots was to give it a place in dialogue, Scots does play some part in his narrative as well. In this he was following his contemporaries. Even though Standard English was the accepted medium for prose, a few literary Scoticisms tended to remain as well as the words which must necessarily be used to describe institutions peculiar to Scotland. All the same the number of Scottish terms not covering Scottish institutions in the narrative is quite small. Some of them are nowadays hard to recognize as Scoticisms since they were later in the nineteenth century adopted into Standard English. This is the case with *untimeous* meaning 'untimely' or 'unseasonable' which, until Scott gave it some currency in English texts, was a Scots word only. As it happens it has now disappeared again from Standard English, having become obsolete. So too *outlay* used as a verb meaning 'expend' found in Scott's narrative (*Wa* 49) and in later nineteenth-century English texts (*OED* outlay v 3) has failed to oust its English equivalent *lay out* used by Falstaff urging Bardolph to spend freely 'Lay out, lay out' (1*HIV* IV ii 5). On the other hand present-day English makes full use of the corresponding noun *outlay* which was also Scottish until the Victorian period. It occurs in the English speech of Jonathan Oldbuck (*An* 165). The adoption of the noun *outlay* has the convenience of giving us a word clearly differentiated from the American borrowing *layout* meaning 'arrangement'.

The word *stance* had the reverse history in its sense 'a standing place, site'. Though found in early Modern English it fell out of use except in Scotland. Scott's use of it did not revive its popularity, although another Scottish sense of the same word 'the position of a sportman's feet' has been accepted into Standard English. It is possible that Scott considered the former sense to be Standard English since it appears in the narrative of *Peveril of the Peak* (*PP* 172) as well as, again, in Jonathan Oldbuck's speech (*An* 43). The meaning of 'bog, swamp' for *moss* is also a Scoticism; it appears in the narrative of both the poems (*LL* I v) and the novels (*GM* 208).

None of these words covers concepts exclusive to Scotland. Scott uses them because they were normal literary usage in Scotland. Valleys and lakes are not limited to Scotland either, but more than just literary usage leads him to use Scottish terms for them. They help create a feeling of the uniquely Scottish setting he wishes to evoke. Nowadays we fall quite naturally into talking about Highland 'lochs' and 'glens'. The Highlands are recognized as having their own special characteristics and have also been invested with a certain glamour – Scott was one of those who helped do this – and we use these Scots borrowings from Gaelic to express our feeling for the distinctive qualities of the Highland landscape rather than making do with terms like 'lake' and 'mountain valley' which are similar in meaning though more mundane in their associations. All the same Scott shows some hesitation in using *loch* and *glen*, as well as the much less familiar *strath*, with English readers in *Waverley*.

> The glen, or dell, was terminated by a sheet of water called Loch Veolan, into which the brook discharged itself, and which now glistened in the western sun . . . there was nothing to interrupt the view until the scene was bounded by a ridge of distant and blue hills, which formed the southern boundary of the strath or valley (*Wa* 112).

Glen and *strath* are explained and *loch* only introduced as a proper name. In later novels *glen* is used freely in the narrative without explanation (*FM* 478, *OM* 5, *Mo* 9) but Scott's practice remains much the same with regard to the two other words. *Strath* is usually explained (*FM* 491) or coupled with the better-known *glen* (*LM* 82, *LL* III iv) and Scott is apparently reluctant to use *loch*. It usually figures as a proper name; in the long description of the funeral of Conachar's father in *The Fair Maid*, Loch Tay is usually referred to as 'the lake' (*FM* 500, 501, 515), only once as 'the Loch' and then with *loch* capitalized as if a place-name. In *The Lady of the Lake* too the normal term is 'lake' (e.g. I vi, vii, xiv), including for one of the most famous of all lochs, Loch Katrine.

When it comes to the Scottish legal system Scott could, once again, had he wanted to, have used English equivalent terms. Not surprisingly, however, he chooses to introduce us to some of the Scottish terminology. In the description of Effie's trial, for example, we find many Scots terms in the narrative. In the court, most of the major participants have names different from the English ones. The accused or prisoner is called the *panel* (*HM* 317), the jurymen are *assizers* (*HM* 353) and the foreman of the jury is called its *chancellor* (*HM* 353). Unlike English practice there are five judges, the 'five Lords of Justiciary' (*HM* 319), and the sentence is not pronounced by the Judge but by a separate official, the *Doomster* (*HM* 356), who is also the public hangman. In fact Scott could, had he wished, have used English terms for some of these: 'the accused, the jurymen, the foreman' – but not without the scene losing something of its atmosphere. Indeed Scott's pride in the Scottish courts shines through; he even points out some of the elements he feels are superior: 'on the other [side] sat the advocates, whom the humanity of the Scottish law (in this particular more liberal than that of the sister-country) not only permits, but enjoins, to appear and assist with their advice and skill all persons under trial' (*HM* 317). We know that Scott saw the legal system as being one of the bastions of the Scottish national identity, so it does not surprise us that he emphasizes its differences by using these terms. At the same time it is significant that he does explain the terms for his English audience even, in one case, giving the English equivalent term primacy: 'The foreman, called in Scotland the chancellor of the jury' (*HM* 353).

The Scottish terms here add to the local colour. Sometimes they are introduced simply because Scott finds the Scottish expression particularly vivid. Talking of Conachar-Eachin after he has left the Battle of the Clans in disgrace, Scott writes:

> His countenance was wild, haggard, and highly excited, or, as the Scottish phrase expresses it, much *raised* (*FM* 675).

I suspect that it was for the same reason, that he found it an effective phrase, that Scott used the phrase 'corbie messenger' to describe a man-servant who was very ineffectual in carrying out his mission (*SRW* 603). But the effectiveness of the phrase is lost on us since we do not understand the allusion. Perhaps Scott was, on the contrary, attracted by its obscurity.

There are other occasions where one feels Scott's love of minutiae and his delight in communicating them is the main force at work, as in his description of Fergus MacIvor's house:

> The chief and his guest had by this time reached the house of Glennaquoich, which consisted of Ian nan Chaistel's mansion, – a high, rude-looking square tower, with the addition of a *lofted* house; that is, a building of two stories (*Wa* 179).

Lofted is a Scottish and northern English dialect word. Or, again, when he tells us that town-gates are 'called in the Scottish language *ports*' (*HM* 74) and on the next page tells us the attendants on these gates were called *waiters* (*HM* 75), we recognize the same impulse at work.

This same role of Scott's is somewhat curiously taken up by Darsie Latimer. Admittedly he is English but he came to Scotland at an early age so that it sounds unnatural when he writes (to a Scotsman, too) that 'the old man now lighted and placed on the table a silver lamp, or *cruisie*, as the Scottish term it' (*Re* 46).

These intrusions of Scots terms into the English narrative can

The Extent of Scots in the Novels

be seen as brief extensions of the local colour of the dialogue and they are often explicitly presented as such. The speech of both Dandie Dinmont and his wife overflows into the narrative. When Bertram-Brown is welcomed to their house a couple of fowls are sacrificed on 'the gridiron, – or "brander", as Mrs Dinmont denominated it' (*GM* 218) and at the end of the meal 'Brown' is pressed to take 'another "cheerer", as Dinmont termed it in his country phrase, of brandy-and-water' (*GM* 219). Of course there are times when no English equivalent exists and Scott is more or less obliged to use the Scots term. So, in accounting for her ability to suddenly appear on the scene when Bradwardine and Balmawhapple come to blows, Scott notes how 'Luckie Macleary . . . sat quietly beyond the hallan, or earthen partition of the cottage' (*Wa* 93), using the Scots term *hallan* in the narrative as he does elsewhere in the dialogue (*An* 357, *HM* 662, *Re* 43). Here he can explain the term in passing; in *Redgauntlet* he adds a footnote (*Re* 43n). Yet on the whole it is not so much necessity which leads Scott to introduce Scottish words into the narrative as a deliberate decision to increase the colour and interest of his language.

Finally we need to note that sometimes it looks as if Scott has simply made a mistake in introducing a Scottish term. In *Kenilworth* he refers in the narrative to 'a large scale-staircase, as they were called' (*K* 78). The term is Scottish, is now obsolete and means 'a staircase with flights and landings'. Probably Scott had it from Burt who explains it in his *Letters from a Gentleman in the North of Scotland* (London, 1754, I 63). It is quite inaccurate to use it in an English setting and probably anachronistic too as the earliest recorded example of the word is dated 1643 (see *SND scale* n³). These objections do not arise with the use of *scale-staircase* (*GM* 341) and *scale-stair* (*GM* 361) in *Guy Mannering*. Another possible mistake in *Kenilworth* is in the phrase 'dink and dainty dame' (*K* 424). Did Scott forget *dink* was a Scots word or could he not resist the attractive alliterative phrase? He recognizes it as Scots in *The Bride of Lammermoor* where it means 'neatly dressed' and occurs in the Scots dialogue and in *The Fair Maid* where it is glossed in a footnote as 'Contemptuous – scornful of others' (*FM* 362). Either meaning could fit the *Kenilworth* context.

SCOTS IN LETTERS

As well as narrative and dialogue there is one other very minor place where Scottish language occurs in the novels – this is in letters. The letters which provide the first third of *Redgauntlet* I have treated as part of the ordinary narrative and dialogue. A possible exception is the short Letter IX from 'Alexander Fairford, W.S., to Mr Darsie Latimer'. It functions less to further the narrative, which it does only slightly, than to expand the character portrayal of the elder Fairford. As we would expect from a writer to the signet (a Scottish solicitor with special privileges), there is a good deal of Scottish legal jargon. On the other hand, his use of everyday Scottish words in his letter is more of a personal idiosyncracy. It is true that Scott himself was willing to use Scoticisms in his letters (though he often comments that they are Scoticisms and explains them) but generally by the 1760s (when *Redgauntlet* is set) educated people tried to avoid them in letters. Saunders' use of phrases like *blawing, bleezing stories* 'bragging, boasting stories' (*Re* 127), *a bit chack of dinner* 'a small dinner' (*Re* 128) and *full of daffing* 'full of fun' (*Re* 128) serves more to reproduce his manner of speaking than to imitate the letter-writing style of an educated Scotsman of the time. Even more unlikely, in realistic terms, is his use of the spelling *Hieland* (*Re* 127) in a letter which uses Standard English spelling throughout except in idioms unknown to English (like *blawing*, the Scots form of English *blowing* but meaning 'bragging'). The word *Highland* was well established in English by this stage and it is not at all likely that Saunders would have gone out of his way to indicate his Scottish pronunciation. In short he is made to write as he speaks.

Realism of speaking also triumphs over realism of writing in the more important and extensive case of Jeanie Deans' letters from England. The first set of letters ends with Jeanie's apology 'Excuse bad spelling and writing, as I have ane ill pen.' Scott continues:

> The orthography of these epistles may seem to the southron to require a better apology than the letter expresses, though a bad pen was the excuse of a certain Galwegian laird for bad spelling; but, on behalf of the heroine, I would have them to know, that thanks to the care of Butler, Jeanie Deans wrote and spelled fifty times better than half the women of rank in Scotland at that period, whose strange orthography and singular diction form the strongest contrast to the good sense which their correspondence usually intimates (*HM* 416).

The Extent of Scots in the Novels

The comment reveals interesting attitudes to a non-standard dialect and unstandardized spelling. While willing to tolerate the occasional Scoticism in his letters, Scott considers it proper that they should be written in Standard English. It is also made clear that Jeanie's letters are *not* presented as typical of her age; instead Scott's a little unconvincing comment about Butler's educative skills allows him to use her letters to reflect her normal style of speech. The spelling is that usually found in the Scots dialogue apart from a few illiterate spellings like *fisycian* (HM 576), *tobaka* (HM 578), *pardun* (HM 578) and *cumming* (HM 579) and a few old-fashioned spellings like *alwaies* (HM 576), *graie* (HM 578) and *fiftie* (HM 579). For the rest there is the usual mixture of Scots and English forms including the usual inconsistency such as *forgie* and *forgive* on one page (HM 413) and *Duke* (HM 578) alongside *Duk* (HM 577). The use of Scottish spelling traditions and not just illiterate spellings aiming at indicating Scottish sounds is, from the point of view of realism, a little strange; Butler would certainly have aimed to teach Jeanie an English spelling and not the modified Scottish spelling used by the eighteenth-century poets. The apostrophe spellings common in Scott's dialogue are especially inappropriate here. If Jeanie knew that words like *a'* (HM 413), *Da'keith* (HM 413), *wi'* (HM 414), *partin'* (HM 415), *huntin'* (HM 577) and *throu'* (HM 577) have a different form in English then she would spell them in the English way not phonetically with an apologetic apostrophe. Even the ending *-in'* for *-ing* which we have seen Scott uses fairly infrequently, is here pressed into service to convey, very unsatisfactorily, the impression of a partially educated woman. What we have here then is really an extension of the dialogue rather than any fully developed separate medium of letters.

APPENDIX I

PERIOD AND PLACE OF SETTING OF THE MAJOR NOVELS AND POEMS

SCARCELY ONE OF SCOTT'S NOVELS is without inconsistencies of dating in the historical events mentioned. Some of the more glaring are given in Lang's introductions to the Border edition. However I have tried to set out here approximate dates for the action of each work; not all historical events worked into the novels and poems will tally with the dates given below but they probably do represent the period in which Scott intended us to imagine the action as taking place. Some works are dominated by one major historical event and for these the dating given is more precise. The date in brackets is the year of publication.

Work	Setting
The Bridal of Triermain (1813)	England; Arthurian and later
Harold the Dauntless (1817)	England; 7th century
Count Robert of Paris (1832)	Constantinople; late 11th century
The Betrothed (1825)	England and Wales; late 12th century
The Talisman (1825)	Palestine; late 12th century
Ivanhoe (1819)	England; late 12th century
Castle Dangerous (1832)	Scotland; early 14th century
The Lord of the Isles (1815)	Scotland; early 14th century
The Fair Maid of Perth (1828)	Scotland; end of 14th, beginning of 15th century
Quentin Durward (1823)	France, Burgundy, Flanders; 1470s
Anne of Geierstein (1829)	Switzerland, Provence, Burgundy; 1470s
Marmion (1808)	Scotland; 1513
The Lady of the Lake (1810)	Scotland; earlier 16th century

Appendix I

The Lay of the Last Minstrel (1805)	Scotland; mid-16th century
The Monastery (1820)	Scotland; 1550s
The Abbot (1820)	Scotland; 1560s
Kenilworth (1821)	England; 1570s
The Fortunes of Nigel (1822)	England; about 1620
Rokeby (1813)	England; 1644
A Legend of Montrose (1819)	Scotland; 1644–5
Woodstock (1826)	England; 1651
Peveril of the Peak (1822)	England and Isle of Man; mostly 1678
Old Mortality (1816)	Scotland; 1679–90
The Pirate (1822)	Shetlands and Orkneys; about 1700
The Bride of Lammermoor (1819)	Scotland; about 1700
The Black Dwarf (1816)	Scotland; early 18th century
Rob Roy (1818)	Scotland; 1715
The Heart of Midlothian (1818)	Scotland; 1736–7 and 1750s
Waverley (1814)	England and Scotland; 1745–6
The Surgeon's Daughter (1827)	Scotland and India; later 18th century
Guy Mannering (1815)	Scotland; later 18th century
Redgauntlet (1824)	Scotland; later 18th century
The Antiquary (1816)	Scotland; near end of 18th century
St Ronan's Well (1824)	Scotland; contemporary

APPENDIX II

IN THE TEXT I have given references to the novels by page numbers of the Border edition since it is widely available in libraries. To allow the words and passages referred to, to be found in other editions, I have included a list of the number of pages of text for each novel in the Border edition. The number of pages given includes introductory chapters but excludes Scott's introductions and notes.

Ab	*The Abbot*	628
AG	*Anne of Geierstein*	697
An	*The Antiquary*	598
Be	*The Betrothed*	454
BD	*The Black Dwarf*	195
BL	*The Bride of Lammermoor*	456
CD	*Castle Dangerous*	298
CRP	*Count Robert of Paris*	582
FM	*The Fair Maid of Perth*	680
GM	*Guy Mannering*	604
HM	*The Heart of Midlothian*	778
Iv	*Ivanhoe*	651
K	*Kenilworth*	659
LM	*The Legend of Montrose*	301
Mo	*The Monastery*	457
OM	*Old Mortality*	597
Pi	*The Pirate*	657
PP	*Peveril of the Peak*	821
QD	*Quentin Durward*	642
Re	*Redgauntlet*	638
RR	*Rob Roy*	582
SD	*The Surgeon's Daughter*	249
SRW	*St Ronan's Well*	621
Ta	*The Talisman*	458

Appendix II

Wa	*Waverley*	651
Wk	*Woodstock*	691

A rough page number in any edition can be calculated by taking the total page number in that edition, comparing it with the figures here and reducing or increasing the page reference given in the text in due proportion.

SELECT BIBLIOGRAPHY

APART FROM PROVIDING INFORMATION about the editions used in citing Scott and other frequently quoted literary texts, this bibliography is confined to work directly on Scott's language and to basic reference works. Books and articles on Scott's work in general are not included, although there are many which have influenced my views on Scott and thus on his language. The best general bibliography of Scott is that of Dr J. C. Corson in *The New Cambridge Bibliography of English Literature* (Vol. III, Cambridge, 1969, 670-92).

Tillyard puts the position succinctly when he says 'the language of Scott's novels has been taken for granted with surprising coolness'. The little which has been written about Scott's language approaches it from four angles: firstly, his debts to other writers, notably Shakespeare; secondly, his contribution to the vocabulary of present-day English; thirdly and fourthly, a relatively small amount of work directly on the subject of this book, his period and Scottish language. Brewer and Skelton are mainly concerned with the non-linguistic influence of Shakespeare on Scott but in the process they cover a number of allusions to Shakespeare in the novels, a subject on which Gordon concentrates in a series of articles. The work on Scott's contribution to present-day English coincides to some degree with our subject since Scott's main contribution has been in the revival of obsolete words and the introduction of Scottish words into Standard English. Weekley was one of the first to point out our debt and he has been followed by Roberts, who has treated the subject exhaustively and produced a list of some two hundred words we owe to Scott. Tillyard is one of the few writers to deal directly with the subject of Scott's period language. He takes *The Monastery*, 'linguistically far the strangest of the novels', as his starting point and I have continued the discussion of the strange language of *The Monastery* in my article on Sir Piercie Shafton, the so-called Euphuist. Murison in his essay 'The Two Languages of Scott' is mainly concerned with his Scottish language (including some interesting comments about Scott's sources and the sociolinguistics of the use of Scots) although, in passing, he makes a few unfavourable comments on Scott's period language. Hendrickson's dissertation is a defence of Scott's style against the largely adverse criticism it has received. It is based on the analysis of selected passages and covers dialect and archaisms as well as other aspects, but concentrates on stylistic qualities. However, in the end, the best commentaries on Scott's language remain *The Oxford English Dictionary* and *The Scottish National Dictionary*. It is an indication of the range and variety of his language that no smaller dictionaries will do him full justice.

A WORKS BY SCOTT

Journal, W. E. K. Anderson ed., Oxford, 1972.
Letters, H. J. C. Grierson ed., in 12 vols, London, 1932–7.
Lives of the Novelists, London, 1906.
The Minstrelsy of the Scottish Border, T. F. Henderson ed., in 4 vols, Edinburgh, 1902. Also referred to: the first edition, in 3 vols, Vols I & II, Kelso, 1802, Vol. III, Edinburgh, 1803.
Poetical Works, J. Logie Robertson ed., London, 1904. Also referred to: *Poetical Works*, J. G. Lockhart ed., in 12 vols, Edinburgh, 1833–4.
Tales of a Grandfather, London, 1911.
The Waverley Novels, Large Type Border Edition, Andrew Lang ed., in 24 vols, London, 1898–9. Also referred to: the 'magnum opus' or Collected Edition, in 48 vols, Edinburgh, 1829–33; the Dryburgh Edition, in 25 vols, London, 1892–4.

B OTHER LITERARY TEXTS

Austen, Jane, *The Novels*, R. W. Chapman ed., in 5 vols, Oxford, 1923.
Chaucer, Geoffrey, *Works*, F. N. Robinson ed., 2nd edn, London, 1957.
Percy, Thomas, *Reliques of Ancient English Poetry*, Everyman's Library, in 2 vols, London, 1906.
Shakespeare, William, *Complete Works*, W. J. Craig ed., London, 1905. Also referred to: *Plays*, Samuel Johnson and George

Select Bibliography

Steevens eds., in 10 vols, London, 1778; 2 supplementary vols, 1780.

C BOOKS ON LANGUAGE, INCLUDING SCOTT'S, AND OTHER REFERENCE WORKS

Abbott, E. A., *A Shakespearian Grammar*, 3rd edn, London, 1883.
Adolphus, John Leycester, *Letters to Richard Heber, Esq., Containing Critical Remarks on the Series of Novels Beginning with 'Waverley' and an Attempt to Ascertain their Author*, 2nd edn, London, 1822.
Bailey, Nathaniel, *A Universal Etymological Dictionary*, 14th edn, London, 1751.
Batho, Edith C., 'Sir Walter Scott and the Sagas: Some Notes', *Modern Language Review*, XXIV, (1929), 409–15. Reprinted, considerably revised, as 'Scott as a Medievalist' in *Sir Walter Scott Today*, H. J. C. Grierson ed., London, 1932, pp. 133–57.
Berkeley, David S., 'Sir Walter Scott and Restoration "Preciosité"'; *Nineteenth-Century Fiction*, X, (1955), 240–2.
Bradley, Henry, 'Shakespeare's English' in *Shakespeare's England*, in 2 vols, Oxford, 1916, II 539–74.
Brewer, Wilmon, *Shakespeare's Influence on Scott*, Boston, 1925.
Brook, G. L., *The Language of Dickens*, London, 1970.
Cochrane, J. G., *Catalogue of the Library at Abbotsford*, Edinburgh, 1838.
Craigie, Sir William and Aitken, A. J., *A Dictionary of the Older Scottish Tongue*, Chicago and London, 1931–.
Franz, Wilhelm, *Die Sprache Shakespeares: Shakespeare-Grammatik*, Halle, 1939.
Gordon, R. K., 'Scott and Shakespeare's Tragedies', *Transactions of the Royal Society of Canada*, 3rd ser., XXXIX, (1945), 111–7.
Gordon, R. K., 'Shakespeare and Some Scenes in the Waverley Novels', *Queen's Quarterly*, XLV, (1939), 478–85.
Gordon, R. K., 'Shakespeare's *Henry IV* and Some Scenes in the Waverley Novels', *Modern Language Review*, XXXVI, (1942), 304–16.
Grant, William and Dixon, James Main, *Manual of Modern Scots*, Cambridge, 1921.
Grant, William and Murison, David D., *The Scottish National Dictionary*, 10 vols, Edinburgh, 1931–76.

Select Bibliography

Grose, Francis, *A Classical Dictionary of the Vulgar Tongue*, Eric Partridge ed., London, 1963.

Haber, Tom B., 'The Chapter Tags in the Waverley Novels', *Modern Language Notes*, XLV, (1930), 1140–9.

Hendrickson, Richard Henry, *The Prose Style of Sir Walter Scott's Waverley Novels*, PhD. dissertation, University of Connecticut, 1968.

Jespersen, Otto, *Chapters on English*, London, 1918.

Jespersen, Otto, *A Modern English Grammar on Historical Principles*, in 7 vols, Vols I–VI, Heidelburg, 1922–31; Vol. VII, Copenhagen, 1949.

Johnson, Samuel, *A Dictionary of the English Language*, rev. by H. J. Todd, London, 1818. Also referred to: 1st edn, London, 1755.

Johnston, George Burke, 'Scott and Jonson', *Notes and Queries*, CXCV, (1950), 521–2.

Kellner, Leon, *Historical Outlines of English Syntax*, London, 1892.

Kersey, John, *Dictionarium Anglo-Britannicum*, London, 1708.

Kurath, Hans, Kuhn, Sherman, M., and Reidy, John, *Middle English Dictionary*, Ann Arbor, 1954–.

Lang, Andrew, *Sir Walter Scott and the Border Minstrelsy*, London, 1910.

Lascelles, Mary, 'Scott and the Art of Revision', in *Imagined Worlds*, M. Mack and I. R. Gregor eds., London, 1968, pp. 139–56.

Latham, R. E., *Revised Medieval Latin Word-List*, London, 1965.

Lockhart, J. G., *Memoirs of the Life of Sir Walter Scott, Bart.*, in 7 vols, Edinburgh, 1837–8.

Mackie, Albert D., 'Fergusson's Language: Braid Scots Then and Now', in *Robert Fergusson 1750–1774*, S. G. Smith ed., Edinburgh, 1952, pp. 123–47.

Murison, David, 'The Two Languages in Scott' in *Scott's Mind and Art*, A. Norman Jeffares ed., Edinburgh, 1969, pp. 206–29.

Murray, Sir James A. H., *The Dialect of the Southern Counties of Scotland: Its Pronunciation, Grammar and Historical Relations*, London, 1873.

Murray, Sir James A. H., *et al.*, *The Oxford English Dictionary*, 12 vols, Oxford, 1884–1928, with *Supplement*, R. W. Burchfield ed., Oxford, 1972–.

Mustanoja, Tauno F., *A Middle English Syntax*, Helsinki, 1960.

Onions, C. T., *A Shakespeare Glossary*, 2nd edn, Oxford, 1958.

Select Bibliography

Parker, W. M., 'Scott's Knowledge of Shakespeare', *Quarterly Review*, CCXC, (1952), 341–54.
Parsons, Coleman Oscar, 'Character Names in the Waverley Novels', *Publications of the Modern Language Society of America*, XLIX, (1934), 276–94.
Partridge, Eric, *A Dictionary of Slang and Unconventional English*, 5th edn, London, 1961.
Partridge, Eric, *A Dictionary of the Underworld*, London, 1961.
Phillipps, K. C., *Jane Austen's English*, London, 1970.
Review of *Woodstock*, or *The Cavalier* in *Westminster Review*, V, (1826), 399–457. Reprinted, in part in *Scott: The Critical Heritage*, J. P. Hayden ed., London, 1970, pp. 290–9.
Roberts, Paul, 'Sir Walter Scott's Contributions to the English Vocabulary', *Publications of the Modern Language Society of America*, LXXVIII, (1953), 189–210.
Roberts, Paul, *The Influence of Sir Walter Scott on the Vocabulary of the Modern English Language*, PhD. dissertation, University of California, Berkeley, 1948.
Scudder, Harold H., 'A Queen at Chesse', *Modern Language Notes*, XLII, (1927), 141–5.
Schultz, J. R., 'Sir Walter Scott and Chaucer', *Modern Language Notes*, XXVIII, (1913), 246–7.
Skelton, L. M., *The Influence of Shakespeare's Plays on the Waverley Novels*, B Litt. dissertation, Oxford University, 1952–3.
Smith, Roland M., 'Chaucer Allusions in the Letters of Sir Walter Scott', *Modern Language Notes*, LXV, (1950), 448–55.
Strang, Barbara, *A History of English*, London, 1970.
Tillyard, E. M. W., 'Scott's Linguistic Vagaries', *Etudes Anglaises*, XI, (1958), 112–8.
Tulloch, Graham, 'Sir Walter Scott's Excursion into Euphuism', *Neuphilologische Mitteilungen*, LXXVIII, (1977), 65–76.
Visser, F.Th., *An Historical Syntax on the English Language*, 4 vols, Leiden, 1963–73.
Warrack, Alexander, *Chambers Scots Dictionary*, with an introduction by William Grant, Edinburgh, 1911.
Weekley, Ernest, 'Walter Scott and the English Language', *Atlantic Monthly*, CXLVII, (1931), 595–601. Reprinted in Weekley's *Something About Words*, London, 1935, pp. 69–84.
Wilson, Sir James, *The Dialects of Central Scotland*, London, 1926.
Withycombe, E. G., *The Oxford Dictionary of English Christian Names*, 2nd edn, Oxford, 1950.

Select Bibliography

Wood, G. A. M., 'Scott's Continuing Revision: the Printed Texts of *Redgauntlet*', *Bibliotheck*, VI, (1971–73), 121–98.

Wood, G. A. M., 'The Manuscripts and Proof Sheets of *Redgauntlet*', in *Scott Bicentenary Essays*, Alan Bell ed., London, 1973, pp. 160–175.

Wright, Joseph, *The English Dialect Dictionary*, 6 vols, Oxford, 1898–1905.

INDEX OF SUBJECTS

Aberdeenshire dialect, 249, 253–4
addressives, Scottish, 216–17, 237, 245–7
adjectives, 132–3, 147–9, 280–1; interrogative, 281–2
adverbs, 149–51, 268, 282–4
anachronisms, 73, 76–8, 90, 93, 103, 108–17, 121, 228–30, 242, 329
arms and armour, 31–3, 39, 62, 109–16, 118
articles, 146–7, 277–80
Austen, Jane, 138, 140, 143, 145, 146, 153, 157–8, 162–3, 223
Authorized Version, 130, 137–8, 144, 148–50, 153, 154, 155–6, 158–9, 271, 288, 321–2

ballads, 61–3
Barbour, John, 23, 107–8
Beattie, James, 175
Berners, Dame Juliana, 27, 35–6
Boswell, James, 171, 178, 223
Burns, Robert, 23, 71, 168, 172, 179–80, 249–51, 298, 301
Burt, Edward, 50–1, 223–4, 329
Byron, Lord, 75, 133, 264

cant, 75–8
Carlyle, Thomas, 177
Chatterton, Thomas, 14–15, 61
Chaucer, Geoffrey, 22, 23, 24, 27, 34–5, 78, 280, 299
christian names, Scottish, 185, 221, 242, 256–9
Cockburn, Lord, 171–2, 176–7
conjunctions, 153–4, 286

dialects, Scottish, 176–7, 182, 249–256

Edinburgh dialect, 176–7, 249–50
etymology, Scott's interest in, 54, 116, 118–19, 228
exclamations, period, 81–97; Scottish, 247–9
extension of meaning, 73–5, 123
eye-dialect, 195–7, 294

Fergusson, Robert, 179–80, 250–251, 301
food, Scottish, 244–5
foreign words, 78–81, 96–7

Gaelic, 223–5, 254–6
Galt, John, 175–6
Gray, Thomas, 61, 111
Grose, Francis, 75–8

Harman, Thomas, 75–7
Highland Scots, 249, 254–6
Hume, David, 52, 54, 179
hunting, 35–6, 122

intelligibility, 14–15, 117–28, 168, 213–14, 259–66, 303, 305–6

James VI, 46–8
Johnson, Dr Samuel, 174–5
Jonson, Ben, 21, 23, 43–5, 142

Keats, John, 111, 133, 142–3, 157

Laneham, Robert, 21, 81
legal language, Scottish, 214, 238–241, 327–8
Lytton, Edward, 38, 43, 80, 86, 161

Milton, John, 18, 23, 45–6, 100, 143

343

Index of Subjects

mistakes, *see also* anachronisms, 61, 74–5, 115–16, 119, 124, 128, 222, 254, 278, 329
money, Scottish, 206, 220, 222, 241–4

Naunton, 20, 48–50, 82, 92
neologisms, Scott's, 65–6, 68–75, 91, 132–3, 166, 221–2
nouns, 129, 134–5, 268–9

oaths, *see* exclamations
Old English in Scott, 36–8, 52–4

Percy, Bishop, 19, 28, 55–7, 61–3, 81
poeticisms, 58–63, 111, 114–15, 130, 138, 142, 152, 155–6, 210–211
prepositions, 151–3, 284–5
pronouns, demonstrative, 267, 274; interrogative, 145–6, 277; personal, 129–33, 135–44, 267–274; relative, 145, 267–8, 275–7
pronunciation, Scottish, 64, 169–179, 182–202, 301–25

Ramsay, Allan, 103, 173, 175, 179–180, 298, 301
Reeve, Clara, 13–14
Ritson, Joseph, 56–8

Saviolo, Vincentio, 44–5
Scott, his reading, 13–24, 29–58, 74–78, 103, 106–8, 114–17; his spoken language, 176–7
Scottish language, attitudes towards, 170–82, 193–4, 303, 309, 315, 317–18, 320, 330–1; definition of, 306–7; extent of use in Scott, 301–31; use in Scott's time, 171–81, 301–31
Shadwell, Thomas, 76–7
Shakespeare, William, 18, 20, 21, 23, 24, 38–42, 45, 51, 53, 78, 98–102, 104–5, 108, 133, 135, 138–140, 143, 145–6, 148, 151, 154, 158, 161, 265–6, 290, 299

Shetland dialect, 249, 252
sociolinguistics of Scots, 169–79, 301–25, 330–1
Southey, Robert, 33
spelling, 15–16, 63, 184, 186–7, 192–204, 265, 301–10, 330–1
Spenser, Edmund, 18, 21, 23, 33, 42–3, 59–60, 78, 133, 153
Spenserian poets, 59–60
Stevenson, Robert Louis, 201

Turner, Sharon, 53–4

verbs, 129–30, 132–4, 154–66, 267, 286–300; auxiliaries, 129–130, 132–4, 157–60, 296–300; ellipsis, 166; imperative, 160; impersonal, 164; infinitive, 165; inflections, 130, 132–4, 154–7, 267, 286–94; negation, 267, 294–296; subjunctive, 162–4; tenses, 132, 157, 296
vocabulary, period: historical accuracy, 76, 103, 105, 108–17; new words, 65–6, 68–75, 91, 132–3, 166; obsolete and obsolescent words, 25–52, 66, 72, 78, 117–28; sources, 34–58, 60, 62–3, 75–8, 104; variant forms, 63–6; vogue words, 66–9, 131; words from historical works, 52–8; words from poetry, 58–63
vocabulary, Scottish: Scottish loan words, 189–92, 211–13, 215, 219, 222–8; Scottish senses of words in Standard English, 204–7, 211–12; Scottish words adopted into Standard English, 29–30, 211, 216, 218–19, 226–8, 230, 232–6, 244–5, 264, 283, 315, 326; variant forms, 64, 182–92; words created in Scots, 213–22; words from place-names, 220; words obsolete in English, 204, 207–13; words obsolete in Scots, then, 30–2, now, 216, 229–32, 297

Walker, Patrick, 230

INDEX OF WORDS

This index does not include forms of words resulting from common sound changes in Scots (see pp. 182–204) or its dialects (see pp. 249–256), Scottish christian names (see pp. 256–9) and words from the two chapters on grammar.

Aberdeen-a-way, 282
aboon, 201
abye, 26
accost, 43–4
acton, 111, 113
Ad-(oaths), 89–91, 95
address, 43–4
-ado, 67–8, 81
advisement, 64
advocate, 238
a'gad, 90
alderman, 52–3
Alicant, 120
Alsatia, 76
ambuscade, 64
ambushment, 33, 64
Andrea, -rew, -ro, -ra Ferrara, 221
arblast, 33, 62, 113, 118
ashet, 227
assizer, 327
assoilzie, 189, 199
'at, 187
attaint, 119
aw, 251
aweel, 247
aw(e)some, 30, 32, 233, 264
awn, 251

backfriend, 123
back-spaul, 215
bailie, 190–1, 241
baldrick, 114–15

ballant, 189
bandog, 26, 118
bane, 40, 125
bannock, 245
barbican, 26
barns-breaking, 311
baron(-), 239–41
bartizan, 65
basnet, 61–2, 110
basset, 121
bastard, 120
bastinado, 68
baudrons, 259
bawbee, 220, 243
Bawty, 259
bear, 208
Beaumont, 36
behove, -uve, 195, 300, 305, 307
belle amie, 78
Benval, 119
berlin(g), 225
bide, 210
bield, 209
big (v), 226
biggonet, 219
bilbo(a), 116
billy, 217–18, 259
bing avast, 76
bink, 187, 260
birkie, 205, 308
bit, 205, 285
bittock, 219
black-jack, 31–2, 115
blackmail, 263

blaw-in-my-lug, 215
bleed-barrel, 70
blood-boltered, 16
blue-bottle, 40
bodin, 31–2
bod(d)le, 243
body, 219–20
bogle, 233, 236, 263
bolt, 113, 118
bona-roba, 40–1, 127
bonnet(-), 221–2
bonny, 203, 232, 236, 246
bookie, 218
bordel, 61, 128
Borrowing Days, 214
botcher, 63
bower-, 56, 62, 71
bowie, 260
brander, 244–5
bransle, 27
braxy mutton, 245, 260
breeks, 187
brigandine, 110
brigg, 187
brock, 261
brod, 188
brose, 245
brownie, 233, 236
bruilzie, 189, 199
bunker, 234–5
burgh, 241
Burn-the-wind, 71, 213

345

Index of Words

burrows-, borough-town, 265, 313
bushment, 64

cad(d)ie, 234–6
caird, 259
caliver, 52, 116
callet, 266
camerado, 68
Cannlemas, 187
canny, 232–3, 312
Cap de diou, 96
carl, 226
carline, 226
carte, 190
carvy-seed, 191
casque, 110, 115
cast out, 216
casting, 35–6
cat(h)eran, 30, 230
ca'throw, -through, 215–16
causey(-way), 265
cavaliero, 40
certes, certie, 42, 60, 96
chainzie, 199
chamfrom, 112
chancellor, 327
change-house, 213
chapelle, 63
chaplain, 125
chappin, 244
charger, 58
chiel(d), 195
chrom, 219
chucky, 244
clachan, 223–4
clack-goose, 214–15
clan, 264
clansman, 221, 264
clary, 120
cleugh, -ch, 186, 199, 253, 262
close, 43–4
cniht, 29, 53–4
cock– (oaths), 89–91
cock-a-leeky, 244
cockatrice, 127

cock-bree, 244
cockernony, 229
cock-up, 229–30
coign of vantage, 232
coistril, 42
college, 237
College of Justice, 214
collegeaner, 237
come o' will, 266
condeshend, 188
conscionable, 25, 125
contrair, 192, 264
contriturating, 47
cookie, 219
coranto, 68
corbie, 227
coronal, 28
corr(e)i, 223, 226
corslet, 126
cote, 74
couching, 73
country, 253
coup, 306
cowardlike, 33
cow-feeder, 174, 213
crack-rope, 70–1
cragsman, 69
craig, 266
crans, 306
crappit-heads, 245
craven, 33
crombie, 219
cross-bow, 115
crouse, 306
crowd, 57
crowdie, 245
cruells, crewels, 192
cruisie, 328
crummie, 219, 259
cuddie, 259
cullionly, 40, 42
culver, 65–6
culverin, 65–6
cummer, 227, 246
cunzie, 190, 232
curious, 25
curliewurlie, 306
curn, 218
curney, 218

curpel, 188
curtal-axe, 112–13
custodier, 64
cut boon whids, 76
cutter, 26

daffing, 330
daft, 209
dam(o)sel, 64–5, 148
danger, 211
danske, 26
da(u)rg(ue), 210
dargle, 222
deacons, 241
deboshed, 64
decay, 232
decored, 64
decus, 76–7
deil, deevil, 202, 248, 256, 312–13
deliverly, 74
den, 253, 262
dependence, 44
derring-do, 42–3
desiderate, 64
despardieux, 96
destrier, 58, 117
devoir, 80
dike-louper, 215
dink, 329
dirgie, drigie, 190
dirks, 262
doggie, 218
doited, 322
donjon(-), 65, 72, 123
doo, dow(n), 186, 246
doomster, 327
dortour, 217
douce, 212
dour, 227, 232–3, 236
dow (v), 208, 291
dowsets, 128
drap-de-berry, 26
dree, drie, 185, 208, 312, 323
drinc hael, 36–7
drouk, 266
dudgeon-dagger, 115, 123–4

Index of Words

duello, 69
dyvour, 232

effeir, 31–2
egad, 89–90, 95
eilding, 226–7
elaboratory, 66
Eldorado, the, 67
emboscata, 45, 64
eme, 217
emprize, 60
errant, 43, 64–5, 147
Erse, 188
esne, 29, 52–3
estramazone, 45, 65
-et, 219
ettle, 226
examinator, 232
exercise, 211

faitour, 42, 60
falchion, 111
fallal, 229
fall-off, 44
falset, 227
fash, 227
fasheous, 227
fasherie, 227
faut, fau't, 196
F(e)ifteen, The, 230
feir, 32
fence-louper, 215, 222
fendy, 219
feu(-), 239
feuar, 239
fey, fie, 207–8
fico, 39
Fifish, 220–1
Fire-the-fagot, 70, 83
firth, frith, 203–4, 226–7
fissenless, fizzenless, 265
fleshers, 231
fley, 263
flichter, 186
flory, 231
folkfree, 29
following, 230

forayer, 27
forbear, 234
forby, 264
forfairn, 232
forsooth, 93
fox, 27, 39, 116
fozy, 228
frack, 231–2
franklin, 53
fray, 60
free-lance, 71–2, 221
friar's chicken, 244
fusionless, 265

gab, 79
gabbart, 212
gaberlunzie, 190
Gad- (oaths), 89, 91
gae, 183, 290
gae-down, 195, 215–216
galliard, 127
gambado, -ade, 68
gang, 208, 290
gang-there-out, 215, 222
gar, 226–7
gauntlets, 112, 115
gay, 205, 282, 308
gentry cove, 76
gillie, 230
girdle, 188
girnel, 188, 231
glamour, 233–4, 236
gled, 227
glee(-), 56–7
gleek, 121
glen, 223, 226, 262, 264, 327
gloaming, 209
gloze, 26
Gog- (oaths), 89–91
golf, gowff, 234
good year, jere, 93–4
gossipred, 74
gouge, 80
gow, 219
gramarye, 27–8
gramercy, 33

Grizzy, 259
gr(o)und officer, 213, 314
grue, grew, 228
gruesome, grewsome, 30, 32, 228, 233
gudedaughter, -mither, -sister, -sire, 216–17, 246
gudeman, 217, 247–9, 313, 317
gudewife, 217, 247, 317
guerdon, 42, 60, 80
guesten, 30
gutter-blood, 213
gutty, 261

haaf, 252
hackbut, hagbut, 115
hacqueton, 111, 125–126
haddie, 218
haet, 248
haggis, 245
ha(i)rst, 186–7, 194, 202, 206
halfling, 73
halidome, 88
hallan, 260, 329
hallion, 261
hamesucken, 238
handicraft, 26
hand-waled, 215
haply, 61
harman beck, 75
harquebus, 115
harrowtry, 64
haugh, 209, 261–2
hause, 187
haven, 252
Hawkie, Hackie, 259
hawkit, hackit, 259
head-piece, 109, 113
heart-spone, 27, 35
heben-wood, 43
hedge-, 78
hellicat(e), 222, 265
helm, 110–11

Index of Words

henchman, 50–1, 72
her nainsell, 255
hership, 30–2
hest, 26
Hieland, 185, 330
High Court of
    Justiciary, 238
hilding, 42
hinny, 184–5, 203,
    237, 246
hoast, 226–7
hoff, 252
holidame, 88
holm(e), 261–2
holytide, 26–7
hope, 252
hout, 247
howff, 228, 252, 266
humorous, 42
hurdies, 266
hurricanoe, 68–9, 81
hyke, 36

-ie, 218–19
ill-fa'ard, -faur'd, 186,
    194
imitashion, 195–6
in and in, 121
ingle, 128
injeer, 26
innocent, 263
inventar, 191
ivy-tod, 33

jack, 31, 62, 113–15,
    118
jackman, 31–2, 62,
    113–14, 118
jalouse, 212
jape, 28, 32
jazeran, 33, 115, 118
jealous, 211
jerry-come-tumbles, 71
jesses, 36
jo, 246
jockie, 259
joctaleg, 259
jongleur, 56
justified, 264–5

juvenal, 40–1

kaisar, 36–7
kale, 183
kemp, 218
kempie, 218
ken, 264, 307–8
kettle of fish, 245
killbuck, 70
kill-cow, 213
kilt, 225, 264
kiltman, 221
kimmer, 227, 246
king-craft, 48, 72
kinrick, 208
kitchener, 55, 120–1
kith, 233
kittle, 226
knap, 77
knight, 118
Knight Ranger, 148
kythe, 208

Lack-a-day, 95
-lad, 220
laddie, 218, 312
Lady, 240
ladye, 63
lady-love, 41
lai, 55–6
laigh-house, -shop,
    214
laird, 239–40, 308
lamour, lammer, 191
lance-knight, 73, 123
lance-prisade, 26
largesse, 81
lassie, 218–19, 246
lassock, 219
lavrock, 188
layout, 326
leap-the-ladder, 70–1
leech, 27
leg bail, 78
leid, 47
leman, 62–3
levin-bolt, 71
levin-brond, 43
levin-fire, 34

light o' love, 127
like (v), 207
-like, 220
Lindabrides, 128
links, 234–5
loch, 186, 199, 223,
    226, 264, 327
Lochaber axe, 220
lockeram, 26
lofted, 328
loot, 201
Lords of (Council
    and) Session, 214,
    238
Lords of Seat, 214
los, 79
losel, 42, 60, 122
loup, 192
loup-the-dike,
    -tether, 215, 222
luckie(-), 216–17, 246
lungie, 227
lustihood, 60
lyme-hound, -dog, 71

mace, 111
Mackenyie, 199
magnum, 244
Mahound, 57–8
main (adj), 123
make-bate, 66, 70
maker, 31–2
malecontent, 67
malvoisie, 27
man, 246, 312
man-at-arms, 33, 114
mangonel, 33, 111–
    113, 120
manner, taken in the,
    41
manty, 189
mar-company,
    -feast, 69–70
marker, 72
marry, marry quep,
    93–4
martialist, 48
massymore,
    massamore, 228

Index of Words

maugre, 60
maun, 264, 308, 315
meat (v), 210
mense(-), 212
menyie, -zie, 190
mettle (adj), 204–5
middle-earth, -world, 29
minish, 63
minnie, 217–18
mirrig und machtigh, 37
miscarry, 25
miscreant, 122
miser, 42
misericord, 55
misproud, 27, 42
mittens, 205
mocado, 68
morat, 54–5, 58, 118
morgue, 47
morion, 110, 112
morning, 206
moss, 253, 326
mosstrooper, 114
moust, 191
mouther, 72
moyle, 64
muist, 191
multiplepoinding, 238, 260
mutchkin, 244
mystery, 58

naggie, 218
needcessity, 189
ne'er, 248
ne'er-be-licket, 248
neibor, neebor, 199
nid(d)ering, 38, 43
night-rail, 127
nolt, 192
nombles, 63–4, 122
nose-of-wax, 66
nouns, 91
nowte, 192
nubbing cheat, 77–8

-ock, 219

Od(d)- (oaths), 83, 89, 91, 247–8
oe, 217, 223–4
ombre, 121
oons, 91
open-steek, 187
ordinar, 191
ou, 247
outcast, 216
outlandish, 124–5
outlay, 216, 234
outrance, 119
outrecuidance, 122–3
outshot, 216
ow, 247
owerta'en, 216
oye, 217, 223–4

Pace, 231
paitrick, 187
palabras, 27, 41
palfrenier, 28–9
panderly, 42
panel, 327
pantaloon, 39
papistrie, 63
paraffle, 192
par amours, 78
parish-top, 123
partan, 223–4
partisan, 109, 112
Pasques-dieu, 96
pasquinado, 68, 81
passado, 45, 68, 122
passage, 25, 121
passage of arms, 72
pass(e)mented, 46
pavesse, -isse, 33, 112–13
pawkie, 232
Paynimrie, 28
pedder-coffe, 30, 32, 46
penneeck, 121
peremptory, 43
petticoat-tails, 227
philabeg, 225
piccadilloe-needle, 69
pigment, 54–5

pilgrimer, 30, 32
pint(-), 244
plack(-), 243–4
plaid, 264
player, 66
pleached, 39
poignado, 67–8
poignet, 116
pokmanty, pockmanky, 189
poldroons, 33, 115
poorful', 202
port, 231, 328
portmantle, 189
pottle-deep, 38–9
pouncet-box, 38
powsoudie, 245
precise, 67
precisian, 67
press, 61
prig a prancer, 75–6
primero, 121
princox, 42
procurator(-), 190
professor, 67
prokitor, 190
proof, 113, 115
provant, 43
provost, 241
pund, 243
put-on, 204
pyot, 219

quacksalver, 66
quaigh, 186
quarrell, 52, 113, 118
queez-maddam, 228

raid, 30, 32, 183
raised, 328
rampallian, 42
rascaille, 64
rascallion, 125
rash-taffeta, 72, 123
ratton, 212
raun, 192
reclaim, 27, 35
red-handed, 221
refectioner, 55, 120–1

349

Index of Words

reformado, 67, 81
reft, 210–11
regard, 43–4
reik, 200
reive, -er, -ing, 200, 211
remeed, remeid, 190–191, 200, 323
rere-supper, 124
ride, -er, -ing, 207
rifler, 35–6
rin-there-out, 215, 222
roisterer, 73
rokelay, 213, 227–8
romaunts, 55
rook, 77
rote, 57
rotten, 212, 261
roy, 78
royne, 78
rudesby, 27, 125

'S (oaths), 89–91
sack, 120
sackbut, 123
sack-butt, 123
sack-spigot, 71
sain, 264
Sapperment, 96
sark, 226
sartie, 96
saulie, 229
scale-staircase, 329
scantly, 234
scart, 188
scathed, 45
scaur, 226
scholar-craft, 72
sclate-stane, 188
sclaveyn, 58
Scotch, 170, 203
Scots, 170, 188, 203
Scottish, 170, 203
sculduddery, 237
sealgh, 198–9
secret, 113
secretary, 27, 125
selcouth, 27

servitor, 31
shabble, 191
sheep-biting, 40
sheriff(-), 241
shirra, 186, 241
siller, 186, 206, 313
single house, 213
singles, 35–6
singults, 42, 60
sirs, 186, 247
six-hooped-pot, 39, 71
skeily, skeely, 200, 219
skene(-), 223–5, 262
skeps, 263
skirl, 187
skriegh, 187–8
skyte, 188, 266
slack, 226–7, 252–3
sleuth-hound, 261
sloan, 253
slogan, 30, 61, 72, 233
slow-hound, 261
slughorn, 61
slur, 77
smelt, 76–7
snaphaunc(h)e, 116
snood, 208
solan, 227
soldado, 27, 67
soldanrie, 28, 73
soldo, 67
sonse, 223–4
sonsy, 223–4
sorra, 248, 306
sort, 206
sounder, 74
Southron, 188
speel, spiel, 200
speer, 264
spence, 212–13
spleuchan, 199
spoil-sport, 70
sponsible, 264
sporran, 224
spreagh, 199
spule-blade, 215

spu(i)lzie, 189, 199, 238
stab, 77
stance, 236, 326
state, 25
statist, 66
steel-jack, 115
stern, 192
stickit stibbler, 185
stilet, 116
stir, 246
stirra, 246
stoccata, 44–5, 122
stot, 261
stouthrief, 238
stramaçon, 45, 65, 122
strath, 223, 226, 327
strathspey, 220
straught, 293
subtrist, 73
suburb-wench, 71
sud, suld, 188, 194, 195, 305, 308
sunk, sunkie, 218
surcoat, 33
swankie, 219
sweer, swear, 209
swill-flagon, 70
sworder, 27
sworn man, 49
sworn servant, 49

tailor-craft, 72
Talbot, 36
Tammy Norie, 185, 259
tartan, 264
tear-cat, 70, 123
tearmouth, 70
Termagaunt, 57–8
Teste-dieu, 96
tête-bleu, 96
thack, 187
thane, thegn, 29, 52–4
theow, 52–3
thunder-dint, 27, 34
tittie, 217–18
tod, 261

Index of Words

toledo, 26, 116
tollbooth, 231
top, 77
toun, town, 201–2, 209–10, 263, 308
tour, 77, 201
township, 210
toy, 228
Tranchefer, 27, 36
trangam, 26
trankum, 26
traveller, -ing, 263
tregetour, 27, 210
trench, 39, 125
trews, 225
trewsman, 221
trine, 77–8
trinidado, 67–8
troth, 93
trouble-mirth, 70
trow, 210, 264
tuck, 26, 116
turn-broche, -spit, 124
tush, 92–3
twalmonth, 186

Ud- (oaths), 83, 90–1
ulyie, 189–90
umquhile, -while, 198, 313–14
uncanny, 223–4
unco, 187, 282
undertaker, 25–6
unfriend, 31–2
upgang, 216
upgive, 216
unhouseled, 40
unthrift, 42, 66

untimeous, 326
upset, 216
uptake, 216

vasquine, 30, 32, 46
vau't, 196
venue, 44
verquire, 121
veshel, 188
vex (n), 204
via, 97
villagio, 119
viretot, 27, 34
vivers, 315
viznomy, 34
voto a dios, 97

wabster, 231
wad, wald, 194–5, 308–9
wadset, 311
wae (adj), 204
waes hael, 36–7
waistcoateer, 127
waiter, 328
wale, 226
wame, 206
wanle, 187
wap, 75
ware, 212
warison, 74–5
warlock, 219
wars(t)le, 187–8, 310
wassail, wassel, 37, 124
wastel-, wassel-, 124
wean, 215

weapon-schaw(ing), wappen-schaw, wappinshaw, 32
weary, 248
weel-far'd, -faurd, 194
weird, 208, 313–14
whaap, 251–2
wheen, 285
whigmaleerie, 306
whilom(e), 60
whisht, 247, 254
whorn, 252
wife, 211
wight, 60
winnock, 219
winsome, 233
witenagemot, 29, 54
wizzened, wizen'd, 233
woodcraft, 27, 35
woodie, 188
wowf, 221
wraith, 236
writer, 238
wuddy, 215
wuzzent, 233

Ye, 184
yearn, 183
yeomanly, 27, 35
yepistle, 184, 313
yerl, 183
yestate, 184
yill, 183, 249–50
yin, yince, 183, 250
yode, 60

Z- (oaths), 89, 91, 95